Digital Cities Roadmap

Scrivener Publishing
100 Cummings Center, Suite 541J
Beverly, MA 01915-6106

Advances in Learning Analytics for Intelligent Cloud-IoT Systems

Series Editor: Dr. Souvik Pal and Dr. Dac-Nhuong Le

The role of adaptation, learning analytics, computational Intelligence, and data analytics in the field of cloud-IoT systems is becoming increasingly essential and intertwined. The capability of an intelligent system depends on various self-decision-making algorithms in IoT devices. IoT-based smart systems generate a large amount of data (big data) that cannot be processed by traditional data processing algorithms and applications. Hence, this book series involves different computational methods incorporated within the system with the help of analytics reasoning and sense-making in big data, which is centered in the cloud and IoT-enabled environments. The series publishes volumes that are empirical studies, theoretical and numerical analysis, and novel research findings.

Submission to the series:
Please send proposals to Dr. Souvik Pal, Department of Computer Science and Engineering, Global Institute of Management and Technology, Krishna Nagar, West Bengal, India.
E-mail: souvikpal22@gmail.com

Publishers at Scrivener
Martin Scrivener (martin@scrivenerpublishing.com)
Phillip Carmical (pcarmical@scrivenerpublishing.com)

Digital Cities Roadmap

IoT-Based Architecture and Sustainable Buildings

Edited by

**Arun Solanki, Adarsh Kumar
and Anand Nayyar**

Scrivener
Publishing

WILEY

This edition first published 2021 by John Wiley & Sons, Inc., 111 River Street, Hoboken, NJ 07030, USA and Scrivener Publishing LLC, 100 Cummings Center, Suite 541J, Beverly, MA 01915, USA
© 2021 Scrivener Publishing LLC
For more information about Scrivener publications please visit www.scrivenerpublishing.com.

Wiley Global Headquarters
111 River Street, Hoboken, NJ 07030, USA

For details of our global editorial offices, customer services, and more information about Wiley products visit us at www.wiley.com.

Limit of Liability/Disclaimer of Warranty
While the publisher and authors have used their best efforts in preparing this work, they make no representations or warranties with respect to the accuracy or completeness of the contents of this work and specifically disclaim all warranties, including without limitation any implied warranties of merchantability or fitness for a particular purpose. No warranty may be created or extended by sales representatives, written sales materials, or promotional statements for this work. The fact that an organization, website, or product is referred to in this work as a citation and/or potential source of further information does not mean that the publisher and authors endorse the information or services the organization, website, or product may provide or recommendations it may make. This work is sold with the understanding that the publisher is not engaged in rendering professional services. The advice and strategies contained herein may not be suitable for your situation. You should consult with a specialist where appropriate. Neither the publisher nor authors shall be liable for any loss of profit or any other commercial damages, including but not limited to special, incidental, consequential, or other damages. Further, readers should be aware that websites listed in this work may have changed or disappeared between when this work was written and when it is read.

Library of Congress Cataloging-in-Publication Data

ISBN 978-1-119-79159-1

Cover image: Pixabay.Com
Cover design by Russell Richardson

Set in size of 11pt and Minion Pro by Manila Typesetting Company, Makati, Philippines

Contents

15 Effects of Green Buildings on the Environment   **477**

Ayushi Nain, Ankita Banerjee and N.P. Melkania

Preface

Due to their continuously growing populations, cities are facing major challenges in providing conditions that will contribute to the development of a healthy sustainable environment. This population growth has increased resource requirements and the demand for large-scale waste management systems and other services. Therefore, the aim of sustainable development is to provide processes for the planning, implementation and development of projects to meet the needs of modern communities without compromising the potential of future generations. Sustainability always includes a balance of priorities in various areas, including economics, community needs and environmental quality, as well as justice, health and well-being, energy, water and material resources, and transportation needs. Also, since communication is of fundamental importance for both internet access and new digital services, an important starting point for smart cities is the introduction of public Wi-Fi.

Another point of significant concern that has contributed to the advent of sustainable smart cities is the energy crisis brought about by the global demand for limited natural resources, which are declining as demand grows. These natural resources are used by the industrial, transport, commercial, and residential sectors. Those living in residential areas use energy mostly for space heating, followed by electronics, lighting and other appliances, water heating, air conditioning, and cooling. Because the global residential sector consumes a significant amount of energy, which is equivalent to one-third of all available primary energy resources, it is necessary to reduce energy consumption by using sustainable buildings. A good management strategy must be expected to mitigate the dangerous consequences of rapid urbanization in modern society, the economy and the environment. Since sustainable smart cities include established structures, infrastructures, communities, institutions, and individuals, the proposed solution should be the result of real interdisciplinary discussions in a multicultural environment that encourages communication and has a real chance of succeeding.

This book provides readers with a platform through which they can simulate all of the requirements for the development of smart sustainable cities. It helps readers interact, brainstorm, and work on common problems or discuss proven solutions and models. Moreover, it also deals with energy consumption. Such energy consumption leads to a rapid depletion of energy resources, an increased need for building maintenance, an improvised comfortable lifestyle, and an increase in time spent on building construction. A sustainable building mainly refers to the renewable sources used for construction that help the structure withstand atmospheric changes. Currently, all countries are looking for ecological materials; that is, renewable plant materials such as straw and clay bricks, wood from forests certified for sustainable management, recycled materials, and other nontoxic, reusable and renewable products. For sustainable and durable construction, energy efficiency is an urgent problem, and researchers are currently actively involved in this area. This book provides an in-depth analysis of design technologies that lay a solid foundation for sustainable buildings. Smart automation technologies that help save energy are also highlighted, as well as various performance indicators needed to make construction easier. The aim of this book is to create a strong research community and to impart a deep understanding of the latest knowledge regarding the field of energy and comfort, along with offering solid ideas in the near future for sustainable buildings. These buildings will help cities grow into smart cities. Since the focus of smart cities is on low energy consumption, renewable energy, and a small carbon footprint, researchers must study optimization methods in order to find the optimal use of energy resources.

The book is organized as follows: Chapter 1, "The Use of Machine Learning for Sustainable and Resilient Buildings," provides insights into intelligent resources, artificial learning and big data analytics. A detailed study of the field of intelligent architecture is presented, which focuses on the role of machine learning and large-scale data analytics technologies. Finally, some of the challenges and opportunities of applying machine learning in the built environment are discussed. Chapter 2, "Fire Hazard Detection and Prediction by Machine Learning Techniques in Smart Buildings (SBs) Using Sensors and Unmanned Aerial Vehicle (UAV)," discusses various time-series methods used to calculate the threshold value of the parameters in UAV-based data, including the Naive Bayes, simple average, moving average, simple exponential smoothing (SES), Holt's linear, Holt-Winters, and autoregressive integrated moving average (ARIMA) methods. Since variation in the degree of value from the threshold range is helpful in predicting different actions, the vector autoregressive (VAR) method is also discussed, which is a multivariate time-series analysis used to calculate the threshold value that considers all the features at once along with their impact on each other.

Chapter 3, "Sustainable Infrastructure Theories and Models," introduces the concepts of data fusion and data fusion approaches with respect to sustainable infrastructure. This work computes and explains various data fusion tools, techniques, and important methods of decentralized and distributed detection. Several smart city infrastructure approaches are highlighted along with the smart city components architecture. Chapter 4, "Blockchain for Sustainable Smart Cities," explains how a sustainable smart city is a key solution for the large-scale urbanization of rural areas. However, urbanization poses a number of challenges for governments and city planners, including increased traffic congestion, reduction in quality health service provision, burden on civic facilities, and data management among others. Blockchain is integrated into smart city applications to improve the standard of living of citizens and overall management of the smart city. With the advantage of blockchain, a smart city can provide efficient and reliable services to people. Chapter 5, "Contextualizing Electronic Governance, Smart City Governance and Sustainable Infrastructure in India: A Study and Framework," surveys and shows the research gaps in various E-governance services developed and implemented in India that are being initiated to achieve the Digital India program launched by the government of India with the help of information and communication technology (ICT). Furthermore, the architectural framework for smart governance-based services for smart cities in India based on transforming electronic governance to governance in a smart city is proposed.

Chapter 6, "Revolutionizing Geriatric Design in Developing Countries: IoT-Enabled Smart Home Design for the Elderly," presents a study that emanated from concern for the growing population of the elderly in our cities who are forced to live alone without much assistance due to shrinking family size and intercity and international migration of their children in search of better job opportunities. The study looks at the middle-class to upper-middle-class elderly population aged 65 and above living in urban cities of India such as Bangalore. This group usually comes from a well-educated background with mid-level financial security. Chapter 7, "Sustainable E-Infrastructure for Blockchain-Based Voting System," explores the blockchain technology used to implement an electronic voting system. E-voting can change the way in which we have voted for decades. The main feature of this system is that voters can cast their vote from anywhere in the world. As this voting process starts going digital and online, voters from outside the country can also vote from wherever they are, which can increase the total voting percentages tremendously. Chapter 8, "Impact of IoT Enabled for Smart Cities: A Systematic Review and Challenges," discusses the way in which the IoT has influenced specific areas of our daily lives. Moreover, the reader will discover the fundamental options that come with smart cities and exactly why a contemporary community is given that name, along with some of its problems and solutions. Additionally, this particular chapter covers the role of 5G technologies in the IoT along with big data analysis. Finally, it includes the primary options that come with the Indian perspective of smart cities by 2030 to enhance the daily lives of humans, along with conceptual and block diagrams.

Chapter 9, "Indoor Air Quality (IAQ) in Green Buildings: A Prerequisite to Human Health and Well-Being," examines why the IAQ inside buildings is one of the most important determining factors of human health as more than half of the air inhaled by a person during his/her lifetime is at home. Illnesses associated with environmental exposure often stem from indoor air exposure. Prominent air pollutants are found indoors, including volatile organic compounds (VOCs), particulate matter (PM), carbon monoxide (CO), lead (Pb), nitrogen oxides (NOx), and asbestos. Smart and sustainable approaches to green building construction should incorporate IAQ as a critical component of building design as the air quality is directly related to the inhabitants' sound well-being. Chapter 10, "An Era of Internet of Things Leads to Smart Cities Initiatives towards Urbanization," outlines the components of smart cities and IoT technologies used in smart cities for establishing relationships between industries and their services, and includes a table showing various sectors providing different services and related principal issues of IoT technologies. Finally, the challenges of smart cities, urbanization, and IoT are highlighted. The perceived concept of the smart city appears to initiate the new standards for urban city planning. Urban planners imagine the city of the future as smart and economical. This initiative will always remain critical for development and sustainability. Chapter 11, "Trip-I-Plan: A Mobile Application for Task Scheduling in Smart City's Sustainable Infrastructure," provides comprehensive, automatic task rescheduling for mobile application. This approach will enhance the growth of smart city workers' planning and boost the growth of smart sustainable infrastructure. Here, a comparative study of existing mobile applications of task scheduling is also presented.

Chapter 12, "Smart Health Monitoring for Elder Care in Indoor Environments," discusses the various technologies that are being used by researchers to measure indoor environmental quality, human health and well-being along with case studies and real-life examples. Technology plays a crucial role in supporting the self-sufficient living of the elderly and their caregivers. However, the environmental quality of the spaces they reside in affects their health. Real-world case studies and their results are discussed in subsequent sections. Finally, available tools and research to aid readers delve further into this vital application area are discussed. Chapter 13, "A Comprehensive Study of IoT Security Risks in Building a Secure Smart City," presents a holistic review of ML/DL algorithms that can be deployed to improve security. The IoT is capable of assimilating a variety of heterogeneous end systems by facilitating seamless access and communication among an expansive range of devices, people and their environment, making it the key feature in developing the idea of smart cities. This chapter delineates the challenges related to the technology's implementation and standardization. It briefly overviews existing IoT architectures and enabling technologies, and also explores the prospects of ML/DL methodologies that can be implemented on the IoT platform to maintain an admissible level of services, security and privacy issues, with the aim of enhancing the overall experience of smart cities.

Chapter 14, "Role of Smart Buildings in Smart City: Components, Technologies, Indicators, Challenges, and Future Research Opportunities," presents various indicators, technologies, components, and features of smart buildings in any smart city. General architectures are subsequently discussed along with the various supporting technologies and requirements of smart buildings for smart cities. The chapter ends with a discussion of the different challenges followed by future research opportunities in the domain of smart buildings in a smart city. Chapter 15, "Effects of Green Buildings on the Environment," discusses concerns related to rapidly increasing environmental and sustainability issues like urbanization, climate change, loss of biodiversity and degradation of resources, which highlight the need for advancements in housing. Green building is the theory, science and styling of buildings planned and constructed in accordance with a minimum impact on the surroundings by reducing utilization of water, energy, and disturbances in the surrounding environment in which the building is located. This contribution is an attempt to appraise the value of green buildings compared to standard buildings. An attempt is also made to illustrate the available good practices regarding green structures in India.

The information provided in this book will be an incentive to the researchers, academicians and industry professionals interested in IoT-based architecture and sustainable buildings. The book also provides a platform to exchange knowledge in the field of energy efficiency and various tools and methods used to develop green technologies for construction in smart cities.

We would like to express our sincere gratitude to the contributors to the book, who supported us with the contribution of their valuable work and dedication to make this book a resounding success. Last but not the least, we thank Scrivener Publishing and associated production editors for handling the project and making this book a reality.

The Editors
January 2021

The Use of Machine Learning for Sustainable and Resilient Buildings

Kuldeep Singh Kaswan[1]* and Jagjit Singh Dhatterwal[2]

[1]School of Computing Science and Engineering, Galgotias University, Greater Noida, India
[2]Department of Computer Science & Applications, PDM University, Bahadurgarh, India

Abstract

The use of Artificial Intelligence to ensure that intelligent and resilient buildings are sustainably developed. The intelligence displayed in buildings by electronic devices and software operated systems is artificial intelligence which perceives the building environment and takes actions aimed at optimizing output in a given context or constraint. A complex, sensitive infrastructure that ensures efficient, cost-effective and environmentally acceptable conditions for every occupant by constantly communicating with its four basic elements: locations (components, frameworks, facilities); processes (automation, control systems), staff (services, users) and management (maintaining, performance) and processes (controlling, systems); and they separate current technologies into two major groups, occupant-centered and energy-centered facilities. The first level approaches that use ML for occupant dimensions, including (1) occupancy and identity estimations, (2) behavior recognition and (3) choice and enforcement estimates. The approach in the second-class category used ML to approximate energy or device-related aspects. It is divided into three categories, (1) estimating the energy profiling and demand, (2) profiling and detection of faults of devices, and (3) sensor inferiority. In this chapter, we focus on guided study, unrestricted learning and improving learning. The main variants, implications of specific parameter choices are explored and we generate standard algorithms. Finally, discuss some of the challenges and opportunities in the built environment to apply machine learning.

*Corresponding author: kaswankuldeep@gmail.com

Arun Solanki, Adarsh Kumar and Anand Nayyar (eds.) Digital Cities Roadmap: IoT-Based Architecture and Sustainable Buildings, (1–62) © 2021 Scrivener Publishing LLC

Keywords: Machine learning, big data analytics, Internet of Things, smart building, resilient building, sustainable building

1.1 Introduction of ML Sustainable Resilient Building

The hyperconnectivity generated by IoT will enhance the assurance of Smart Sustainable Resilient Building (SSRB) as all basic construction facilities and goods from your home electronics to your plant vessels have now been connected [1–5]. Nevertheless, this hyperconnectivity could hinder the control of SSRBs at the same time. In particular, massive quantities of streaming data are required from SSRB and its residents. The management of large data streams is becoming more and more relevant with ML, testing, compaction, learning and filtration technologies. In order to obtain a greater interpretation of human beings than their environment computers, the amount of sensory data obtained by sensors and devices needs to be processed by algorithms, converted into details and derived expertise [6–8]. This awareness can also contribute, and most significantly, innovative goods and services that change our lives drastically. For starters, smart meter readings may be used to help estimate and control power usage. To optimize this convenience, reduce expenses adapting to requirements of its residents, the SSRB requires sophisticated tools to understand, anticipate and make intelligent decisions. SSRB must also provide a variety of wearable sensor data linked to its patients and produce new remote sensors. SSRB algorithms include estimation, decision analysis, robots, smart devices, wireless sensor networks, interactive, web computing and cloud computing and include several other developments. Cognitive maintenance of offices is necessary in several SSRB programs for starters, fitness, safety, energy management, illumination, repair, the elderly and digital entertainment through these technologies.

1.2 Related Works

While several SB-focused survey papers have been released, none focuses on the role of data analysis and ML within SBs. All the relevant survey papers are comprehensively presented in Table 1.1.

Table 1.1 Report data of a survey.

Cite	Purpose	Limitations
Chan *et al.* [12]	A country and continent arranged project SH Review as well as the associated technologies for monitoring systems and assistive robotics.	It not emphasized on the importance of ML and big data analytics, it does not review and classify the papers according to the applications of SH
Alam *et al.* [13]	Research objectives and services-based review of SH projects; namely, comfort, healthcare, and security.	It not emphasized on the importance of ML and big data analytics for SB.
Lobaccaro *et al.* [14]	Review of existing software, hardware, and communications control systems for S.H and smart grid.	It not emphasized on the importance of ML and big data analytics. It also does not focus on reviewing and categorizing papers according to the applications of SH.
Pan *et al.* [15]	The energy efficiency and the vision of microgrids topics research review in SBs.	The emphasis of the paper is not the ML and big data analytics for SB services. It does not consist of the other applications of SB rather than energy efficiency.
Ni *et al.* [16]	Propose a classification of activities considered in SH for older peoples independent living, they also classify sensors and data processing techniques in SH.	Does not cover all the services in SH. It also does not categorize the research according to different ML model styles.

(Continued)

Table 1.1 Report data of a survey. (*Continued*)

Cite	Purpose	Limitations
Rashidi and Mi-hailidis [17]	Review AAL technologies, tools, and techniques.	The paper focuses only on AAL in healthcare, and does not cover the other applications in SH or SB; in addition, there is no classifying of the researches according to ML model styles.
Peetoom et al. [18]	The monitoring technologies that detect ADL or significant events in SH based review.	Does not focus on the role of ML in SB.
Salih and Abraham [19]	The ambient intelligence assisted healthcare monitoring focuses only on AAL in healthcare, and does not cover the other applications in SH or SB in the review.	The challenges and the future research directions in the field not covered in the research.
Perera et al. [20]	Discuss and analyzed the works in context awareness from an IoT perspective	Not emphasized specifically on the SB domain and its application services.
Tsai et al. [21]	Data mining technologies for IoT applications data reviewed.	SB applications not emphasized.
Mahdavinejad et al. [22]	Discussed and analyzed some ML methods applied to IoT data by studying smart cities as a use case scenario.	Not concentrated on SB and its applications as a use case.

Chan *et al.* in 2008 [12] gave a description of intelligent home study. It even speaks about smart and friendly robotics. The article examines the nation and the continent's smart home programs. Alam *et al.* [13] presented information on sensors, apps, algorithms and protocols of communication used in smart homes. The paper explores intelligent homes focused on their facilities and study aims: protection, fitness and comfort.

Lobaccaro *et al.* [14] shared the notion of a smart house but smart grid technology and address obstacles, advantages and potential developments of intelligent home technology. Pan *et al.* [15] analyzed the research of SBs with microgrids on efficient energy usage. The study explores subjects for analysis and latest developments in SBs and microgrid vision.

For multiple study articles research on making the autonomous lives of seniors for smart homes simpler has been checked. Ni *et al.* [16] have reported on sensing machine features including practices which can help elderly people reside peacefully in intelligent residences. Rashidi and Mihailidis provided a study on environmental assistance systems for elderly people [17]. Peetoom *et al.* [18] concentrated software tracking that understands householder existence, including reduced identification and changes of safety condition. Salih *et al.* [19] proposed a health-assisted urban knowledge report surveillance system identifying different methods included in current research literature, as well as connectivity and wireless sensor network technology.

1.3   Machine Learning

A brief list of the different algorithms for machine learning [49] in sustainable and resilient building is obtained below.

- Decision Tree—Decision Tree is a supervised learning system used for classification or regression. A training model is built in Decision Tree Learning and the importance of the results is determined through the learning decision rules derived from the data attributes. In Big data there are many drawbacks to these decision tree algorithms. Firstly, if the data are very large, it is very time to build a decision tree.

Secondly, there is no optimal solution to the distribution of data that contributes to higher communication cost.

- Support Vector Machine (SVM)—Support Vector Machine is a supervised learning approach that can be used for either regression or classification. When used on big data, due to its high machine complexity, the SVM technique is not successful. The demand for measurement and storage is increased considerably for enormous amount of data.
- K-Nearest Neighbor (KNN)—For regression and classification problems, K-Nearest Neighbor (KNN) algorithms are used. KNN approaches are using data and graded use similar steps to different data points. The information is reserved for the class with the closest neighbors. The value of k increases with the increase of the number of closest neighbors. KNN is not realistic on big data applications because of the high cost of calculation and memory.
- Naive Bayes Classifier—For classification function Naive Bayes Classifier is commonly used. For any class or data point that belongs to a certain class, they define membership probabilities. The most probable class is the one with the highest likelihood. The efficiency of Naive Bayes is not possible in text classification tasks due to text redundant features and rough parameter estimation.
- Neural Networks—A semi-supervised technique for classification and regression, the Neural networks. Neural Nets is a computing device consisting of highly interrelated processing elements that process data via their dynamic state response. Back Propagation is one of the best-known algorithms in the neural network. Neural networks have few challenges for big data with the growing scale of information. The huge quantity of information makes it difficult for the technique to maintain both reliability and efficiency and also increases the system operating load.

1.4   What is Resilience?

Over the last couple of decades, the concept of resilience has received increasing attention in several ways and is now viewed as a desirable feature of physical systems and communities. A popular feature in both meanings is that resilience "is the system's capacity to tolerate external disturbance(s), adjust and rapidly return to the initial or a new stage," and also offers a multi-disciplinary concept in resilience within the engineering sector [9−15].

Resilience can be described as an ability to reach a desired level of reliability or provide a desired level of service or features in the physical systems, Q, immediately after a risk arises.

1.4.1 Sustainability and Resiliency Conditions

Most societies choose to be resilient and sustainable [50]. When priorities and plans are formulated separately in order to enhance resilience and sustainability, there are strong risks that the targets may overlap and may also clash. This chapter looks at the principles of safe and durable cities, how increasing environmental and constructed environments and stressors will need different approaches and resources to improve stability and longevity for the environment.

When their resilience and sustainable strategies align themselves, the best results for communities occur. However, sustainable and resilient advancement must be accomplished before promising future generations are delivered. Challenges include reduction of impacts on environmental systems, management and the time it takes to change current practices and replace existing infrastructure with standard renewal rates. Nevertheless, while the governance potential and sustainability and adaptation strategies are open, intergenerational wealth is undermined by expectations that natural environments (our atmosphere, habitats, and climate) are secure and healthy [16−20]. Introduction to sustainability and the resilience of buildings, the dynamic nature of natural systems has not been fully understood through their intricate interrelationships across time and space and their preference for inclination points and threshold values. Many experts face the challenge of developing dangerous model infrastructure that does not involve potential improvements in risk magnitude or frequency, because scientific consensus is not yet formed on this topic. In fact, today's construction methodology does not take into consideration the harm rates and related impacts on building operation recovery—a critical aspect of resilience.

1.4.2 Paradigm and Challenges of Sustainability and Resilience

A basic yet strong definition is sustainable development to ensuring that society "combines the present need without compromising potential generations' capacity to fulfill their needs" (UN 1987). The groundbreaking

Bruntland Commission study on sustainable growth presented this Sustainable development concept for the first time. With the implementation of the Sustainable Development Goals in 2015, sustainable development remains an international initiative which has motivated policy and individuals worldwide to alleviate some of the more drastic consequences of mankind on the global operation of the environment.

The idea of cohesive societies emerged concurrently. Application and special concept of resilience to a variety of subjects and dimensions, include psychology, economics, public safety, protection, business continuity, disaster preparation and reaction, risk reduction and ability of the building system (i.e. design, transport, services and other infrastructure) to physically resist and rapidly recover. In terms of populations and dangerous incidents, "the capacity to adjust and withstand and recover rapidly from damage" is specified (PPD-21 2013). The idea of building resilience and infrastructure systems, in order to minimize damage to the environment, restore and reconstruct expenses as well as economic impacts, is to be avoided until a certain point, then improve or recover over a certain period of time [21, 22, 26–28]. In reality there also are situations where the constructed system cannot avoid only threshold hazard in terms of the different facilities age and circumstances around a

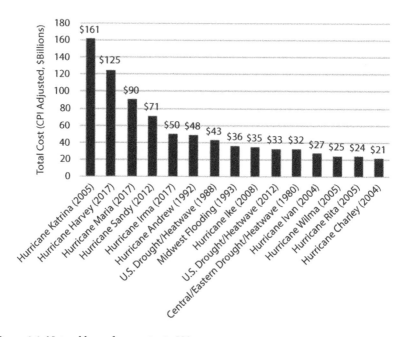

Figure 1.1 Natural hazard year wise in US.

city. Throughout these situations, contingency preparation may be used to recognize performance gaps and transitional measures which would allow the society to continue to deliver services, if the building(s) or network system(s) impacted is not willing to do so. Such performance holes often present the possibility of beginning an innovative cycle to enhance construct environments efficiency.

Natural disasters will affect societies by human loss, relocation, death, property harm and economic impacts. Such consequences and sluggish group rebounder may be amplificated by structural stressors like high unemployment, inadequate services or food shortages. The National Environmental Awareness Centers (NOAA, 2018a) report that 218 extreme weather events happened in the USA between 1980 and 2017 worth at least $1 billion. The degree to which societies have been affected and lost their work from natural disasters is seen in Figure 1.1. The enhancement of construction and infrastructure's robust and sustainable efficiency will help cities escape major economic loss and long-term consequences.

1.4.3   Perspectives of Local Community

There are a number of communities in the United States which recover each year from a dangerous event. Over the last 50 years, an annual average of 40 declarations of presidential hazardous events has been issued (FEMA 2013). Hazardous results are first experienced and first handled in populations. While governments cannot eliminate natural threats, long-term planning and prioritized initiatives that are enforced over time will mitigate their effects. The level of recovery and the eventual outcome would rely on the scope and magnitude of the incident and on the action taken by government to mitigate harm, preserve properties, react in a timely and organized manner and restore government functionality within a given time period. Such activities collectively assess the strength of a group.

Resilience provides a holistic solution to risk handling catastrophic incidents, as well as environmental problems, through structures that allow new generations the same opportunities to prosper. Communities will move for a more socially and economically equitable and prosperous environment by resolving skill differences and essential threats through a systemic integrated and systematic strategy [29−35]. Approaches include: introduction into City planning and network projects with adaptability, resilience and regeneration, utilizing a framework methodology that tackles multi-scale connections and dependency and methodologies that resolve the complexity of the potential severity of hazards (Table 1.2).

Table 1.2 Planning for community resilience [55].

Planning steps	Key activities
1. Form a collaborative Planning Team	• Identify resilience leader for the community • Identify team members, and their roles and responsibilities • Identify key public and private stakeholders for all phases of planning and implementation

2. Understand the situation	Social Dimensions
	
	• Identify and characterize functions and dependencies of social institutions, including business, industry, and financial systems, based on individual/social needs met by these institutions and social vulnerabilities
	• Identify how social functions are supported by the built environment
	• Identify key contacts and representatives for evaluation, coordination, and decision nuking activities
	• Built Environment
	  ➢ Identify and characterize buildings and infrastructure systems, including condition, location, and dependencies between and among systems
	  ➢ Identify key contacts/representatives for evaluation, coordination, and decision-making activities
	  ➢ Identify existing plans to be coordinated with the resilience plan
	• Link social functions to the supporting built environment
	• Define building clusters and supporting infrastructure

(Continued)

Table 1.2 Planning for community resilience. (*Continued*)

Planning steps	Key activities
3. Determine goals and objectives	• Establish long-term community goals • Establish desired recovery performance goals for the built environment at the comma level based on social needs, and dependencies and cascading effects between systems • Define community hazards and levels • Determine anticipated performance during and after a hazards event to support social functions • Summarize the results
4. Plan development	• Evaluate gaps between the desired and anticipated performance of the built environment to improve community resilience and summarize results • Identify solutions to address gaps including both administrative and construction options • Prioritize solutions and develop an implementation strategy
5. Plan preparation, review and approval	• Document the community plan and implementation strategy • Obtain feedback and approval Mon stakeholders and community • Finalize and approve the plan
6. Plan implementation and maintenance	• Execute approved administrative and construction solutions • Evaluate and update on a periodic basis • Modify short or long-term implementation strategy to achieve performance goals as needed

1.5 Sustainability and Resilience of Engineered System

The word "anthroposphere" has more and more been used by scientists to emphasize the impact of human existence in the new geological era. The accelerated demographic increase, technical advances and industrialization have reached a state in which the relations of human enterprises, the global environment of the world and the surroundings have a devastating effect on potential social changes at local level. The lack of natural capital, arable and inhabitable property, potable water and life-threats in general, are increasingly impacting civilization-culminating in civil instability and migration. Human environmental emissions are widely accepted to adversely affect the earth's geology and biosphere itself, thereby affecting the same living conditions which enable human civilization to be promoted in various ways, including global climate change. Regions and towns are not merely at danger, but are also a fact for millions. Environmental contamination, clean water and land, significant damage to the safety, well-being and livelihoods of current and future generations are a hazard. A global catastrophically danger must be taken seriously at all stages of society's policy-making in the absence of sustainable social growth.

Earth structure and individual behavior on the functionalities of health organizations. It is therefore clear that the relation between sustainable growth and resilience is powerful and that the two concepts are essentially similar from two separate viewpoints, see also Figure 1.2.

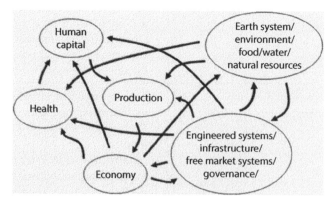

Figure 1.2 Societal principle of resilience and sustainability.

1.5.1 Resilience and Sustainable Development Framework for Decision-Making

A program delegate must be developed to encourage the creation of decision-making resources for the resiliency, healthy community and to promote the rating of decision-making options in line with the information required, compatible with priorities and goals and conforming to potential requirements. The following introduces a structure representation paradigm, which fits closely Faber *et al.* [58].

- Analysis system representation of hierarchical decisions

In order to help decisions about the management of processes, it is essential to create structure representations that regularly chart potential alternative options for decision-makers and the stakeholders involved in achieving their priorities. This assumes that the nature of the structures is decided by the policy makers, stakeholders and their choice, time-boundary and spatial limits, the functional features and functionality of the systems and their impact on system efficiency, and feasible and appropriate decision-making alternatives.

In other governance contexts, such as private organizations, or industrial practices, the overarching concept which underlies the hierarchical governance system seen in Figure 1.3 may be extended.

Theoretically, it is important for decisions to be rated in accordance with their anticipated worth (or benefit) in accordance with the Bavarian Decision Analytics and the axioms to be made in order to automate the design and/or the management of engineering systems subject to complexity and inadequate information in a normative decision sense.

The structure as outlined in Figure 1.4 incorporates not just threats in terms of potential negative value in various applicable indicators (e.g. negative in life, disruption to environmental values and financial losses) but also gains linked to decision-making options—the key goal of optimized structures—as opposed to more traditional risk-informed solutions to decision-making. The expansion supported the way *Section 4* discusses durability and longevity as a framework for evaluation for stability outlined by Linkov *et al.* [59], thus accurately correcting typical risk modeling limitations. Specific decision alternatives to designed device architecture and management in accordance with the predicted utility benefit or any particular metrical requirements can be assessed and classified according to the device modeling paradigm as outlined in Figure 1.5.

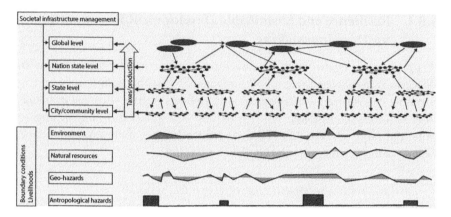

Figure 1.3 Decision making resilience and sustainable development framework.

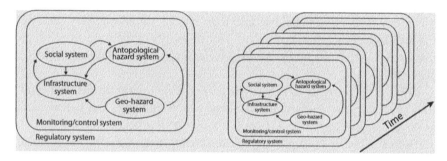

Figure 1.4 Bavarian decision analytics.

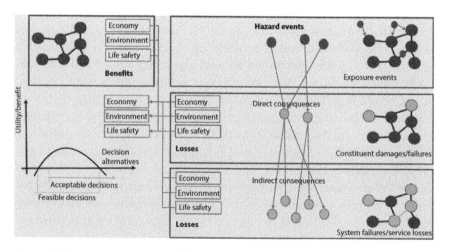

Figure 1.5 Framework system modeling.

1.5.2   Exposures and Disturbance Events

As seen in Figure 1.5, exposure incidents (disturbances) are considered to reflect, in theory, all future occurrences that may have implications. Resiliency, ecological models and analyses can include exposures.

Type-1 Hazards: The related threats are manageable in broad enough time and room, rendering their management far simpler. Geohazards such as earthquakes, flooding, waves, etc. are common manifestations of this form of hazards [37, 41, 43, 44].

Type-2 Hazards: They may be correlated with catastrophic combined effects on adequate time and space scales. Furthermore, their cumulative effects may cause the same characteristics as the hazards of type 3 to have more disastrous consequences. Typical cases include biological pollution, misuse of land, plant destruction, ineffective or poor management, insufficient financial planning, human mistakes, etc.

Type-3 Hazards: Very unusual and possibly catastrophic occurrences, also in broad sections of time and space, that are unforeseen and about which little evidence is practically available. The cumulative effects of type 2 hazards may be triggered. Examples include volcano eruptions, meteor collisions, solar storms of extreme severity, rapid temperature change as well as significant terrorist activities.

1.5.3   Quantification of Resilience

The literature includes a fairly wide number of ideas for modeling and quantifying network durability, e.g. Cimellaro *et al.* [60], Linkov *et al.* [59], Sharma *et al.* [61] and Tamvakis and Xenedis [62]. The proposed models are more commonly aimed at the short-term reflection of the system's capacity to withstand and rebound from disruptions, without major output loss and without outside assistance, usually, the emphasis on the portrayal of resilience models.

For impact on service delivery of the stated perturbations and on recovery characteristics in relation to service grade recovered against period and overall service failure, see Figure 1.6.

Until recently only the modeling of processes to rebound from disruptions has been granted tacit attention. Neither the functional failure nor rather the production of capability that is critical to the productive, yet quick reorganization, change, yet recovery following disruptions and danger events will take account of processes flexibility providing a life cycle gain in the flexibility model described in Faber and Qin [57]. See Figure 1.6.

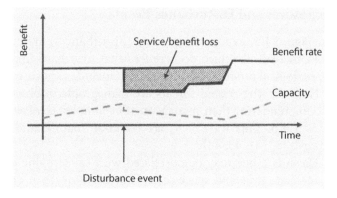

Figure 1.6 Quantification of resilience.

1.5.4   Quantification of Sustainability

Addressing biodiversity includes a shared analysis of the implications of inter-generational and intra-generational inequality on the environment, public safety and wellbeing, financial circumstances and extension of natural capital [45, 46, 48, 49]. In relation to the consequences currently discussed in resilience models, the emphasis is on whether changes on the ecosystem should be taken into consideration.

The theory behind this is to extend the Planetary Boundaries principle as a way to reflect the Earth's capabilities which are essential to continuing social growth, as we know it today. The Planet Life Support System (ELSS) is the following features of the Earth system. It is often believed that device states and the associated effects linked to the effect on the environmental quality, which put strain on the ELSS, may be attributed to every alternate decision concerning the configuration and the management of an integrated system. This relationship may be built in the sense of product production following Hauschild [63], by Life Cycle Analysis, as implemented in support of QSAs. Figure 1.7 demonstrates the definition.

Another important point of this article is that due to lack of knowledge and inherent natural variability the resilience and sustainability of engineered systems can only be proven and probabilistically modeled in a meaningful way. As a result, resilience and sustainability criteria need to be described in terms, for example, of appropriate annual resilience probabilities and sustainability failures. It quickly becomes apparent from this point of view that tradeoffs occur.

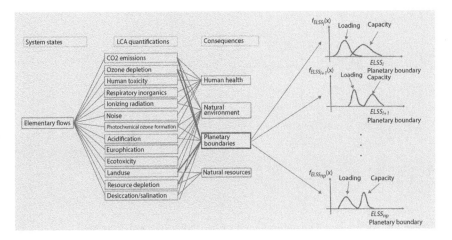

Figure 1.7 Mapping of quantification of sustainability and resilience.

The problem of how robust built structures and efficient society innovations should be taken into consideration when choosing. The short-term social security may rely on what are perceived as appropriate threats linked to local adaptation failures (e.g. at neighborhood level) as well as society's tolerance for the possibility of global mitigation failures. In order to promote effective and educated collective decision-making, more work on this solution will be carried out to the immediate future.

1.6   Community and Quantification Metrics, Resilience and Sustainability Objectives

The impact of natural (and anthropogenic) dangers can be significant in communities. Objectives must be described in terms of their appropriate after-effects. Resilience and sustainability objectives can be defined explicitly in assessing the impact on the well-being of recovery times, environmental justice, and social justice (i.e., international and inter-generational justice) [58]. We ought to identify quantification measures to assess the effect of a harmful occurrence on the well-being. These quantification indicators may be described at various intervals in order to reflect improvements in the health directly after and after the rehabilitation period, even until a danger arises [55, 64]. The individual's well-being is dynamic and relies on several aspects, including resources, social

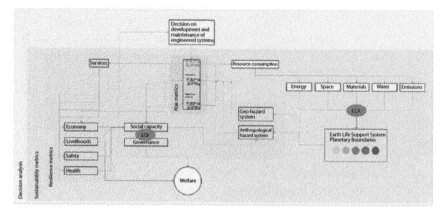

Figure 1.8 Techniques of quantification of sustainability and resilience [58].

expectations and socioeconomic status that are open to the society. Social standards and status are commonly referred to as factors of social vulnerability [71]. Such principles ought to compensate for priorities and quantification in order to correctly forecast and measure the impact of a natural catastrophe on health (Figure 1.8).

1.6.1 Definition of Quantification Metric

These indicators can be measured by means of the disaster impact and the recuperation as quantification metrics for the various capacities and functions. Issues of data access make ideal metrics and regressors challenging to create. For starters, the household regressors are usually desirable. Nonetheless, socio-economic details including employment, ethnicity or age is also not accessible at the household level. Furthermore, the nature of the capacities makes it harder to identify a measure that is always indicative in the context of disparities within populations and infrastructure roles and socio-economic conditions before a harmful event occurs. For example, access to clean water in a developed country can provide a desired indicator, whereas it may be more useful to study different sources of drinking water, for example water tanks or wells in a developing country. Indicators will also be chosen on the grounds of data quality and importance to the area of concern. For the development of exact predictive models, the collection of data sources for indicators/regressors is important. In order for models to be used in the future, the data source should be reliable and frequently actualized. The US census, which is frequently revised and freely accessible, may be an indicator of a data base. If real-time data is available, updates to Bayesian models can be used.

1.6.2   Considering and Community

We find the City of Seaside, Oregon, vulnerable to potential seismic hazards to highlight some of the ideas explored in this segment. Seaside is a coastal city with a population of 6,000 to 14,000 based on the season of the year. According to the 2010 Decades Census estimates [65], 6,440 people are dispersed across the city to different houses. The seismic risk is Mw = 70 and a 25 km southwest epicenter of the area.

Equations [66] are used to build graphs of the amplitude of the ground motion measurements across the appropriate field of research.

For each residential building on the Seaside, Figure 1.9 shows the mean injury. In Figure 1.9, Bai *et al.* [67] describes insignificant, moderate, weighted and complete definitions.

A logistical model predicts the likelihood of dislocation of a household [65]. The likelihood of community dislocation is estimated in Figure 1.10.

Figure 1.9 Paradigm of damage of building.

Figure 1.10 Estimation of household dislocation.

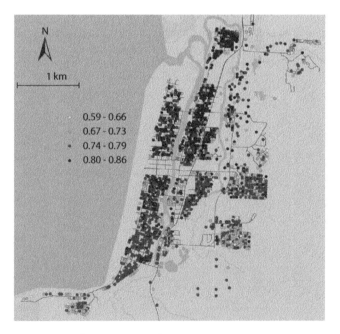

Figure 1.11 Estimation of permanent residence.

An even weaker importance in the case that an adult does not dislocate in a temporary residence (the dislocation capacity knowledge is focused on the dislocation model). Figure 1.11 indicates the probability of individuals getting access to a permanent residence.

1.7 Structure Engineering Dilemmas and Resilient Epcot

Throughout the 15 years after the seminal efforts of this taskforce, new projects have arisen almost everywhere, under the umbrella of the 'resilience' of vital (and uncritical) networks. In 2003, the weekend of resilience in San Francisco celebrated in Tokyo, where a "low carbon and resilient city" initiative was developed, New York was using its logos as "strengthen and resilient New York" initiative, while a "100 towns and cities" initiative was founded by the Rockefeller Foundation. In 2013, the Distinguished Lecturer Award was awarded to Mary Comerio for her lecture on 'resilience and technological issues' and inside the qualified earthquake engineers' group, and the theme for the 16th World Earthquake Technological Conference was 'resilience, the latest problem of the earthquake engineering' (which can be translated in more than one way, interestingly).

1.7.1 Dilation of Resilience Essence

Throughout the course of 15 years, "resilience" has evolved from an extraordinary term to define the "capability," including in accident cases, to rebound from damage, pain or deformation, to becoming an increasingly commonly known "buzz word." Google searches can informally evaluate the emerging popularity of the term (not strictly scientifically, but informatively). In July 2016, 47,000,000 "hits" were checked for "resilience" alone, up from 7,880,000,000 six years before. The most notable aspect, in adding 'Obama' and 'resilience' almost 3/4 million hits, is that six years ago there were only 0.4 million hits, which is no surprise, because President Obama released a presidential order compelling all federal departments to enact resilience-enhancing policies (White House, 2013). 17,300 findings were reported, up from 6,200 six years earlier for the quest for the mixture of "technical resilience." Just 2,470 times, up from 953 six years ago, was identified for the combination "quantifying resiliency" and only three times was identified for the "quantification of tech resilience" up from just one result six years earlier (a quest for Google that offers one single hit is considered "Google's wake," and is a uncommon event). Surprisingly enough,

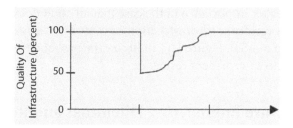

Figure 1.12 Resilience seismic concept [58].

the hits received from such queries indicate that, except for the case of "resilience" alone, such findings have tripled roughly from 2010 to 2016.

Either the word "resilience," though staying important, has grown with an unprecedented elasticity (Figure 1.12), or the above indicate that "resilience" may have been the base of a modern Tower of Babel, in which all inhabitants speak without comprehension. A term of resilience which implies everything and all to everyone is definitely not an especially useful concept since it avoids meaning, consistency and therefore renders it intangible for practical purposes when the aim is to increase group resilience in the way can be calculated. It highlights the importance that such values and the stringent application of 'resilience' be re-established in this unique sense. This is discussed below and reflects in a way important to engineers on durability.

1.7.2   Quality of Life

The only approach to measure the quality of life as a proportion of the general population (Figure 1.13(a), (b)) is to calculate the quality of life as a feature. Using the whole stable community without an earthquake.

That figure does not alter at State level, except for such fatalities that happened in seismically deficient hospitals. In the case of hospitals that are seismically remodeled or not. Injuries suffered after the disaster will periodically contribute to a continued decline in the stable community. All these injuries would cure, and deaths would no longer be added to the toll, in the best case, in the absence of hospital loss.

First Dilemma

Until a disaster happens, most of the people don't care about resilience to the designed infrastructure.

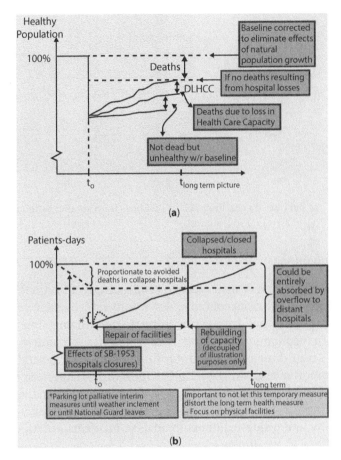

Figure 1.13 (a) Healthy population (b) Patients-days treatment.

As seen, for instance, in Figure 1.14(a)—and in the hotel rooms, belongings and passports. However, it was as harshly attacked as this tight regulation was. A significant portion of the central business area was already blocked down on the second anniversary of the disaster. Additional forms of destruction were resulting from unfinished repairs/rebuild (Figure 1.14(b)).

Some rocking frames (note that the standard for Christchurch new buildings before the earthquake is reinforced concrete buildings). Surprisingly enough, there is also a big controversy on the wish of parishioners to construct again the severely destroyed cathedral in the same steel-making framework on which it was originally designed, but probably reinforced to ensure a degree of 'collapse protection.'

Figure 1.14 (a) Building after earthquake, (b) Building two years after earthquake.

Second Dilemma

How does a structural designer lead to resilience quantification?

Population and socioeconomic, environment/ecosystem, integrated municipal systems, build-up urban infrastructure, living style and civic competence, economic growth, as well as social and cultural resources define all seven dimensions of group functioning (not generally by any order of importance as expressed in PEOPLES). The suggested PEOPLES Readiness Model offers the foundation for creation of quantitative and consistency temporal–spatial models that continually assess improvements in functionality and group readiness to adverse incidents or hazards across some of all the above dimensions.

Strategies of Resilience

"Mitigation," requiring either the re-building of current structures or the development of modern construction projects, is essential to achive the goal of sustainable cities, but sometimes neglected or dismissed in the assumption that it is "too expensive". There appears to be very reasonable cost appetite to remove some danger in some other controlled areas, for example by ordering the elimination of traces of asbestos from crews in hazmat suits or by allowing the elimination after several years of baby car seats due to plastic ageing.

Nation would stay trapped in the constant process of devastation–reconstruction. However, if the nation wants to see vital services and life-lines working following a tragedy, that is not always the case—the majority of the network should not be overlooked (Figure 1.15).

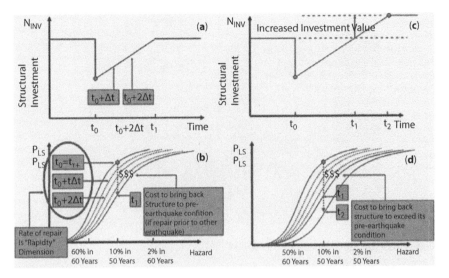

Figure 1.15 (a) Improve resilience structure, (b) Reduce probability structural loss, (c) Increase resilience pre earthquake and (d) Improve the structural loss.

Third Dilemma

Various owners and stakeholders—with differing goals, interests and purpose—will simultaneously support resilience in the creation of a disaster-resilient society. Some research has been conducted on quantifying resiliency in network environments, such as road networks, electricity grids, delivery structures and the like. For a variety of factors, such networks are radically different from the group of buildings in a city [23, 24].

- First, the network device properties are usually either held by an individual alone or by a group of several broad interdependent shareholders. The highways in one state, for example, are the responsibility of the State Transport Department, with a few exceptions.
- Second, the architecture of such networks is often self-regulated such that the implementation committees for which even such owners are allowed to vote follow the design specifications of such facilities.
- As a consequence of the first two points mentioned above, these owners are willing to step ahead and develop goals for their infrastructural durability. State Transport Ministers, for instance, took the initiative to define vital routes for the

Figure 1.16 Building damage by earthquake [55].

network to function during an earthquake which is usually referred to as roads and bridges on lifelines.

As seen in Figure 1.16, the building with a low-rise stage may have done well alone during the earthquakes but it was nevertheless demolished by the brick shower triggered by the out-of-plan collapse of an unreinforced maçonery wall in the neighboring house. Many well-performing buildings after the earthquake in Christchurch were still unavailable (and thus without functionality) because the owners were refused after the earthquake in the Christchurch Business District. For these reasons, genuinely resilient communities may be at risk for several decades.

Possible Solution to the Core Resilience Problem

There will also be a process to guarantee that stability becomes part of the negotiations in the construction of every building if durability is to be accomplished. Given the context of the unlikelihood of durability in architecture coding and requirements in the near future and the belief in constructing robust facilities continues to decline as time from past dangerous earthquakes decreases, it is not obvious what such a debate would achieve. It's commendable that the US Resiliency Council (USRC) has suggested to implement Earthquake Building Rating System similar to the LEED Green Building Rating System, in which buildings voluntarily evaluated will receive a 1 to 5-star rating for their respective safety, damage (in terms of repair costs) and recovery measures.

1.8   Development of Risk Informed Criteria for Building Design Hurricane Resilient on Building

To maintain the best distribution of services in the city there is a de-aggregation method to maximize the efficiency of the buildings and building groups in order to meet the City output objectives. Degradation is the process through which the community's performance objectives are converted into performance goals that are relevant for developing practice-based design criteria as described in the paragraph below. The tiered de-combination structure [69] as seen in Figure 1.17 will help to establish a connection between group priorities and PBE targets for specific buildings. The upper de-aggregation (ULD) can be formulated to define minimum output requirements as an inverse multinational optimization problem.

Inventories and service networks of growing group organization, when satisfied at the same time achieve the overall community resilience goals.

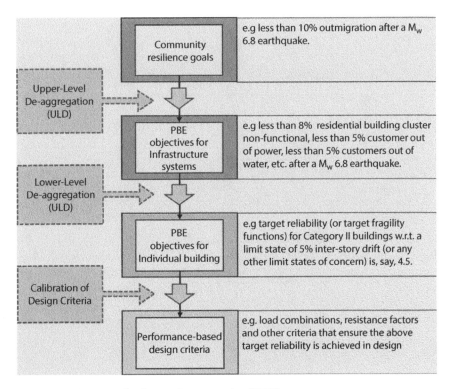

Figure 1.17 Framework of upper de-aggregation (ULD).

1.9   Resilient Infrastructures Against Earthquake and Tsunami Multi-Hazard

Hurricanes are one of America's most expensive natural disaster [47]. Between 1970 and 2016, the U.S. sustained seven of the world's 10 most expensive hurricane due to this the insurance company face huge losses for next five years.

In order to recognize the unavoidable interdependencies between vital infrastructure structures in the world, the quantification of vulnerability for populations prone to natural disasters (such as hurricanes) is important [70]. The vital infrastructure networks have effects on the environmental and economic stability of the nation because of their breakdown. Examples include communication networks, transport systems, water delivery schemes, etc. While interdependencies will boost the operating efficiencies of critical infrastructure networks, the network instability should be increased [68]. Such rise in device instability is triggered by cascade malfunction phenomena. Figure 1.18 provides an example of the

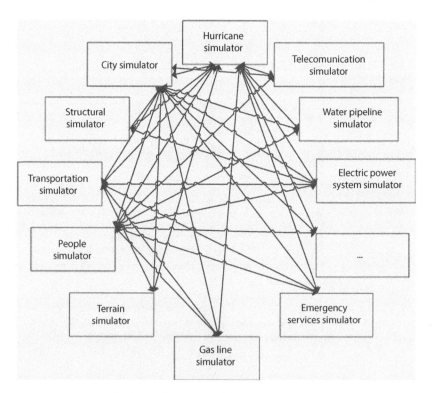

Figure 1.18 Framework of critical system modeling.

interdependencies that typically occur inside a computational setting and thus involve modeling.

To measure the vulnerability of hurricane-prone communities where a computational simulator models each vital structure, for various types of hazards, similar diagrams can be drawn.

1.10   Machine Learning With Smart Building

While the word "Smart Building" (SB) may offer a focus on a futuristic intelligent space in science fiction films, the truth SBs still occur yet are its amount that. Standard buildings can be converted efficiently into SBs with limited infrastructural improvements due to recent developments in Machine intelligence (ML, large amounts of data Analysis, Items Network camera technology (IoT)) [51]. Smart workplaces, smart schools, intelligent residences, intelligent health facilities, intelligent hospitals and a broad range of other SBs provide digital systems that provide a vast assortment of value-added services, such as energy conservation, and often maintain occupant convenience, safety and protection.

1.10.1   Smart Building Appliances

SBs are also incorporated into a single framework, including a wide variety of programs and facilities including energy management systems, temperature controls, access protection systems, fire protection and defense, light and life regulation, telephone infrastructure, bureau automation, computer networks, region position systems, LANs, informatic management. The SB devices, including air temperatures, lighting systems, solar panels, energy storage systems, temperature sensors, power sensors and tracking cameras, will be shown in Figure 1.19.

Central management of these components, for example, will facilitate efficient energy consumption by smart monitoring of the air-conditioners and lights and good management of various sources of green and brown electricity. In most instances, SB requires a Controller Area Network (CAN) connection to Ethernet backend.

1.10.2   Intelligent Tools, Cameras and Electronic Controls in a Connected House (SRB)

Compared with commercial buildings, intelligent systems are simpler to incorporate in residential buildings because residential buildings have

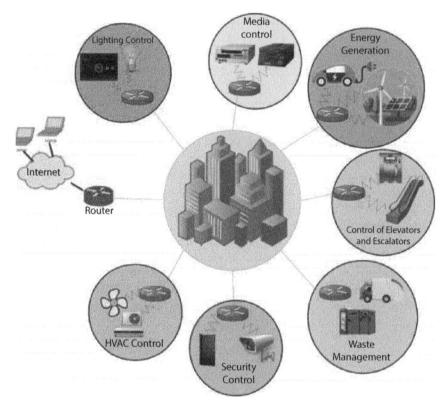

Figure 1.19 Smart building appliances [52].

fewer technological infrastructure and less strict quality specifications. Because industrial buildings typically receive more public tourists, design projects are generally more complex than development models for private buildings [25].

For apartment buildings typically have the bulk of the time with a small number of inhabitants. Rather than residential houses, the expenses involved with the procurement and development of intelligent equipment and services with industrial buildings are higher. Figure 1.20 shows an embedded socialized housing framework using an intelligent sensor network. Sensors include energy supply, estimation, HVAC, illumination and protection control systems. A building automation network operates a range of interconnected tools, sensors and actuators that together offer facilities for the well-being of citizens. Of starters, washers and drives, refrigerators, thermostats, lighting systems, power outlets, energy meters, smoke alarms, TVs, game consoles, window/door controls and alarms, air conditioning systems, video cameras and sound-detectors [36, 38, 39],

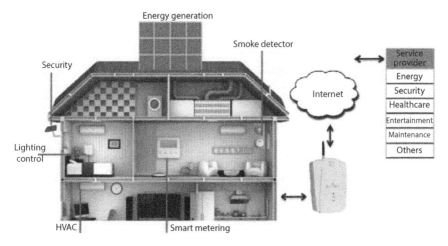

Figure 1.20 Smart Residential Building Connected Sensors and Actuators.

are examples of these electronic appliances, sensors and actuators. These include advanced electronic systems like sophisticated floors and smart furnishings are continuously being built [40, 42].

1.10.3   Level if Clouds are the IoT Institute Level With SBs

To order to maintain optimum monitoring and activity of the design, the IoT enables the convergence Interconnection and transfer of data processing capacities in embedded devices to SBs in high definition. IoTs are based on a layer-dependent design as seen in Figure 1.21. Data collected from different sensing devices is obtained, which are able to track environmental conditions, gather data on the civilian community and identification of disturbances (e.g., bursts of flames and water pipes). This layer also contains actuators to be monitored for energy conservation, water usage minimization and so on.

In the network layer (second layer in Figure 1.21), there is a clear access and core networking potential. This layer is used to link the smart grid with the top layers accountable for the processing of data. An intermediate software layer known as the middleware layer (the third layer in Figure 1.21) is required to incorporate the design sensing layer smoothly into heteroscope devices and networks. The layer acts as a link between the embedded devices operating intelligent sensors and network backend services.

The context and the somaticized discovery layer (Figure 1.21, fourth layer) is responsible for the management of context and semanticized

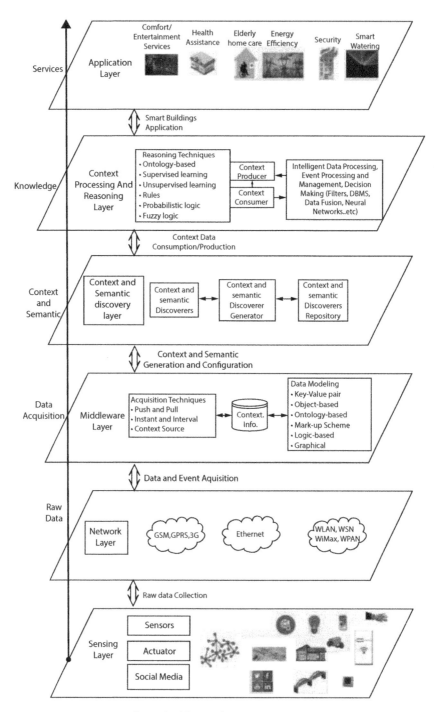

Figure 1.21 IoT smart resilience building architecture.

discovery, including context and semanticization generation. The analysis and reasoning layer (fifth layer in Figure 1.21) processes extracted knowledge from the middleware and takes decisions according to the application level. Various information retrieval systems are implemented in this layer to combine, retrieve and contextualize massive knowledge into practical know-how.

These included exceptional facilities and initiatives, an OSI model (Figure 1.20's biggest layer). This layer offers a context with clear links to the fundamental functions for various forms of applications. In addition, panels for managing automatic, the residence will create confined environments and infrastructure for a regional human–computer interface. The residence will create confined environments and infrastructure for a regional human–computer interface.

Knowledge and the retrieval of information in the sense of implementation and decision-making and the last layer of operation, including health care and home elderly care, convenience and entertainment facilities, protection, tele-management, intelligent watering, and resource output etc. analyze the core features of residential and industrial structures.

1.10.4   Component of Smart Buildings (SB)

Advances in intelligent design technologies contribute to widespread production of SBs, with the integration of IT and building automation systems, creating advantages for housing developers efficient and sustainable. The core elements of SB systems are seen in Figure 1.6, which involve vast sensors and drives, networks and connectivity structures, a software interface framework and a smart control device [54]. Figure 1.22 reveals different smart building components.

New solutions use smart sensors and control units attached to a central network. Such control systems and intelligent sensors are installed in the whole area. Each device has its own network and communications array that enables the central system to interact. SBs run linked networks that act for several structures as a connectivity backbone.

Sensors and Actuators for SBs

Mechanical elements calculating and monitoring environmental values of their system are sensors and actuators. Sensors collect and make information ready for the system from the environment. IR sensors can, for example, be used in a room for detecting human presence. While the actuator is an instrument for converting an electronic power signal for physical

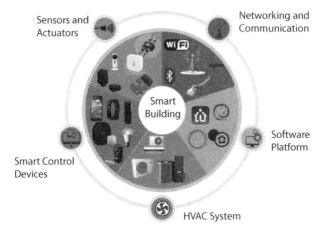

Figure 1.22 Smart building components.

activity, determines and then executes ecological acts that enable automated interaction, remotely and with the environment. For examples, one or more control lights may be turned on and off by an actuator.

1. Environmental Sensors: Data obtained from environmental sensors may be used to shape valuable details for tracking human behavior inside an SB.
2. Wearable Sensors and Biosensors: Such sensors are linked to the consumer body directly or indirectly. The compact scale allows it easy to mount such sensors to clothing, wristwatches, shoes, ties, slippers, etc.
3. Heating, Ventilation, and Air Conditioning (HVAC): In SB infrastructure, the HVAC program plays a significant function. The HVAC device plays a significant function in the efficient usage of electricity in SBs and provides innovative operational solutions in order to increase the health of inhabitants.

Smart Control Devices

Smart tracking systems capture, process and enable data from a range of sensors to respond to sensor–sensor events. An intelligent control system may be run independently without a central server order. Nevertheless, different control devices that require connectivity or they are able to link to one another via the intelligent gateway (Table 1.3).

Table 1.3 Smart control devices [56].

Sensor	Measurement	Calory
IR sensor	User presence in a room	Environmental sensors (ES)
Video cameras	Human actions	(ES)
RFID	Object identification	(ES)
Motion sensor	Object/User presence/ location	(ES)
Contact switch	Detect users' interaction with the object	(ES)
Pressure sensor	Tracking movements and location of the user	(ES)
Light sensor	Intensity 01 light	(ES)
Temperature sensor	Temperature of surrounding environment	(ES)
Humidity sensor	Detect the air humidity in a specific area	(ES)
Power sensor	Detect the usage of electric devices	(ES)
Accelerometer	The rate of acceleration accompanying a sensitive axis	Wearable-mental sensors (WMS)
Gyroscope	Angular velocity and maintain orientation	(WMS)
Electroencephalography	Observing electrical brain activity	(WMS)
Electrooculography	Observing eye movement of ocular activity	(WMS)

(Continued)

Table 1.3 Smart control devices [56]. (*Continued*)

Sensor	Measurement	Calory
Electromyography	Observing muscle activity	(WMS)
Electrocardiography	Observing cardiac activity, pressure sensors for observing blood pressure	(WMS)
CO2 gas sensors	Observing respiration	(WMS)
Thermal sensors	Observing body temperature	(WMS)
Galvanic skin response	Observing skin sweating	(WMS)

Automatically, life and seasons shift. Try it on your own for a week. These study the temperatures expected by the inhabitants and generate a personalized routine in the background.

WeMo is a Wi-Fi mechanism that enables mobile devices to be enabled/disabled everywhere. It monitors the orientation sensors of lamps, light bulbs, marts and connections and lighting devices, all from the mobile program or client.

The Nest thermostat, a mobile tool that Nest has built and purchased by google, adjusts seamlessly to your life and the seasons.

Lockitron is a door lock that enables the door to be unlocked and closed by telephone remotely on the Computer. Every iOS or Android device can install and use the Lockitron software.

A wireless hub that connects multiple mobile appliances and applications is part of the SmartThings SB management system; the wireless hub incorporates numerous protocols and Protocols including ZigBee, Z-Wave, and open IP apps that allow them to power over Wi-Fi than Bluetooth connectivity.

Philips Hue is a blend of mobile LED illumination, a smartphone device accompanying using WLAN apps for the mood-based control of artificial lighting and color packages. This device tracks users' drinking patterns and gives them reminders as to the amount and quantity of the water they can consume to keep them safe and hydrated.

Canary is a home protection device that incorporates a variety of atmospheric pressure, air pollution, noise & activity indicators detection, and a single unit HD video camera [53].

Amazon Echo is a tiny cylindrical device that enables users to monitor something at home through their voices. Amazon Echo provides a versatile capacity for speech identification which the customer needs to think about their voice's sophistication. Table 1.4 shows the difference between various smart control devices in SB.

Table 1.4 Difference Between Various Smart Control Devices in SB [56].

	Technology	Platform used	Pros	Cons
WeMo	Wi-Fi	Android, iOS, Windows Phone	Affordable hardware options. Can expand using Smart Things hob. Can expand using IFT1T.	No color bulbs, no dimmer switches. Experienced some latency issues.
Nest Thermostat	Wi-Fi, Zigbee, Thread	Android, iOS, MAC OS, Windows Phone	Easy to program. It learns the user daily routine; it could set itself up for the user lifestyle after the first work of use.	More expensive than other smart thermostats. The Nest might not be for you if you are a sticker for temperatures that are "lust right".
Lockitron	Bluetooth	Android, iOS	Affordable, Easy to install, quick operation. Offers proximity locking and unlocking.	Wi-Fi bridge costs extra. Does not work with other devices.
SmartThings	Wi-Fi, Zigbee, Z-Wave, Bluetooth	Android. iOS, Windows Phone	Affordable, Easy to install, quick operation. Offers proximity locking and unlocking.	Compatibility issues with other devices, workarounds for non-natively supported devices will be difficult for some.

(Continued)

Table 1.4 Difference Between Various Smart Control Devices in SB [56].
(*Continued*)

	Technology	Platform used	Pros	Cons
Philips Hue	Wi-Fi	Android, iOS	Modest list of 3rd party integrations. Offers own proprietary *hardware*. Active web community for help. Deep customization for power user.	Least user-friendly app, Complex to configure simple task. Missing some "key" integrations.
Blufitbottle	Bluetooth	iOS and Android	Easy to set up and use. Excellent Light quality	High Cost.
Canary	Wi-Fi	iOS and Android device	Simple and easy to set up.	Expensive.
Amazon Echo	Wi-Fi, Bluetooth	Fire OS, Android, and iOS	High-quality voice recognition. Integrations with all of the "key players", works for all users. regardless of phone brand.	The system only detects the intruder once they are inside premises.
Honeywell	Wi-Fi, Z-Wave	iOS and Android	Easy installation.	Priced higher than other smart thermostats with similar functionality.

This system blends smart home automation with a safety management function, with Honeywell Complete Link Remote Services. This helps us to track and regulate things through decorations and windshield covers to home security devices and smoke alarms.

Networking and Home Gateway

An SB incorporates a contact network to monitor the building's electronic devices and services. The information network in an intelligent city, such as the conventional computing networks, will be focused on different networking channels.

Software Platform

In order to be a "smart" house, all the computers and structures of the house will safely connect and exchange knowledge, as well as through laptops, tablets and cloud servers. In sharing, archiving and disseminating knowledge via numerous protocols, web systems play a key role.

Machine Learning Framework

Massive information generated by detectors, wearables and other technologies have comprehensive knowledge regarding the product background and construction status, which can be used to construct SB management.

The ML algorithms can be split between walking and jogging lessons between potential data points. Without any human intervention, it is fairly straightforward for ML to build sophisticated software systems. They are applicable in SB environments to many real-life issues. Self-learning and collaboration frameworks may also be built and created. ML algorithms can research and render input data predictions.

The furnace of both the nesting is an illustration of a device that, like the resident desired, maintains a different climate in a certain location and at those periods of the day. These are applications like the Amazon's Alexa that can understand from words, whereas some learn from even more nuanced behaviors. In order to create intelligent systems that can sense and respond according to contextual shifts, ML strategies have been used extensively.

The four main categories of Machine Learning are: Supervised Learning, Semi-Supervised learning, Unsupervised Learning and Reinforcement Learning. Figure 1.23 shows ML styles. The next explanation of these groups is the integration of this methodology in Table 1.5.

Supervised Learning: The ML model is built through an input-training cycle which continues until the model achieves the required accuracy. Some of the examples of commonly monitored ML algorithms include: Naive Bayes model, decision-making tree, linear discriminatory functions (SVMs), hidden Markov models (HMMs), instance education (for instance, k neighbor learning), ensembles (bagging, boosting, random forest), logistic regression, genetic algorithms and so on. ML algorithms are also common to use as an alternative algorithm. Monitored methods of learning are commonly used to solve different problems in SB.

Classification: Classification algorithms are intended to classify an instance into specific discreet categories. Due to two data sets (labeled and unscheduled data sets), the labeled data set is used to train.

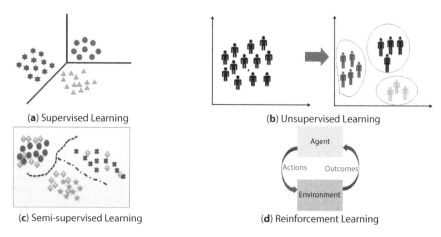

(a) Supervised Learning

(b) Unsupervised Learning

(c) Semi-supervised Learning

(d) Reinforcement Learning

Figure 1.23 Machine learning techniques.

Decision Tree Algorithms: The decision tree approach is a key predictive ML modeling approach, which constructs a decision model based on the real values of the data's features. For both classification and regression issues, decision trees can be used.

Bayesian Algorithms: For classification and regression questions, the Bayesian approaches use Bayes' theorem. Naive Bayes, Naive Gauss, Bayesian beliefs network, Bayesian Network and Bayesian Network are most general.

Support Vector Machine (SVM): SVM is one of the most commonly used for a large range of problems of statistical learning, including the identification of the face and object, classification of messages, spam-related detection and handwriting analysis.

Artificial Neural Network Algorithms (ANNs): The mechanism of the biologic neural networks inspires the ANN models. For regression and classification problems, ANN models are frequently used. The major algorithms are: perceptron, back-propagation (back-propagation), Hopefield network and radial feature network (RBFN).

Deep Learning Algorithms: Deep learning techniques reflect a type of advanced NANs in which deep (many layers consisting of several linear and non-linear transformations) architecture is used.

Hidden Markov Models (HMM): An HMM is a twice stochastic cycle with a secret corresponding stochastic system that can be found in the series of symbols that another stochastic mechanism generated.

Statistical Analysis: A critical path is a collection of scenarios; sets typically contain high dimensionality, a wide range of cases and continuous changes.

Table 1.5 Difference between of ML techniques.

Category	Type	Algorithms	Pros	Cons	Applicability in SBs
Supervised Learning	Classification	Neural networks	Request little statistical training; Can detect complex non-linear relationships	Computational burden; Prone to Overfitting; Picking the correct topology is difficult; Training can take a lot of data	Used for classification control and automated home, appliances, next step/action prediction
		SVM	Can avoid overfitting using the regularization; expert knowledge using appropriate kernels	Computationally expensive; Slow: Choice of kernel models and parameter, sensitive to overfitting	Classification and regression problems in SBs such as activity recognitions, human tracking, energy efficiency services
		Bayesian networks	Very simple representation does not allow for rich hypothesis	You should train a loge training set to me it well	Energy management and human activity recognition

(Continued)

Table 1.5 Difference between of ML techniques. (*Continued*)

Category	Type	Algorithms	Pros	Cons	Applicability in SBs
		Decision trees	Non-parametric algorithm that it easy to interpret and explain	Can easily overfit	Patient monitoring, healthcare services, awareness and notification service
		Hidden Markov	Flexible generalization of sequence profiles; can handle	Requires training using annotated data: Many unstructured parameters	Daily living activities recognition classification
		Deep Learning	Enables learning of feature rather than hand tuning: Reduce the need for feature engineering	Requires a very large amount of labeled data. computationally really expensive, and extremely *hard to tune*	Modeling occupied a behavior, and in human voice recognition and monitoring systems; Context-aware SB services

(Continued)

Table 1.5 Difference between of ML techniques. (*Continued*)

Category	Type	Algorithms	Pros	Cons	Applicability in SBs
	Regression	Orthogonal matching pursuit	Fast	Can go seriously wrong if there are severe outliers or influential cases	For regression problem such as energy efficiency services in SBs
		clustered based	Straightforward to understand and explain, and can be regularized to avoid overfitting	It is not flexible enough to capture complex patterns	Gesture recognition.
	Ensemble methods	N/A	Increased model accuracy through averaging as the number of model increases	Difficulties in interpreting decisions; Large computational requirements	Human activity recognition and energy efficiency services

(*Continued*)

Table 1.5 Difference between of ML techniques. (*Continued*)

Category	Type	Algorithms	Pros	Cons	Applicability in SBs
	Time Series	N/A	Can model temporal relationships; Applicable to settings where traditional between subject design are impossible or difficult to implement	Model identification is difficult; Traditional measures may be inappropriate for TS designs; Generalizability cannot be inferred from a single study	Occupant comfort services and energy efficiency services in SBs
Unsupervised learning	Clustering	KNN	Simplicity: Easy to implement and interpret; Fast and computationally efficient	High computation cost; lazy learner	Human activity recognition.
		K-pattern clustering	Simple; Easy to implement and interpret; Fast and computationally efficient	Only locally optimal and sensitive to initial points; Difficult to predict K-Value	Predict user activities in smart environments
		Others	N/A	N/A	N/A

(Continued)

Table 1.5 Difference between of ML techniques. (*Continued*)

Category	Type	Algorithms	Pros	Cons	Applicability in SBs
Semi-Supervised Learning	N/A	N/A	Overcome the problem of supervised learning having not enough labeled data	False labeling problems and incapable of utilizing out-of-domain samples	Provide context aware services such as health monitoring and elderly care services
Reinforcement learning	N/A	N/A	Used "deeper" knowledge about domain	Must have a model of environment; must know where actions lead in order to evaluate actions	Lighting control services and learning the occupants, preferences of music and lighting services.

Ensemble Methods: The community of classification models that are educated separately and then predictions are merged in a way that generates the ultimate prevision, also referred to as classifier ensemble.

Unsupervised learning implies designing algorithms to use data that have no labeling to evaluate the behavior or structure being analyzed. The algorithm is the best techniques to work on its own to discover patterns and information that was previously undetected. Clustering, anomaly, detection, Neural Networks etc. are all the examples of unsupervised learning.

Clustering: The internal groupings in the products, such as the grouping of customers, are investigated through a clustering problem. Modeling approaches including centroid-based and hierarchical are typically organized through clustering techniques.

Association: The question of the association rule is used to classify laws that describe significant quantities of input data, such as individuals who purchase X products, who also purchase Y objects. Association research can be achieved by evaluating rules for repeated if/then statement inputs and utilizing help requirements and trust to distinguish associations between unconnected data in a relational database.

Semi-Supervised Learning: Semi-controlled instruction is between approaches regulated and unregulated. Information is a labeled and blank experimental combination. Such architectures are synthetic are intended to consider and counteract the weaknesses of the main groups.

Reinforcement Learning: To order to optimize the principle of accrual compensation, enhanced learning, an ML area influenced by behavioral science, is concerned with the way virtual agents are to work to an environment. RL algorithms are used to learn policy of control, particularly if no prior information exists and a large amount of training data are available.

1.10.5   Machine Learning Tasks in Smart Building Environment

The key ML activities that are applicable to SB will be identified. For the general description of ML activities in SBs and measures to incorporate ML in an SB setting the reader is alluded to in Figure 1.24.

Collecting and collecting data: A range of methods were used to collect data, each of varying resources, energy consumption and networking deals. Sensors and related artifacts in SBs simultaneously produce raw information and these devices can store or record the information on monitored components for a specified period of time.

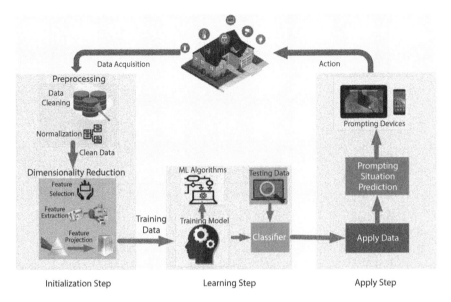

Figure 1.24 ML tasks in SB Environment.

It can be utilized by decision-makers, planners, running and sustaining staff and building customers, many healthcare services and so on.

Data Pre-processing: Much data is generated in SBs by sensors from various sources with specific formats and architectures. The data come from different sources. This knowledge is not usually ready to be evaluated, since its poor battery capacity, bad tuning, access to numerous harmful elements and intervention may be incomplete or redundant.

Dimensionality Reduction: Raising volumes of raw data from heterogenous and all-embracing sensors used in SBs are enormous. The bulk of data from these sensors is redundant and needs to be minimized by utilizing techniques to limit their dimensionality to a smaller number of features without missing any valuable details.

1.10.6   ML Tools and Services for Smart Building

The learning method is facilitated across a number of ML frameworks and resources. The challenge of choosing the best platform in order to data analytics flow sharing can also be achieved from alternative viewpoints challenging despite the growing amount of such toolkits. There is generally no one toolkit that completely suits all challenges (Table 1.6) and

Table 1.6 Difference between deep learning and machine learning tools [56].

Tool	Creator	OS	Open source?	Written In	Interface	CUDA support?	Algorithms	Release date
Tensor Flow	Google Brain team	Linux, Mac OS X (Windows support on road map	Yes	C++, Python	Python, C/C++	Yes	Deep learning algorithm: RNN, CN, RBM and DUN.	Novembeir 2015
Theano	Universit de Montral	Cross-platform	Yes	Python	Python	Yes	Deep learning algorithm: RNN, CN, RBM and DBN.	September 2007
H20	H20.ai	Linux, Mac OS, Microsoft Windows And Cross-platform inch Apache HDFS; Amazon EC2, Google Compute Engine, and Microsoft Azure.	Yes	Java, Scala, Python, R	Python, R	No	Algorithms for classification, clustering, generalized linear models, statistical analysis, ensembles, optimization tools, data pre-processing options and deep neural networks.	August 2011

(Continued)

Table 1.6 Difference between deep learning and machine learning tools [56]. (*Continued*)

Tool	Creator	OS	Open source?	Written In	Interface	CUDA support?	Algorithms	Release date
Deeplearning4j	Various. Original author Adam Gibson	Linux, OSX, Windows, Android, CyanogenMod (Cross-platform)	Yes	Java, Scala, C, CUDA	Java, Scala, Clo-jure	Yes	Deep learning algorithms including: RBM, DBN. RNN. deep autoencoder	August 2013
MLlib Spark	Apache Software Foundation. UC Berkeley AMPLab, Databricks	Microsoft Windows, OS X, Linux	Yes	Scala. Java, Python, R	Scala, Java, Python. R	No	Classification, regression, clustering, dimensionality reduction, and collaborative filtering	May 2014
Azure	Dave Cutler from Microsoft	Microsoft Windows, Linux	No	C++	C++, Java. ASP.NET, PHP. Nodejs, Python	Yes	Classification, regression, clustering	October 2010
Torch	Ronan Collobert, Koray Kavukcuoglu, Clement Farabet	Linux. Android, Mac OS X, iOS	Yes	C, Lua	Lua, LuaJIT. C, utility library for C++/ OpenCL	Yes	Deep algorithms	October 2002

(*Continued*)

Table 1.6 Difference between deep learning and machine learning tools [56]. (*Continued*)

Tool	Creator	OS	Open source?	Written In	Interface	CUDA support?	Algorithms	Release date
MOA	University of Waikato	Cross-platform	Yes	Java	GUI, the command-line and Java	No	ML algorithms (classification, regression, clustering, outlier detection, concept drift detection and recommender systems)	November 2014
Caffe	Berkeley Vision and Learning Center. community contributors	Ubuntu, OS X, AWS, unofficial Android port, Windows support by Microsoft Research, unofficial Windows port	Yes	C++, Python	C++, command line. Python, MATLAB	Yes	Deep learning algorithms: CN, and RNN	December 2012

includes remedies. Some of the toolkits available could overlap, with benefits and drawbacks.

1.10.7   Big Data Research Applications for SBs in Real-Time

Many systems need a stream data processing in real time, so it is not feasible for this form of program to wait for data to be stored so evaluated. Stream processing is typically configured to interpret large volumes of data and operate on data streaming in real time by using constant queries, including SQL queries, to manage streaming data in real time, using an interface that is robust, accessible and fault resistant (Table 1.7).

1.10.8   Implementation of the ML Concept in the SB Context

Figure 1.25 illustrates specific measures to forecast an event in the SB sense by utilizing ML methods.

On the other hand, the aim of optimization is to optimize long-lasting gains by proper decisions. Strengthening learning with these issues can be used. Many optimization issues may be treated as predicting issues such that benefit is estimated for different activities and the activity with the largest income is chosen. The most important form in optimization is decision-making. A variety of factors and compromises about the effects of specific environmental locations need to be addressed.

Smart Building Services Taxonomy

The taxonomy of SB resources essential domains is shown in Figure 1.26. Lighting service connects the well-being of occupants in SBs that have sensors that save energy when lights are not needed, based on their operation. Power and electricity can supply a percentage of SB power consumption with renewable energy sources. HVAC implies the heating, ventilation and air conditioning device, built for the comfort of citizens and an efficient ambient contact. The water resources program aims at growing conservation and maximizing resource recovery for water supply.

Smart building service taxonomy is related to the maintenance of electronic doors, biometrics and SB security cameras devices. The Control Center offers management and decision-making for apps. The automated apps include a description of the state of building capital resources and HR managers. These interfaces enable occupants to set optimum criteria to boost everyday business comfort and productivity. Ultimately, the Control Center, in the house like in the service control room, refers to linking sensors and actuators (Table 1.8).

Table 1.7 Difference between real time data analysis tools [56].

Tool	First released in	Main Owner	Platform	Written in	API languages	Auto-Scaling?	Event Size	fault Tolerance	Type
Storm	Sept. 2011	BacLtvpc. Twitter	Cross-platform	Clojure and Java	Any programming language	No	Single	Yes	Distributed stream processing
Kafka	Jan. 2011	LinkedIn. Confluent	Cross-platform	Scala	Java, C++, Node.js	Yes	Single	Yes	Message broker
Oracle	Jan. 2013	Oracle	Cross-platform	Java	Java, Node.js, Python, PHP, and Rubv	YES	NA	Yes	Distributed stream processing
Spark	May 2014	AMPLab. Databricks	Microsoft Wmdous, OS X. Linux	Scala, Java, Python, R	Scala, Java, Python, R	Yes	Minii-batch	Yes	Streaming analytics
Amazon Kinesis	Dec. 2013	AWS	Microsoft Windows, OS X, Linux	C++	C++, Java, Python, Ruby. Node.js, .NET	Yes	Data blob of 1 MB size	Yes	Real-time streaming data
Flume	Jan. 2012	Apple, Cloudera	Cross-platform	Java	Java	No	Single	Just with file channel only	Distributed stream processing
SAMOA	May 2013	Created at Yahoo Labs	Cross-platform	Java	Java	Yes	NA	Yes	Distributed stream processing

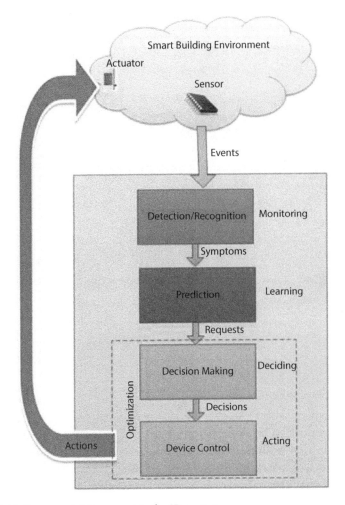

Figure 1.25 Framework ML concept in the SB context.

1.11 Conclusion and Future Research

Research results in this study revealed the value of establishing a sustainable framework for emerging development on the basis of green design and automated project execution in smart buildings. It will be achieved before artificial intelligence is used to accomplish smart buildings in the context of nanotechnology, structural knowledge simulation and Lean Architecture. The challenge of global change remains a major concern, given new technologies and smart buildings in developing countries.

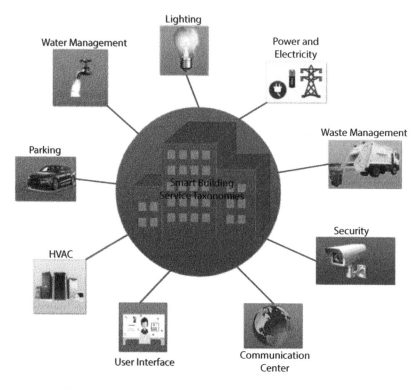

Figure 1.26 Taxonomy of SB Services.

In Africa, however, we will ensure that the efficient use of green infra-structure is first addressed in emerging technology, including artificial intelligence and smart buildings. The coordinated project execution often guarantees that the various sources of knowledge recorded in building information models and lean design are adequately applied by the presence at a strategic level of specific categories of practitioners. For starters, IT specialists are often an important part of the strategic design team as a case study, Eko Atlantic City has reported that Eko Atlantic City and Victoria Island now cover more than five million square meters of Great Wall of Lagos, which is developed more than two miles offshore. One big problem was the possibility of extreme floods. The tidal waves used to spray water and scrap daily on the major coastal path called the Ahmadu Bello route until the Great Wall Builder of the modern community design during development to use environmentally sustainable products and state-of-the-art technology. Further analysis will demonstrate when the first build-ings are complete, the essence of smart buildings and level of automated project execution at the location.

Table 1.8 Application of smart buildings [56].

Application category	Characteristics	ML algorithm	Technology used
Elderly Population's Home Care	Recognition of basic five activities, as feeding, grooming, dressing mobility and stairs	SVM	Wrist worn multi-sensors
	Framework covers both sensing and the monitoring services for assisting elders at smart homes environment	NA	RFID
	Elderly monitoring subsystem, home monitoring subsystem and the caretaker monitoring subsystem	NA	Vital sign sensors, GPS
	Support elderly people in carrying out a longer independent life at home	Neural Network	Illumination sensor, temperature sensor, door sensors and RFID

(Continued)

Table 1.8 Application of smart buildings [56]. (*Continued*)

Application category	Characteristics	ML algorithm	Technology used
Energy Efficiency	It becomes functional on a knowledge base that stores all information needed to fulfill the goals of energy efficiency and user comfort	NA	Household appliances
	Stationary and mobile user interfaces for monitoring and controlling the smart environment	NA	Wireless power metering plugs, household devices.
	Designing and evaluating end consumer energy efficient services	NA	Smart meters, Different types of sensors and actuators
	Gateway system architecture to support home-automation, energy use management, and smart-grid operations.	Classification algorithms such as C4.5 and RIPPER	Smart gateway
Safety and Security	Computer vision platform for security surveillance in smart homes	CNN	Surveillance cameras
	Composed of two methods: web *camera* to detect the Intruder, and GSM technology that sends SMS.	NA	Web camera and GSM technology
	Inexpensive, less power consumption	NA	GSM/GPRS

(*Continued*)

Table 1.8 Application of smart buildings [56]. (*Continued*)

Application category	Characteristics	ML algorithm	Technology used
Comfort and Entertainments	Deliver the service based on context-aware feature of the user	k nearest neighbors' classifier	Environment monitoring sensors
	Detect the atmospheric changes and predict the indoor air quality	Deep learning	CO_2, fine dust, temperature, humidity, and light quantity seniors
Miscellaneous Protects	Medical monitoring, green living, and general comfort.	Classification regression and clustering algorithms.	Wearable sensors
	SB services in the fields of health and well-being, digital media and entertainment, and sustainability	NA	Smart floor sensors, assistive robots
	Control people to control their environment. save resources. Remain mentally and physically active	NA	Home environmental sensors
	Context-aware computing services through video tracking and recognition	NA	Contains myriad devices that work together

References

1. Guikema, S. and Gardoni, P., Reliability estimation for networks of reinforced concrete bridges. *ASCE J. Infrastruct. Syst.*, 15, 61–69, 2009.
2. Kajitani, Y., Okada, N., Tatano, H., Measuring quality of human community life by spatial temporal age group distributions—Case study of recovery process in a disaster-affected region. *Nat. Hazards Rev.*, 6, 1, 41–47, 2005.
3. Kang, W.H., Song, J., Gardoni, P., Matrix-based system reliability method and applications to bridge networks. *Reliab. Eng. Syst. Safe.*, 93, 1584–93, 2008.
4. Koliou, M., Van De Lindt, J.W., McAllister, T.P., Ellingwood, B.R., Dillard, M., Cutler, H., State of the research in community resilience: Progress and challenges. *Sustain. Resilient Infrastruct.*, 5, 3, 131–151, 2018.
5. Lee, Y.-J., Song, J., Gardoni, P., Lim, H.-W., Post-hazard flow capacity of bridge transportation networks considering structural deterioration of bridges. *Struct. Infrastruct. Eng.*, 7, 7, 509–21, 2011.
6. MacLean, D., Gardoni, P., Murphy, C., Rowell, A. (Eds.), *Societal Risk Management of Natural Hazards*, Springer, New York, 2016.
7. Mardfekri, M. and Gardoni, P., Probabilistic demand models and fragility estimates for offshore wind turbine support structures. *Eng. Struct.*, 52, 2013, 478–87, 2013.
8. Mardfekri, M. and Gardoni, P., Multi-hazard reliability assessment of offshore wind turbines. *Wind Energy*, 18, 8, 1433–50, 2015.
9. Mardfekri, M., Gardoni, P., Bisadi, V., Service reliability of offshore wind turbines. *Int. J. Sustainable Energy*, 34, 7, 468–84, 2015.
10. Martins, N., Sustainability economics, ontology and the capability approach. *Ecol. Econ.*, 72, 1–4, 2011.
11. May, P., *Organizational and Societal Consequences for Performance-Based Earthquake Engineering*, PEER 2001/04, Pacific Earthquake Engineering Research Center, College of Engineering, University of California, Berkeley, Berkeley, CA, 2011.
12. Chan, M., Estve, D., Escriba, C., Campo, E., A review of smart homes present state and future challenges. *Comput. Methods Programs Biomed.*, 91, 1, 55–81, [Online]. http://www.sciencedirect.com/science/article/pii/S0169260708000436, Jul. 2008.
13. Alam, M.R., Reaz, M.B.I., Ali, M.A.M., A Review of Smart Homes—Past, Present, and Future. *IEEE Trans. Syst. Man Cybern. Part C (Appl. Rev.)*, 42, 6, 1190–1203, Nov. 2012.
14. Lobaccaro, G., Carlucci, S., Lfstrm, E., Lobaccaro, G., Carlucci, S., Lfstrm, E., A Review of Systems and Technologies for Smart Homes and Smart Grids. *Energies*, 9, 5, 348, [Online] https://www.mdpi.com/1996-1073/9/5/348, May 2016.

15. Pan, J., Jain, R., Paul, S., A Survey of Energy Efficiency in Buildings and Microgrids using Networking Technologies. *IEEE Commun. Surv. Tut.*, 16, 3, 1709–1731, 2014.

16. Ni, Q., Garca Hernando, A.B., de la Cruz, I.P., The Elderlys Independent Living in Smart Homes: A Characterization of Activities and Sensing Infrastructure Survey to Facilitate Services Development. *Sensors*, 15, 5, 11 312–11 362, [Online] Available: http://www.mdpi.com/1424-8220/15/5/11312, May 2015.

17. Rashidi, P. and Mihailidis, A., A Survey on Ambient-Assisted Living Tools for Older Adults. *IEEE J. Biomed. Health Inform.*, 17, 3, 579–590, May 2013.

18. Peetoom, K.K.B., Lexis, M.A.S., Joore, M., Dirksen, C.D., De Witte, L.P., Literature review on monitoring technologies and their outcomes in independently living elderly people, *Disability and Rehabilitation. Assist. Technol.*, 10, 4, 271–294, 2015.

19. Salih, A. and Abraham, A., A review of ambient intelligence assisted health-care monitoring. *Int. J. Comput. Inf. Syst. Ind. Manage. (IJCISIM)*, 5, 2013.

20. Perera, C., Zaslavsky, A., Christen, P., Georgakopoulos, D., Context Aware Computing for The Internet of Things: A Survey. *IEEE Commun. Surv. Tut.*, 16, 1, 414–454, 2014.

21. Tsai, C.W., Lai, C.F., Chiang, M.C., Yang, L.T., Data Mining for Internet of Things: A Survey. *IEEE Commun. Surv. Tut.*, 16, 1, 77–97, 2014.

22. Mahdavinejad, M.S., Rezvan, M., Barekatain, M., Adibi, P., Barnaghi, P., Sheth, A.P., Machine learning for internet of things data analysis: A survey. *Digit. Commun. Netw.*, 4, 3, 161–175, [Online] Available: http://www.sciencedirect.com/science/article/pii/S235286481730247X, Aug. 2018.

23. McAllister, T., *Developing guidelines and standards for disaster resilience of the built environment: A research needs assessment*, NIST Technical Note 1795, Gaithersburg, MD, 2013.

24. Mileti, D.S., *Disasters by Design: A Reassessment of Natural Hazards in the United States*, Joseph Henry Press, Washington, DC, 1999.

25. *Intelligent CRE for Enterprise: Smart Buildings, Intelligent Workplace, and Management Systems 2018-2023*, Research and Markets, Technical Report, 4559384, Business Wire, Dublin, Jun. 2018, [Online] Available: https://www.researchandmarkets.com/reports/4559384/intelligent-cre-for-enterprise-smart-buildings.

26. Chan, M., Estve, D., Escriba, C., Campo, E., A review of smart homes Present state and future challenges. *Comput. Methods Programs Biomed.*, 91, 1, 55–81, [Online], Available: http://www.sciencedirect.com/science/article/pii/ S0169260708000436, Jul. 2008.

27. Alam, M.R., Reaz, M.B.I., Ali, M.A.M., A Review of Smart Homes—Past, Present, and Future. *IEEE Trans. Syst. Man Cybern. Part C (Appl. Rev.)*, 42, 6, 1190–1203, Nov. 2012.

28. Lobaccaro, G., Carlucci, S., Lfstrm, E., Lobaccaro, G., Carlucci, S., Lfstrm, E., A Review of Systems and Technologies for Smart Homes and Smart Grids. *Energies*, 9, 5, 348, [Online] Available: https://www.mdpi.com/1996-1073/9/5/348, May 2016.
29. Pan, J., Jain, R., Paul, S., A Survey of Energy Efficiency in Buildings and Microgrids using Networking Technologies. *IEEE Commun. Surv. Tut.*, 16, 3, 1709–1731, 2014.
30. Rashidi, P. and Mihailidis, A., A Survey on Ambient-Assisted Living Tools for Older Adults. *IEEE J. Biomed. Health Inform.*, 17, 3, 579–590, May 2013.
31. Peetoom, K.K.B., Lexis, M.A.S., Joore, M., Dirksen, C.D., De Witte, L.P., Literature review on monitoring technologies and their outcomes in independently living elderly people, *Disability and Rehabilitation. Assist. Technol.*, 10, 4, 271–294, Jul. 2015.
32. Salih, A. and Abraham, A., A review of ambient intelligence assisted healthcare monitoring. *Int. J. Comput. Inf. Syst. Ind. Manage. (IJCISIM)*, 5, 741–750, 2013.
33. Perera, C., Zaslavsky, A., Christen, P., Georgakopoulos, D., Context Aware Computing for The Internet of Things: A Survey. *IEEE Commun. Surv. Tut.*, 16, 1, 414–454, 2014.
34. Tsai, C.W., Lai, C.F., Chiang, M.C., Yang, L.T., Data Mining for Internet of Things: A Survey. *IEEE Commun. Surv. Tut.*, 16, 1, 77–97, 2014.
35. Mahdavinejad, M.S., Rezvan, M., Barekatain, M., Adibi, P., Barnaghi, P., Sheth, A.P., Machine learning for internet of things data analysis: A survey. *Digit. Commun. Netw.*, 4, 3, 161–175, [Online] Available: http://www.sciencedirect.com/science/article/pii/S235286481730247X, Aug. 2018.
36. Institute for Building Efficiency, Sep. 2018, [Online] Available: https://buildingefficiencyinitiative.org/.
37. Zafari, F., Papapanagiotou, I., Christidis, K., Microlocation for Internet-of-Things-Equipped Smart Buildings. *IEEE Internet Things J.*, 3, 1, 96–112, Feb. 2016.
38. Kehoe, M., Cosgrove, M., Gennaro, S., Harrison, C., Harthoorn, W., Hogan, J., Meegan, J., Nesbitt, P., Peters, C., Smarter cities series: A foundation for understanding IBM smarter cities, *Redguides for Business Leaders*, IBM, 2011, https://www.computer.org/csdl/proceedings-article/hpcc/2016/07828528/12OmNz6iONv.
39. European Commission and Directorate-General for the Information Society and Media. *ICT for a low carbon economy: Smart electricity distribution networks*, EUR-OP, Luxembourg, 2009.
40. Badica, C., Brezovan, M., Bdic, A., An Overview of Smart Home Environments: Architectures, Technologies and Applications, in *CEUR Workshop Proceedings*, Thessaloniki, Greece, Volume 1036, pp. 78–85, Sep. 2013.
41. Flax, B.M., Intelligent buildings. *IEEE Commun. Mag.*, 29, 4, 24–27, Apr. 1991.
42. The Introduction to Smart Home Technologies Information Technology Essay, Dec. 2017, [Online] Available: https://www.uniassignment.com/essay-

samples/informationtechnology/theintroduction-to-smart-home-technologies-informationtechnology-essay.php.

43. Murphy, C. and Gardoni, P., The role of society in engineering risk analysis: A capabilities-based approach. *Risk Anal.*, 26, 4, 1073–83, 2006.

44. Murphy, C. and Gardoni, P., Determining public policy and resource allocation priorities for mitigating natural hazards: A capability-based approach. *Sci. Eng. Ethics*, 13, 4, 489–504, 2007.

45. Murphy, C. and Gardoni, P., The acceptability and the tolerability of societal risks: A capabilities-based approach. *Sci. Eng. Ethics*, 14, 1, 77–92, 2008.

46. Murphy, C. and Gardoni, P., Assessing capability instead of achieved functioning's in risk analysis. *J. Risk Res.*, 13, 2, 137–47, 2010.

47. Murphy, C. and Gardoni, P., Design, risk and capabilities, in: *Human Capabilities, Technology, and Design*, J. van den Hoven and I. Oosterlaken (Eds.), Springer, Heidelberg, 2011a.

48. Murphy, C. and Gardoni, P., Evaluating the source of the risks associated with natural events. *Res Publ.*, 17, 2, 125–40, 2011b.

49. Alzubi, J., Nayyar, A., Kumar, A., Machine learning from theory to algorithms: An overview. *J. Phys.: Conf. Ser.*, 1142, 2018.

50. Rameshwar, R., Solanki, A., Nayyar, A., Mahapatra, B., Green and smart buildings: A key to sustainable global solutions, in: *Green Building Management and Smart Automation*, pp. 146–163, IGI Global, 2020, https://www.igi-global.com/chapter/green-and-smart-buildings/231678.

51. Solanki, A. and Nayyar, A., Green internet of things (G-IoT): ICT technologies, principles, applications, projects, and challenges, in: *Handbook of Research on Big Data and the IoT*, pp. 379-405, IGI Global, 2019, https://www.igi-global.com/chapter/green-internet-of-things-g-iot/224280.

52. Krishnamurthi, R., Nayyar, A., Solanki, A., *Innovation Opportunities through Internet of Things (IoT) for Smart Cities, Green and Smart Technologies for Smart Cities*, pp. 261–292, CRC Press, Boca Raton, FL, USA, 2019.

53. Mahapatra, B. and Nayyar, A., Home energy management system (HEMS): Concept, architecture, infrastructure, challenges and energy management schemes. *Energy Syst.*, 1–27, 2019.

54. Das, S. and Nayyar, A., Innovative Ideas to Manage Urban Traffic Congestion in Cognitive Cities, in: *Driving the Development, Management, and Sustainability of Cognitive Cities*, pp. 139–162, IGI Global, 2019, https://www.igi-global.com/chapter/innovative-ideas-to-manage-urban-traffic-congestion-in-cognitive-cities/226920.

55. Gardoni, P., *Routledge Handbook of Sustainable and Resilient Structure*, Taylor & Francis, 2018, https://doi.org/10.4324/9781315142074.

56. Qolomany, B., Al-Fuqaha, A., Gupta, A., Benhaddou, D., Alwajidi, S., Qadir, J., Fong, A.C., Leveraging Machine Learning and Big Data for Smart Buildings: A Comprehensive Survey, *IEEE conference*, 7, 90316–90356, 2019.

57. Faber, M.H. and Qin, J., On the relationship between resilience and sustainability for infrastructure systems. In *International Symposium on*

Sustainability and Resiliency of Infrastructure (ISSRI2016), S.-S. Chen and A.H.-S. Ang (eds.), Taiwan Tech, Taipei, Taiwan, 2016.

58. Faber, M.H. *et al.*, Bridging resilience and sustainability decision analysis for design and management of infrastructure systems. *Journal for Sustainable and Resilient Infrastructure*, Taylor and Francis, 5, 102–124, 2018.

59. Linkov, I., Bridges, T., Creutzig, F., Decker, J., Fox-Lent, C., Kröger, W., Lambert, J. H., Levermann, A., Montreuil, B., Nathwani, J., Nyer, R., Renn, O., Scharte, B., Scheffler, A., Schreurs, M., Thiel-Clemen, T., Changing the resilience paradigm. *Nat. Clim. Change*, 4, 407–409, 2014.

60. Cimellaro, G.P., Reinhorn, A.M., Bruneau, M., Framework for analytical quantification of disaster resilience. *Eng. Struct.*, 32, 3639–49, 2009.

61. Sharma, N., Tabandeh, A., Gardoni, P., Resilience analysis: A mathematical formulation to model resilience of engineering systems. *Sustainable and Resilient Infrastructure*, 3, 2, 49–67, 2017.

62. Tamvakis, P. and Xenidis, Y., Comparative evaluation of resilience quantification methods for infrastructure systems, 26th IPMA World Congress, Crete, Greece, 2012, Elsevier. *Procedia – Soc. Behav. Sci.*, 74, 339–48, 2013.

63. Hauschild, M.Z., Better – but is it good enough? On the need to consider both eco-efficiency and eco-effectiveness to gauge industrial sustainability. In *The 22nd CIRP conference on Life Cycle Engineering – Procedia CIRP*, 29, 1– 7, 2015.

64. Gardoni, P. and Murphy, C., Society-based design: Developing sustainable and resilient communities. *Sustainable and Resilient Infrastructure*, 10, 1–16, 2018, https://www.tandfonline.com/doi/abs/10.1080/23789689.2018.1448667?journalCode=tsri20.

65. Guidotti, R., Gardoni, P., Rosenheim, N., Integration of physical infrastructure and social systems in communities' reliability and resilience analysis. *Reliab. Eng. Syst. Saf.*, 185, 476–492, 2018.

66. Boore, D.M. and Atkinson, G.M., Ground-motion prediction equations for the average horizontal component of PGA, PGV, and 5%-damped PSA at spectral periods between 0.01 s and 10.0 s. *Earthq. Spectra*, 24, 99–138, 2008.

67. Bai, J.-W., Hueste, M.B.D., Gardoni, P., Probabilistic assessment of structural damage due to earthquakes for buildings in mid-America. *J. Struct. Eng.*, 135, 1155–63, 2009.

69. Wang, Y., Gardoni, P., Murphy, C., Guerrier, S., Predicting fatality rates due to earthquakes accounting for community vulnerability. *Earthq. v*, 35(2), 502–513, 2019.

68. Dueñas-Osorio, L., and Vemuru, Seismic response of critical interdependent networks. *Earthq. Eng. Struct. Dyn.*, 36, 285–306, 2009.

70. Ouyang, M., Review on modeling and simulation of interdependent critical infrastructure systems. *Reliab. Eng. Syst. Saf.*, 121, 43–60, 2014.

71. Bates, F.L. and Peacock, W.G., Measuring disaster impact on household living conditions: The domestic assets approach. *IJMED*, 10, 1, 133–160, 1992.

2

Fire Hazard Detection and Prediction by Machine Learning Techniques in Smart Buildings (SBs) Using Sensors and Unmanned Aerial Vehicles (UAVs)

Sandhya Tarar* and Namisha Bhasin

School of Information and Communication Technology, Gautam Buddha University, Greater Noida, India

Abstract

Smart Building is a cost-effective way of managing different operations by integrating and automating activities effectively. In that direction one such requirement is to predict and take action automatically when a fire outbreak occurs at a SB. The task is performed with the help of sensors which collect analog signals and transfer the data to the drones using Bluetooth. Drones provide a 360-degree view of the building and after collecting data take necessary action. Here, threshold value plays an important role for predicting fire incidents and which is calculated based on various methods. Variation in degree of actual values from the threshold provides a range which is helpful for predicting different actions. The aim is to reduce False Rejection Rate (FRR) and make the system capable of predicting fire before danger point.

Keywords: Smart building, machine learning, time-series, fire detection, Hidden Markov Model (HMM), Artificial Neural Network (ANN), Back Propagation (BP), Unmanned Aerial Vehicle (UAV)

*Corresponding author: namishabhasin@gmail.com

Arun Solanki, Adarsh Kumar and Anand Nayyar (eds.) Digital Cities Roadmap: IoT-Based Architecture and Sustainable Buildings, (63–96) © 2021 Scrivener Publishing LLC

2.1   Introduction

In a smart building there are some major concerns that need to be addressed like: 1) safety and security of occupants, 2) accurate and early detection of any major hazardous event, etc. One of the major concerns is fire incidents which can be dangerous for lives along with having a commercial impact also. Three major factors leading to a fire incident are: heat, oxygen and fuel. Fire produces: light, various hazardous gases, plumes, heat and flame [1]. Most of the research is focused [2] on the process of detecting or sensing some elements like smoke, temperature, gas, infrared light radiation or heat. Fire hazard detection was earlier performed by humans which turned out to be time-consuming and could be harmful for someone's life. There are various types of research going on in this field and the main objective of them all is to ensure early and accurate detection of a fire incident. Authors [3] in this research classify the collected data with Support Vector Machine (SVM) algorithm received from smoke sensors but as in some fire incidents smoke comes out very late hence, will not be able to timely detect the fire outbreak cases where flaming occurs. In another paper, authors [4] detect fire outbreak by employing vision sensor and Support vector machine. Fire regions have higher intensity of light as compared to neighbouring regions which is used to make a luminance map. Then on this luminous map a model with wavelet coefficient and radial basis function (RBF) kernel with two-class SVM classifier is applied. But this suffers from many drawbacks as fire regions are detected by fire-coloured pixel methods. The whole process is very time consuming and does not take smoke into account which can be a major component while detecting fire. As incident of fire outbreak is very sensitive hence, early detection of the incident plays an important role. For these there is a requirement of smart [5] devices as they can be connected to the place of incident, can perform autonomously, having the quality of context-awareness, mobility, data storage and user-interaction. Fire incidents can occur anywhere but the objective of this chapter is to detect fire at smart building. And one of the issues with smart building is collecting data from the whole building. To achieve this, an unmanned aerial vehicle (UAV) is used which connects with the sensors through Bluetooth technology and can be helpful in collecting data with a 360° view. Drones are connected to analyzing center which can transmit information to the fire-fighting unit.

2.1.1   Bluetooth

Bluetooth [6] is an ideal solution which is inexpensive, capable of integrating applications, and universally accepted by every vendor. It uses single-chip which can operate in the 2.4-GHz industrial, scientific, and medical (ISM) RF band. The receiver sensitivity for Bluetooth is much better as compared to IEEE 802.11 Wireless LANs (WLAN) which is about −90 dBm while Bluetooth's is −70 dBm. Hence, Bluetooth is having the same transmitting power as WLAN but with a shorter range. Bluetooth provides 3-bit address hence at a time 8 devices can be connected together forming a piconet. If more than 8 devices have to be connected this can be accomplished by forming scatter nets.

2.1.2   Unmanned Aerial Vehicle

Small UAVs can be used in monitoring, transport, safety and disaster management. An autonomous [7] network consists of UAVs having the capabilities of sensing, processing, coordinating, and networking. Drones can be connected to sensors and actuators and can communicate with a central server through Wi-Fi using User Datagram Protocol (UDP) and web applications. Collecting data by IoT devices [8] stored and processed at local fog nodes in Edge computing critically impacts and increases the response time of user requests. But [9] if drone base stations (DBS) are located near to the drone [27] flying zone it will result in its latency being reduced.

2.1.3   Sensors

Sensors are small devices capable of detecting changes in the environment. The data is collected in the form of analog signals which is then converted into useful information. They are helpful to measure parameters such as lighting levels, temperature, humidity and room occupancy. Sensors [10–15] are wirelessly connected to each other. Sensors can communicate with each other using Internet. There are various types of sensors that collect information from their environment, process it and transmit [11] the information to the cluster head. Major limitations in a sensor are: 1) limited energy hence charging is required frequently; 2) small main memory which can store only a few kilobytes [12] hence for processing part they have to be dependent upon the service centre; 3) Compared to traditional processing units the micro-controller used in a wireless sensor node operates at low frequency. They are also known as [13] "System on Chip" (SoC). Multi-sensor nodes in the sensing field and distributed processing through multi-hop communication among sensor nodes can provide high quality and fault tolerance services in Wireless Sensor Networks. A sensor is a device that receives a stimulus and responds with an electrical [14] signal. Electrical signals like voltage, current, charge can be channelized, amplified and modified [15] by electronic devices. These signals can be described based on amplitude, frequency, phase and digital code. Some sensors directly convert stimulus into electrical signals while some perform this action with the help of transducers as shown in Figure 2.1. For different environments different sensors are there as follows:

Motion sensors: used to measure the motion of human in the vicinity, can be helpful in many ways as if no human is there it can switch off the lights, if someone tries to approach a no entry zone it can be detected. There are various motion sensors like 1) Passive infrared sensors: work on IR radiations which is emitted by all warm blood animals, 2) ultrasonic sensors: work on the concept of sound, 3) microwave sensors: generate microwave radiations and observe the reflection waves to know whether the object is moving or not and 4) tomographic sensors: work on the radio waves generated by these sensors and based on the calculation of reflected waves they detect the motion.

Temperature sensors: these sensors monitor the individual spaces and compare this value with the set point for the local system or with facility wide settings. Based on this the decision is taken whether the temperature needs to be increased (heating) or brought down (cooling) as needed in each given area.

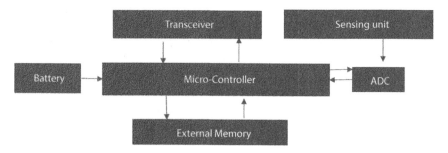

Figure 2.1 Block diagram of a sensor [10].

Humidity Sensors: calculate humidity level of the building area. Used to maintain a comfortable space as target value is dynamic due to frequent change in occupants and environment.

Ambient light sensors: are able to measure light intensity and depending upon the required amount of brightness the same is adjusted. Placement of sensor plays an important role in order to get accurate result. For example, if photometric sensors are placed close to the window, they dim the artificial light according to the daylight availability, hence they are placed at the ceiling for better results.

WSNs based on IEEE 802.15.4 is a collection of sensors and there is always a need for multiple sensors to communicate and aggregate information before it is sent to the Internet to save bandwidth and power consumption. Sensors are easy to install. The response time of sensors is approximate 11 ms to get into an active state from the power down state [16].

2.1.4   Problem Description

A survey revealed [17] that workplaces which were not managed properly lead to stress and health issues even when the environment [18] being equipped with greenery [21–24] which necessitates the need of smart building. Smart Buildings [19] are supposed to be adaptive and not reactive by integrating intelligence, control and construction to fulfil the requirement of energy with efficiency, longevity, comfort and satisfaction. Smart building is a concept of transformation from static to dynamic approach. Here changes occur every second as the situation in the environment develops. Smart building should be capable of managing the changes [20] in temperature and light [24] intensity according to changes in the number of people and space occupied. It is ideally supposed to be a comfortable space where all the factors affecting the occupant are monitored and controlled on the basis of individual need that too in a cost-effective way. It is a concept which considers HVAC system, lighting and is user friendly. Smart building following HVAC system uses sensors to [25, 26] measures occupancy, temperature, air quality, humidity and duct static pressure to maintain a comfortable and productive place. Efforts are put into smart building concept to detect the faults in the system as early as possible. According to the authors [26] if the variation in values of parameters are in a small range then it might be a minor issue but if difference is large then it is an indication of a serious problem. Smart building [26] is a concept where there is no wastage of electricity and to maintain the building energy-efficient different steps are implemented. Energy consumption is calculated based on occupants, room size, weather and by understanding the pattern as to when and where power consumption will be more. There is also monitoring of CO_2 so that a smart ventilation system can be provided. To maintain all these factors required data is collected by sensors. These values are analysed and action is taken accordingly. The sensors [72] used in HVAC system are 1) temperature: to know the temperature of room; 2) Pressure: to measure the pressure; 3) Smoke: to have a check on CO_2 level; 4) humidity: to measure the amount of humidity in the building and 5) Light: to measure the quantum of lighting in the building. Now the problem faced here is that for detection of fire also same sensors are used. And experiments show as fire incident occur temperature and CO_2 will increase; pressure and humidity will decrease. So, HVAC system will increase the temperature of cooling system and because of increased level of CO_2 ventilation system will also be activated. Hence, system will not be able to provide accurate fire information at the right time. These limitations are removed in the proposed system by using same sensors. Hence, no extra cost is incurred on the proposed architecture.

The rest of this chapter is organized as follows: Section 2.2 describes the review of existing literature which discusses how fire incidents can be detected. Section 2.3 discusses experimental methods for detecting, predicting and taking proper action for the fire incidents. Section 2.4 discusses experimental evaluation and results. Section 2.5 concludes the chapter with future scope.

2.2   Literature Review

This section discusses the contribution of various techniques for fire detection and prediction. Fire is a chemical and physical phenomenon that produces smoke, light and heat. Some fire detection systems are dependent on single sensor which produces false results because fire incidents have multiple factors which cannot be measured by a single sensor. As in fire incidents when dataset is analyzed then it was found that fire incidents data values show an unusual pattern which Shahid *et al.* [28] described as 'outlier'. Hence, any data value that comes in the category of outlier is considered as fire incident. The authors [28] proposed nearest neighbors and clustering approach to differentiate between the patterns but they were unable to justify the threshold value which is crucial for the classification of outlier and normal data. So, they were not able to classify the data correctly. Threshold value plays an important role as if taken too low then false negative rate is more. Similarly, clustering techniques face difficulties in dynamic environment where data changes over time. As in many researches gas sensors are used to detect fire incidents but, as they are sensitive to ionization or obscuration hence events like smoking a cigarette or toasting a bread can also trigger the fire alarm. So, Andrew et al. [29] used the approach probabilistic neural network to classify different smells with e-nose and an accuracy of 94.18%. Fire detection by Mahdipour and Dadkhah [30] used image processing RGB based chromatic to take decision of the incident. Based upon the intensity of color, in flame-oriented incidents red color and in smoke-oriented Chen et al. [31] considered grayish color. Further analysis is done to understand whether red color or grayish color is because of fire or by another object and verified. Chen et al. [32] proposed fuzzy logic for differentiating between fire and fire like coloured objects with an accuracy of 99%. For smoke detection two basic decision rules were followed 1) chromaticity-based static and 2) diffusion-based dynamic decision rules. The decision rule of smoke for chromatic considers intensity of grayish color and for dynamic the spreading attributes. The biggest drawback of this approach is that it is time consuming and in fire incidents time plays an important role. Further, Horng et al. [33] used temperature sensor to find the temperature in the vicinity. If critical value is informed by temperature sensor then system issue a fire alarm and in all the discussed cases of fire authors were able to get correct results. But as environment under observation is dynamic hence, just using one sensor will not be able to provide correct results which are not considered in the research work. Predicting behaviour of fire can be helpful for saving many lives. In that direction, two approaches were used (1) genetic algorithms where authors Denham et al. [34] proposed dynamic data driven approach to automatically adjust input values and improve quality of prediction in the calibration stage; (2) expert, knowledge and rule-based systems—authors used genetic algorithm to automatically evolve fuzzy rules and membership functions. As most of the situations are dynamic hence authors Fowler et al. [35] found it difficult to detect fire with static parameters, therefore they used fuzzy logic and genetic algorithm to predict the incident with RMSE of 50.3. Bahrepour et al. [36] found suitable threshold of the parameters play an important role. In that direction they used Naïve Bayes and Feed-Forward Neural Network for fire detection with an accuracy of 100 and 98.45% respectively. Rasyid et al. [37]

applied fuzzy logic on the data received from temperature, humidity, CO, smoke sensors with an error rate of 3.33%. Sowah *et al.* [38] applied fuzzy logic on the data received from smoke, temperature and flame sensor with an accuracy of 90%. Wang *et al.* [39] proposed multisensory fire detection level, fire hazard distribution level, fire hazard ranking level and system fire hazard ranking level to provide fire location, fire development intensity and fire situation of an entire building. Park *et al.* [40] proposed fire detection system using Convolutional Neural Network (CNN), Deep neural network (DNN), and adaptive fuzzy algorithm with a multifunctional artificial intelligence framework and an accuracy of 95% and a data transfer delay using Direct-MQTT based on SDN by an average of 72%. Chen *et al.* [41] used data from temperature, smoke and combustion products (CO, CO2) to calculate the dynamic threshold using linear regression and moving average method. Cheng *et al.* [42] used three sensors temperature, smoke and sensor to measure CO concentration and applied neural network to calculate the threshold values of these parameters depending upon the environment in which they are implemented with an error rate of 5%. Wang *et al.* [43] proposed time-independent information collected by fusion algorithm for Artificial Neural Network (ANN) models, namely Radial basis function (RBF), Back propagation (BP), Probabilistic neural network (PNN) to find the step size and observation window duration for feature extraction in multi-sensor fire detection technology and found that observation window duration of 90 s with step size of 25 to 200 s provides best result for all three ANN models. Umoh *et al.* [44] applied Support Vector Machine (SVM) classification algorithm using Fire Outbreak Capture Device which is equipped with MQ-2 smoke sensor, DHT11 temperature sensor, LM393 Flame sensor, and ESP8266 Wi-Fi module with 100% accuracy. Khooban *et al.* [45] used video based on 3D point cloud fire pixel samples, Gaussian mixture model to select static and dynamic features and for that three types of fire colors are labeled. They further used colour distributions, texture parameters and shape roundness for static and flickering frequency from temporal wavelet-based Fourier descriptors analysis for dynamic features and classify the result with Support Vector Machine (SVM). Vigneshwara *et al.* [46] used the approach adaptive fusion on three sensors Temperature, Flame and Gas and use Arduino IDE for system implementation. Khule *et al.* [47] used the approach SVM algorithms and compared the results with logistic regression and found that SVM performs better in Fire detection scenarios. Torabnezhad and Aghagolzadeh [48] proposed fire detection based upon smoke and found detecting fire based upon smoke is not fully reliable hence consider other feature shape for it. But Yuan *et al.* [49] found that other features like shade, motion and density were also not able to provide reliable results and found that low saturation color of smoke plays an important role. Rong *et al.* [50] proposed rule based generic flame colored model for motion detection which was capable of detecting the fire incidents without any requirement of static background and further author used a BP model to successfully detect the fire incidents accurately and timely. Wang *et al.* [51] proposed early detection of smoke using swaying and diffusion with a processing speed of 25 frames per second and also described that smoke tends to progress rather than backtrack and it develops in different ways. Toreyin *et al.* [52] found that as fire progresses the images of smoke slowly start losing the smoothness of the edges which leads to decrease in chrominance values.

2.3 Experimental Methods

In HVAC system [53, 54] various types of sensors covering a wide range of areas are deployed which can improve reliability and productivity. But if a single senor is deployed it produces false results as operating environment is dynamic. For example, if smoke sensor is deployed to detect the fire then it can produce wrong results because wood as compared to plastic produces less smoke. If the number of sensors increases, the accuracy of result will also increase. Different sensors are combined to improve the quality of performance. Temperature sensor measures the amount of heat energy and coldness in the environment. Temperature sensors are able to detect difference in temperature of the surroundings. All hot-blooded objects have temperature above absolute zero and they emit energy in the form of electromagnetic radiations. Different objects reflect different amount of energy, which can be measured as a wavelength and known as spectral reflectance. According to Stefan–Boltzmann Law the total energy (E) being radiated increases rapidly as the temperature (T) increases as shown below:

$$E \propto T^4 \tag{2.1}$$

The open wood and plastic fires have apparent source temperatures that range from 1,400 to 1,700 K. As fire outbreak occurs temperature rises in the vicinity which can be an indication of fire in the surrounding. It works on the concept of 1) thermocouple where electromotive force (emf) is used to find the temperature, where emf is defined as the work dW done per charge dq; 2) Resistance Temperature detector (RTD) where small current generate voltage is used to calculate temperature and 3) Thermistors work on the same concept of RTD. As rise in temperature can be because of some other aspects like using stove for preparing food also, hence for true prediction of fire outbreak other factors are also required. A flame is the visible, gaseous part of a fire. Flame sensors confirm whether flame is burning or not. A small current is sent out from the sensor to know whether flame is there or not. Flame sensors work on the concept of infrared rays. Quantum infrared sensors produce good results for flame detection. As some fire incidents happen because of smouldering alone flame sensors are not sufficient to produce correct results. The smouldering wood fire has intensity value which is lower than other substance by around three orders of magnitude. Third sensor used is smoke sensor which works on the concept of measurements of light scattering or smoke ionization. Smoke sensors are of two types: 1) optical smoke sensor and 2) ionization sensor. Fourth sensor used is for measuring humidity. Humidity represents the moisture present in the surroundings environment. As fire outbreak occurs temperature increases which results in lower relative humidity. Types of humidity sensors are 1) capacitive, 2) resistive and 3) thermal. But they can also be affected by environmental changes. Fifth sensor used is for measuring pressure. Pressure sensors are used to measure the pressure of the environment. Various types of pressure sensors are 1) gauge pressure sensor and 2) differential pressure sensor. Same sensors are used in detecting fire incidents. Hence as temperature or CO2 level increases or humidity and pressure decreases HVAC system will try to reach at equilibrium point and will not be able to detect fire incidents early. The type and number of sensors used should be able to detect the changes in the indoor environment when fire incident occurs. In the proposed system different sensors used are 1) temperature, 2) smoke, 3) flame, 4) humidity and 5) pressure which are already implemented for HVAC [55] enabled building.

In solving the problem, dynamic threshold values plays an important role. This problem is solved by using time-series based forecasting where a value is estimated depending upon the previous values. Hence, can be used to find a threshold value for the parameters and any changes in the current situation will have a corresponding impact on the threshold value. Changes [56] can be minor or major; minor changes can be accepted but for major changes a reflect action is required. Further, forecasting

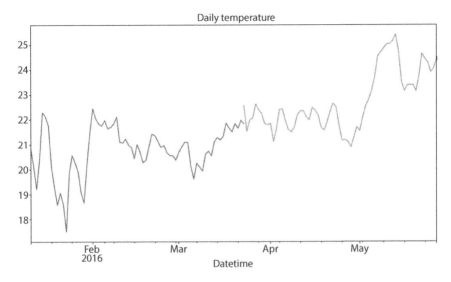

Figure 2.2 Blue color represents training data and red color test data.

technique can be univariate or multivariate time-series-based. In univariate time-series analysis only one variable is considered for prediction. In multivariate multiple variables are used for prediction. In the proposed work both forecasting techniques are used to calculate the threshold value. By using univariate variable threshold value of single parameter is predicted and taken as threshold. If vicinity temperature is more than the threshold value by some range then that is taken as fire outbreak. Various cases have been discussed. For this the dataset is divided into training and testing data. In Figure 2.2 temperature feature data used for training and testing is plotted in blue and red respectively. The dataset is taken from Kaggle [57].

2.3.1 Univariate Time-Series

Univariate time-series is used to predict the threshold value of a parameter. This is a simple time-series method where parameters are supposed to have no influence on other parameter's value. Any deviation from the threshold produces a different range of values. Depending upon that range a proper action is taken. If parameter values increase or decrease by small range then no action is taken but if this is not the case then proper action is taken as shown below.

2.3.1.1   Naïve Bayes

Naïve Bayes—Equation 2.2 prediction algorithm [58, 59] is used which is able to forecast data based on previous value and provide results in real-time as it is a fast technique. But it is unable to consider other factors. In this case, next 17 days temperature data is predicted based on Naïve Bayes shown in Figure 2.3. Accuracy is checked with root mean square error (RMSE) value and R^2 values. The RMSE and R^2 scores are calculated with predicted and test data. R^2 close to value 1 is appreciated.

$$P(X|C)\ P(X) = P(C|X)\ P(C) \tag{2.2}$$

2.3.1.2   Simple Average

Second technique [60] used is Simple Average as shown in Figure 2.4. In many cases data values increase or decrease with time but average remains constant. Therefore, past average values are considered for prediction. In simple average next value is predicted based on previous average result.

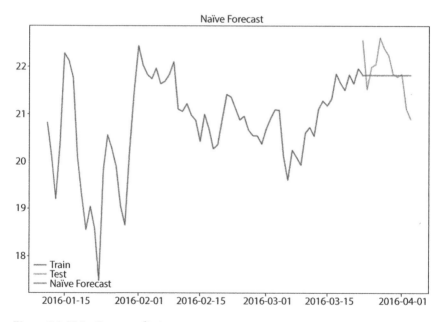

Figure 2.3 Naïve Bayes prediction.

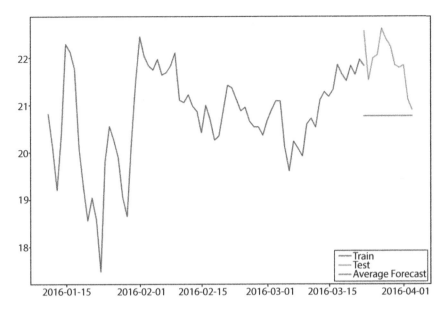

Figure 2.4 Forecasting with simple average.

2.3.1.3 Moving Average

Prediction based on Moving Average [61] as shown in Figure 2.5 is used to get an overall idea of data. As some values behave differently from the previous pattern in those cases moving average is helpful to predict next values.

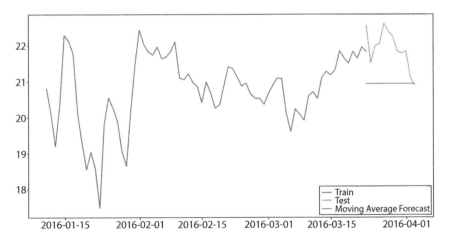

Figure 2.5 Prediction based on moving average.

2.3.1.4   Simple Exponential Smoothing (SES)

Prediction based on SES [62] as shown in Figure 2.6 consider overall data and not just dependent upon a special pattern and results are calculated with weighted averages. If data is old one then less weightage is given as compared to recent values. Weights decrease exponentially if the observed data is from the past.

2.3.1.5   Holt's Linear Trend

This [63] method as shown in Figure 2.7 is used when values are increasing continuously. It is a three-layer method. In first layer smoothing equation used to adjust last value for the last periods trend. Second layer update this value overtime using the difference between the last two values and third layer is used for prediction of values by making use of first-layer and second-layer values.

2.3.1.6   Holt–Winters Method

This method [64] as shown in Figure 2.8 consider seasons as a special feature. For the method four-layer prediction concept is used. For the first layer level smoothing value; for second layer trend smoothing value and for third seasonal component is consider and forth layer is used to predict these lower layer values.

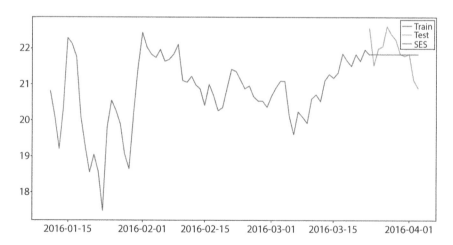

Figure 2.6 Simple Exponential Smoothing.

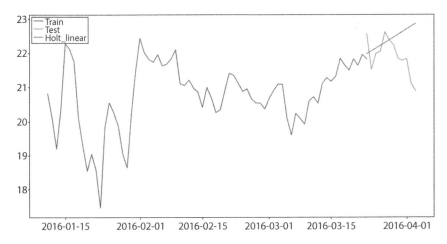

Figure 2.7 Holt's Linear Trend.

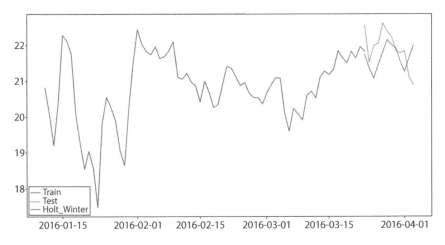

Figure 2.8 Holt–Winters Method.

2.3.1.7 *Autoregressive Integrated Moving Average Model (ARIMA)*

In this method [65, 66] autocorrelations in the data are considered. It uses dependent relationship between observed and lagged observed value and uses differences of raw observations to convert the series into stationary one, after that uses moving average between observed and residual error values. By having a series as stationary make the properties of data independent of time. There are various ways to make a series from non-stationary to stationary like 1) differencing method, 2) random walk method, 3) second order differencing and 4) seasonal differencing. The predicted result is shown in Figure 2.9.

From the above used time-series prediction methods best result has been produced with ARIMA model. As in univariate time-series based on single parameter prediction for next few hours, days or months can be calculated and those values can be taken as threshold. The results are discussed in Table 2.1.

Further, these threshold values can be improved by using Artificial neural method (ANN) [67] as shown in Figure 2.10 or Back Propagation method [68]. Here predicted values by threshold are used as input (I1)

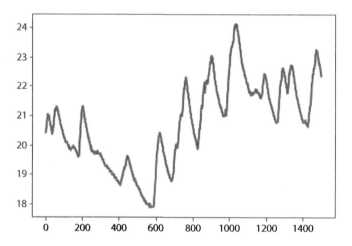

Figure 2.9 Auto Regressive Integrated Moving Average model.

Table 2.1 Results of different techniques.

Technique/Result	RMSE	R² score
Naïve Bayes	0.516023603770526	−0.023542814334042816
Simple average	1.2441947059014173	−4.950364595821548
Moving average	1.089542433854416	−3.5630494700878623
Simple Exponential Smoothing	0.5149310532505095	−0.019213212372246158
Holt's Linear Trend	0.8863720488433394	−2.0199446532847016
Holt–Winters Method	0.614896359830968	−0.45335169995983193
ARIMA	0.042227031760264946	0.9991440622360026

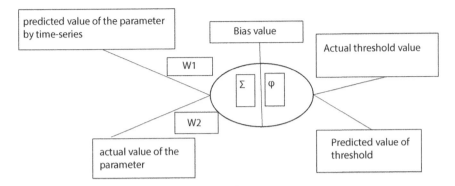

Figure 2.10 Artificial neural network [67].

with weightage w1 and actual value of parameter (I2) by w2 with bias value (b) and sigmoid activation function (φ). Initially weights are taken as randomly and sigmoid function acts as catalyst which has no impact on the results. The output produced is compare with actual value that value is known as error in Back Propagation to reduce the error these values are back propagated to adjust the weight values. $\phi((I1 * w1 + I2 * w2) + b) =$ prediction of threshold and error = actual result – prediction result.

Comparing to predicted thresholds values with the actual values and knowing the difference provides a glimpse of what is going on in the environment. Major difference in the range of values is a reflection of fire outbreak. As shown in Table 2.2 where *th* acts as threshold value and t acts ac temperature, p as pressure, s as smoke, h as humidity, l as light intensity. Output depends upon the degree of diversion from the current value.

Table 2.2 Action taken for different range of values.

Input					Output
Temperature	**Smoke**	**Pressure**	**Humidity**	**Light intensity**	
$th \geq t$	$th \geq s$	$th \leq p$	$th \leq h$	$th \geq 1$	**Normal**
$3 + t \geq th \geq t$	$s + 5 \geq th \geq s$	$th \geq p - 3$	$th \geq h - 3$	$1 + 50 \geq th \geq 1$	**Normal**
$5 + t \geq th \geq 2 + t$	$s + 7 \geq th \geq s + 5$	$th \geq p - 5$	$th \geq h - 7$	$1 + 150 \geq th \geq 1 + 50$	**Get ready**
$7 + t \geq th \geq 5 + t$	$s + 9 \geq th \geq s + 7$	$th \geq p - 9$	$th \geq h - 10$	$1 + 250 \geq th \geq 1 + 150$	**Get ready**
$t \geq th + 10$	$\geq th + 10$	$th > p - 12$	$th > h - 15$	$1 \geq th + 350$	**Outbreak**

2.3.2   Multivariate Time-Series Prediction

Next time-series prediction is based on more than one variable and also considers how one parameter is affecting the other parameters.

2.3.2.1   *Vector Autoregressive (VAR)*

There are more than [69] two variables which are affecting each other as temperature value increases pressure and humidity decrease. Hence, multivariate time series can be used to predict fire outbreak. Each variable value is predicted based on past values. VAR model R2 score is −528.7642948354535. In VAR variables influence each other this factor is also considered as given below:

$$Y_{1,t} = f_1(y_{1t-1}, y_{kt-1}, ..., y_{1t-p}, ..., y_{k,t-p}, X_{t-1}, X_{t-2}, ...) \qquad (2.3)$$

$$Y_{k,t} = f_k(y_{1t-1}, y_{kt-1}, ..., y_{1t-p}, ..., y_{k,t-p}, X_{t-1}, X_{t-2}, ...) \qquad (2.4)$$

The results of predicted and actual for overall values is shown in Figure 2.11.

For individual parameters results are shown in Table 2.3. MPE close to 0 and RMSE minimum are consider as ideal values.

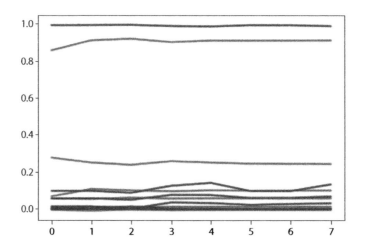

Figure 2.11 Artificial neural network [67].

Table 2.3 Forecast accuracy of different variables.

	Temperature	Smoke	Flame	Humidity	Light intensity
Mean Absolute Percentage Error (MAPE)	1.719	1.7591	1.7734	6.7966	Inf
Mean Error (ME)	74.84.09	132.6282	1218.2469	−190.1885	−746.5679
Mean Absolute Error (MAE)	74.8409	132.6282	1218.2469	243.5354	746.5679
Mean Percentage Error (MPE)	1.719	1.7591	1.7734	−5.9221	−Inf
Root Mean Square Error (RMSE)	82.5684	143.0441	1339.4318	278.1665	790.815
CORR	.3996	−0.0421	0.8531	0.1103	Nan
MINMAX	.5848	0.595	0.5996	6.5184	Inf

2.3.3   Hidden Markov Model (HMM)

The limitation with the above algorithms is that threshold values are adjustable according to the environment and they change their threshold values depending upon the previous values of the time-series. But as the system is HVAC enabled and try to make the system to reach the comfort level also uses previous data. If in the HVAC enabled SB temperature rises air conditioner will try to make the environment cool which will act on previous data in the time-series. Hence, system will not be capable to provide the required values [70]. So, system has to be independent of these values. To make the system more reliable other factors should also be consider like room temperature is different from the outer temperature by 2 4 °C. Hence, these factors should also be considered to make the system work properly. As outside temperature increases so inside temperature will also increase and air conditioner will try to lower the temperature inside. Similarly, if smoke outside the building is more will increase smoke inside the building hence, ventilation system will be activated to lower the smoke value. In the same way light intensity if outside is more than inside area will require less intensity of artificial light. If temperature is more outside pressure and humidity values will be relatively low. Hence, outside environment can be consider as a reference for inside values and any increase in these values than expected; depending upon the range of value proper action can be taken. The features used in proposal are shown in Table 2.4.

Table 2.4 Features to be considered for fire detection.

Temperature	Smoke	Flames	Pressure	Light intensity

As outside environment values change relatively but in case of fire inside values changes drastically.

$a1$ = temperature of air conditioner inside the building at time t_i.

$a2$ = temperature of air conditioner inside the building calculated at time $t_i + 1$.

$a3$ = temperature outside the building at time t_i.

$a4$ = temperature outside the building calculated at time $t_i + 1$.

$a5$ = temperature of air conditioner inside the building calculated at time $t_i + 1$ using Hidden Markov Model i.e. $p(a2|a4)$.

Use steps (1–5) to calculate values for smoke (s), light intensity (l), humidity (h) and pressure (p).

Step1: if ((a2>a5) and (s2>s5) and (l2>l5) and (h2<h5) and (p2<p5)) values difference is more than 10 then fire is there.
Step2: if ((a2>a5) and (s2>s5) and (l2>l5) and (h2<h5) and (p2<p5)) values difference is up to 5 then alarming situation is there.
Step3: if ((a2>a5) and (s2>s5) and (l2>l5) and (h2<h5) and (p2<p5)) values difference is up to 2 then situation is normal and no action is required.

Algorithm

Step1: if ((a2 > a5) and (s2 > s5) and (l2 > l5) and (h2 < h5) and (p2 < p5)) values difference is more than 10 then fire is there.

Step2: if ((a2 > a5) and (s2 > s5) and (l2 > l5) and (h2 < h5) and (p2 < p5)) values difference is up to 5 then alarming situation is there.

Step3: if ((a2 > a5) and (s2 > s5) and (l2 > l5) and (h2 < h5) and (p2 < p5)) values difference is up to 2 then situation is normal and no action is required.

Case Study: Relevant cases are discussed further:

Case 1:

Temperature of air conditioner inside the building at   Outside Temperature

tᵢ a1 = 25.08   tᵢ a3 = 26.1

t_{i+1} a2 = 25.977 t_{i+1} a4 = 27.1

t_{i+1} a5 = 26.0

Case 2:

Temperature of air conditioner inside the building at   Outside Temperature

tᵢ a1 = 25.08   tᵢ a3 = 26.1

t_{i+1} a2 = 45.977 t_{i+1} a4 = 26.5

t_{i+1} a5 = 26.6

Case 3:

Smoke inside the building at   Outside Smoke

tᵢ s1 = 50.529   tᵢ s3 = 50

t_{i+1} s2 = 52.345 t_{i+1} s4 = 52.8

t_{i+1} s5 = 52.66

Case 4:

Smoke inside the building at   Outside Smoke

tᵢ s1 = 50.529   tᵢ s3 = 50

t_{i+1} s2 = 81.57 t_{i+1} s4 = 52.8

t_{i+1} s5 = 52.66

Case 5:

Flames/Light intensity inside the   Flames/Light intensity
building at   outside the building at

tᵢ l1 = 464.37   tᵢ l3 = 10,000

t_{i+1} l2 = 462.3 t_{i+1} l4 = 10,000

t_{i+1} l5 = 462.3

Case 6:

Flames/Light intensity the building at

Flames/Light intensity outside the building at

ti l1 = 464.37

ti l3 = 10,000

t_{i+1} l2 = 753.5

t_{i+1} l4 = 10,000

t_{i+1} l5 = 462.3

Case 7:

Pressure level inside the building at
ti p1 = 1017

Pressure outside the building at
ti p3 = 1,019

t_{i+1} p2 = 1,019

t_{i+1} p4 = 1,019

t_{i+1} p5 = 1,019

Case 8:

Pressure level inside the building at
ti p1 = 1,017

Pressure outside the building at
ti p3 = 1,019

t_{i+1} p2 = 998

t_{i+1} p4 = 1,020

t_{i+1} p5 = 1,020

Case 9:

Humidity level inside the building at
ti h1 = 880

Humidity outside the building at
ti h3 = 650

t_{i+1} h2 = 880

t_{i+1} h4 = 650

t_{i+1} h5 = 880

Case 10:

Humidity level inside the building at
ti h1 = 670

Humidity outside the building at
ti h3 = 619

t_{i+1} h2 = 298

t_{i+1} h4 = 620

t_{i+1} h5 = 650

Data analysis:
  Rule 1: {Case1, Case3, Case5, Case7, Case9} occurs
  Result   No fire breakout
  Rule 2: {Case2, Case3, Case 5, Case7, Case9} occurs
  Result   No fire breakout
  Rule 3: {Case1, Case4, Case 5, Case7, Case9} occurs
  Result   No fire breakout
  Rule 4: {Case1, Case3, Case 6, Case7, Case9} occurs
  Result   No fire breakout

Rule 5: {Case1, Case3, Case 5, Case8, Case9} occurs
Result   No fire breakout
Rule 6: {Case1, Case3, Case 5, Case7, Case10} occurs
Result   No fire breakout
Rule 7: {Case2, Case4, Case6, Case8, Case10} occurs
Result   Fire breakout is there.
Rule 8: For other combination of Rules except mentioned above
Result   Fire Outbreak

2.3.4   Fuzzy Logic

For fire detection fuzzy logic [71–73] concept is used where temperature value is range is [20,70], pressure range [970,1,020], smoke range [23, 73], light intensity [300,800], humidity range [230,880] is taken and converted into triangular membership into 5 ranges into and fire range [0,1] into 3 ranges as shown in Figures 2.12-2.15.

Step 1: membership function values are taken as shown below:

For temperature
temp_lo = fuzz.trimf(x_temp, [20, 25, 30]), temp_lo_more = fuzz. trimf(x_temp, [30,35, 40]),
temp_md = fuzz.trimf(x_temp, [35,45 , 50]),temp_md_more = fuzz. trimf(x_temp, [45,55, 60])
temp_hi = fuzz.trimf(x_temp, [60, 65, 70])

For smoke
s_lo = fuzz.trimf(x_s, [23, 28, 33]), s_lo_more = fuzz.trimf(x_s, [33, 38, 43])
s_md = fuzz.trimf(x_s, [38,43, 53]), s_md_more = fuzz.trimf(x_s, [43, 53, 63])
s_hi = fuzz.trimf(x_s, [63,68, 73])

For light intensity
l_lo = fuzz.trimf(x_l, [300, 350, 400]), l_lo_more = fuzz.trimf(x_l, [400, 450, 500])
l_md = fuzz.trimf(x_l, [450, 550, 600]), l_md_more = fuzz. trimf(x_l, [550, 650, 700])
l_hi = fuzz.trimf(x_l, [700, 750, 800])

For pressure

p_lo = fuzz.trimf(x_p, [970, 975, 980]), p_lo_more = fuzz.trimf(x_p, [980, 985, 990])

p_md = fuzz.trimf(x_p, [985, 995, 1000]), p_md_more = fuzz.trimf(x_p, [995, 1,005, 1,010])

p_hi = fuzz.trimf(x_p, [1,010, 1,015, 1,020])

For humidity

h_lo = fuzz.trimf(x_h, [230,295, 360]), h_lo_more = fuzz.trimf(x_h, [360, 425, 490])

h_md = fuzz.trimf(x_h, [425, 525, 620]), h_md_more = fuzz.trimf(x_h, [525, 620,750])

h_hi = fuzz.trimf(x_h, [750,815 , 880])

For fire

f_lo = fuzz.trimf(x_f, [0, 0.165, 0.333]), f_md = fuzz.trimf(x_f, [0.333, 0.500,0.665])

f_hi = fuzz.trimf(x_f, [.665,.835, 1])

Step 2: Active rules

active_rule1 = np.logical_and(s_level_lo,np.logical_and(np.logical_and(p_level_hi,l_level_lo),np.logical_and(temp_level_lo, h_level_hi)))

active_rule2 = np.logical_or(temp_level_md,np.logical_or(np.logical_or(np.logical_or(np.logical_or(np.logical_or(np.logical_or(np.logical_or(temp_level_md_more,temp_level_lo_more), p_level_md), p_level_md_more),p_level_lo_more), s_level_md),np.logical_or(s_level_md_more,s_level_lo_more)), np.logical_or(l_level_md, l_level_md_more)),np.logical_or(l_level_lo_more, h_level_md)),np.logical_or(h_level_md_more,h_level_lo_more)))

active_rule3 = np.logical_and(temp_level_hi,np.logical_and(np.logical_and(p_level_lo, s_level_hi),np.logical_and(l_level_hi, h_level_lo)))

Step 3: defuzzification: converts fuzzy values into crisp values.

The whole data is collected by UAVs [5, 74] produced by sensors which are connected to it through Bluetooth. The received data is send by UAV [75] to nearest control system for proper action as shown in Figure 2.16, as UAVs [76] can move around the whole building. The pattern [77] of movement can be regular or irregular. In regular pattern [78] UAVs visit each location according to a predefined pattern only and in irregular pattern there is no fixed [79] pattern to visit a location. UAVs can visit randomly at any location.

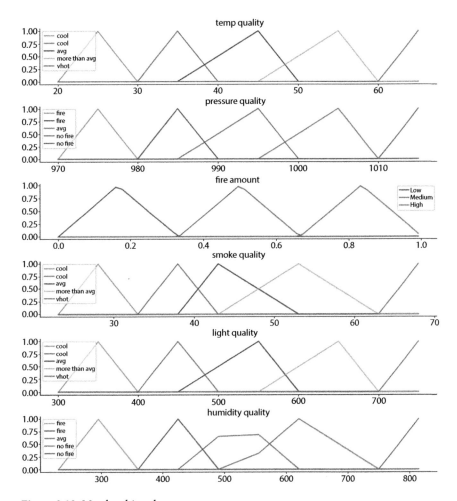

Figure 2.12 Membership values.

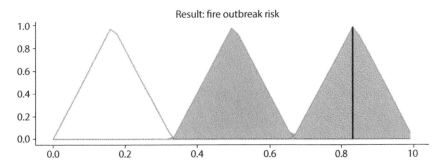

Figure 2.13 The result when parameters values are high.

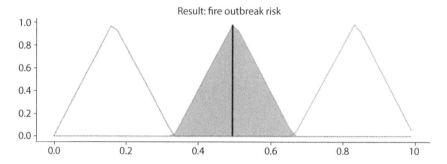

Figure 2.14 The results at average values of the parameters.

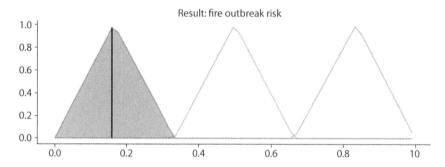

Figure 2.15 The results at low values of the parameters.

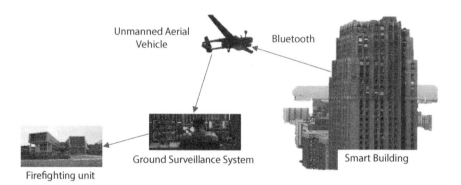

Figure 2.16 Information collected by UAV from smart building for processing.

2.4   Results

In many systems to work properly a threshold value is required depending upon which it can be checked that these variables are behaving differently or not. In this chapter, these threshold values are calculated based on time-series method using Naïve Bayes, Simple Averaging, Moving Averaging, Holt's–Winter and linear trend, ARIMA univariate models are implemented. ARIMA model R^2 score is close to 1 which is very encouraging, where ARIMA model represents the less value of RMSE which is 0.042227031760264946 and R^2 score which is 0.9991440622360026 close to 1. These values are further improved by using ANN or BP model with an error of 1.5 and .65% respectively. VAR for multivariate model is implemented with RMSE value −528.7642948354535. In this proposed work, fire outbreak problem faced in a Smart building enabled with HVAC system is discussed. In a HVAC mentioned system, sensors observe temperature, ventilation observe CO2 level and any changes in these values means system will try to approach the required point. But if fire has occurred then it will not be able to recognized as the system will try to compensate all the values. To solve this problem two approaches are used 1) Hidden Markov Model used to calculate the threshold value depending upon the external environment and results of actual values are close to predicted values; 2) Fuzzy logic method which is using a range of values to predict. Fuzzy logic is implemented to detect the fire incident and results are 100%.

2.5   Conclusion and Future Work

In this approach various methods are discussed to solve the problem of fire outbreak. In first approach dynamic threshold value is calculated based on time-series method. The threshold value for these parameters is calculated using different time-series models. For this, univariate time-series methods like Naïve Bayes, simple average, moving average, Holt's linear, Holt's–Winter, simple exponential smoothing, Auto Regressive Integrated Moving Average model (ARIMA) are implemented and there RMSE and R^2 score is calculated. Further, the values are improved by using ANN or BP model. Vector Autoregressive (VAR) model is implemented where all the parameters and their impact on each other is considered. For second approach Smart Building enabled with HVAC system problem is solved by considering the threshold values depending upon the features value's from outside the building. SB is synonym of comfort and a place which understands the requirement of the end-users and provides the facilities accordingly. To maintain the comfort level room temperature, light intensity, humidity level and $CO2$ values are checked. For these values system uses different sensors. When any change in the environment is noticed by the sensors the system tries to reach the comfort value of the system. But if fire incident occurred in the building the system will try to increase the temperature of air conditioner, ventilation system will also work different from its pattern. The problem is solved by Hidden Markov Model (HMM) and Fuzzy Logic. HMM model helps to find the threshold values with respect to outer environment as outer world always impact the inner environment of the building. With a range of values Fuzzy logic is also implemented which is able to provide ample preparations time for the incident. In the proposed architecture the data is collected through sensors by UAVs through Bluetooth, as sensors are easy to implement, reliable and cheap. UAVs can collect data from the whole building and can submit to nearest station for analysis. Smart building is a concept of providing comfort with balancing all the factors. But while maintaining comfort some serious issues can arises. Hence, need to be addressed. One of them was no able to differentiate either temperature rise because of fire or environmental reasons. In future work, more reliable time-series forecasting method considering HVAC system and fire incidents is required so that more accurate threshold values can be calculated.

References

1. Mobin, M.I., Abid-Ar-Rafi, M., Islam, M.N., Hasan, M.R., An intelligent fire detection and mitigation system safe from fire (SFF). *Int. J. Comput. Appl.*, 133, 6, 1–7, 2016.
2. Alkhatib, A.A., A review on forest fire detection techniques. *Int. J. Distrib. Sens. Netw.*, 10, 3, 597368, 2014.
3. Zhao, J., Zhang, Z., Han, S., Qu, C., Yuan, Z., Zhang, D., SVM based forest fire detection using static and dynamic features. *Comput. Sci. Inf. Syst.*, 8, 3, 821–841, 2011.
4. Luck, H.O., Dedicated detection algorithms for automatic fire detection. *Fire Saf. Sci.*, 3, 135–148, 1991.
5. Davy, A., *Components of a smart device and smart device interactions*, pp. 1–18, Telecommunications Software and Systems Group, Waterford, Ireland, 2003.
6. Bhagwat, P., Bluetooth: technology for short-range wireless apps. *IEEE Internet Comput.*, 5, 3, 96–103, 2001.

7. Yanmaz, E., Yahyanejad, S., Rinner, B., Hellwagner, H., Bettstetter, C., Drone networks: Communications, coordination, and sensing. *Ad Hoc Networks*, 68, 1–15, 2018.

8. Pereira, A.A., Espada, J.P., Crespo, R.G., Aguilar, S.R., Platform for controlling and getting data from network connected drones in indoor environments. *Future Gener. Comput. Syst.*, 92, 656–662, 2019.

9. Caillouet, C., Giroire, F., Razafindralambo, T., Efficient data collection and tracking with flying drones. *Ad Hoc Networks*, 89, 35–46, 2019.

10. Sensor node, 2020, September 21, Retrieved September 1, 2020, from https://en.wikipedia.org/wiki/Sensor_node.

11. Levis, P., Madden, S., Polastre, J., Szewczyk, R., Whitehouse, K., Woo, A., & Culler, D., TinyOS: An operating system for sensor networks, in: *Ambient intelligence*, pp. 115–148, Springer, Berlin, Heidelberg, 2005.

12. Pandey, M. and Mishra, G., Types of Sensor and Their Applications, Advantages, and Disadvantages, in: *Emerging Technologies in Data Mining and Information Security*, pp. 791–804, Springer, Singapore, 2019.

13. Vetelino, J. and Reghu, A., *Introduction to sensors*, CRC Press, Boca Raton, Florida, 2017.

14. Liu, S.C., Tomizuka, M., Ulsoy, G., Strategic issues in sensors and smart structures. *Struct. Control Health Monit.: The Official Journal of the International Association for Structural Control and Monitoring and of the European Association for the Control of Structures*, 13, 6, 946–957, 2006.

15. Da Xu, L., He, W., Li, S., Internet of things in industries: A survey. *IEEE Trans. Industr. Inform.*, 10, 4, 2233–2243, 2014.

16. Papkovsky, D.B., New oxygen sensors and their application to biosensing. *Sens. Actuators B: Chem.*, 29, 1–3, 213–218, 1995.

17. Gray, T. and Birrell, C., Are biophilic-designed site office buildings linked to health benefits and high performing occupants? *Int. J. Environ. Res. Public Health*, 11, 12, 12204–12222, 2014.

18. Altomonte, S. and Schiavon, S., Occupant satisfaction in LEED and non-LEED certified buildings. *Build. Environ.*, 68, 66–76, 2013.

19. Buckman, A.H., Mayfield, M., Beck, S.B., What is a smart building?, in: *Smart and Sustainable Built Environment*, 2014.

20. Dutta, J. and Roy, S., IoT-fog-cloud based architecture for smart city: Prototype of a smart building, in: *2017 7th International Conference on Cloud Computing, Data Science & Engineering-Confluence*, Noida, India, 2017, January IEEE, pp. 237–242.

21. Krishnamurthi, R., Nayyar, A., Solanki, A., *Innovation Opportunities through Internet of Things (IoT) for Smart Cities. Green and Smart Technologies for Smart Cities*, pp. 261–292, CRC Press, Boca Raton, FL, USA, 2019.

22. Solanki, A. and Nayyar, A., Green internet of things (G-IoT): ICT technologies, principles, applications, projects, and challenges, in: *Handbook of Research on Big Data and the IoT*, pp. 379–405, IGI Global, Hershey, Pennsylvania, 2019.

23. Ullah, F., Al-Turjman, F., Nayyar, A., IoT-based green city architecture using secured and sustainable android services. *Environ. Technol. Innov.*, 20, 101091, 2020.

24. Silverio-Fernández, M., Renukappa, S., Suresh, S., What is a smart device?-a conceptualisation within the paradigm of the internet of things. *Vis. Eng.*, 6, 1, 3, 2018.

25. Malkin, R., Measurement and Data Analysis for Engineering and Science (Dunn, PF; 2004)[Book Review]. *IEEE Eng. Med. Biol. Mag.*, 26, 6, 9–11, 2007.

26. Katipamula, S., Kim, W., Lutes, R.G., Underhill, R.M., *Rooftop unit embedded diagnostics: Automated fault detection and diagnostics (AFDD) development, field testing and validation (No. PNNL-23790)*, Pacific Northwest National Lab (PNNL), Richland, WA United States, 2015.

27. Fan, Q. and Ansari, N., Towards traffic load balancing in drone-assisted communications for IoT. *IEEE Internet Things J.*, 6, 2, 3633–3640, 2018.

28. Shahid, N., Naqvi, I.H., Qaisar, S.B., Characteristics and classification of outlier detection techniques for wireless sensor networks in harsh environments: A survey. *Artif. Intell. Rev.*, 43, 2, 193–228, 2015.

29. Andrew, A.M., Zakaria, A., Mad Saad, S., Md Shakaff, A.Y., Multi-stage feature selection based intelligent classifier for classification of incipient stage fire in building. *Sensors*, 16, 1, 31, 2016.

30. Mahdipour, E. and Dadkhah, C., Automatic fire detection based on soft computing techniques: Review from 2000 to 2010. *Artif. Intell. Rev.*, 42, 4, 895–934, 2014.

31. Chen, T.H., Wu, P.H., Chiou, Y.C., An early fire-detection method based on image processing, in: *2004 International Conference on Image Processing, 2004. ICIP'04*, vol. 3, 2004, October, IEEE, Singapore, Singapore, pp. 1707–1710.

32. Chen, T.H., Yin, Y.H., Huang, S.F., Ye, Y.T., The smoke detection for early fire-alarming system base on video processing, in: *2006 International Conference on Intelligent Information Hiding and Multimedia*, 2006, December, IEEE, Pasadena, CA, USA, pp. 427–430.

33. Horng, M.F., Shih, C.C., Hsieh, W.H., Lin, L.C., A temperature surveillance system based on zigbee technology for blaze detection, in: *2009 Fourth International Conference on Innovative Computing, Information and Control (ICICIC)*, Kaohsiung, Taiwan, 2009, December, IEEE, pp. 1277–1280.

34. Denham, M., Cortés, A., Margalef, T., Luque, E., Applying a dynamic data driven genetic algorithm to improve forest fire spread prediction, in: *International Conference on Computational Science*, 2008, June, Springer, Berlin, Heidelberg, pp. 36–45, 2009.

35. Fowler, A., Teredesai, A.M., De Cock, M., An evolved fuzzy logic system for fire size prediction, in: *NAFIPS 2009-2009 Annual Meeting of the North American Fuzzy Information Processing Society*, 2009, June, IEEE, Cincinnati, OH, USA, pp. 1–6.

36. Bahrepour, M., Meratnia, N., Havinga, P.J., Use of AI Techniques for Residential Fire Detection in Wireless Sensor Networks, in: *AIAI Workshops*, 2009, April, pp. 311–321.

37. Al Rasyid, M.U.H., Enda, D., Saputra, F.A., Smart Home System for Fire Detection Monitoring Based on Wireless Sensor Network, in: *2019 International Electronics Symposium (IES)*, IEEE, Surabaya, Indonesia, Indonesia, 2019, September, pp. 189–194.

38. Sowah, R., Ofoli, A.R., Krakani, S., Fiawoo, S., Hardware module design of a real-time multi-sensor fire detection and notification system using fuzzy logic, In *2014 IEEE Industry Application Society Annual Meeting*, 2014, October, IEEE, Vancouver, BC, Canada, pp. 1–6.

39. Wang, X.G., Lo, S.M., Zhang, H.P., Wang, W.L., A novel conceptual fire hazard ranking distribution system based on multisensory technology. *Procedia Eng.*, 71, 567–576, 2014.

40. Park, J.H., Lee, S., Yun, S., Kim, H., Kim, W.T., Dependable fire detection system with multifunctional artificial intelligence framework. *Sensors*, 19, 9, 2025, 2019.

41. Chen, S.J., Hovde, D.C., Peterson, K.A., Marshall, A.W., Fire detection using smoke and gas sensors. *Fire Saf. J.*, 42, 8, 507–515, 2007.

42. Cheng, C., Sun, F., Zhou, X., One fire detection method using neural networks. *Tsinghua Sci. Technol.*, 16, 1, 31–35, 2011.

43. Wang, X.G., Lo, S.M., Zhang, H.P., Influence of feature extraction duration and step size on ANN based multisensor fire detection performance. *Procedia Eng.*, 52, 413–421, 2013.

44. Umoh, U., Udo, E., Emmanuel, N., Support Vector Machine-Based Fire Outbreak Detection System, *arXiv preprint arXiv:1906.05655*, 2019.

45. Khooban, M.H., Abadi, D.N.M., Alfi, A., Siahi, M., Swarm optimization tuned Mamdani fuzzy controller for diabetes delayed model. *Turk. J. Elect. Eng. Comp. Sci.*, 21, Sup. 1, 2110–2126, 2013.

46. Vigneshwara, S.R., Shanthakumari, S.S., Ranganathan, V., Fire Detection using Support Vector Machine (SVM). *Int. J. Sci. Res. (IJSR)*, 6, 1607⁻1618, 2017.

47. Khule, V. and Jangle, N.N., Design and implementation of a fire and obstacle detection and control system using fuzzy logic with notification system to avoid automobile accidents, in: *10th International Conference on Recent Trends in Engineering Science and Management. India: Newton's School of Science and Technology*, vol. 10, pp. 307–313, 2017.

48. Torabnezhad, M. and Aghagolzadeh, A., Visible and IR image fusion algorithm for short range smoke detection, in: *2013 First RSI/ISM International Conference on Robotics and Mechatronics (ICRoM)*, IEEE, Tehran, Iran, 2013, February, pp. 38–42.

49. Yuan, F., Fang, Z., Wu, S., Yang, Y., Fang, Y., Real-time image smoke detection using staircase searching-based dual threshold AdaBoost and dynamic analysis. *IET Image Process.*, 9, 10, 849–856, 2015.

50. Rong, J., Zhou, D., Yao, W., Gao, W., Chen, J., Wang, J., Fire flame detection based on GICA and target tracking. *Opt. Laser Technol.*, 47, 283–291, 2013.

51. Wang, S., He, Y., Zou, J.J., Zhou, D., Wang, J., Early smoke detection in video using swaying and diffusion feature. *J. Intell. Fuzzy Syst.*, 26, 1, 267–275, 2014.

52. Töreyin, B.U., Dedeoğlu, Y., Cetin, A.E., Wavelet based real-time smoke detection in video, in: *2005 13th European Signal Processing Conference*, IEEE, Antalya, Turkey, 2005, September, pp. 1–4.

53. Wu, X., Lu, X., Leung, H., A video based fire smoke detection using robust AdaBoost. *Sensors*, 18, 11, 3780, 2018.

54. Jung, W. and Jazizadeh, F., Comparative assessment of HVAC control strategies using personal thermal comfort and sensitivity models. *Build. Environ.*, 158, 104–119, 2019.

55. Yu, L., Sun, Y., Xu, Z., Shen, C., Yue, D., Jiang, T., Guan, X., Multi-agent deep reinforcement learning for HVAC control in commercial buildings. *IEEE Trans. Smart Grid*, 1, 2020.

56. Chen, B., Cai, Z., Bergés, M., Gnu-rl: A precocial reinforcement learning solution for building hvac control using a differentiable MPC policy, in: *Proceedings of the 6th ACM International Conference on Systems for Energy-Efficient Buildings, Cities, and Transportation*, pp. 316–325, November, 2019.

57. Qiriro (2019, August 27), Affective thermal comfort. Retrieved September 11, 2020, 2019, from https://www.kaggle.com/qiriro/comfort

58. Rish, I., An empirical study of the Naive Bayes classifier, in: *IJCAI 2001 workshop on empirical methods in artificial intelligence*, August, Vol. 3, No. 22, pp. 41–46.

59. Nam, S. and Hur, J., Probabilistic forecasting model of solar power outputs based on the Naive Bayes classifier and Kriging models. *Energies*, 11, 11, 2982, 2018.

60. Genre, V., Kenny, G., Meyler, A., Timmermann, A., Combining expert forecasts: Can anything beat the simple average? *Int. J. Forecast.*, 29, 1, 108–121, 2013.

61. Makridakis, S. and Wheelwright, S.C., Adaptive filtering: An integrated autoregressive/moving average filter for time series forecasting. *J. Oper. Res. Soc.*, 28, 2, 425–437, 1977.

62. Ostertagova, E. and Ostertag, O., Forecasting using simple exponential smoothing method. *Acta Electrotech. Inform.*, 12, 3, 62, 2012.

63. Yapar, G., Capar, S., Selamlar, H.T., Yavuz, I., Modified Holt's linear trend method. *Hacet. J. Math. Stat.*, 47, 5, 1394–1403, 2018.

64. Kalekar, P.S., Time series forecasting using Holt–Winters exponential smoothing. *Kanwal Rekhi School of Information Technology*, 4329008, 13, 1–13, 2004.

65. Khashei, M., Bijari, M., Ardali, G.A.R., Hybridization of autoregressive integrated moving average (ARIMA) with probabilistic neural networks (PNNs). *Comput. Ind. Eng.*, 63, 1, 37–45, 2012.

66. Valipour, M., Banihabib, M.E., Behbahani, S.M.R., Parameters estimate of autoregressive moving average and autoregressive integrated moving average models and compare their ability for inflow forecasting. *J. Math. Stat.*, 8, 3, 330–338, 2012.

67. Yegnanarayana, B., *Artificial neural networks*, PHI Learning Pvt. Ltd, Patparganj Industrial Area, New Delhi, Delhi, 2009.

68. Vogl, T.P., Mangis, J.K., Rigler, A.K., Zink, W.T., Alkon, D.L., Accelerating the convergence of the back-propagation method. *Biol. Cybern.*, 59, 4–5, 257–263, 1988.

69. Zivot, E. and Wang, J., Vector autoregressive models for multivariate time series, in: *Modeling Financial Time Series With S-PLUS®*, pp. 385–429, 2006.

70. Rabiner, L. and Juang, B., An introduction to hidden Markov models. *IEEE Assp Mag.*, 3, 1, 4–16, 1986.

71. Dernoncourt, F., *Introduction to fuzzy logic*, p. 21, Massachusetts Institute of Technology, Avenue, Cambridge, MA, USA, 2013.

72. *Introduction Fuzzy Inference Systems*, Massey University, Centennial Drive, Hokowhitu, Palmerston North 4410, New Zealand. University of New Zealand. 2020, September 30, Retrieved September 1, 2020, from https://www.massey.ac.nz/~nhreyes/MASSEY/159741/Lectures/Lec2012-3-159741-FuzzyLogic-v.2.pdf.

73. Revathi, G.K., Amudhambigai, B., Narmadha, V., Poornima, T., Identification of Social Problems of Farmers Using Fuzzy Mathematics. *Int. J. Eng. Technol.*, 7, 4.10, 624–628, 2018.

74. Nayyar, A., Jain, R., Mahapatra, B., Singh, A., Cyber security challenges for smart cities, in: *Driving the Development, Management, and Sustainability of Cognitive Cities*, pp. 27–54, IGI Global, Hershey, Pennsylvania, 2019.

75. Singh, S.P., Nayyar, A., Kumar, R., Sharma, A., Fog computing: from architecture to edge computing and big data processing. *J. Supercomput.*, 75, 4, 2070–2105, 2019.

76. Anavangot, V., Menon, V.G., Nayyar, A., Distributed big data analytics in the Internet of signals, in: *2018 International Conference on System Modeling & Advancement in Research Trends (SMART)*, IEEE, Moradabad, India, India, 2018, November, pp. 73–77.

77. Navid Ali Khan, N.Z. Jhanjhi, Sarfraz Nawaz Brohi, Raja Sher Afgun Usmani, Anand Nayyar, Smart traffic monitoring system using Unmanned Aerial Vehicles (UAVs), *Comput. Commun.*, 157, 434–443, 2020, https://doi.org/10.1016/j.comcom.2020.04.049

78. Puri, V., Nayyar, A., Raja, L., Agriculture drones: A modern breakthrough in precision agriculture. *J. Stat. Manag. Syst.*, 20, 4, 507–518, 2017.

79. Nayyar, A., Nguyen, B.L., Nguyen, N.G., The Internet of Drone Things (IoDT): Future Envision of Smart Drones, in: *First International Conference on Sustainable Technologies for Computational Intelligence*, pp. 563–580, Springer, Singapore, 2020.

3

Sustainable Infrastructure Theories and Models

Saurabh Jain[1], Keshav Kaushik[1], Deepak Kumar Sharma[1], Rajalakshmi Krishnamurthi[2] and Adarsh Kumar[1]*

[1]School of Computer Science, University of Petroleum and Energy Studies, Dehradun, India
[2]Department of Computer Science and Engineering, Jaypee Institute of Information Technology, Noida, India

Abstract

In this chapter, we introduce the concepts data fusion and data fusion approaches concerning sustainable infrastructure. First, it classify various data fusion techniques based on relationships between different data sources, based on abstraction levels of utilized data, based on the nature of input/output data types, based on various data fusion levels, and architecture types. Thereafter, this work describe smart city application with sustainable infrastructures based on different data fusion techniques. The monitoring framework is also needed for smart city infrastructure development and is used with GIS for information retrieval and analysis. Latest technology like Low Power Wide Area Network is used for IoT deployment that helps in several smart city applications and air quality monitoring as well. Intelligent control and monitoring centres helps in assisting the smart parking, waste management, healthcare, sewage systems etc. Furthermore, a unified city modelling for smart infrastructure helps in setting a benchmarks and following the common standards. The smart city operational modelling focuses on collecting and accessing data, checking financial viability of various solutions and promoting an end-user utility. Some case studies and simulation results are discussed at the end of this work.

Keywords: Smart city, smart infrastructure, sensor-technology, Industry 4.0, infrastructure theories, infrastructure models

Corresponding author: adarsh.kumar@ddn.upes.ac.in

Arun Solanki, Adarsh Kumar and Anand Nayyar (eds.) Digital Cities Roadmap: IoT-Based Architecture and Sustainable Buildings, (97–126) © 2021 Scrivener Publishing LLC

3.1   Introduction to Data Fusion Approaches in Sustainable Infrastructure

In this chapter, the authors introduce the concept of data fusion and data fusion approaches in relation to sustainable infrastructure and smart cities. We first described the IoT scenario with respect to data fusion and various data fusion infrastructure based on alignment, association and estimation techniques and their pros and cons [1–5]. Then we describe the application of various smart cities, which are based on the relation of sustainable infrastructure and different fusion technologies and their future aspects.

3.1.1   The Need for Sustainable Infrastructure

The progression of various research areas for example machine learning, Internet of Things (IoT), mining of data, artificial Intelligence, communication technology and Big Data has revealed some insight into changing the urban city infrastructure, integrating the aforesaid technologies into a common known structure—sustainable infrastructure. With the development of Sustainable Infrastructure, a plenty of information sources have been accessible for a various applications [6–12]. The data fusion is a technique, which handle the multiple data sources, where it maximizes information yield, quality or concentrates information from crude information. To cater to the ever-increasing complex applications, studies in Sustainable Infrastructure and Smart Cities need to utilize information from different sources and assess their presentation depending on a few angles [13–18].

According to United Nations estimates [19–28], a significant number of people will live in smart cities by 2050. Therefore, it is prudent to manage the current resources and infrastructure to meet the daily needs of sustainable urban development. Fortunately, advances in the Internet of Things (IoT), information and communications technology (ICT), data mining, big data, and data fusion are gradually paving the way for sustainable infrastructure and the emergence of smart cities. If we understand its maximum potential, then sustainable infrastructure [29] is one of the major technological developments of our time. IoT plays an important role in sustainable infrastructure development. It is a global infrastructure for a data society, which relies on existing data and communication technologies to empower interconnected things. The number of IoT-enabled devices is expected to increase to 50 billion by 2020 due to the large outflow of diversified goods.

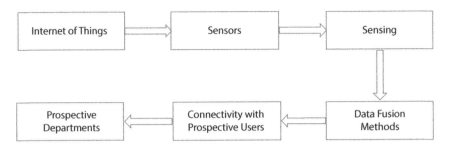

Figure 3.1 Internet of things landscape concerning data fusion.

Figure 3.1 shows the application areas IoT: Smart Gadget, Intelligent Shopping, Healthcare, Smart Home, Warning System, Hazard Identification System, Smart City, Smart Road, Fire System, Tracking & Monitoring. The main objective of these increasing numbers is to provide useful information around us and to make the infrastructure of society smart and sustainable. IoT is relied upon to be a significant manufacturer of this large data. This information will be created by different vendors, information and other support resources will be important to enable sustainable ubiquitous environments such as smart cities, smart communication, smart buildings, home, and smart societies [30]. A combination of different types of data, to be specific data fusion, are used to expand information excellence and dynamic decision making, so a sustainable ubiquitous infrastructure will have a significant role.

3.1.2   Data Fusion

Data fusion is the process of combining data to evaluate the state of a unit in a common representation format for data derived from sensor data, or sensory data [31, 32]. It is a multi-disciplinary field that has many advantages, for example, improving reliability, increasing confidence, and reducing the ambiguity of measurements to evaluate the position of objects in engineering frameworks. It can also maximize the completeness of fused data, which can be important for computing the state of the engineering framework. Data fusion has been implemented in various fields such as intelligence automation and robotics. In most cases, the object or entity state reflects the state of the physical state, the identity or identification of the entity, or the motion during the unit's time [33]. The brain of a human is the best example of information or data fusion in real life. As indicated by the underlying US Joint Directors of Laboratories (JDL) data fusion lexicon, Information Fusion characterizes it as "a process that measures single and different sources of position and computation and to achieve completeness, deals with correlations, associations, and combinations of information, and complete timely assessment of malicious threats and various situations and their importance [34]." There are several general benefits of data fusion, of which very important is to increase confidence and therefore increase reliability and reduce data ambiguity by expanding measurement reliability, spatial and temporal coverage [35]. Data fusion likewise gives benefits for certain application areas. For example, the sensor network consists of countless diverse sensor nodes creating a new scalability issue due to the possible transmission of data and unnecessary data collisions.

3.1.3   Different Types of Data Fusion Architecture

Data fusion architecture is divided into four categories—centralized architecture, decentralized architecture, distributed architecture, and hybrid data fusion architecture.

3.1.3.1   *Centralized Architecture*

In this design architecture, a fusion node resides in a central processor that gathers information from all information sources. Therefore, all fusion processes are evaluated in a central processor that uses raw estimates given from sources [36, 37]. In this blueprint, the sources only obtain observational estimates and pass them to a central processor, where information fusion measures are performed. The drawback of this scheme is that too much bandwidth is required to send raw data through the system network. Such an issue turns into a bottleneck when such design plots are used to measure information in a visual sensor based organization. Figure 3.2 shows an example of centralized architecture.

Figure 3.2 Centralized architecture.

3.1.3.2   Decentralized Architecture

A decentralized fusion architecture consists of a network of nodes; in this type of architecture, each node has its own data processing power and no single point of information fusion. Therefore, each node processes its local data with data received from its neighboring peers [38]. The main issue of this scheme is the high data communication cost, which is consumed at each data communication stage, where there is a quantity of nodes. What's more, an exceptional case is thought, in which each node communicates data with all its neighboring peers. Therefore, when the volume of nodes expands, such architecture can mess up scalability issues. Figure 3.3 shows an example of decentralized architecture.

3.1.3.3   Distributed Architecture

In a distributed design, architecture, projections from each source node are processed autonomously before a data fusion is sent to the node. The fusion node represents the data received from various nodes. In other words, data association and the state are evaluated in the source node before communicating the fusion node [39]. Accordingly, each node only gives a gauge of the object position based on its local computation, and this data is contributed as an input to the fusion process, giving a fused global view. Such design, architecture provides various options and varieties that range from just one fusion node to various intermediate fusion nodes. Figure 3.4 shows an example of distributed architecture.

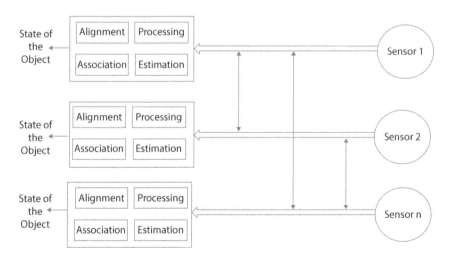

Figure 3.3 Decentralized architecture.

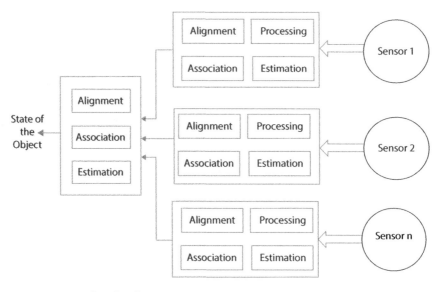

Figure 3.4 Distributed architecture.

3.1.3.4 Hierarchical Architecture

Hierarchical architecture involves a mixture of distributed nodes and decentralized nodes from which hierarchical designs are designed, in which information fusion measures are evaluated at different levels in the designed hierarchy. In theory, decentralized fusion architecture systems are structures that are more difficult to execute due to computing power and communication requirements. In any case, there is not another good design, architecture, and the most appropriate design, architecture should depend on requirements, demand, existing communication networks, information access, node data processing and handling capability, and the design of the data fusion framework.

3.1.4 Smart Cities Application With Sustainable Infrastructures Based on Different Data Fusion Techniques

In this section, we introduced the Smart City's application with a sustainable infrastructure based on information fusion technologies from various cities. In smart cities, sustainable infrastructure is intended to facilitate the public by supplying critical resources such as electricity, gas, and water, or by offering basic services such as communication systems. Here, we outline three specific sub-domains, which are smart communication, smart grid, smart buildings.

Smart Communication: Communication in urban areas remains an infrastructure for various application platforms to communicate with each other. Various guidelines and protocols are designed to meet different requirements. In the research [40, 41] the authors introduced technologies for the integration of the upcoming 5G technology and continued customer experiences to provide consistent interfaces for older generation technologies such as Wi-Fi and LTE. Raw data signals are regular data sources in 5G network protocols, and the main motivation behind this is that information fusion occurs only at the edge level. On the Internet of things area, wireless sensor networks are seen as a regular communication medium due to its low power consumption and large area coverage. Later, various nodes can be connected for the encoding–decoding purpose of the received data packets. The main goal is to focus on the reliability of the communication network channel while maintaining coverage and low power consumption. The fundamental objective is to design reliable and efficient and communication network protocols to meet the diverse needs of applications. Alternatively, low power communication costs are another objective for IoT to accomplish long-term sensory activity [42, 43].

Smart Grid: The power grid serves as an intermediate platform for the transfer of electricity from the power grid plant to the residential and industrial areas. The purpose of this sub-domain is to move a stable and reliable power supply with the inclusion of ICT, commonly known as a smart grid. In research work [44] authors have largely focused on smart grid infrastructure and its purpose is to focus on the balance of power demand and load in specific areas or buildings. The basic method implemented in this subdomain is forecasting, and an example of such an application can be found in the discussion in this work, which collects data derived from private meters and predicts the load bill of electricity usage.

Smart Building: Urban Building Administration provides a resource interface for building management to understand the energy consumption ratio of a building while automating resource management. The current trend is widely concentrated in Refs. [45, 46] such as optimization of hot water structures, power consumption charges and units, and construction resources such as ventilation and air conditioning. Luo and Su [47] combined three diverse information sources (temperature, fire, and smoke sensors) to identify any potential fire event and to minimize inaccurate alarms. In addition, if an emergency event occurs, a warning-based framework is executed to advise the owner/supervisor of the land/property.

In the future, robots may be involved to manage fire hazards and two-way liability as security risks to uncover potential risks.

3.2   Smart City Infrastructure Approaches

This section explores the feasibility of smart city infrastructure construction. The various approaches that are recently studied and adapted in literature are discussed as follows.

3.2.1   Smart City Infrastructure

Infrastructure has a few implications that rely upon the term of setting utilized in regarding utility and office useful activities, the foundation speaks to the underground and over-the-ground links and channels systems bolstered with every single related resource. While structural architects worried about other urban zone administration capacities, for example, street systems, spans, train/transport stations, schools, medical clinics, colleges, and other open administrations. While the distant framework is a key portion of a smart city foundation, it is just a basic development. In a smart city, the structures of multiple infrastructures should be constructed in a way to improve the overall growth of handling the interoperability and working of cross disciplines departments. A smart city gives fast connectivity and accessibility driven affiliations that empower unavoidable availability to change key government structures, both inside work environments and agents and indirectly to tenants and affiliations. Smart city associations are open through distant PDAs and are locked in by association's orchestrated undertaking planning including Web benefits, the Extensible Markup Language (XML), and impelled programming applications. Examination on sharp urban locales has been driven by different affiliations. The execution of the Enterprise Resource Planning (ERP) framework helps in making a sharp idea in the city foundation level. The motivation behind the SAP is to normalize all conceivable plans of action and every single operational procedure in one stage. Figure 3.5 represents the framework for smart city infrastructure development in which all the related components are shown that are used for communicating the concept of smart in city infrastructure [16].

The entire framework for smart city infrastructure development is divided into two sub-categories—Geo-spatial applications and network data models. The geo-spatial part takes care of the several models related to the location like Network Analysis Model, Facility Sitting Model, and a

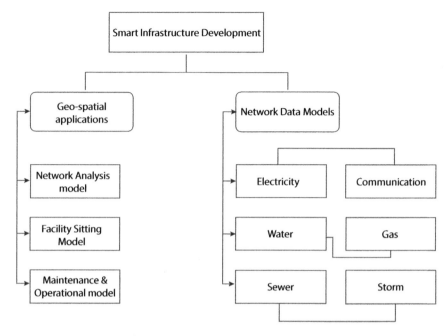

Figure 3.5 Smart city infrastructure development framework.

model for maintenance & operations. On the other hand, Network Data Models are related to interlinked communication with electricity, connectivity of water and gas, and interlinked entities like sewer and storm.

3.2.2   Smart City IoT Deployments

Smart city IoT affiliations are driving movements and evaluation in long-expand low force inaccessible correspondence structures. Past Wireless Sensor Network (WSN) plans would have utilized custom equipment and show to help correspondence. The redesigns around there have incited such a removed correspondence plan, LPWANs [17]. Bardyn *et al.* express the standard attributes of a LPWAN [18] are: ultra-low-power activity, unimportant effort, no persuading inspiration to wake an end gadget to keep up form compose, straightforwardness of approach of the framework the nation over, and secure information move. While disallowed from this diagram, then since a long time ago run is likewise a depicting highlight of the structures. This gathers these LPWAN advancements are not contenders to Bluetooth, Wi-Fi, Zigbee, or other short-broaden far off correspondence movements. Present-day urban networks and metropolitan regions wherever all through the world face new organization challenges in the 21st century in a general sense as a result of growing solicitations on desires for ordinary solaces by the urban people. These difficulties extend from environmental change, contamination, transportation, and resident commitment, to urban arrangement, and security dangers. The essential objective of a Smart City is to check these issues and relieve their belongings by methods for current ICT to improve urban organization and foundation. Key thoughts are to use organize correspondence to between interface open specialists; yet in addition to convey and incorporate various sensors and actuators all through the city foundation—which is additionally generally known as the Internet of Things (IoT). Therefore, IoT advances will be a fundamental part and key empowering influence to accomplish numerous destinations of the Smart City vision. Smart Governance, for example, speaks to an assortment of advances, individuals, strategies, rehearses, assets, normal practices, and data that interface to help city overseeing exercises. In a keen city, the coordination of data and correspondence advances into a city's diverse specialized frameworks and foundations are the reason for imaginative arrangements in the fields of vitality, organization, well-being, portability, and security. A key thought of the Internet of Things (IoT) [19] is to upgrade this present reality with associated gadgets, i.e., sensors and actuators, to empower new administrations and applications. As such, IoT advancements for the most part fit into the Smart City vision and will supplement existing urban foundations to empower imaginative answers for address the previously mentioned difficulties. Internet of Things (IoT) broadens the customary Internet into the universe of implanted, asset imperative gadgets utilizing machine-to-machine correspondence dependent on remote, low-power radio principles. Consequently, the IoT requires committed models and advancements specifically intended to be agreeable with such limitation situations, however, that additionally take into account adaptability and strength.

3.2.3   Smart City Control and Monitoring Centers

A smart city is a reconciliation of heterogeneous parts [20] of a city robotized it might be said to make a perceptive domain and are interconnected inside a system. The smart city is an assortment of keen articles sent at better places inside a city that sense information at specific places, store, and decipher it to settle on significant choices. Smart urban communities are actualized in each field of life including clinical foundations, industry, medical clinics, workplaces, transportations, sewerage frameworks, stopping, and keen matrices. Smart urban areas are demonstrated utilizing innovative innovations of Wireless Sensor Networks (WSNs), for example, distributed computing, customer worker model, and focal database the board frameworks. A smart city is a need of present day registering to make the earth computerized, responsive, productive, dependable, and mechanized. A smart city is executed in true situations by utilizing shrewd hubs, sensors, and actuators. Scientists to address shrewd city parts yet at the same time, there are a few imperfections that are not illuminated by specialists introduce numerous models. Smart traffic checking and direction framework is a significant segment of smart cities. The far off correspondence utilizing complex arranged sensors and Programmable Logic Controllers (PLC) will be utilized to group the system status in a predefined coordinated structure that would bolster the system's operational stage. The GIS operational stage will be the base for dealing with the foundation sensors and programmable rationale regulators with the interoperability of the frameworks for all accessible/related frameworks. The GIS operational stage will discuss all prospects of frameworks combinations, for example, SCADA frameworks and computerized sensors. The fixation will be on the accessible utility systems to build up a far reaching, normal, normalized geospatial information models. The systems are spoken to the positional area for all system resources, for example, pressurized, gravity funnels, and framework valves appended with all data including the availability resources rules. Web of Things is an interconnection of genuine situations with actuators, brilliant hubs, sensors, programming, and systems that empower correspondence, translation, gather and trade the information. Smart city is the computerization of genuine situations into brilliant conditions for urban turn of events and to oversee city resources electronically. Conveying sensors at streets, structures, schools, banks, lodgings, houses, petroleum siphons, medical clinics, and workplaces making viable, responsive, and brilliant framework, robotize the framework. Different sorts of sensors are accepted for looking through a spot inside a brilliant city, discovering substantial traffic zones, stay away from to utilize streets of school timings and emergency clinics, and to discover the most limited way towards the goal as for separation and time. In overwhelming rush hour gridlock circumstances, our proposed model will be more compelling as a manual framework does not work in crisis circumstances to control substantial traffic on streets. Further, the vehicle drivers are educated to pick an elective way to their goal if there should be an occurrence of uncommon timings. In Figure 3.6, connected components of smart city control and monitoring center are shown in which it is classified under surveying activities and updates related to data communication. The surveying activities are also categorized further into two major components of radar installed for ground penetration and monitoring that are used mainly for surveillance. The other category is of

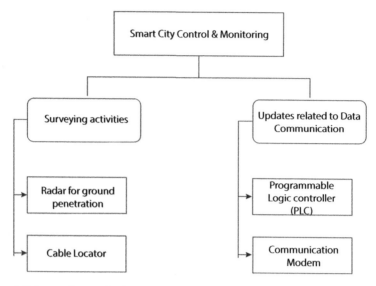

Figure 3.6 Smart city monitoring center.

Cable Locator that is responsible for locating the various cables installed in the smart city architecture and is also used for the control center. On the other hand, there are updates related to data communication that is connected with the technical components like Programmable Logic Controller (PLC) and several communication devices like modem, routers, etc.

3.2.4   Theory of Unified City Modeling for Smart Infrastructure

Smart urban communities have pulled in a broad and rising enthusiasm from both science and industry with an expanding number of worldwide models rising out of everywhere throughout the world. Nonetheless, regardless of the noteworthy job that shrewd urban communities can play to manage ongoing urban difficulties, the idea has been being condemned for not having the option to understand its latent capacity and for being seller publicity. As of late, there have been numerous ways to deal with conceptualizing and benchmark keen urban areas. Conceptualization is a noteworthy philosophy for keen city definition, which has been beginning late wrapped up by normalization bodies. The keen city field has gone to a uniform definition, which supervises headway (less yet ICT-orchestrated) in the urban space that means to improve the 6 city estimations (individuals, economy, government, movability, living, and condition). This is a particularly broad definition to cover the difference and assortment of activities in this field; in any case, it will as a rule be regarded when the further assessment is head. In that limit, smart urban systems are an umbrella term for a wide extent of types of progress in the urban condition. Dexterous urban systems have been perceived as smart modernized regular structures introduced in the urban space. Regardless, keen urban zones have not been restricted to ICT and they moved to impressive individuals and they are taking a gander at the inventive brain. Starting here of view, they are spun around improving urban presence concerning six estimations: individuals, government, economy, portability, condition, and living. Over 150 sharp city cases can be seen the world over, which can be engineered in (a) with no arranging city cases; (b) hard ICT foundation centered cases; and (c) delicate ICT structures in the urban space [21]. Since there is no reasonable shrewd city approach yet, there have been two or three attempts by overall relationship to normalize sharp city strategies, for example, for mind blowing water, vitality, transportation, structures, and so on. To reveal information [22] into the shrewd urban region's considerations, different models for comprehension and conceptualizing sharp urban areas have been made, which expect to depict their degree, targets, and plans. In like way, benchmarking techniques for separating keen city practices and each other have been made.

3.2.5   Smart City Operational Modeling

Smart City has made some amazing progress foundations as "Business index" postings gave by nearby experts during the 1970s to the organization of innovative data and correspondence innovation (ICT) and fabricated reasoning (AI) applications. The latest advances are in universal processing what's more, PC vision, with advanced advances (e.g., profound neural systems) getting more productive at perceiving and deciphering pictures/recordings information, combined with quick dynamic advances, for example, profound fortification learning (DRL) that misuse data at scale to make better reactions to city issues. Urban areas everywhere throughout the world are utilizing best in class advanced innovations to fabricate open and insightful control frameworks as the show-stopper of their brilliant city activities, utilizing constant data for open traffic, crisis the executives, and open security. Seemingly, the most striking instances of brilliant city tasks are ongoing urban portability arrangements. For instance, Alibaba's cloud offering, City Brain, influences information accumulated through video takes care of at traffic signals to ease gridlock and gridlock in Hangzhou, China. As per Alibaba, its traffic management is 92% precise in recognizing petty criminal offenses, empowers crisis vehicles to arrive at the goals in a fraction of the time, and has empowered traffic speed to increment by 15% [23]. Numerous urban transportation arrangements rely upon the commitment of residents, city transportation organizations, controllers and administrators, portability new businesses, and tech organizations. Heap versatility new businesses and tech organizations have prevailing concerning getting end clients to contribute information to improve the estimation of their contributions. Some have set up stage based arrangements (through application programming interfaces) to impart the information to government and transport offices. Urban areas face the test of encouraging expanded monetary open doors energized by the populace increment while improving personal satisfaction by diminishing the city's ecological impression, expanding open division profitability, improving wellbeing and keen portability, expanding vitality effectiveness, improving air quality, security, and so forth., which each require a blend of open and private segment speculations. Nevertheless [24], keen city speculation cases contrast from standard personal business improvement and open area the board. As the two expenses and advantages, just as vulnerabilities and hazards, rise and end up with various gatherings, which are not generally and naturally associated with the dynamic procedure, city pioneers must build up an unmistakable keen city speculation plan and imaginatively structure the plans of action to share costs, advantages, and dangers among open, helpful, and highlight entertainers.

3.3   Theories and Models

The following sections shows the sustainable infrastructure theories and models adopted in recent infrastructure developed in developed and developing countries [48–55]. These theories and models are explained as follows.

3.3.1   Sustainable Infrastructure Theories

Timmermans and Beroggi [25] studied the planning infrastructures in any organization. An organization needs a systematic way of resolving technological and social issues. In these issues, the economic, potential and environmental issues/concerns are major challenges. To handle these challenges it is recommended to have smart and sustainable infrastructure solutions that are acceptable and easily adaptable to developers without any unrealistic assumptions. To identify the systematic approach in sustainable building development, there is a need to identify the actors that are helpful in planning and constructing the buildings. In the proposed work, a similar study is performed with melioration project for Alphen in Netherlands. In this project, fourteen actors were identified with seven planning agencies, government departments, and private business associates. In this project, advanced sustainable infrastructure technologies are used to gain insights into mutual dependencies. Here, it aims to apply more workshops that configure more actors and provide potentials for reducing the conflicts in objectives. This smoothens the development and construction processes. Similar approaches could be applied in other urban center amelioration projects with multiple actors, objective conflicts, and planning issues.

Kumar et al. [15] mentioned the need for sustainable building in the healthcare system. This work has broadly explained the need of Industry 4.0-based solutions in healthcare. As the demand of patient centric system is increasing day by day in developed and developing countries, the requirements to construct an advanced solution for handling patients is increasing as well. With the advancement of technology like Industry 4.0-based solutions to healthcare, sustainable infrastructure is also required. This infrastructure with sensor technology helps in identifying the environment conditions, patients monitoring abilities, automating the patient monitoring and reporting system, enhances the infrastructure capabilities to handle unexpected conditions like fire, earthquake, collapse, etc. Sensor-based solution is helpful in pre-determining the building conditions. This kind of determination is very much helpful in congested areas where there are always chances of building collapsing either due to quality of building or heavy rains.

González-Ruiz et al. [26] proposed a financial sustainable infrastructure framework based on mezzanine-type debt. This work has realized that a significant exploration is required for post-positivist approach. The financial eco-innovations are helpful in analysing the knowledge of how a mezzanine-debt type could work in sustainable criteria like system. The financing process is helpful in understanding the proposed framework and identify the gaps in development of sustainable and financial resources required process to have an efficient infrastructure [56–60]. The discussions and conclusions are found to be helpful in finalising the practical solution using academic ways. The proposed framework provides a choice to exchange outstanding debts if sustainability criteria objectives are achieved. This proposes a model where 100% of equity shares is possible in capital structure. Here, lenders can capture corporate value in a project and improve business practices. In the proposed framework, relationships among different system entities are analyzed. These entities include financial terms public private partnerships, funding sources. All are important to analyze the possibilities of developing sustainable infrastructure. The development is possible if significant contribution and attentions are given to overall framework in integrating with real-time development environment. The sustainable issues are discussed in detail for expanding the feasibility of investors which enhances the overall growth. To highlight the contributions based on the necessities of innovation, the designed framework provide solution and new approaches. This way of developing the research construct theories that are helpful in understanding the infrastructure financing and strategic planning. A new financial strategic hybrid debt planning framework is unique in itself in terms of creating a new financial system for sustainable development. The testing of the framework is necessary that is not yet done as specified in the proposal. Thus, case studies are required to be designed and implemented to ensure that the proposed framework is validated before its actual use.

3.3.2   Sustainable Infrastructure Models

Sensor-based technology is popular for tracking the target. Various target tracking approaches are proposed in recent times. In multi-sensor data fusion, information complexity is dependent over information complementarity, improving the tracking accuracy, and recognize various capabilities. In single-tracking system information fusion is capable of optimal data processing. Various optimization techniques are available to process the data in a way that maximum profits can be achieved. For example, Kumar et al. [13] proposed simulation optimization in IT-based application to improve the performance. Here, lightweight and optimized solution is targeted to achieve with minimum cost and maximum benefits. The cost and benefits are multi-constraint function to have optimized solution. In multi constraint functions, the objectivity is achievable through defining the constraints with maximized and minimized solution probabilities. The maximized probability aim in maximizing the profits with minimum cost. For example, minimum deployment of sensor with maximum profit of getting the data and interpretations. The interpretations should be useful to gain maximum data presentation. Similarly, the data fusion approaches in infrastructure model can be classified as: (i) single target tracking, (ii) multi-target tracking, (iii) multi-target and multi-sensor tracking, (iv) application tracking and legal requirements, (v) information fusion tools, techniques and theory, and (vi) decentralized and distributed detection and data fusion methods.

3.4   Case Studies

This section presents case studies for data analysis approaches in different domains. More details of these case studies and their association with sustainable models and theories are explained as follows.

3.4.1   Case Studies-1: Web Browsing History Analysis

The report is focused on extracting user's history from a text file and then aims to analyze the browsing history to find out User's Browsing behavior by using Apriori Algorithm. Browsers have a method through which user's history can be analyzed by finding out the occurrences of websites individually and with other possible websites in a single transaction. Data is being extracted at runtime from a text file using the concepts of File Handling. It will give a clear and better insight of user's browsing behavior. Browsing is done heavily these days but there is still an important need to check how the user is investing time on internet. Some Sites are not directly related to each other but sometimes users frequently visits the second website. If the user visited the first one so it creates some indirect relation between these websites and it is needed to be analyzed to know the browsing pattern. Using Apriori Algorithm Implementation, browsing data can be read and then analyzed in order to find out how many websites are visited together and how much time they are being visited in a single Transaction. All this information can be helpful in learning more about one's own browsing pattern.

Requirement in the field of cost calculation helps the user to choose the path with least traveling cost and also the least congested path. User gets the facility to choose the cost optimized path i.e. the path with the least traveling expenses are associated with. Traveling expenses are calculated by the values of gasoline price, mileage associated with the vehicle and the toll price during the journey [61]. Nearby scenic sites and monuments are also displayed as a suggestion to the user. For this approach, file handling is used to display details and Image processing to display the BMP image of the scenic sites. Runtime results are calculated as the inputs given by the user.

Figure 3.7 shows the use case diagram for data operations. In these operations, a system can extract the data and analyze using an algorithm for load estimation. The proposed system is based on file system that uses text files for operations. A user is slowed to enter or retrieve data at any stage. Figure 3.8 shows the system flow chart. In this flow, the system contains the data in files and processed through C– interfaces. The processes data

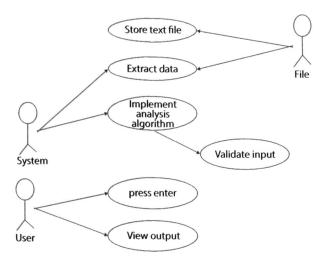

Figure 3.7 System use case diagram.

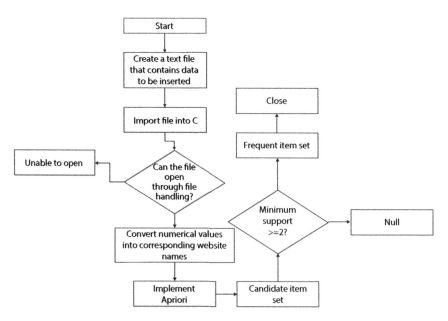

Figure 3.8 System flow chart explaining the working.

is handled to name the websites and implement the Apriori algorithm for filtering and candidature creation. Here, the minimum support of two persons is required to have a frequent item set with unconditional operations.

3.4.1.1   Objective

- Find out how many times the user has visited two websites in a single transaction by performing the possible combination of different websites to see if they are visited frequently.
- Using association rule to find out occurrences of websites by the user in a single transaction and filter the display by showing websites that are visited frequently.

This work is to get a better insight of user's browsing history so that the browsing behavior can be predicted for the user. Data analysis tool is needed to analyze user's browsing history and display websites frequently visited by the user and to find out what are the frequent combination of websites visited by the user in a single transaction. This work analyzes the browsing history of user and finds out frequency of individual websites and additional and more important and crucial feature is to find out occurrences of more than one websites together in a single transaction. The data is being taken from a text file at runtime. The sequence followed in this work is as follows.

- *Analyzing the data using different steps:* It involves a series of steps starting from taking the data from the file and then performing certain operations including Apriori Implementation on the data.
- *File Input/output:* The program asks for file and Data. If the File is present then the rest of implementation starts beginning else the program displays output saying that the file is not found.
- *Apriori Algorithm:* Apriori takes the data from text file as input and then create candidate item set for individual websites. After applying Minimum Support creation of frequency item set is done. This Frequency item set serves as input for the second list of Candidate item set. Now the second list of item set created which is served as input for Third list of item set. Then display all the lists of item set in output.

Various case scenarios generated in implementing the proposed system are explained as follows.

Scenario-1: First Candidate and Frequent List
This involves storing the data extracted from text file and storing it into 2-dimensional array. Thus taking those data as input. A total 5 number of transactions are being considered here each transaction involving number of websites to be visited between 0 and 5. The text file contains integers between 1 and 10 as the reference to websites visited by users. The website name corresponding to the integer will be defined in program. Now Program takes data from file at runtime and counts the number of times websites are visited and first Candidate and Frequent list gets Generated.

Scenario-2: Second Candidate and Frequent List
This involves taking input as the frequent list created in the first list and array and counter to count occurrences of two websites together.

Scenario-3: Third Candidate and Frequent List
This involves creation of third item set that is able to show the occurrences of three websites together creating the Third and Final Candidate and Frequency item set which takes Second list as input in order to perform deeper analysis.

Figures 3.9 to 3.12 show the implementation screenshots. In Figure 3.9, first page output is shown. Here, data related to multiple websites is displayed. The data in numerical shows the number assigned to website

```
Please Note that :
Here
 Facebook is denoted by 1

 Google is denoted by 2

 Quora is denoted by 3

 Youtube is denoted by 4

 Wikipedia is denoted by 5

 Gmail is denoted by 6

Javatpoint is denoted by 7

bankersadda is denoted by 8

w3school is denoted by 9

tutorialspoint is denoted by 10
```

Figure 3.9 First page.

```
History :

Transaction     websites
1       :       Facebook    google      quora       youtube
2       :       Wikipedia   youtube     google      Facebook
3       :       quora       youtube     Wikipedia   google
4       :       JavaTpoint  Bankersadda w3school    tutorialspt   Gmail
5       :       Gmail       JavaTpoint  Bankersadda w3school      tutorialspt

We have minimum support: 2

Generating First Candidate Itemset from data
Facebook : 2
Google : 3
Quora : 2
Youtube : 3
Wikipedia : 2


Generating First Frequent Itemset from Candidate Itemset
Facebook : 2
google : 3
quora : 2
youtube : 3
Wikipedia : 2
```

Figure 3.10 Firstcandidate and frequent list.

for further analysis. Figure 3.10 shows the candidate wise accessibility list and sequence of website. This analysis is important to fetch the sustainable infrastructure models and theories. Figure 3.11 shows the different statistics at second and third candidate list traced according to algorithm. Thereafter, the importance and accessibility of website to candidate can be read. Figure 3.12 shows the input text file considered as explained in system flow (Figure 3.8).

3.4.2 Case Study-2: Data Model for Group Construction in Student's Industrial Placement

The aim of this project is to design and implement a pooling system that differentiated students based on various parameters like CGPA, projects, training and certifications, interests, mobility, expectations etc for easy placement venture. There is one large cluster of students (say n). At each subsequent step, the largest available cluster is split into two clusters according to the needs of the placement cell. This technique used is DIANA (Divisive Analysis)—Hierarchical clustering. Gone are the days when students didn't pay attention to the rate of placement of college before taking admission. Now time is changed and the future market of the college depends on today's placement record. Campus placement season is a high-stakes game which destines students' lives for at least the next year or two. As we know, the placement of students is the most looked

```
Generating Second List
Facebook          google         2
Facebook          quora          1
Facebook          youtube        2
Facebook          Wikipedia      1
google            quora          2
google            youtube        3
google            Wikipedia      2
quora             youtube        2
quora             Wikipedia      1
youtube           Wikipedia      2


Generating frequent Itemset for Second List
Facebook          google         2

Facebook          youtube        2

google            quora          2
google            youtube        3
google            Wikipedia      2
quora             youtube        2

youtube           Wikipedia      2


Generating Third List
Facebook          youtube        quora          1
google            youtube        quora          2
google            quora          Wikipedia      1


Generating Frequent Itemset from Third List

google            youtube        quora          2
```

Figure 3.11 Second and third candidate and frequent list.

```
1 2 3 4 0
5 4 0 2 1
3 4 5 0 2
7 8 9 10 6
6 7 8 9 10
```

Figure 3.12 Input data from text file.

after process of any college or university. Hence we decided to make a project that would eventually help the career services to make things easy. This project categorises students into different groups based on different parameters such as CGPA, projects, trainings and certifications, interests, mobility, expectations, etc; so that the entire venture can be accomplished beyond the shadow of a doubt, thus improvising the placement record.

In institution study practices, student's learning abilities with respect to industrial placement is considered in curriculum development. Students understand the importance of content that they are learning and more likely to be actively involved in learning process and less likely to be passively participating in classroom activities. But sometimes the highly reputed colleges are failed to place their students in good and reputed MNCs. There could be any reason behind the failure. To increase the reputation of college in the market and to increase the placement rate, proper strategy is required to be followed. Gone are the days when students didn't pay attention to the rate of placement of college before taking admission. Now time is changed and the future market of the college depends on today's placement record. Placement cell has been facing difficulty in the previous years. We are developing a project to segregate students according to their capabilities apart from their pointer based division. Suppose a student having a pointer less than other students but has more industrial knowledge and is thus much more deserving than the student qualified. We analyzed this situation that the students have been facing all these years and thus thought of designing a project which would eventually better the records and brings positive feedback from the companies as well. The aim of the project is to group students as a means of raising attainment. Through survey we will be collecting student information and create our own dummy data set. Performing data mining and using hierarchical clustering technique: DIANA (Divisive Analysis) we will classify students into different pools and suggest areas to be worked upon. Understanding characteristics of students from multifarious backgrounds is essential. This research is the first attempt to apply hierarchical clustering technique, DIANA in particular, to aid administration of placement activities to identify different clusters of students and to allow characteristics of each cluster to be further extracted. The research also improves DIANA further resulting in better clustering performance. It is yet another affirmation of the application of knowledge discovery, especially in clustering, in the field of education. Such future attempts may result in a new paradigm in the advancement in the field of knowledge discovery in general and higher placement dossier. Placement cell has been facing difficulty in the previous years. Suppose a student having a pointer less than other students but has more industrial knowledge and is thus much more deserving than the student qualified. We are developing a project to segregate students according to their capabilities apart from their pointer based division. The work objectives are:

(i) To group students into different pools A, B & C based on various parameters using hierarchical clustering, and (ii) To improve placement record of the university. Figure 3.13 and 3.14 show the overall results. The statistics shows the implementation of various outcomes in student's accessibility.

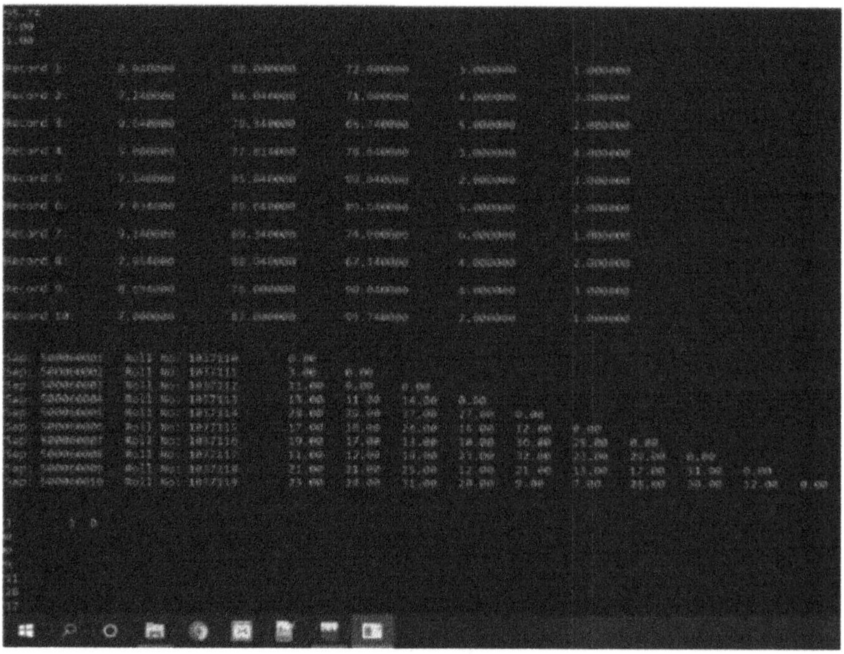

Figure 3.13 Display of data and euclidean distance matrix.

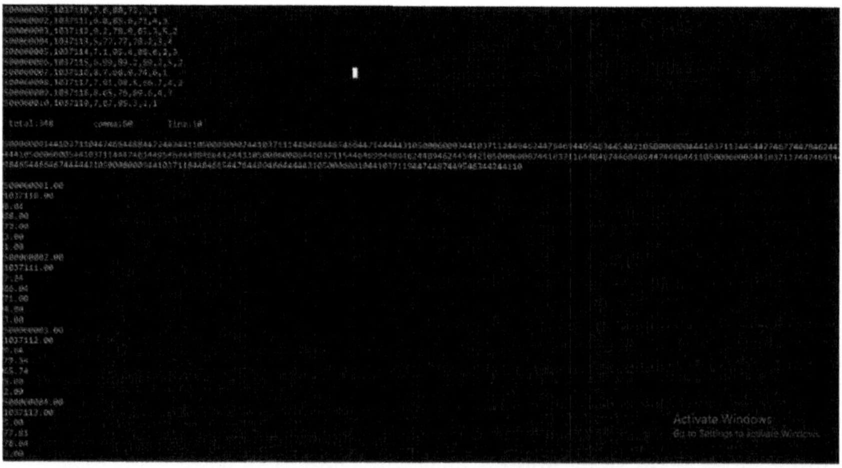

Figure 3.14 Final result.

3.5   Conclusion and Future Scope

In this work, data fusion models and techniques are studies that show the use of recent technologies in self-healing concrete and forces the convergence of technology of civil infrastructure development to future smart infrastructure. The success of technology and its adoption in civil infrastructure development require external interventions for inspection and repair with sensors. Sensors are smart and intelligent devices to have regular automated monitoring and repair. This implicates the economic impact over environmental sustainability and quality of life in broad perspectives. Thus, the importance to study these aspects increases with an increase in time and development of smart environment friendly infrastructure. The technological approaches need to be investigated from the vision of self-repairing infrastructure. The self-repairing infrastructure will have the ability to make it impossible in attaining robustness in civil tasks. The significance of the approach needs investigation with wide-range of sensors. Sensors generate a huge amount of data. Thus, there is a need to analyze the patterns in light of building in states changes with time, and cracks observed with concrete development. Here, data fusion techniques with respect to infrastructure models are discussed. In future, various designs to enhance the infrastructure capabilities will be explored. The possibilities of integrating Industry 4.0 solutions require attention. Thus, new proposal will be designed and analyzed keeping the latest infrastructure trends into consideration. This work has presented two case studies in relation to sustainable theories and models for website accessibility and student's placement activities.

The shortcomings in existing work and future directions are discussed as follows.

In web-based case study, Turbo C Compiler just permits access to 1MB of memory so in a heavy memory allocated C program the compiler runs out of memory resulting in a trap mode. Turbo C does not support dynamic and dynamic loaded library. Turbo C graphics does not support 32-bit graphics resulting in a poor display. It can open a limited number of files at a time.

The future directions (in web-based case study) are discussed as follows.

- *More transactions:* This project could be extended to add more transactions to analyze quantity of data and improved results.
- *Ad companies:* This Project could be used by Different websites that will be able to provide more better and relevant ads to the user at less cost and more accuracy.
- *Real Time Analytics:* It can be linked with browser and provide real time analytics of user's browsing.

References

1. Hall, D.L. and Llinas, J., An introduction to multisensor data fusion. *Proc. IEEE*, 85, 1, 6–23, 1997.
2. Liggins, I.I.M., Hall, D., Llinas, J. (Eds.), *Handbook of multisensor data fusion: Theory and practice*, CRC Press, 2017.
3. Yokoya, N., Grohnfeldt, C., Chanussot, J., Hyperspectral and multispectral data fusion: A comparative review of the recent literature. *IEEE Geosci. Remote Sens. Mag.*, 5, 2, 29–56, 2017.
4. Alam, F., Mehmood, R., Katib, I., Albogami, N.N., Albeshri, A., Data fusion and IoT for smart ubiquitous environments: A survey. *IEEE Access*, 5, 9533–54, 2017 Apr 25.
5. Chen, F.C. and Jahanshahi, M.R., NB-CNN: Deep learning-based crack detection using convolutional neural network and Naïve Bayes data fusion. *IEEE Trans. Ind. Electron.*, 65, 5, 4392–400, 2017 Oct 19.
6. Wang, M., Perera, C., Jayaraman, P.P., Zhang, M., Strazdins, P., Shyamsundar, R.K., Ranjan, R., City data fusion: Sensor data fusion in the Internet of Things. *Int. J. Distrib. Syst. Technol. (IJDST)*, 7, 1, 15–36, 2016.
7. Xiao, F., Multi-sensor data fusion based on the belief divergence measure of evidences and the belief entropy. *Inf. Fusion*, 46, 23–32, 2019.
8. Schmitt, M. and Zhu, X.X., Data fusion and remote sensing: An ever-growing relationship. *IEEE Geosci. Remote Sens. Mag.*, 4, 4, 6–23, 2016.
9. Smilde, A.K., Måge, I., Naes, T., Hankemeier, T., Lips, M.A., Kiers, H.A., Acar, E., Bro, R., Common and distinct components in data fusion. *J. Chemom.*, 31, 7, e2900, 2017.
10. T.P. Blackadar and D.P. Monahan, inventors; Lumiradx Uk Ltd, assignee, Versatile sensors with data fusion functionality, United States patent application US 15/645,305, 2017.
11. Noack, B., Sijs, J., Reinhardt, M., Hanebeck, U.D., Decentralized data fusion with inverse covariance intersection. *Automatica*, 79, 35–41, 2017.
12. Zhou, D., Al-Durra, A., Gao, F., Ravey, A., Matraji, I., Simoes, M.G., Online energy management strategy of fuel cell hybrid electric vehicles based on data fusion approach. *J. Power Sources*, 366, 278–91, 2017.
13. Kumar, A., Srikanth, P., Nayyar, A., Sharma, G., Krishnamurthi, R., Alazab, M., A Novel Simulated-Annealing Based Electric Bus System Design, Simulation, and Analysis for Dehradun Smart City. *IEEE Access*, 8, 89395–424, 2020.
14. Kumar, A. and Jain, S., Proof of Game (PoG): A Game Theory Based Consensus Model, in: *International Conference on Sustainable Communication Networks and Application*, Springer, Cham, pp. 755–764.
15. Kumar, A., Krishnamurthi, R., Nayyar, A., Sharma, K., Grover, V., Hossain, E., A Novel Smart Healthcare Design, Simulation, and Implementation Using Healthcare 4.0 Processes. *IEEE Access*, 8, 118433–71, 2020.

16. Al-Hader, M. and Rodzi, A., The smart city infrastructure development & monitoring. *Theor. Empir. Res. Urban Manag.*, 4 2, 11, 87–94, 2009.

17. Basford, P.J., Bulot, F.M., Apetroaie-Cristea, M., Cox, S.J., Ossont, S.J., LoRaWAN for smart city IoT deployments: A long term evaluation. *Sensors*, 20, 3, 648, 2020.

18. Bardyn, J.P., Melly, T., Seller, O., Sornin, N., IoT: The era of LPWAN is starting now, in: *ESSCIRC Conference 2016: 42nd European Solid-State Circuits Conference*, IEEE, pp. 25–30, 2016.

19. Atzori, L., Iera, A., Morabito, G., The internet of things: A survey. *Comput. Networks*, 54, 15, 2787–805, 2010.

20. Latif, S., Afzaal, H., Zafar, N.A., Intelligent traffic monitoring and guidance system for smart city, in: *2018 International Conference on Computing, Mathematics and Engineering Technologies (iCoMET)*, IEEE, pp. 1–6, 2018.

21. Anthopoulos, L., Smart utopia VS smart reality: Learning by experience from 10 smart city cases. *Cities*, 63, 128–48, 2017.

22. Anthopoulos, L., Janssen, M., Weerakkody, V., A Unified Smart City Model (USCM) for smart city conceptualization and benchmarking, in: *Smart Cities and Smart Spaces: Concepts, Methodologies, Tools, and Applications*, pp. 247–264, IGI Global, 2019.

23. Stop Saying 'Smart Cities' Digital stardust won't magically make future cities more affordable or resilient, https://www.theatlantic.com/technology/archive/2018/02/stupid-cities/553052/, 2018.

24. Giourka, P., Sanders, M.W., Angelakoglou, K., Pramangioulis, D., Nikolopoulos, N., Rakopoulos, D., Tryferidis, A., Tzovaras, D., The smart city business model canvas—A smart city business modeling framework and practical tool. *Energies*, 12, 24, 4798, 2019.

25. Timmermans, J.S. and Beroggi, G.E., Conflict resolution in sustainable infrastructure management. *Saf. Sci.*, 35, 1–3, 175–92, 2000.

26. González-Ruiz, J.D., Botero-Botero, S., Duque-Grisales, E., Financial eco-innovation as a mechanism for fostering the development of sustainable infrastructure systems. *Sustainability*, 10, 12, 4463, 2018.

27. Kumar, A., Gopal, K., Aggarwal, A., Novel Trusted Hierarchy Construction for RFID Sensor-Based MANETs Using ECCs. *ETRI J.*, 37, 1, 186–96, 2015.

28. Mwaniki, V., *Policy Brief on the State of Taxation on the Digital Economy*, 2015.

29. Choguill, C.L., Ten steps to sustainable infrastructure. *Habitat Int.*, 20, 3, 389–404, 1996.

30. Mehmood, R., Alam, F., Albogami, N.N., Katib, I., Albeshri, A., Altowaijri, S.M., UTiLearn: A personalised ubiquitous teaching and learning system for smart societies. *IEEE Access*, 5, 2615–35, 2017.

31. Mitchell, H.B., *Multi-sensor data fusion: An introduction*, Springer Science & Business Media, 2007.

32. Hall, D. and Llinas, J. (Eds.), *Multisensor data fusion*, CRC Press, 2001 Jun 20.
33. Khaleghi, B., Razavi, S.N., Khamis, A., Karray, F.O., Kamel, M., Multisensor data fusion: Antecedents and directions, in: *2009 3rd International Conference on Signals, Circuits and Systems (SCS)*, IEEE, 2009 Nov 6, pp. 1–6.
34. White, F.E. and Data fusion lexicon, joint directors of laboratories, Technical panel for C; 3, 1987.
35. Waltz, E.L. and Data fusion for C3I: A tutorial, *Command, Control, Communications Intelligence (C3I) Handbook*, pp. 217–226, EW Communications, Palo Alto, CA, 1986.
36. Zhu, C., Xia, Y., Yan, L., Fu, M., Centralised fusion over unreliable networks. *Int. J. Control*, 85, 4, 409–18, 2012.
37. Esteban, J., Starr, A., Willetts, R., Hannah, P., Bryanston-Cross, P., A review of data fusion models and architectures: Towards engineering guidelines. *Neural Comput. Appl.*, 14, 4, 273–81, 2005.
38. Utete, S. and Durrant-Whyte, H.F., Reliability in decentralised data fusion networks, in: *Proceedings of 1994 IEEE International Conference on MFI'94. Multisensor Fusion and Integration for Intelligent Systems*, IEEE, 1994 Oct 2, pp. 215–221.
39. Kumar, R., Wolenetz, M., Agarwalla, B., Shin, J., Hutto, P., Paul, A., Ramachandran, U., DFuse: A framework for distributed data fusion, in: *Proceedings of the 1st international conference on Embedded networked sensor systems*, 2003 Nov 5, pp. 114–125.
40. Andrews, J.G., Buzzi, S., Choi, W., Hanly, S.V., Lozano, A., Soong, A.C., Zhang, J.C., What will 5G be? *IEEE J. Sel. Areas Commun.*, 32, 6, 1065–82, 2014.
41. Rappaport, T.S., Sun, S., Mayzus, R., Zhao, H., Azar, Y., Wang, K., Wong, G.N., Schulz, J.K., Samimi, M., Gutierrez, F., Millimeter wave mobile communications for 5G cellular: It will work! *IEEE Access*, 1, 335–49, 2013.
42. Kreibich, O., Neuzil, J., Smid, R., Quality-based multiple-sensor fusion in an industrial wireless sensor network for MCM. *IEEE Trans. Ind. Electron.*, 61, 9, 4903–11, 2013.
43. Luo, X., Zhang, D., Yang, L.T., Liu, J., Chang, X., Ning, H., A kernel machine-based secure data sensing and fusion scheme in wireless sensor networks for the cyber-physical systems. *Future Gener. Comput. Syst.*, 61, 85–96, 2016.
44. Lau, B.P., Marakkalage, S.H., Zhou, Y., Hassan, N.U., Yuen, C., Zhang, M., Tan, U.X., A survey of data fusion in smart city applications. *Inf. Fusion*, 52, 357–74, 2019.
45. Raza, M.Q. and Khosravi, A., A review on artificial intelligence based load demand forecasting techniques for smart grid and buildings. *Renewable Sustainable Energy Rev.*, 50, 1352–72, 2015.
46. Baetens, R., Jelle, B.P., Gustavsen, A., Properties, requirements and possibilities of smart windows for dynamic daylight and solar energy control

in buildings: A state-of-the-art review. *Sol. Energy Mater. Solar Cells*, 94, 2, 87–105, 2010.

47. Luo, R.C. and Su, K.L., Autonomous fire-detection system using adaptive sensory fusion for intelligent security robot. *IEEE/ASME Trans. Mechatron.*, 12, 3, 274–81, 2007.

48. Kumar, A., Sharma, K., Singh, H., Naugriya, S.G., Gill, S.S., Buyya, R., drone-based networked system and methods for combating coronavirus disease (COVID-19) pandemic. *Future Gener. Comput. Syst.*, 2020.

49. Kumar, A., Gopal, K., Aggarwal, A., Design and Analysis of Lightweight Trust Mechanism for Accessing Data in MANETs. *KSII Trans. Internet Inf. Syst.*, 8, 3, 2014.

50. Kumar, A., Aggarwal, A., Gopal, K., A novel and efficient reader-to-reader and tag-to-tag anti-collision protocol. *IETE J. Res.*, 1–2, 2018.

51. Kumar, A., Rajalakshmi, K., Jain, S., Nayyar, A., Abouhawwash, M., A novel heuristic simulation–optimization method for critical infrastructure in smart transportation systems. *Int. J. Commun. Syst.*, e4397, 2020.

52. Kumar, A., Kumar Sharma, D., Nayyar, A., Singh, S., Yoon, B., Lightweight Proof of Game (LPoG): A Proof of Work (PoW)'s Extended Lightweight Consensus Algorithm for Wearable Kidneys. *Sensors*, 20, 10, 2868, 2020.

53. Kumar, A. and Aggarwal, A., Comparative Analysis of Elliptic Curve Cryptography Based Lightweight Authentication Protocols for RFID-Sensor Integrated MANETs, in: *International Conference on Intelligent Systems Design and Applications*, Springer, Cham, 2018 Dec 6, pp. 934–944.

54. Chugh, N., Kumar, A., Aggarwal, A., Availability Aspects Through Optimization Techniques Based Outlier Detection Mechanism in Wireless and Mobile Networks. *Int. J. Comput. Netw. Commun. (IJCNC)*, 10, 2018.

55. Kumar, A., Gopal, K., Aggarwal, A., A Novel Cross-Layer Network Architecture and Its Performance Analysis Using Mobile Ad Hoc Network Routing Protocol. *J. Adv. Comput. Netw.*, 1, 3, 2013.

56. Kumar, A., Jain, S., Aggarwal, A., Comparative Analysis of Multi-round Cryptographic Primitives based Lightweight Authentication Protocols for RFID-Sensor Integrated MANETs. *J. Inf. Assur. Secur.*, 14, 1, 2019.

57. Kumar, A. and Aggarwal, A., Analysis of DCNS anti-collision protocol with contiguous channel allocation, in: *2016 Ninth International Conference on Contemporary Computing (IC3)*, IEEE, 2016 Aug 11, pp. 1–7.

58. Kumar, A., Gopal, K., Aggarwal, A., Lightweight trust propagation scheme for resource constraint mobile ad-hoc networks (MANETs), in: *2013 Sixth International Conference on Contemporary Computing (IC3)*, IEEE, 2013 Aug 8, pp. 421–426.

59. Kumar, A. and Jain, S., Proof of Game (PoG): A Proof of Work (PoW)'s Extended Consensus Algorithm for Healthcare Application, in: *International Conference on Innovative Computing and Communications*, Springer, Singapore, pp. 23–36.

60. Manjulata, A.K., Survey on lightweight primitives and protocols for RFID in wireless sensor networks. *Int. J. Commun. Netw. Inf. Secur.*, 6, 1, 29, 2014.

61. Kumar, A., Gopal, K., Aggarwal, A., Outlier detection and treatment for lightweight mobile ad hoc networks, in: *International Conference on Heterogeneous Networking for Quality, Reliability, Security and Robustness*, Springer, Berlin, Heidelberg, 2013 Jan 11, pp. 750–763.

4

Blockchain for Sustainable Smart Cities

Iftikhar Ahmad*, Syeda Warda Ashar, Umamma Khalid, Anmol Irfan
and Wajeeha Khalil

*Department of Computer Science & Information Technology, University of
Engineering & Technology, Peshawar, Pakistan*

Abstract

Large scale urbanization posed a number of challenges for the government and city planner. Smart city concept can be applied to overcome these challenges. However, the concept of smart city by itself faces numerous challenges most prominently data handling challenge. The data handling challenge includes data formatting, information sharing, data quality, security and privacy, and scalability. Blockchain is a novel technology mainly associated with the cryptocurrencies. Blockchain is integrated in smart city applications to improve the living standard of citizens and the overall management of the smart city. In this chapter, we present an overview of smart city and discuss the challenges faced for the realization of smart city dream. Specifically, we focus on data handling challenges faced by the smart city. We present blockchain as enabling technology, and present uses cases where blockchain is employed to address the key challenges of a smart city. We observed that the intrinsic properties (such as public/private key combination, time stamped record management, immutability etc.) of the blockchain has the ability to address key challenges of a smart city such as data sharing, privacy and security, health applications, and smart infrastructure management. We conclude the work by discussing potential open research questions.

Keywords: Smart city, sustainable city, blockchain, smart living, smart economy, smart contracts

Corresponding author: ia@uetpeshawar.edu.pk

Arun Solanki, Adarsh Kumar and Anand Nayyar (eds.) Digital Cities Roadmap: IoT-Based Architecture and Sustainable Buildings, (127–162) © 2021 Scrivener Publishing LLC

4.1   Introduction

"The most profound technologies are those that disappear. They weave themselves into the fabric of everyday life until they are indistinguishable from it" [1]. As the world is advancing in the field of technology, smart city has become a widespread term that is interpreted by several communities in various ways, primarily targeting the introduction of smartness concept in the life of individuals. The concept of smartness is linked to intelligent operations and independent working of the technology in decision making to facilitate people [2]. The concept of smart cities emerged as a consequence of the requirement of efficient management of city's resources. The smart city concept introduced the use of Information and Communication Technology (ICT) in all aspects of life such as health, safety, infrastructure, transport, etc. [2].

The need for smart city grew when people started migration from rural to urban areas. With increased population, the cities were poorly managed causing the over burdening of resources such as healthcare, housing, education, energy, and water [2]. The speedy increase in population also effected the environment, resulting in higher pollution (both air and water), and thus causing health issues. Other effects include over burdening of infrastructure, such as roads, bridges and public transportation system.

These issues motivated the researchers and authorities to focus on the city management standards and improvement in the quality of life of citizens. Thus, the concept of smart city was introduced. The concept promises to provide social benefits to people and solve the above mentioned challenges by introducing a proper management systems. The idea of smart city providing facilities to its citizens requires huge amount of data gathering for smart decisions. It requires technologies that will fulfill the data handling requirements of a smart city. Beside data gathering, data integrity, confidentiality, and transparency are the other key aspects that must be taken into account when storing and handling citizens' data.

Data handling techniques play a key role in successful automation of information and decision making. Multiple techniques have been adopted in response to variable needs that appeared from time to time. Currently, popular data handling technologies include cloud storage, blockchain, fog storage etc. [3]. Among them, blockchain is the leading technology that can help in the development of smart cities by connecting different services of a city and providing security, confidentiality and transparency to all processes. It can also address the social, economic, environmental, mobility, security, and governance issues of the city. Numerous research efforts have been made for the development and working of a smart city [4].

The efforts are directed to decide on the types of applications to be developed for a smart city environment as well as the technologies and architecture to support these applications [4]. However, implementation of smart city with blockchain is rarely discussed.

Due to a lack of research and implementation work in the field of blockchain as an enabling technology for smart cities for data handling, this chapter aims to explore the possibilities. We conducted a thorough review of the literature related to the smart city. Based on the literature review, we present an overview of smart city, its origin and categories. Based on these categories, six major domains of a smart city are discussed. The challenges faced by smart city in different situations are presented. In addition, the introduction to blockchain technology and the way it helps smart city grow is also discussed. The main focus of this work is on the use cases of blockchain in smart city. Several use cases of blockchain in various domains of smart city is presented. Each use case explains how it implements blockchain in the smart city domain to improve living standards of the citizens.

A number of research articles presented surveys related to either smart city or blockchain. da Silva *et al.* [5] focused on the need of a robust architecture to meet the requirements of a smart city. A number of architectures from the literature are surveyed and presented. The authors argued that none of the proposed architecture met the key requirements of a smart city. Yin *et al.* [6] presented a thorough review of smart city literature by discussing the origin and challenges of smart city. A data-centric view of smart city architecture is discussed, and key enabling technologies to address the challenges are presented. Petrolo *et al.* [7] introduced the concept of Cloud of Things (CoT) for smart city. The authors presented the benefits of integrating various IoT eco-systems within CoT. Panarello *et al.* [8] presented a thorough review of the literature on blockchain and Internet of Things integration. The authors analyzed the existing research trends of blockchain and IoT integration and briefly discussed the integration of IoT and blockchain for the smart city. Other major works include Refs. [9–15]. We differentiate our work by focusing on the challenges of smart city and how blockchain is used to address these challenges by presenting the use cases of blockchain in a smart city.

Chapter Organization

The chapter is organized into sections as follows: In Section 4.2, we introduce smart city by discussing its evolution, categories, domains and challenges. We present blockchain, its emergence and working in Section 4.3. In Section 4.4, we present domains of smart city with the support of various use cases which implements blockchain. Finally, the chapter concludes with directions for future research in Section 4.5.

4.2   Smart City

4.2.1   Overview of Smart City

IBM defines smart city as the use of information and communication technology to sense, analyze and integrate the key information of core system in running cities while at the same time making an intelligent response to heterogeneous needs and livelihood [4]. Smart city becomes smart with the use of smart computing technologies such as client devices, hardware and software, network and server infrastructure that connects the components of city infrastructure and services like health care, education, city administration, public safety, transportation, real estate, etc. [2, 16, 17]. However, the definition of smart city is not consistent, and includes various dimensions of urban life based on the perceived meaning of smart [18]. Some of the synonyms of smart city include intelligent city [19], ubiquitous city [20], knowledge city [21], and digital city [22].

4.2.2   Evolution

The concept of smart cities can be tracked back to Smart Growth movement that promoted intelligent policy designs for urban infrastructure planning. Recognized example of smart growth is Portland, Oregon. Smart growth advocates policies that will lessen the congestion, clean the air and protect the open space, provide affordable housing, and reduce urban-service costs [23]. The phrase smart cities is also used by technology companies since 2005 referring to the use of state-of-the-art information systems to streamline various operations of the urban society. Such operations may include buildings, health infrastructure and services, citizen safety, and various distributions channels (such as electricity and water). The concept has since refined to encompass the use of innovative technologies in various aspects of cities' operations.

4.2.3   Smart City's Sub Systems

Smart city is not a stand-alone unit, but instead consists of multiple heterogeneous sub-systems that work together in tandem to make a city smart. We divide these sub-systems into different categories. We assume these categories as the basic components that communicate in a heterogeneous environment to transform a city into a smart city. Following are the general categories of the sub system of a smart city.

Smart Health

Smart health care systems store patients' record on electronic devices that are retrieved as and when required. The databank thus created can be used for various research purposes [2, 24]. Further, applications can be developed to assist individuals in case of emergency and recommend medication. Examples of such system includes telemedicine applications [25].

Smart Infrastructure and Smart Home

Smart infrastructure such as smart and sustainable buildings use ICT and supporting technologies to assist residents in keeping track of different aspects of their living. For instance, using Internet of Things (IoT) and cellphone applications, the residents can control the temperature of a building. They can also keep electronic record of energy consumption of various devices and can regulate their use remotely as well. Further, sustainability can also be achieved by monitoring the health of the buildings using IoT devices which can warn residents of any degradation well in time [26]. The US Green Building Council (USGBC) advocates policies that encourage real-estate developers and homeowners to install smart technologies for managing various aspects of homes [2]. The technology can be used to control home appliances remotely helping to reduce the cost of living. Further, the aggregated data from a locality can be used by the government and other agencies in decision making as well.

Smart Grid

Smart grid ensures to use the limited energy resources in an efficient manner. It is connected with numerous components of the smart city including smart home, smart metering system, smart streetlights, transformers, distribution channels, etc. [27, 28].

Smart Environment

Smart environment refers to the use of technology to monitor various aspects of the environment and record information that can be used in decision making. For instance, a smart city can use ICT technologies to monitor the pollution level in different parts of the city and inform residents accordingly when pollution level reaches a threshold value. The information is useful for residents who face health issues such allergy or asthma who can plan their visit accordingly. Further, temperature, humidity, and concentration of various toxic gasses can also be monitored.

Smart Street Lights

Energy is an important and scarce resource, and therefore, must be used efficiently. One key aspect in smart city is the proper utilization of streetlights to reduce the energy usage. Smart sensors can be deployed to monitor the pedestrian and vehicles and turn on the lights as and when necessary. Veena *et al.* [29] proposed a smart framework for streetlights management using live video to identify the movement of people and vehicles and switch on the streetlights accordingly. If no movement is detected for a specific interval, the lights are turned off.

Smart Traffic

Smart traffic is another key aspect of the smart city infrastructure. Smart traffic monitoring ensures that traffic flow is smooth, and congestions are avoided to the possible extent. Smart traffic can also provide near real time updates to drivers to avoid road congestions and use alternate routes to reach their destinations [30]. The traffic data can be obtained by using smart sensors. For instance, vehicle detection can be achieved by the use of magnetic field or applying machine learning techniques on live video streams.

4.2.4   Domains of Smart City

So far, we have discussed categories that describes the ways which can transform a locality into a smart city. However, separating each of these categories into mutually exclusive sets is not possible as they contain overlapping sub-categories. For instance, achieving the goal of smart security is not possible without achieving the objectives of smart governance and smart infrastructure. We group these categories into six domains that fully define various aspects of a smart city. These domains are summarized in Figure 4.1 and are described in the following text.

Smart Economy

Smart economy can be regarded as the main pillar of urban development. Smart economy is also referred to as DNA of the smart city. Smart economy advocates the concepts of sustainable development, investor friendliness and growth. The investments can be made in a broad spectrum of

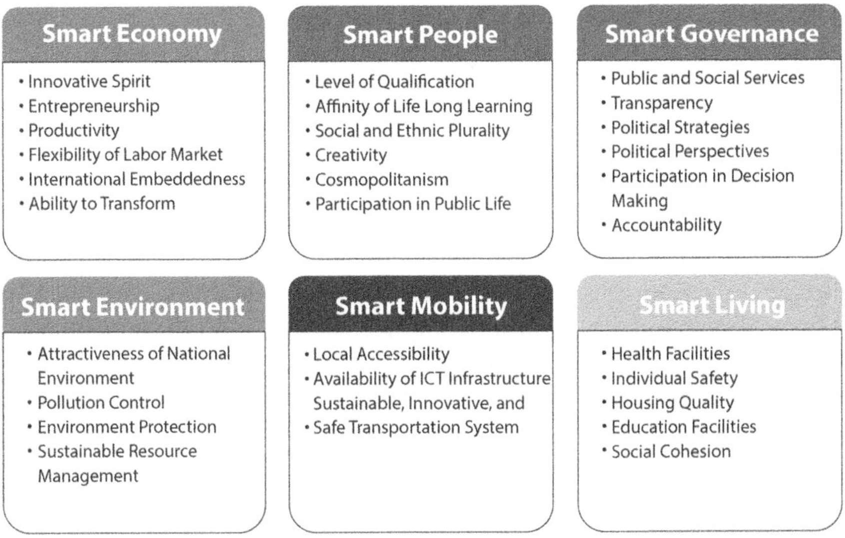

Smart Economy	Smart People	Smart Governance
• Innovative Spirit • Entrepreneurship • Productivity • Flexibility of Labor Market • International Embeddedness • Ability to Transform	• Level of Qualification • Affinity of Life Long Learning • Social and Ethnic Plurality • Creativity • Cosmopolitanism • Participation in Public Life	• Public and Social Services • Transparency • Political Strategies • Political Perspectives • Participation in Decision Making • Accountability
Smart Environment	Smart Mobility	Smart Living
• Attractiveness of National Environment • Pollution Control • Environment Protection • Sustainable Resource Management	• Local Accessibility • Availability of ICT Infrastructure Sustainable, Innovative, and • Safe Transportation System	• Health Facilities • Individual Safety • Housing Quality • Education Facilities • Social Cohesion

Figure 4.1 Domains of smart city [31].

businesses to decrease unemployment rate and increase the productivity. The objective of the smart economy is to stimulate sustainable economic growth leading to higher economic activity and lower unemployment rates.

Smart People

Smart people form the core of a smart city. The dream of smart city cannot be achieved without smart people. For people to become smart, they must regularly and frequently improve and update their skill sets. They should differentiate themselves by acquiring and maintaining state of the art skills in various disciplines of life. A smart city needs to streamline the curricula of their educational institute with the requirement of the society. Smart people can contribute towards long term sustainable growth of the city.

Smart Governance

Smooth functioning of government is of utmost importance for a smart city. The government should introduce set of rules encouraging and facilitating people to achieve the goal of smart city. A smart government relies on modern technologies and infrastructure to deliver various services to its residents [32]. Technologies are integrated in decision making to ensure that people are involved in key decisions. For citizens and businesses, the procedures and approval process become simplified and easy. For government employees and agencies, it facilitates the appropriate and timely decision-making, the coordination and collaboration among the cross-agency [33].

Smart Mobility/Transportation

An important characteristic of any smart city is the presence of smart mobility/transportation system. Smart mobility includes both vehicles and people, and encourages healthy mobility including walking and cycling. To achieve smart mobility, appropriate infrastructure and government supported legislation is a key requirement. The objective of smart mobility is to ensure the hassle-free movement of people across the city and ensuring smooth flow of the traffic. Intelligent transportation systems are included in the city infrastructure [34, 35].

Smart Environment

Sustainability is a key consideration of a smart city. Smart environment aims to achieve the objective of sustainability by offering clean, pollution free and healthy environment to its residents. ICT technologies are used to measure various aspects of the environment such as pollution and noise level and relevant authorities are informed to take immediate remedial actions if residents are exposed to high level of pollution/noise levels. Further, national phenomenon such as earthquakes, flash floods, sudden eruption of volcano are regularly monitored, and early warning is released when an imminent threat is detected.

Smart Living

Living a standard life is the dream of every resident of a locality. Smart living incorporates various aspect of a resident's daily life routine to offer high standard of living enriched in local customs, culture and history. Smart living caters the need of every age group and provide the necessary services accordingly. For instance, for women, children and senior citizens safety and security is ensured. The overall objective is to enhance the living experience of the residents.

4.2.5   Challenges

A smart city is not just a set of various ICT technologies but comprises of highly integrated state of the art living solution that combines various aspects of life in a ubiquitous manner. Smart city manages all the resources intelligently and efficiently to offer a sustainable and improved quality of life. Smart city is focusing on the aforementioned six domains as well as its applications such as smart education, smart energy, smart transportation and smart housing, etc. These applications require large computation and storage as the data is being gathered from different data sources like smart phones, environmental sensors, GPS (Geographical Positioning Systems), computers, cameras and from applications like social media sites, images and videos, etc. Data acquisition, storage and processing is one of the key challenges of smart city as it is very difficult to handle and manage massive amount of data which is then required by the smart city applications to work efficiently. Some of the challenges associated with the data handling are discussed below.

Data Sources and Formats

In smart city applications, the data needs to be in an organized format so it can be easily accessible for the use of a variety of applications. A smart city gathers data from various sources which results in a heterogeneous data. The data can thus be structured and unstructured posing storage, and processing challenges. Therefore, to leverage the best use of huge amount of data available by virtue of smart city's data development and gathering abilities, a proper storage, processing and computational mechanism must be developed [36].

Data and Information Sharing

In smart city, applications require data and information sharing [37]; for example, patient health records need to be shared among various medical facilities, and possibly with the researchers for future research purposes. This poses a serious challenge as ensuring the citizens' rights of privacy is collecting and sharing the data among various entities of city requires careful consideration [36].

Security and Privacy

One of the challenges in smart city is the security and privacy issues of users' data [37]. As confidential information of citizens and government is stored using various data storage technologies (such as cloud), proper security measures must be implemented to safeguard the confidential data against malicious attacks and unauthorized access. The systems should be resistant against different types of attacks. In the absence of a secure system, citizens will not trust the government and it will be difficult to gather the information for various purposes such as census. Therefore, the security and privacy problems must be handled with proper security measures to avoid data leakages [36–38].

Data Quality

Smart city deals with heterogeneous data that originate from numerous sources, each having different source, encoding and format. The data lacks proper structure, and validation mechanism. Thus, the resultant heterogeneous data poses several challenges for its efficient storage, retrieval and processing. In the absence of a unified system that can collect the diverse data and store it into a common structure for decision making, data handling is found to be a key technological challenge for smart city. Smart city is driven by data, which requires a number of safety and security mechanism to ensure safe storage and authorized access. Likewise, ensuring data integrity, confidentiality and availability is a key challenge as well [36].

Scalability of Applications

Smart city applications are developed in order to provide better and efficient services to the people of a city. People are positively influenced by smart city applications as they provide ease to their life. The growth in population results in the growth of data produced by the city's residents. Smart city applications should be scalable and needs to evolve quickly according to the growth of population so they can handle huge amount of big data [36].

4.3   Blockchain

Blockchain in an emerging technology for managing (recording, authentication, and retrieving) the financial transactions of companies. The term Blockchain refers to the chain of blocks that are linked and secured through cryptographic mechanisms. It is defined as a shared and distributed ledger that eases keeping track of assets in a network while providing security and transparency. An asset can be anything that as has an associated value with it, e.g., cash, property and land, etc. Assets can be tracked, shared, and traded using blockchain [39, 40].

4.3.1 Motivation

Blockchain emerged to address the flaws of historical transaction systems [39]. For instance, the cash is only useful when used locally and is a nuisance when used outside the country of issue. Similarity, the transfer of money involves a third party usually banks which charge a fee for the transaction to take place. The growing online banking, e-commerce, and in-app purchases, and the increasing mobility of people around the world have fueled the transaction volumes [39]. This increase in the digital market coupled with exponential growth of transactions magnified complexities, inefficiencies, vulnerabilities and the cost of the current financial systems [39, 41].

4.3.2 The Birth of Blockchain

In order to address the aforementioned challenges, a novel payment system was desired. The system should be fast, trust-worthy, commission-free, transparent and open with no central authority in command [40, 39]. Hence the blockchain was born. Blockchain transformed the dynamics of business. It provisioned fast, secure and trusted system for global business for transaction management. Satoshi Nakamoto introduced the concept of blockchain linked with the famous cryptocurrency bitcoin in 2008 [40].

4.3.3 System of Blockchain

In its simple form, a blockchain is a public registry to store all cryptocurrency transaction [40]. The public nature of the registry means that it is accessible to anyone who wishes to join the eco-system, allowing individuals to monitor the records [40]. Figure 4.2 is a simplistic view of a blockchain. Blockchain consists of several blocks, whereas Block is the basic unit of a blockchain. Each block is composed of two parts, data part and a cryptographic hash pointer. Data field stores time-stamped transaction data, whereas the hash pointer stores the address of the previous block as well as the hash of contents of the previous block. A block is added to the blockchain once the required formalities are completed. Once added to the blockchain, the contents of the blockchain cannot be modified. Any node (participating entity) can read, write and make a copy of the block. Any node/user (also called miner) can suggest a block to be added to the blockchain. However, for a block to be accepted in the blockchain, the miner has to solve a mathematical computational puzzle [40]. The miner collects

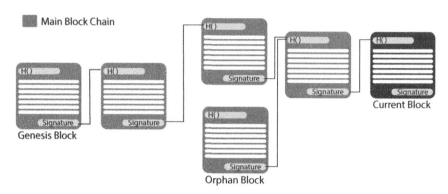

Figure 4.2 Simplistic view of blockchain.

the transactions from the network, creates a block from the transactions, and attempts to solve the computational puzzle. Upon successfully solving the computational puzzle, the miner earns the right to suggest a block to be added to the blockchain [40]. If the block is proved as a valid block, an incentive is given to the miner. A valid block follows the longest blockchain path from the genesis block to the current block [40]. Genesis block refers to the first block of a blockchain. The block that is not valid and added outside of the blockchain forming the shortest path is called orphan block.

Note that the design mechanism of the blockchain ensures that its contents are immutable, i.e., the contents cannot be changed once they are recorded [40]. A major issue with the blockchain is its increasing size which can cause issues related to storage and synchronization [40].

4.4   Use Cases of Smart City Implementing Blockchain

Smart city uses information technologies to help people improve their standards of living [42]. It uses digital services to build a digital society in both developed and developing countries. In this section we will discuss how a digital technology—blockchain—plays its role in different domains of smart cities.

4.4.1   Blockchain-Based Smart Economy

The inherent nature of blockchain facilitates economic growth by omitting the need of intermediary for financial transactions. Blockchain can facilitate economic growth as following.

4.4.1.1   Facilitating Faster and Cheaper International Payment

In the current financial system, delay and higher transaction fee are inevitable whenever cross border financial transactions are made, forming an invisible barrier for economic growth and development. Such scenarios are observed when an individual wants to send remittances back home or an organization wants to transfer money across the border for investment in a project [43]. In such situations, bank payments are the go-to method. However, bank's procedures are complicated and involve a number of steps such as the involvement of intermediary bank (at times different than the sender and beneficiary bank), record keeping, statement/transaction reconciliation, and fee deductions. The whole process of initiating a cross border financial transaction to its completion can take 3–5 business days [44]. Blockchain reinvented the banking system by omitting the need of third party (intermediary bank), thus reducing the high transactional costs as well as delay in the processing of transactions [44]. Ripple lab—a blockchain based global payment protocol facilitates the banking sector to use their platform for efficient financial transactions across geographic borders. McKinsey estimated that the cost of cross border financial transactions has decreased by the introduction of blockchain based applications [44]. A notable example is Standard Chartered Bank use of Ripple allowing 10-second payment transfer from one account to another across different geographical boundaries. Ripple is also used by The National Australian bank [44–46].

4.4.1.2   Distributed Innovations in Financial Transactions

Trade finance is used for the import and export of goods across the borders. For example, Company A of one country wants to import a shipment of goods from the exporting Company B of another country. The buyer has to pay for the goods but is uncertain whether the goods will arrive or not. Similarly, the seller is also uncertain about the payments whether she will be paid or not after the shipment of the goods. To resolve uncertainty between both the parties, the trade finance system uses letter of credit. A letter of credit is a bank document issued by the buyer through buyer's bank to the seller through the seller's bank; providing protection to both the buyer and the seller and guarantees a payment after certain conditions are met based on the letter of credit [47]. In trade finance system banks, an intermediary act as an escrow and holds the payment between the parties. The finance of supply-chain involves high manual work and the transactions are based on the paper documents moving forth and back among different parties (buyer and buyer's bank, seller and seller's bank, shipping and receiving companies, local shippers and insurers) requiring confirmation of documents by all the parties in order to ensure the accuracy. This involves many intermediaries, resulting in a high cost. Blockchain based smart contracts are used to digitize the laborious processes of paperwork, resulting in improved process management of the financial transactions [44]. Blockchain eliminates the need of different copies of same document stored on different databases across different entities. Blockchain stores all the information in a single digital document which is constantly updated and viewable by all the parties on the network. Smart contracts ensure that payments are made automatically by sharing the contractual information on the blockchain.

Using blockchain based applications for supply chain finances has reduced the associated costs for the concerned parties. Barclays Bank and an Israeli startup company conducted the first blockchain based trade transaction which involved export of butter and cheese products from Ornua (Irish company) to the Seychelles Trading Company [44]. The trade value of the transaction was 100,000 USD. In contrast to traditional approach which can take over 10 days, the blockchain based approach took merely 4 h [44]. Union Bank of Switzerland also intends to deploy blockchain based application to simplify the process of international trade transactions.

4.4.1.3   Enhancing the Transparency of Supply/Global Commodity Chains

Supply chain process is complicated as goods move from one channel to other involving various companies. The process is often opaque to end users who are not aware about the origin of the raw material. Likewise, the consumers are also not informed about the process and if the processing of the material is conducted as per the required regulatory guidelines. i.e., lack of transparency and information are the major problems for end users in the current supply chain process. As blockchain is an immutable technology that offers to store each record in an open registry, it can be used to keep track of the product in various stages of production/processing. It can record the information related to the transformation of raw material to end product and store all the necessary details of the intermediate processing [46]. Integrating IoT with blockchain to keep track of the key elements such as temperature, humidity can also provide a novel and indisputable mechanism for storing information about the supply chain process.

4.4.1.4   Equity Crowd Funding

In the recent past equity crowdfunding has attained attention of the investors and companies alike. In equity crowdfunding a startup company initiates an investment opportunity for common public by offering the company's shares as reward in exchange of monetary investment in the company. One impediment in the crowdfunding is the differences in regulatory laws of countries, causing uncertainty in cross border investment. For an individual to make an investment in a company, the law requires the individual to be listed as shareholder on the company shareholder list, which should be approved by the registration authority. Generally, registration on the shareholder lists requires a successive task of paperwork. However, in case where an investor from outside the country wants to invest in a company, the paperwork involves a lengthy process requiring document back and forth movement over postal services. This results in a tedious process involving third party document verifications [48].

Blockchain can facilitate the crowdfunding by omitting the need of intermediary for funds transfer and document verification. The start-ups can offer IPO by releasing their own digital currency [49]. Administrative overhead of paper-based record management can be avoided by using blockchain based systems, eliminating the need of paper signing and postal delivery of the documents, facilitating share- holders from different geographical locations to invest in the startup. Likewise, smart contracts can be deployed to ensure trusted and transparent investment and payment to shareholders as per the agreed set of rules [48]. Blockchain can register all the investors as shareholders after successful receipt of payment [48, 49]. The blockchain based platforms for equity management can facilitate the regulators as they can keep track of all the investment made by various investors, thereby reducing the chances of money laundering [48].

4.4.2   Blockchain for Smart People

Blockchain helps citizens of smart city in many ways. Following are few use cases of blockchain in smart city which facilitates people.

4.4.2.1   Elections through Blockchain Technology

The traditional election system has many draw backs. These elections occur from time to time and involves huge expenditure and requires huge human resource mobilization [50]. In the current system of elections, candidates and voters complain about irregularities in the elections process. So, a transparent election process is required which should be fair, inexpensive and requires less manpower. Blockchain provides a solution for these problems by providing a certifiable election process. In blockchain, a vote can be a transaction. Blockchain will keep track of all the vote tallies. The votes can be viewed by all the users as blockchain has a public ledger, thus everybody will be able to count all the votes. However, voters will not know about another voters' choice. Thus, the voters are assured that their votes are not changed or removed and that no vote is added illegally.

Hegadekatti [50] proposed a solution for voting system and named it as Blockchain Voting Program (BVP). This voting procedure takes place in the following manner (see Figure 4.3 for pictorial summary). In the blockchain voting system, the Blockchain Voting Program (BVP) will be downloaded on a phone or a device of choice by a voter. Election Commission, or the department of government responsible for overseeing the process, will confirm the identities of the voters after they provide a verifiable identity. Once the identity verification process has taken place, the voter would be free to request their ballot, which will be issued in the form of a token by the Election Commission. The ballot (token) will then be casted by the voter and the vote will be safely submitted to the Blockchain-based voting program. This is akin to transacting a token. With the vote cast on the Blockchain the voter will print out a receipt with transaction ID in order to obtain evidence of the vote. The voters will also have the ability to monitor their vote to ensure it is casted as per their will after the voting process closes on the election day. Each voter can also audit other votes in the ballot box (with the voter identities not being subject to revelation to the auditor). One can satisfy oneself of the total votes being counted by the Blockchain Voting Program as accurate or not. All this is done with keeping voter identities anonymous. A closer look at the process reveals

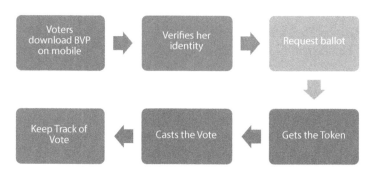

Figure 4.3 Electronic voting process [50].

the wide spectrum the BVP can be applied to. A representative or member of a nation's parliament can directly be in contact with his constituents. The said member can put up certain issues of his constituency for opinion on a poll. Interested people can provide their opinion via the BVP. The office holder will thus remain aware of the mood of the public. Based on the poll, an issue can be brought up in the parliament for consideration.

Blockchain technology makes it possible to attain a highly credible and verifiable election process at a fraction of the cost relative to contemporary systems in place. This technology jumps on the 21st century accessibility bandwagon makes voting possible from the comfort of one's home. Moreover, public opinion can be routinely sought on a host of challenging issues that plague society. This will in turn lead to grass-root participation in the governance process and usher in an era of democracy where Blockchain technology can put power back in the hands of people currently divorced from governance [50].

4.4.2.2 Smart Contract

A smart contract is a self-executing computer protocol between two parties (e.g., a buyer and a seller) [51]. This protocol works across a distributed and a decentralized blockchain network. Smart contract does not require any central manager, nor any external enforcement mechanism [51]. It is a contract between two anonymous parties who do not want to rely on intermediaries. The transactions in smart contract are irreversible, but traceable and transparent. The concept of smart contract can get clearer from its applications. Below are few applications of smart contract.

- *Smart Will:* Traditionally when a person dies her will is disclosed to the successor. However, making changes in the will are easier without the knowledge of the authorized person. It can create chaos among successors as one can turn the will in his/her favor and others will not get what they should. Blockchain can resolve the issue by providing a platform where a person adds her will in blockchain. The will remains immutable. A user can use a platform to write her will as a smart contract and the contract will be executed after her death. The process limits the role of intermediaries and thus avoids the possibility of unauthorized modification [51].
- *Smart Betting System:* Smart contract can also be used for betting system. In traditional betting system a carrier controls the bets. In smart betting system there is no need for

such carriers or controllers. The betting system uses smart contract in a way that both parties must create a virtual contract [51]. The contract holds information such as conditions of winning/losing, and the total reward amount in a digital account. The result from the real world will be updated on a database and then according to the contract whoever wins the bet, the amount from digital account will be shifted to the winner's account [51].

- *Smart Lottery:* Currently all lottery games depend on centralized box about which no one knows of what is inside? This causes distrust in players in many ways. There are few questions about lotteries which are frequently asked by people, such as;

1. Is the lottery ticket real or fake?
2. Is the draw happening random or fixed?
3. Is it possible to add winning ticket after the draw?
4. Are those jackpot winners real?
5. Are funds distributed fairly or not?

In order to bring transparency and mitigate fraud in the lottery system, blockchain's services can be used. In lieu of being under the influence of a centralized authority, it utilizes innovative techniques of decentralizing and forwards services with autonomous interacting codes called smart contracts [52]. When blockchain is used, programs that earlier (old or traditional programs) ran solely via a trusted intermediary, will now be able to function free of those shackles, rendering a centralized authority redundant. This translates to a quicker and increased reconciliation between transacting groups. An incremental quality of blockchain is reliance of cryptography that brings authoritativeness as a force overseeing every blockchain interaction [52].

4.4.2.3   Protecting Personal Data

The amount of data in the world is rapidly increasing. According to a recent report [53], the top four internet-based companies (Amazon, Facebook, Google, Microsoft) amassed 1.2 million terabytes of data among them. According to another report [54], 300 million photos are uploaded to Facebook every day. Each minute results in 510,000 new comments, and 293,000 new status updates. In the current era of big data, an enormous of data is collected using various channels such as social media, cellphone and IoT devices, etc. The data is used by the concerned companies to offer personalized services to its customers leading to better user experience. The same data is also used by the top management in their decision making. Therefore, data is categorized as an asset for the modern economy [55]. Protecting such a huge amount of data is very difficult. However, blockchain can help us in achieving the goal of data protection. The main advantage of blockchain is that it keeps user's identities anonymous. The user does not have to login in any social media website from real name but instead has to use combination of public and secret keys to sign-up and sign-in. Bitcoin (or any other digital currency) can be used for payment purposes. The transaction can be done with smart contracts as well. As soon as contract is completed the amount will itself transfer to another user's wallet.

4.4.2.4   E-Health: Storing Health Records on Blockchain

Blockchain technology can help ease the burden of the complexities and affordability that surrounds healthcare with its implementation on medical records and insurance companies [56]. In 2016, Estonia's government announced that it would use blockchain technology to secure the health records of over a million citizens [56]. Blockchain's use for storing medical records can make healthcare resistant to tampering, safe and scalable. Its dispersed nature can allow data to be shared more conveniently among the authorized personnel and connect contemporary data storage, consequently increasing efficiency and improving coordination of care [57]. A more efficient way of insurance claim coordination will also lead to scaling down the costs. A marked improvement will also be seen via the unchanged records held by blockchain. Blockchain mining's connoted costs can also be mitigated by allowing anonymous metadata incentives for medicinal science researcher [58].

4.4.2.5   Intellectual Property Rights

Registry of IP rights is a common application of blockchain. On internet, ownership is hard to prove, and it becomes difficult for authors to keep track of their work and check who is using their work. Thus, the authors cannot make most of the money from their work and they are unable to stop this [59].

A key advantage of using blockchain as an IP registry is the clarity and transparency it provides to the stakeholders including authors, owners and users. Once an author registers her work on a blockchain, she has irrefutable evidence of ownership. A website "Binded" helps authors in IP rights using a blockchain. An author uploads her image on internet through Binded. The website creates a fingerprint unique to each user, incorporating the contents of image as well as owners' details such as her name and email address. Blinded updates the blockchain on regular basis, ensuring a secure chain of non-editable time stamped records. Using the unique fingerprint, the owner can monitor the online space for any infringement of the copyright of the original work [60].

4.4.2.6   Digital Payments

The contemporary method of payment lacks the quality of having a permanent record. Due to the tangible nature of currency, it cannot be spent twice, however its record can be tampered and erased causing problems for people. With the help of blockchain, information can be permanently stored and relied upon due to a lack of reliance on third parties. It is also integrated on blockchain and the transaction therefore become part of the eco system. A blockchain system is employed by Bitcoin with the exact purpose of eliminating third-party intermediaries. Other digital payment systems can be made using the blockchain technology to help reduce the reliance on third party intermediaries for processing of payments transactions.

4.4.2.7   Other Use Cases

Smart property is the combination of blockchain and Internet-of-Things (IoT). IoT is an ever-expanding platform that allows connection of every household device across the globe, and blockchain infrastructure helps to form a physical asset bound by smart contracts. Blockchain can help to maintain the record of our property and IoT can help in accessing or controlling the property easily. A simple car can be an example of smart property. If a person rents his car, she will sign a smart contract with the second party. In case if second party missed a payment on vehicle loan then the cars digital keys can be blocked using IoT services. Some other potential uses can be keys for hotel rooms, safety deposit boxes, lockers, houses and apartments [51].

By digitizing land titles discrepancies and issues between successors can be significantly mitigated. Any property could be inspected in real-time by a user of blockchain based system. Cost reduction will be an added benefit of the technology as well as ease of holder verification [51].

4.4.3   Blockchain-Based Smart Governance

Blockchain based smart governance aims to provide its community with decentralized government. It allows the government to follow the slogan services choose your government and choose your services. This enables offering of border-less and decentralized government services through blockchain. A true democracy might be achieved or enhanced by the use of blockchain as a base of government. This refers to a democracy setup without involvement of humans as representatives. Moreover, the use of smart contracts reduces the cost of government. The goals of smart government comprise of concepts like fraud-free voting, tamper-free registries, transparent record keeping and tracking of records, smart contract administration, and merit-based decision-making. Services such as disabling financial frauds, voting, registration of legal documents e.g., identification cards, childcare contracts, land deeds, wedding contracts, wills and many wide varieties of services are enabled by the use of blockchain platform in governance. By using the blockchain technology, Government services can be provided in a distributed and cost-effective manner.

4.4.3.1   *Transparent Record Keeping and Tracking of Records*

Double taxation is a problem faced by many residing in the foreign countries. They investment in foreign countries where the investment is subject to local tax laws. However, they also need to pay taxes in their country of residence as well. This result in double tax problem as the investors have to pay dividend amount on both i.e., where they reside and where they invest. Countries use bilateral double taxation treaties (DTT) in order to facilitate such investors. The investor has to pay withholding tax to country from where the profit is generated. This can be claim as refund of a tax to the country of their residence. With the stakeholder providing documentation and proof of refund eligibility, there are possibilities of falsified/fraudulent applications. The current system is unable to monitor the dividend flow of payments efficiently. It allows the submission of application for refunding money that has already been refunded to them. This happens due to use of forged bank statements due to inability of current system to track it down. It is essential for the taxation authorities to keep track of tax refund in order to avoid and prevent stakeholders and banks from obtaining the false claims. There is no proper infrastructure of these treaties to enable information exchange between the tax authorities about the investors. In Denmark the Danish Tax Authorities (SKAT) were faced with a huge loss of 1.8 billion USD due to a fake application of tax return. No central information system is available that can reliably check and manage the entitlement of a stakeholder for tax refund.

Blockchain technology resolves the problem of double taxation, supports various information providers, and spending guarantees immutable log of historical transactional records. Tokens represents dividend that is are issued by a company. These tokens then track the payments of dividend on the blockchain. Blockchain traces the dividends flow and the exchange of the documents, in addition to providing transparency, to prove the claim for the tax reimbursement.

In Figure 4.4, Alice (the stakeholder) is paid her dividends by the Dansake company via the agent's financial institution (Bank). Three accounts are created in the system, one each for Alice, VP Securities, and Bank. VP Securities is responsible to report the dividend payment event, including information about dividend amount, resulting in execution of smart contract that produces tokens for Dansake company. The number of tokens match the dividend amount and are stored in VP Securities account which is afterwards transferred to Bank's account. Bank can now transfer the tokens to Alice. Alice can apply for refund at SKAT, which can verify the authenticity of refund claim by obtaining tokens of Dansake company from Alice. The tokens are matched with Dansake company, and upon success the exact amount is refunded to Alice account. In order to ensure transparency, SKAT can has the authority to review the transaction chain. The double spending (or double refund) scam is also avoided as tokens can only be reclaimed once [61].

4.4.3.2   Fraud Free Voting

The traditional voting is subjected to manipulation and lacks trusts of its users. A blockchain based voting system reduces the trust issue by logging every vote on blockchain in form of a secure cryptographical hash, thus, offering better transparency. This enables everyone to view the absolute transaction while the system runs independently without the interference from outside. Everyone is mapped to a vote and identities are kept anonymous. Hence, a voting system based on blockchain technology is a better option for e-elections. First voting system of based on blockchain was implemented by a Danish political party for their internal elections purposes [46].

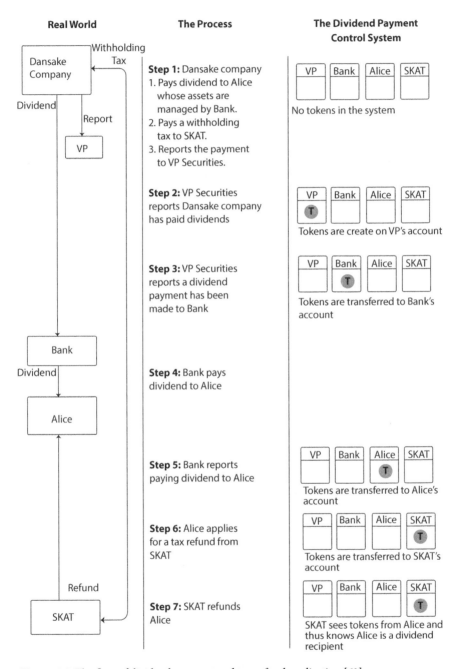

Figure 4.4 The flow of dividend payment and tax refund application [61].

4.4.3.3 Decision Making

Blockchain is being used to strengthen democracy and make it more effective by allowing citizens to directly get involve in process of decision making. New models are being implemented for allowing citizens to participate directly in the decision-making process. This allows individuals full decisional control in a collective decision-making form. One of such implementations is in liquid democracy where an individual can vote directly regarding all issues. In addition, citizens can delegate their voting power to a representative, allowing them to vote on their behalf. Blockchain serves as a platform in this delegated decision making [49].

4.4.4 Blockchain-Based Smart Transport

4.4.4.1 Digitizing Driving License

Among the several properties of blockchain that can benefit people as per the requirements, identification is the most straightforward [62]. Licenses of drivers can serve as a decent example. If, for instance, car club 'A' needs to know their customers have a valid license, they would require the person to send his/her picture for verification. If the same person is asked to do the similar task by car club 'B', the task has to be repeated. A blockchain can ensure the data is authentic by a certain entity's approval at a specified moment. This would translate to 'B' being automatically informed if 'A' has verified the license of a person. A fee can be levied by 'A' on 'B' for the service or both can outsource the task to a third party. Obviously, this is if we assume the organization issues a digital copy of all licenses on a blockchain platform. This example can be applied to other types of identifications too [63].

4.4.4.2 Smart Ride Sharing

Real time ride sharing is positively distinct among the benchmark application situations which have room for Block-VN model integration [64]. This technology of constant travel sharing creates a platform for private car owners to lend vacant seats to travelers on bound to similar destinations. For riders to switch between vehicles, an option of multi-rebound is included which allows expansion in number of shared rides. In comparison to popular platform such as Uber and Lyft, Block-VN offers a more robust privacy focus, decentralization of the technology, and the added benefit of less volatile prices [64]. Further, many ride sharing applications

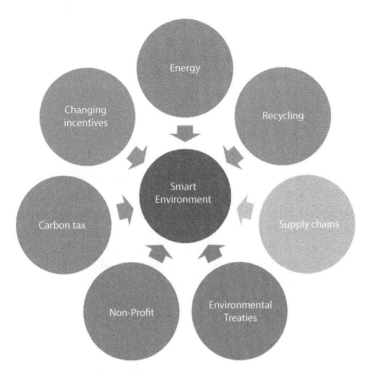

Figure 4.5 Blockchain and environment.

like rideshare[†] and smart-ride[‡] enhances trust on the platform by keeping the public profiles of drivers in the blockchain, thus allowing the user to verify the track record of their driver's rides.

4.4.5   Blockchain-Based Smart Environment

In this section, we summarize some of the use case to achieve the smart environment requirement of a smart city. Figure 4.5 summarizes the key aspect of smart environment.

4.4.5.1   Social Plastic

Recycling programs that uses blockchain gives users motivation and encouragement to recycle plastic bags, and cans, etc., by providing them

---

[†] www.rideshare.org
[‡] www.thesmartride.org

financial reward in return. Every time a user deposits something for recycling, she gets a cryptographic token in exchange for it. These kinds of applications make it easy for the city management to track data transparently. One such notable example is Social Plastic [65]. Social plastic project aims to change plastics into currency and services in order to clean up plastic waste from the world while reducing poverty.

4.4.5.2   Energy

One of the key aspects of smart environment, and by extension of smart city is the use of renewable (or green) energy. Renewable energy generation and consumption poses several challenges, most notably the implementation of proper distribution mechanism and audit system to ensure transparency. In a smart city, the residents can also produce their own energy (for example, using photovoltaic cells on roof), and the extra energy can be added to city grid system. The challenge is the design of mechanism to properly compensate the residents who contribute towards the city grid energy system. In this domain, a number of solutions are proposed in the literature which are based on blockchain [27, 66].

Mengelkamp *et al.* [66] presented a decentralized platform based on private blockchain where people can buy and sell local energy from one another without the involvement of third party. In order to safeguard the privacy of the users in a smart grid environment, Guan *et al.* [27] presented a blockchain based privacy-preserving data aggregation scheme. The objective is to preserve the privacy of the user in near real time data sharing in a smart grid environment.

4.4.5.3   Environmental Treaties

In the real world, it is nearly impossible to track real time effect of environmental treaties. Data can easily be manipulated, and fraud is a common occurrence. Governments are also not provided with incentives to keep their promises. Blockchain can hold key to solve the aforementioned problems. Due to its public ledger, no one will be able to manipulate the data as the data once entered will stay there forever [67]. A naive solution will be to use mix of Internet of Things (IoT) and blockchain. IoT devices can be used to record real time data (such as air quality index, pollution level, etc.) and blockchain can be used to store the data. The data will be immutable and cannot be edited by any party. Likewise, a business model can be developed to sell the data to various organizations (such as research organization, NGOs, universities, etc.) based on their needs, making the model not only transparent but self-sustainable as well.

4.4.5.4   Carbon Tax

Today majority of the products contains carbon which is a major environmental pollutant. No incentives are given to companies to produce carbon-free products and no inducements are given to buyers to buy products which are carbon-free. Using blockchain, we can track the footprints of carbon in each product. It can also be used to charge carbon tax on its sale [67].

4.4.6   Blockchain-Based Smart Living

The goal of enhancing the lives of the citizens can only be achieved by improving the living standards of the people. The integration of blockchain technology in different aspects of life is greatly enhancing the quality of living in a smart city. To achieve the goal of smart living, a multitude of emerging technologies are used in coherence (such as Internet of Things, and blockchain). Figure 4.6 graphically depicts the various technologies required to realize the dream of smart living. In the following, we present some of the use cases of blockchain applications to achieve the objective of smart living.

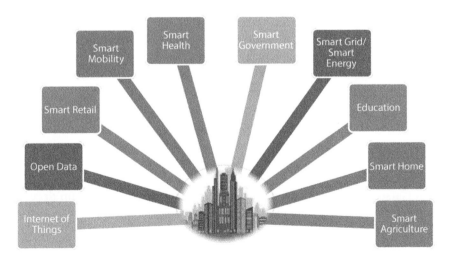

Figure 4.6 Smart living.

4.4.6.1   Fighting Against Frauds and Discriminatory Policies and Practices

Using blockchain, it is possible to keep an audit trail of transactions providing accountability and transparency in the data-exchange process. This can eliminate discriminatory practices, thus preventing unauthorized access to financial information. It becomes practically impossible for one to manipulate data without getting caught. Blockchain can possibly prevent frauds such as those observed in Qingdao and the Adoor Sree Narayana Dharma Paripalana Union [68]. This enhances people's trust over the policies and thus they invest in different domains which results in enhancing the economy and the living standards of the people.

4.4.6.2   Managing Change in Ownership

There are many types of assets and it is important to verify the corresponding ownership. A number of applications are designed to verify such ownerships. One such application based on blockchain is THAT'S MINE 3 used for automotive ownership. The basic idea of the application is to certify any change of ownership through transactions made by the respective parties. In these transactions the basic information relating to the vehicle is transmitted and committed into a blockchain. Once on the blockchain, the records can no longer hold a chance of modification and are publicly accessible for verification purposes. Transactions are recorded by an identifier including a timestamp [69].

The idea of the application can be extended to include other assets such as real estate etc. One of the major challenges in real estate is the complicated bureaucratic process involved in the transfer of property. Even for the verification of ownership, the traditional method can take days as it needs approval of a number of personnel. Using blockchain will considerably reduce the reliance on intermediary and will help in the transparent transfer of ownership between the two parties.

4.4.6.3   Sustainable Buildings

Van Cutsem *et al.* [70] proposed a framework that use blockchain decentralized characteristics to manage the daily energy exchanges within the community of smart buildings. Using blockchain in the system, autonomous monitoring and billing via the smart contract is enabled in addition to trusted communication among the participants. As a result, the smart contract allowed participants to collaboratively decide on a planning profile which minimizes the overall cost. The framework reduced the grid demand by its forecasting facility. Moreover, the simulation showed that the framework is scalable up to 100 smart buildings.

Park *et al.* [71] aims to achieve a power trade system in order to encourage a sustainable electrical energy transaction ecosystem. The work discusses a blockchain-based peer-to-peer (P2P) energy transaction platform be implemented to enable efficient electrical energy transaction between prosumers. The suggested platform is built on the blockchain to use its decentralized and distributed trading system, and allow a more transparent, trustworthy and secure P2P environment. As smart home aims to enhance user comfort and security, along with energy conservation and cost-savings these features of a blockchain will add on a boost to achieve the efficient electrical energy transactions. Initially, a comparative study of two different types of P2P was to identify the one from which the aim will be most benefited. A smart contract is embedded in the blockchain referred as an energy tag. It sets conditions for making energy transaction more cost-efficient while maintaining the most ideal and high-quality energy selection. This energy tag is based on blockchain with the main purpose to democratically connect appliances and provide users with high-quality, low-cost energy always and locations. The IoT applications within the smart home collect data on whether an energy consumer needs to purchase more energy, or a prosumer has spare energy to sell. Based on the need to purchase or sell energy, a purchase or selling tag is formed, which is then sent to all participants of the suggested energy-transaction platform. This tag is confirmed by a participant and assigned to a block to make transaction valid. The proposed scheme publishes information that is permanent, transparent and secure.

Wu and Tran [72] discussed the problems associated with sustainable energy and proposes "Energy Internet through Block-chain Technology". The main purpose of the work is to review the development of block-chain and the Energy Internet and provide some references for the possible applications of block-chain technology to the Energy Internet. For more related works, the reader is referred to Refs. [73–75].

4.4.6.4   *Other Use Cases*

Blockchain is used in various other aspects of smart living such as education [76], smart home [77], smart agriculture [78], smart real estate [79] and smart mobility [80].

4.5 Conclusion

In this work, a comprehensive overview of smart city and blockchain is presented focusing on the use cases of blockchain in the smart city. The use cases include efficient and faster payments, transparency in global supply chain, crowd funding, smart contracts and smart property, protection and storage of personal and health care records, fraud free voting, traffic management and smart ride sharing etc. A number of open issues still remains at large and requires the attention of researchers. For example, the blockchain technology by itself is still new. A customized version of blockchain is a key requirement for all the use cases of blockchain in smart city. For instance, the consensus mechanism of bit coin blockchain is computationally very intensive and might not be feasible for use in smart city applications where the number of users is far less than those in bit coin blockchain. An alternate consensus mechanism must thus be developed. Regulatory amendments must also be made in local laws to accept blockchain as valid technology/tool for the smart city. However, making the regulatory changes can prove to be very difficult in developing countries where the infrastructure to support such drastic changes is minimum. Another key challenge in integration of blockchain in smart city is the introduction and adaptation of the supporting technologies such as Internet of Things (IoT). Without IoT adaptation, the potential of blockchain in smart city cannot be realized to the fullest. IoT devices can be used to monitor various aspects of smart city such as air quality index, and structural strength of the key infrastructure assets. Beside that IoT devices can be used to control personal home appliances, streetlights, and cars etc. Blockchain can be used as supporting technology to ensure that the data collected through IoT devices is stored in a secure way to ensure the integrity, confidentiality, and security of the data. This requires new mechanisms and policies for effective data sharing among various stakeholders.

References

1. Weiser, M., The computer for the 21st century. *Sci. Am.*, 265, 3, 94–105, 1991.
2. Washburn, D., Sindhu, U., Balaouras, S., Dines, R.A., Hayes, N., Nelson, L.E., Helping CIOs understand "smart city" initiatives. *Growth*, 17, 2, 1–17, 2009.
3. Singh, S.P., Nayyar, A., Kumar, R., Sharma, A., Fog computing: From architecture to edge computing and big data processing. *J. Supercomput.*, 75, 4, 2070–2105, 2019.

4. Su, K., Li, J., Fu, H., Smart city and the applications, in: *Electronics, Communications and Control (ICECC), 2011 International Conference on,* IEEE, pp. 1028–1031, 2011.

5. da Silva, W.M., Alvaro, A., Tomas, G.H.R.P., Afonso, R.A., Dias, K.L., Garcia, V.C., Smart cities software architectures: A survey, in: *Proceedings of the 28th Annual ACM Symposium on Applied Computing, SAC '13,* ACM, New York, NY, USA, pp. 1722–1727, 2013.

6. Yin, C., Xiong, Z., Chen, H., Wang, J., Cooper, D., David, B., A literature survey on smart cities. *Sci. China Inform. Sci.,* 58, 10, 1–18, Oct 2015.

7. Petrolo, R., Loscr, V., Mitton, N., Towards a smart city based on cloud of things, a survey on the smart city vision and paradigms. *Trans. Emerg. Telecommun. Technol.,* 28, 1, e2931, 2017.

8. Panarello, A., Tapas, N., Merlino, G., Longo, F., Puliafito, A., Blockchain and IoT integration: A systematic survey. *Sensors,* 18, 8, 2018.

9. De La Rosa, J.L., Torres-Padrosa, V., El-Fakdi, A., Gibovic, D., Hornyák, O., Maicher, L., Miralles, F., A survey of blockchain technologies for open innovation, in: *Proceedings of the 4th Annual World Open Innovation Conference,* pp. 14–15, 2017.

10. Aras, S.T. and Kulkarni, V., Blockchain and its applications—A detailed survey. *Int. J. Comput. Appl.,* 180, 3, 29–35, 2017.

11. Li, X., Jiang, P., Chen, T., Luo, X., Wen, Q., A survey on the security of blockchain systems. *Future Gener. Comput. Syst.,* 107, 841–853, 2020.

12. Lu, Y., Blockchain: A survey on functions, applications and open issues. *J. Ind. Integr. Manage.,* 3, 04, 1850015, 2018.

13. Sharma, P.K. and Park, J.H., Blockchain based hybrid network architecture for the smart city. *Future Gener. Comput. Syst.,* 86, 650–655, 2018.

14. Singh, P., Nayyar, A., Kaur, A., Ghosh, U., Blockchain and Fog Based Architecture for Internet of Everything in Smart Cities. *Future Internet,* 12, 4, 61, 2020.

15. Ghandour, A.G., Elhoseny, M., Hassanien, A.E., Blockchains for smart cities: A survey, in: *Security in Smart Cities: Models, Applications, and Challenges,* pp. 193–210, Springer, Cham, 2019.

16. Krishnamurthi, R., Nayyar, A., Solanki, A., Innovation Opportunities through Internet of Things (IoT) for Smart Cities, in: *Green and Smart Technologies for Smart Cities,* pp. 261–292, CRC Press, Boca Raton, FL, USA, 2019.

17. Vora, J., Nayyar, A., Tanwar, S., Tyagi, S., Kumar, N., Obaidat, M.S., Rodrigues, J.J., BHEEM: A blockchain-based framework for securing electronic health records, in: *2018 IEEE Globecom Workshops (GC Wkshps),* pp. 1–6, 2018.

18. Sun, J., Yan, J., Zhang, K.Z., Blockchain-based sharing services: What blockchain technology can contribute to smart cities. *Financial Innov.,* 2, 1, 1–9, 2016.

19. Komninos, N., The architecture of intelligent cities: Integrating human, collective and artificial intelligence to enhance knowledge and innovation,

in: *The IEEE 2nd IET International Conference on Intelligent Environments*, pp. 13–20, 2006.

20. Anthopoulos, L. and Fitsilis, P., From digital to ubiquitous cities: Defining a common architecture for urban development, in: *2010 Sixth International Conference on Intelligent Environments*, pp. 301–306, 2010.

21. Ergazakis, K., Metaxiotis, K., Psarras, J., Towards knowledge cities: Conceptual analysis and success stories. *J. Knowl. Manag.*, 8, 5, 5–15, 2004.

22. Couclelis, H., The construction of the digital city. *Environ. Plann. B: Plann. Des.*, 31, 1, 5–19, 2004.

23. Geller, A.L., Smart growth: A prescription for livable cities. *Am. J. Public Health*, 93, 9, 1410–1415, 2003.

24. Pramanik, P.K.D., Pareek, G., Nayyar, A., Security and privacy in remote healthcare: Issues, solutions, and standards, in: *Telemedicine Technologies*, pp. 201–225, Elsevier, 2019.

25. Shubbar, S., *Ultrasound medical imaging systems using telemedicine and blockchain for remote monitoring of responses to neoadjuvant chemotherapy in women's breast cancer: concept and implementation*, Doctoral dissertation, Kent State University, Kent, Ohio, 2017.

26. Balakrishna, C., Enabling technologies for smart city services and applications, in: *2012 Sixth International Conference on Next Generation Mobile Applications, Services and Technologies*, pp. 223–227, 2012.

27. Guan, Z., Si, G., Zhang, X., Wu, L., Guizani, N., Du, X., Ma, Y., Privacy-preserving and efficient aggregation based on blockchain for power grid communications in smart communities. *IEEE Commun. Mag.*, 56, 7, 82–88, 2018.

28. Su, K., Li, J., Fu, H., Smart city and the applications, in: *2011 International Conference on Electronics, Communications and Control (ICECC)*, pp. 1028–1031, 2011.

29. Veena, P.C., Tharakan, P., Haridas, H., Ramya, K., Joju, R., Jyothis, T.S., Smart street light system based on image processing, in: *2016 International Conference on Circuit, Power and Computing Technologies (ICCPCT)*, pp. 1–5, 2016.

30. Gharaibeh, A., Salahuddin, M.A., Hussini, S.J., Khreishah, A., Khalil, I., Guizani, M., Al-Fuqaha, A., Smart cities: A survey on data management, security, and enabling technologies. *IEEE Commun. Surv. Tut.*, 19, 4, 2456–2501, 2017.

31. Pieroni, A., Scarpato, N., Di Nunzio, L., Fallucchi, F., Raso, M., Smarter city: Smart energy grid based on blockchain technology. *Int. J. Adv. Sci. Eng. Inf. Technol.*, 8, 1, 298–306, 2018.

32. Bhattacharya, K. and Suri, T., The curious case of e-governance. *IEEE Internet Comput.*, 21, 1, 62–67, 2017.

33. Longo, J., *Open Government. What's in a name?*, The GobLab, Agosto [en línea], 2013, http://thegovlab.org/open-government-whats-in-a-name.

34. Eckhoff, D. and Wagner, I., Privacy in the smart city—Applications, technologies, challenges, and solutions. *IEEE Commun. Surv. Tut.*, 20, 1, 489–516, 2017.

35. Kumar, A., Srikanth, P., Nayyar, A., Sharma, G., Krishnamurthi, R., Alazab, M., Novel Simulated-Annealing Based Electric Bus System Design, A., Simulation, and Analysis for Dehradun Smart City. *IEEE Access*, 8, 89395–89424, 2020.

36. Al Nuaimi, E., Al Neyadi, H., Mohamed, N., Al-Jaroodi, J., Applications of big data to smart cities. *J. Internet Serv. Appl.*, 6, 1, 25, 2015.

37. Zhang, K., Ni, J., Yang, K., Liang, X., Ren, J., Shen, X.S., Security and privacy in smart city applications: Challenges and solutions. *IEEE Commun. Mag.*, 55, 1, 122–129, 2017.

38. Nayyar, A., Jain, R., Mahapatra, B., Singh, A., Cyber security challenges for smart cities, in: *Driving the Development, Management, and Sustainability of Cognitive Cities*, pp. 27–54, IGI Global, Hershey, Pennsylvania, USA, 2019.

39. Gupta, M., *Blockchain for dummies*, IBM Limited Edition, US, 2017.

40. Narayanan, A., Bonneau, J., Felten, E., Miller, A., Goldfeder, S., *Bitcoin and cryptocurrency technologies: A comprehensive introduction*, Princeton University Press, Princeton, New Jersey, 2016.

41. Kaur, A., Nayyar, A., Singh, P., Blockchain: A path to the future, in: *Cryptocurrencies and Blockchain Technology Applications*, pp. 25–42, 2020.

42. Harrison, C. and Donnelly, I.A., A theory of smart cities, in: *Proceedings of the 55th Annual Meeting of the ISSS-2011*, Hull, UK, 2011.

43. Pisa, M. and Juden, M., *Blockchain and economic development: Hype vs. reality*, Center for Global Development Policy Paper, Washington DC, USA, 107, p. 150, 2017.

44. Guo, Y. and Liang, C., Blockchain application and outlook in the banking industry. *Financial Innov.*, 2, 1, 24, 2016.

45. Swan, M., *Blockchain: Blueprint for a new economy*, O'Reilly Media, Inc, Sebastopol, CA, 2015.

46. Pilkington, M., Blockchain technology: Principles and applications, in: *Research Handbook on Digital Transformations*, Edward Elgar Publishing, Cheltenham, UK, 2016.

47. What is trade finance? Center for Global Development, Washington DC, USA, http://gtrventures.vc/resources/trade-finance/journal =GTRVentures.

48. Zhu, H. and Zhou, Z.Z., Analysis and outlook of applications of blockchain technology to equity crowdfunding in China. *Financial Innov.*, 2, 1, 29, 2016.

49. Atzori, M., *Blockchain technology and decentralized governance: Is the state still necessary?*, Available at SSRN 2709713, Journal of Governance and Regulation, 6, 1, 2017, 45–62, 2015.

50. Hegadekatti, K., *Analysis of present day election processes vis-à-vis elections through Blockchain technology*, https://ssrn.com/abstract=2904868 or http://dx.doi.org/10.2139/ssrn.2904868, 2017.

51. Foroglou, G. and Tsilidou, A.L., Further applications of the blockchain, in: *12th Student Conference on Managerial Science and Technology*, pp. 1–8, 2015.
52. Liao, D.Y. and Wang, X., Design of a blockchain-based lottery system for smart cities applications, in: *2017 IEEE 3rd International Conference on Collaboration and Internet Computing (CIC)*, pp. 275–282, 2017.
53. Mitchell., G., *How much data is on the internet?*, https://www.sciencefocus.com/future-technology/how-much-data-is-on-the-internet/, 2020. Last Accessed 9 Mar, 2020.
54. Zephoria, *The top 20 valuable Facebook statistics*, https://zephoria.com/top-15-valuable-facebook-statistics/, 2020. Last Accessed 9 Mar, 2020.
55. Schwab, K., Marcus, A., Oyola, J.O., Hoffman, W., Luzi, M., Personal data: The emergence of a new asset class, in: *an Initiative of the World Economic Forum*, 2011.
56. Heston, T., A case study in blockchain healthcare innovation. *Int. J. Curr. Res.*, 9, 11, 60587–60588, 2017.
57. Editorial Team, Blockchain in healthcare: Make the industry better, 2017.
58. Ekblaw, A. and Azaria, A., *MedRec: Medical data management on the blockchain*, Viral Communications, 2016.
59. Shinner, S., *Blockchain Technology and IP*, Taylor Wessing, 2017.
60. Kulik, T., How blockchain just may transform online copyright protection, 2018.
61. Hyvärinen, H., Risius, M., Friis, G., A blockchain-based approach towards overcoming financial fraud in public sector services. *Bus. Inform. Syst. Eng.*, 59, 6, 441–456, 2017.
62. Angelis, J. and da Silva, E.R., Blockchain adoption: A value driver perspective. *Bus. Horiz.*, 62, 3, 307–314, 2019.
63. Torstensson, J. and Andersson, P., *Exploring the role of blockchain technology in Mobility as a Service-Towards a fair Combined Mobility Service*, Master's thesis, Chalmers University of Technology, Gothenburg, Sweden, 2017.
64. Sharma, P.K., Moon, S.Y., Park, J.H., Block-VN: A distributed Blockchain based vehicular network architecture in smart city. *J. Inf. Process. Syst.*, 13, 1, 2017.
65. Social Plastic, Social plastic, http://socialplastic.org/, 2018. [Online; accessed 9 Mar 2020.].
66. Mengelkamp, E., Notheisen, B., Beer, C., Dauer, D., Weinhardt, C., A blockchain-based smart grid: Towards sustainable local energy markets. *Comput. Sci.-Res. Dev.*, 33, 1–2, 207–214, 2018.
67. 7 ways blockchain can save the environment and stop climate change, https://wp.me/p7k5oK-2S2, 2017, Last accessed 9 Mar 2020.
68. Kshetri, N., Potential roles of blockchain in fighting poverty and reducing financial exclusion in the global south. *JGIM*, 20, 4, 201–204, 2017.

69. Reply, Blockchain applications for retail, http://www.reply.com/en/content/retail, 2018, Last accessed 09 Mar 2020.

70. Van Cutsem, O., Dac, D.H., Boudou, P., Kayal, M., Cooperative energy management of a community of smart buildings: A Blockchain approach. *Int. J. Electr. Power Energy Syst.*, 117, 105643, 2020.

71. Park, L.W., Lee, S., Chang, H., A sustainable home energy prosumer-chain methodology with energy tags over the blockchain. *Sustainability*, 10, 3, 658, 2018.

72. Wu, J. and Tran, N.K., Application of blockchain technology in sustainable energy systems: An overview. *Sustainability*, 10, 9, 3067, 2018.

73. Liu, Z., Jiang, L., Osmani, M., Demian, P., Building information management (BIM) and blockchain (BC) for sustainable building design information management framework. *Electronics*, 8, 7, 724, 2019.

74. Li, J., Greenwood, D., Kassem, M., Blockchain in the built environment and construction industry: A systematic review, conceptual models and practical use cases. *Autom. Constr.*, 102, 288–307, 2019.

75. Imbault, F., Swiatek, M., De Beaufort, R., Plana, R., The green blockchain: Managing decentralized energy production and consumption, in: *2017 IEEE International Conference on Environment and Electrical Engineering and 2017 IEEE Industrial and Commercial Power Systems Europe (EEEIC/I&CPS Europe)*, pp. 1–5, 2017.

76. Gräther, W., Kolvenbach, S., Ruland, R., Schütte, J., Torres, C., Wendland, F., Blockchain for education: lifelong learning passport, in: *Proceedings of 1st ERCIM Blockchain Workshop 2018. European Society for Socially Embedded Technologies (EUSSET)*, 2018.

77. Dorri, A., Kanhere, S.S., Jurdak, R., Gauravaram, P., Blockchain for IoT security and privacy: The case study of a smart home, in: *2017 IEEE International Conference on Pervasive Computing and Communications Workshops (PerCom workshops)*, pp. 618–623, 2017.

78. Lin, J., Shen, Z., Zhang, A., Chai, Y., Blockchain and IoT based food traceability for smart agriculture, in: *Proceedings of the 3rd International Conference on Crowd Science and Engineering*, pp. 1–6, 2018.

79. Karamitsos, I., Papadaki, M., Al Barghuthi, N.B., Design of the blockchain smart contract: A use case for real estate. *J. Inf. Secur.*, 9, 3, 177–190, 2018.

80. López, D. and Farooq, B., A blockchain framework for smart mobility, in: *2018 IEEE International Smart Cities Conference (ISC2)*, pp. 1–7, 2018.

5

Contextualizing Electronic Governance, Smart City Governance and Sustainable Infrastructure in India: A Study and Framework

Nitin K. Tyagi[1]* and Mukta Goyal[2]

[1]*National Informatics Centre (NIC), Government of India, New Delhi, India*
[2]*Jaypee Institute of Information Technology (JIIT), Noida, UP, India*

Abstract

Traditional government services were not in the electronic form. Citizens have to visit to government offices for availing government services. So there is a scope of missing information, that citizen may face. With the introduction of Internet, web applications and smart mobile phones, government is very keen to implement various government services in the electronic form for achieving transparency, speed and coordination among government, citizens and external agencies interacting with government. Thus, this chapter surveys and represents the research gap of various E-governance services developed, implemented in India that is initiative taken the concept of achieving digital India program announced by Indian govt. with the help of information and communication technology (ICT). Further, architectural framework for smart governance based services for smart cities in India based on transforming electronic governance to smart city governance with the use of blockchain, artificial intelligence (AI) techniques, intelligent data mining methods, cloud computing, service oriented architecture (SOA), application program interface (APIs) are proposed. After study and framework, we observed that during application design for smart city governance, focus should be on interactive user interface and user experience, documentation, integration of local language, performance monitoring, feedback form, digital service standard factors defined by government of India open source technology based development and information technology act should be modified.

Corresponding author: nktyagi2007@gmail.com

Arun Solanki, Adarsh Kumar and Anand Nayyar (eds.) Digital Cities Roadmap: IoT-Based Architecture and Sustainable Buildings, (163–192) © 2021 Scrivener Publishing LLC

Keywords: Electronic governance, e-services, e-democracy, smart governance, open governance, smart cities, civilian services

5.1   Introduction

Electronic governance is process of delivering of e-services to their citizens, their businesses as well as the employees of country with the implementation of ICT across country. There are various types of various deliverables of Government services to its peoples, businesses, and their staff electronically by ICT. E-governance services can further be extended to e-services, e-democracy, smart governance, open governance and smart cities implementation. If all the citizens are accessing the government services electronically rather than visiting government office complexes, then it is called E-governance. E-governance is totally dependent upon connectivity, speed, performance, reliability of internet across country. The concept of Smart cities comes from Smart Governance while local government uses technology for public issues [1]. The concept of smart city is considered much bigger than smart governance but is adjacent to it. The Europe Council defined E-Gov. as using electronic methods, techniques and technologies in three dimensions referred as relations linking public authorities with civilians, carrying out of administration at all steps of governance process and providing the public convenience [2]. The objectives of Electronic Govt. executions are to achieve the transparency, convenience, cost reduction, accountability, democracy, public services and responsibility. Once E-Gov. services like transparency means that it is very easy for government to track the inputs and outputs as well as for citizens, accessing the government services at their convenience without visiting government offices complexes. These services also help to government to analysis the data through which predication and requirement of citizens can be known without spending heavy amount of money (cost reduction). E-Government services also fix the responsibility of individual officers through accountability. The electronic government services in India are implemented in various areas named as Electronic Trading, Electronic Passport, Electronic Transport, Electronic Customs, Electronic Health, Electronic Ports, Electronic Districts, and Electronic Results. Government has approved National Electronic Govt. Plan known as NeGP in which 27 Mission Mode Projects (MMPs) are identified after that all projects are implemented under Indian government's Department Of Electronic and Information Technology (Deity), since year 2006. These MMPs include the various sectors such as transport, land records, treasuries, gaon panchayat, police, employee exchange etc. One major sector of MMP Education is also included. The E-Government services implementation majorly depends upon the internet infrastructure within country, private sector and citizens. If any country has high availability of internet, then the peoples can easily use electronic technologies and methods at any instant of time and any geographical place. In various research papers, E-Governance models are proposed. These models mainly divided into four parts named as (G2C—Govt. to Citizen, G2G—Govt. to Govt., G2B—Govt. to Business, and G2E—Govt. to Employee). The model is used to represent that how many types of interaction are being done under Electronic Governance services. Basic E-Governance model is presented in Figure 5.1.

Based on the above literature survey in various directions of the research, some of the issues are identified. These issues are as follows:

1. What are the policies, laws and rules for successful implementation of electronic services among citizens?
2. Evaluation of Electronic governance adoption factors using effective ranking system.
3. How to handle the scalability issues i.e. to incorporate multiple Agencies?
4. How to manage the data in a complex permission setting?

Considering these issues, the contribution of chapter includes to propose a framework which has following points:

- Adopt the open source packages for development and implementation the e-gov. applications for effective cost control.
- Once data is collected in structured or unstructured manner, data analytics techniques can be applied.

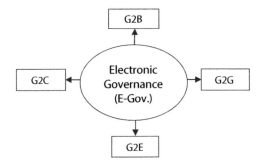

Figure 5.1 Basic E-Governance model.

- Framing of IT polices/laws/cyber laws.
- Blockchain network for e-governance to handle security and immutability of data.

Thus, this chapter is divided in following sections: Section 5.2 argues about related works, literature survey based on research questions to improve the traditional governance. Section 5.3 presents some related E-governance frameworks which are in current use. Section 5.4 proposed the framework for smart e-Governance. Section 5.5 discusses results. Section 5.6 concludes the chapter.

5.2   Related Works

The main objective of this review is consolidating areas of E-governance, Smart Governance in Smart cities. To achieve this, discussions have been made about some recent dimensions of related research areas in Table 5.1.

Based on these research dimensions, some research questions and answers have been formulated.

5.2.1   Research Questions

The term E-governance is the way to enhance transactions for government services, dealing with public, businesses and different parts of administration with aim of formulation of electronic governance applications and smoothening flow of information between citizen, business, bi-directional state to central government and system. A system is able to handle the future large volumes of transactions and frequencies [21]. It has been questioned that what exclusive benefits E-governance can offer? After considering this as a research subject, it is required to first describe what type of entity E-Gov. is? These points help in describing the research questions:

Q1) In what way and for what phenomena is e-governance and smart city governance a more effective framework for various E-services in various areas named as Electronic Trading, Electronic Passport, Electronic Transport, Electronic Customs, Electronic Health, Electronic Ports, Electronic Districts, Electronic Results rather than traditional government services?

The E-Government services implementation majorly depends upon the internet infrastructure within country, private sector and citizens. If any country has high availability of internet then the citizens can access

Table 5.1 E-Governance and Smart Cities Governance related work area dimensions.

Authors	Work Area Dimensions of Electronic Governance and Smart Cities Governance
Layne & Lee [3]	Proposed four stage model of Electronic Governance.
Odendaal [4]	E-Gov. is capability of Administration to interact their citizens electronically with delivery of all government services.
Zouridis and Thaens [5]	Enabling E-society.
Michel [6]	Citizenship management such as Electronic administration, Electronic Government, Electronic Governance and learning city.
Caragliu et al. [7]	Societal addition of citizens in general public services is known as the dimension of Smart Electronic governance.
Mukherjee & Sahoo [8]	Cloud computing in E-Gov.
Al-Shafi & Weerakkody [9]	Discussed E-Gov. adoption factors.
Batty et al. [10]	A government management of a city is termed as Smart governance.
Yadav & Singh [11]	Described four major pillars of E-Gov. named as connectivity, knowledge, data content and capital.
Joshi & Tiwari [12]	Discussed security issues in E-Gov.
Azam et al. [13]	Discussed role of IoT devices and analyzing data generated for smart way of governance activities.
Lee and Lee [14]	Discussed the development of societal based protocols and topology for smart way of governance in Smart cities.
Morabito [15]	Data Analytics for effective E-Governance.
Santana et al. [16]	Cyber physical system can be used for smart city as initiate Smart E-Gov.

(Continued)

Table 5.1 E-Governance and Smart Cities Governance related work area dimensions. (*Continued*)

Authors	Work Area Dimensions of Electronic Governance and Smart Cities Governance
Meijer and Bolivar [17]	Presented Smart city based research contextual, electronic governance model and civilian value evaluation.
Mehr [18]	Artificial Intelligence in E-Gov.
Shrivastava & Pal [19]	Proposed an Ecosystem based data analytics framework for electronic governance.
Mahdi *et al.* [20]	Use of Block chain in E-Gov. for secure transaction.
Proposed Work	Framework proposed for Smart City Governance application with the use of blockchain, AI, data mining, APIs, SOA architecture, cloud computing and found the qualitative and quantitative factors affecting smart city governance applications.

the government electronic services anytime and anywhere. E-Governance is defined as usage of ICT for SMART (Simple, Moral, Accountable, Responsive and Transparent) way of governance that has the capability to increase the interaction relations with peoples, businesses, and different areas of administration [2]. The four major pillars of Electronic Governance are connectivity, knowledge, data content and capital [11]. E-Government applications can be effectively implemented to use the government facilities in effective manner with global recognition. To achieve this, interoperability of information and communication among different department of government including central/state/territories with different domain/platforms, is mandatory. Zouridis and Thaens [5] described Government as enabler of e-society. Citizens and society participates in e-society development. E-governance means e-participation of central government to local government, organizations and departments, government and employees. Michel [6] described the methods of citizenship management with the help of ICT named as E-management, E-govt., Electronic way of governance and city of learning. Dutta and Devi [22] pointed out that government has introduced India.gov.in, Mygov.gov.in, Dial.gov.in portals to interact its own citizens. Government also introduced the technology to converting physical files to digital files under the project digital office. The adaptive governance deals with allocation of judgment power and answerability among govt. management and non-government management actors.

E-Governance brought the way of governance is more proficient and more apparent for their civilians. The Indian government established National Informatics Centre (NIC) in 1976 for the purpose to implement electronic way of Governance that helped citizens of country with 'information' and its communication flow in country. In year 1987, NICNET is launched—national satellite based computer network and further followed by DISNIC (District Information System NIC) to computerize all districts of India [23]. The summary of Electronic Governance applications that has been implemented in India as Open Government Data (OGD) Platform, E-office, Swachh Bharat Mission-Gramin, eCounselling, eVidhan, Target public distributed System, Public Financial Management System (ePFMS), eProcurement, eTransport, eHospital, ePrison, eCustoms, eCourts, MyGov, eLand records, eRail, eSocial service—marriage, birth, death certificate, S3WaaS—secure, scalable and sugamya website as service Platform etc. E-governance has improved its working using open source and cloud computing. Singh *et al.* [24] discussed the automated self scaling techniques of websites at cloud environment with issues, challenges and upcoming prospects. There are various countries which are in the race of E-governance i.e. USA, UK, New Zealand, Brazil, etc. USA introduced various projects EZ Tax filing, Federal Assets sales, E-payroll/HR, E-authentication, etc. towards the step of E-Gov. in 2002–03 [11]. UK also started many projects such as Cornwall Electronic Health Record Pilot (2000), Go-between Project, Integrating Transport: Started in South West Hertfordshire (2008). Due to importance of ICT, New Zealand published E-Governance vision document and e-Governance unit also established [11].

Q2) What are the challenges and failures of Government policies/medium/ procedure for electronically/ digitally improvement in citizen's service of delivery?

Electronically/digitally public service delivery consists of seven examples of innovation i.e.

1. Peoples must aware about service decisions taken by its govt.—transparent;
2. Society must contribute in decision making—participatory;
3. Government's managers begin service delivery to their people—anticipatory;
4. Peoples can find the way to receive services—personalized;

5. Government and people are busy in collaborative service delivery—co-created;

6. Service providers have information regarding service delivery context—context-aware; and

7. Service providers employ situation awareness to improve service deliverables—context-smart.

These public services are accessed by diverse citizen's needs, matured societies, electronically informed citizens, cost effective pressure and asymmetrical circumstances for people service delivery offering within and every corner of countries. Sometimes, no success of public service delivery is due to scarcity of resources, problem of advantages, answerability and management that can depend from one context to another. This requires an improvement in citizen's service deliverables that helps maintaining an ecosystem of government, businesses, non-profits, colleges, peoples and other entities that contribute in the provisioning, using and intermediating in citizen's delivery and bringing methods understandable to consumers. Malik *et al.* [25] described the some assessment factors which can increase the chance of non-success of Electronic projects in governance such as over budgeting, unable to adapt the technology and delay in delivery of services. The other factors are poverty, technology illiteracy, language dominance, unawareness, inequality, infrastructure, etc. Mergel [26] discusses the six challenges for digital service development and implementation teams that face for E-governance projects such as unable to adopt agile technology, selection of IT professional from private industry, upgrading the traditional government culture, improved the process of acquiring innovative IT, Payment to digital service team, decision regarding to build or bought solutions.

Q3) What are the efficient data techniques to analyze the hidden facts and trends?

Earlier applications were developed and implemented with static schema with basic SQL database which is not optimized in terms of high performance, speed, scalability and availability. Most of E-government applications were developed to handle the structured data and collected data for statistical analysis. Big data Analytic techniques plays a major role to handle unstructured data. Today social sites are a convenient medium for a public to share the opinion about government which cannot ignore to make the effective system. Morabito [15] discussed the usage of various unstructured data sources such as crowdsourcing, Internet of Things (IoT), and engagement of citizen things, institutionalizes peoples and private partnership and seeks novel way of value for money to public provision considering Smart City (Barcelona) and Emergency Support in Haiti in year 2010 due to earthquake. Cloud computing is one of the technique to tackle the non-opaqueness, contribution and partnership in the midst its agencies and citizens. The concept behind cloud computing is the availability of computing resources available over internet on need basis so there is no requirement to purchase large servers. The challenge for the government is to data management and to prevent the data from misuse. Big data analysis can help to analyze poor data and make it available for use and prediction of hidden facts and trends. The stored data may be defective, fragmented as well as partially complete due to various sources of data, so data quality is major part for data analytics. Large sectors such as public/private banks, online retailer, insurances and consultants are contending to show their talent.

Big data analytics framework [19] has been proposed for big scale organization service ecosystem for Electronic/digital government that is event driven and time-series graph analytics techniques can be applied for real time information findings. The ecosystem parts carry out pre defined operations and store events concerning to those operations. The event data is made of entity named as citizens, business, service and tools running or starting the operation, time information of the event, associated operation, geographical location and other relevant information. There is an explicit or discovered relationship between actors and events of the component which would contribute to the graph structure [19]. The diffusion or aggregation is done based on these relationship or dependency within a component and termed as local structures [19]. These local structures when diffused would form the system-level structure which may also be termed as global structure [19].

Many big scale computer graphics techniques applications named as Graphlab and Pregel that can help in breaking down bigger structure. Aadhar authentications and electronic governance information exchange are known applications of organization service ecosystem. This type of systems ensures the unauthorized disclosure of stakeholder sensitive information. Munne [27] discussed technical requirements of big data analytics application are blueprint discovery, information distribution, information incorporation, data analytics, transmission, natural language understanding, prediction analysis, modeling and simulation. The pattern blueprint can be done using semantic pattern discovery technologies and cross checking of outcome with peoples. Real time insights can be done by linking data to machine learning based analysis in-memory database.

Real time data can be transmitted using data acquit ion: storm and writing optimex storage solution. Analytical database helps in predictive analytics. Natural language processing techniques can be applied to understand human language. Temporal Database helps in modeling and simulation. Wei and Xiaofeng [28] applied the mining method with the help of rough set theory on road traffic data that could help to find hidden facts about data for better and intelligent traffic management. Das and Nayyar [29] proposed the solution to handle urban traffic management of cognitive cities. Corrêa *et al.* [30] proposed conceptual architectural building block framework for interoperability of government big data which automated ontologies from rough data. Agarwal and Sureka [31] applied data mining techniques and machine learning techniques on tweets to forecast civil unrest or protects. The fuzzy based methods are applied to get the definition of ontology besides searching the set of characters. Kumar *et al.* [32] studied multimedia social big data mining techniques with taxonomy.

Most of E-Gov. applications are developed to handle the structured data and collect data and statics analysis [16]. To handle unstructured data, big data played a major role in E-Gov. [33]. The analysis of prediction, behavior, comparison, scam, threat and sentimental are best examples of this part of framework [34]. The big data analysis is also required in various Indian government departments such as data analysis for drug discovery, health care, public sector and E-Gov. [35].

Q4) Impact factors for adopting of E-govt./digital services by citizens as part of smart governance.

The main objective of Electronic govt. is to transform the public sector in transparent, efficient and accessible manner [36]. But in this process, some nations adopted faster while some lacked behind. For e.g. Germany has advance telecommunication network but the adoption of E-government services is not as per expectation [36]. It has been seen that societal and artistic norms give impact on adoption of ICT [36]. Common studies cannot be thought as to all cultures so carefulness should be taken for getting result. Due to unpredictability of internet for doing transaction and infrastructure spawns risks. Citizens have awareness regarding the personal information collection by government. A lot of research regarding vagueness avoidance is considered as most important national artistic factor which may affect adoption of ICT [36]: Trust of Internet (ToI), faith of government, risk, relative benefit, and difficulty level. Al-Shafi and Weerakkody [9] discussed about impact of factors for accessing of E-govt. services such as performance anticipation, effort determining, social impact, facilitating circumstances, behavioral nature to take, using behavior, gender of people, age of citizens, education of people, etc. Sidek *et al.* [37] analyzed the Malaysian government website adoption analysis using fuzzy techniques based on attractiveness, control, efficiency, helpfulness and learn ability.

Q5) What is role of intelligent techniques in e-governance and smart city governance scenario?

Intelligent techniques are used in e-govt. system to recommend the smart trading for better value of government to business online digital services. Mehr [18] concerned the role of AI in citizen services such as prompt response in emergency, enabling customs and cost effective education, detecting scams and frauds, instant crime information report, prediction to goal and anticipate citizen services interaction, and guiding pre-active repairing of infrastructure and determining cyber-attacks and personal details theft on government websites and service applications. Nayyar *et al.* [38] listed cyber security issues surrounding IoT devices for research and simulation tools.

In E-governance framework analytical layer is responsible of analyzing data collected from various sources. The data format may be in structured or non-structured form. Statistical techniques for structured data can be applied for analyzing the data and further decision making. Analysis may help knowledge data discovery and prediction. But in the case of non-structured information, Big Data analysis was applied to know the trends and hidden facts about data. The citizens give various suggestions/complaints in running text at social websites so analyzing all such texts is not easy process. The Machine Leaning (ML) techniques, Genetic Algorithms (GA), Natural Language Processing (NLP) can be applied for analyzing useful texts. After analyzing all such texts and statistical analysis, it helps government in taking citizen perspective decisions, amend laws and formulate policies and rules. This type of framework helps to transform traditional Governance to Digital Governance.

The machine learning and Natural Language Processing based frameworks are tools and methodologies for Open Source Social Media Intelligence (OSSMInt) for E-Gov [39]. Jain and Nayyar [40] discussed about analyzing security threats and privacy of data. Data mining techniques based on Rough Set theory using MapReduce is presented [41]. Rough set theory helps in retrieving information and finding trends and hidden facts. Rough sets technique is also applied for analyzing traffic accidents [42]. The incremental Rough Set Learning has been applied for intelligent Traffic System [43] that may help government for developing intelligent traffic application for common citizens. The performance of E-Gov has been evaluated using interval Values Intuitionistic fuzzy set (IFS) [44].

Q6) Role of Security in E-governance and smart city governance.

Joshi and Tiwari [12] discussed the security issues for government at user level, transport level, security at ICT access level, information security protection of privacy of individuals, electronic security. Singh and Singh Karaulia [45] also discussed the security of government contents as well as personal information. Author also mentioned the security tools for government such as one time passwords, firewalls, encryptions, monitoring tools for network security, analysis tools for intruders, operational technology for intruder protection and data security. Syamsuddin and Hwang [46] evaluated the fuzzy based security strategy of government websites based on multi criteria decision making which will help policymaker to conduct proper assessment of e-government security.

Q7) Role of enabling technology in current software development architectural framework for Electronic Governance and Smart City Governance.

Aazam *et al.* [13] that Internet of Things (IoT) is generating large volume of data on time series basis so it is need of time to store and determine pattern of data on incremental need basis. Krishnamurthy *et al.* [47] discussed the technology requirements for smart towns/cities, challenges with limitations, IoT-based framework, technology for smart city growth. Cloud computing ensures the availability of resources on need basis over internet. Wu *et al.* [48] proposed the Heterogeneous Autonomous sources with distributed and decentralized control that seeks to explore Complex and Evolving relationship among data (HACE) theorem [48] for big data processing model with respect to data mining. Hou [49] discussed that Blockchain technology can help to develop credit system among society, institutions and government but due to new technology adoption, it is required to establish standards, policies and measure security threat and to ensure of reliability, authoritative and long term record preservations. Internet of Things is to access human use of things over internet directly or indirectly. A huge quantity of IoT devices were made following various architectures is proposed [50]. There are two types of IoT research. One is top down and other one is bottom up. Top down approach is based on web application system based Service Oriented Architecture (SOA) that uses physical service using physical web services [51, 52]. The bottom up method begins with the structure of numerous things can be accessed over internet [53]. So, IoT is basically collection of hardware, sensors, and physical devices, middleware which collects data and can be accessed over internet. Cyber physical system is a combination of computation, networking and physical processes can be used to develop Smart cities as initiative of Smart Governance [16]. Cloud computing platform are also used for E-Gov. applications development. In some research, combination of IoT based systems using cloud computing make new name as cloud of every things. The idea behind to store and processing of data collected through smart digital cities network (IoT network) implemented at a cloud environment. The cloud is having a collection of commodity machines and software layer for distributing application across machines [8].

Blockchain technology ensures the security and privacy for various applications including Internet of Things (IoT) ecosystem [20]. Blockchain has method of public key to store user personal information which provides extra layer of privacy. Blockchain adopted in different non-monetary processes named as online voting system, decentralized based message exchange, and distributed cloud based storage system, proof of geographical location detail, health related applications and so on [20]. Block chain has two major components named as transaction and block. Transaction means some operation triggered by connecting nodes whereas block is collecting of data related to transaction and other relevant details including sequence or ordering number, timestamp information of transaction, etc. Operation of blockchain is triggering transaction, validation and verification, creating new block and adding block to chain. For Government application different types of platform are used such as IoT & Cloud (IC), Big Data & Cloud (BC), CPS & Cloud (CC) and Block Chain & Cloud (BCC) (Figure 5.2). These platforms are discussed below:

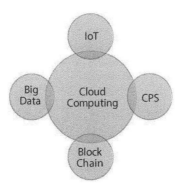

Figure 5.2 Platform types for Electronic Governance.

A) IoT & Cloud (IC) Platform

IoT uses machine to machine learning algorithm without human intervention. If device is not connected, then that device can be component of IoT communication system devices such as bar based coding or RFID based tag. The objects having non-intelligence can be considered as elements of IoT-based system [13]. The numbers of connected devices have been crossed to number of people and connected devices are closed to 9 billion and may reach 24 billion by 2020 [13]. All the devices are generating a huge amount of heterogeneous data contents so it is very hard to store locally and their rental space for storing this data with any time accessibility. There is also requirement of rental processing and computation of data. Cloud computing fulfills all the needs as shown in Figure 5.3. Mukhopadhyay *et al.* [54] discussed the facial emotion detection for online learning systems. Nayyar [54] discussed the cloud computing applications in different area.

B) Big Data & Cloud (BC) Platform

The large volume, high velocity and various varieties of data generated the requirement of analytics of dataset to know trend and highlights of dataset. So the need of high computational infrastructure is generated. Nowadays, big data is transforming healthcare, industry, science, transportation, geographical, societies etc. So, major issue is to design such environment for data analysis and distribute workload with low cost. Cloud computing helps in minimize operational cost, resource sharing, parallel processing, information security, privacy with information/data service integration with scalable storage of data [56]. Figure 5.4 represents big data and cloud blockchain based platform.

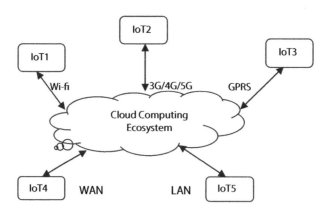

Figure 5.3 IoT and Cloud (IC) Platform.

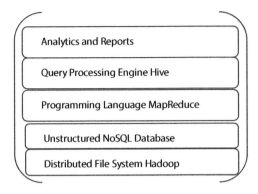

Figure 5.4 Big Data & Cloud (BC) Platform.

C) Block Chain & Cloud (BCC) Platform

The Block chain technology has given attractive alternative for addressing security issues in distributed systems. This technology is based on publically distributed peer to peer ledger maintenance give rise to need of cloud computing services such as auditing, management of digital assets, data privacy and integrity and temper proof security. Blocks of transaction are aligned in chain to enable immutability on the records [57]. Kaur *et al.* [58] discussed the blockchain systems and applications with consensus algorithms involved in it. Singh *et al.* [59] proposed the framework based on fog for internet of thing (IoT) in smart towns/cities.

D) CPS & Cloud (CC) Platform

Cyber physical system and cloud computing provides the platform for E-Gov applications. The platform focuses on the implementation, configuration and running of CPS devices, collection of data from devices. But this system does not ensure the monitoring and publication of data [16]. All Cyber physical system can be deployed configured on cloud network with centralized control of system in effective, transparent manner. Figure 5.5 shows the architecture of cloud computing network connected with cyber physical devices.

Figure 5.5 CPS and Cloud (CC) Platform.

5.3   Related E-Governance Frameworks

In this section of chapter, the discussion about the frameworks of E-governance has been done. Hiller *et al.* [60] represented the E-governance stages and categories of relationship between government and other stake holders. At very early stage 1, the objective of government is to disseminate of information by putting on websites. At Stage 2, two way communications such as email service between government and other agencies had been started. At next stage 3, transaction is being started such as pay tax online; receive election funds, electronic pay check and electronic fund transfer. At next stage number 4, incorporation of digital services so citizens can interact to government online. At Stage 5, government website allows voting online, registering online or giving comments electronically. The discussed step is subset of two-way communication. Table 5.2 shows stages of E-Governance framework.

Mukherjee and Sahoo [8] proposed (as shown in Figure 5.6) cloud based E-governance data analytics framework. In this framework, thin clients and mobiles are generating the request to Hadoop software hosted at cloud environment. Hadoop looks the relevance of request. If this is a valid request, Hadoop sends the request inference engines through volunteer nodes. The inference engine interacts to the knowledge base (KBs) and takes the knowledge data, passed to inference engine then to user via Hadoop.

Shrivastava and Pal [19] proposed Ecosystem based data analytics framework for electronic governance (Figure 5.7). This framework is divided into four parts named as ecosystem transport layer, Data Layer, Mining and Analytics layer and User interface layer [19]. At Ecosystem Transport layer (ETL), ecosystem will be polled from time to time for event data on fixed time interval or event based manner [19]. The required information would be get loaded into data layer. At data layer, data will be stored at data repository such as event related data, service related rules and user profile related data. Complex event processing will handle immediate response. The output will be passed to real time based analysis techniques. At mining and analytics layer, relevant data would be mined; graphs can be prepared with mined data or real data. Reporting tools would also be available. At user interface layer, the web based and mobile based interface would help to interact with end users.

Some researchers discussed dimensions/areas of E-governance [3]. This four stage model shows in Figure 5.8 that complexity increase with the

Table 5.2 Stages of E-governance framework [60].

Govt. Type	Stage1 Information	Stage2 2-way communication	Stage3 Transaction	Stage4 Integration	Stage5 Political Partnership
Government to individual services	Description of medical benefits	Request and receive individual benefit information	Pay taxes online	All services and entitlements	N/A
Government to individual Political	Date of elections	Receive election forms	Receive election finds and disbursements	Register and vote. Federal, state and local	Voting online
Government to Business—Citizen	Regulations online	SEC filing	Pay taxes online Receive program funds (SBA, etc.) Agricultural allotments	All regulatory information on site	Filing comments online
Government to Business—Marketplace	Posting request for proposals	Request clarification or specs	Online vouchers and payments	Marketplace for vendors	N/A
Government to Employees	Pay dates, holidays information	Request for employment benefits statements	Electronic paychecks	One stop job, grade, vacation time, retirement information, etc.	N/A
Government to Government	Agency filing requirements	Request from local governments	Electronic funds transfers		N/A

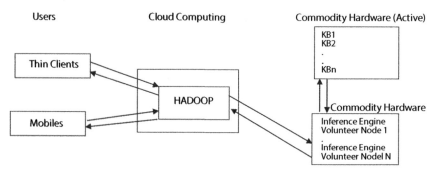

Figure 5.6 Ecosystem based data analytics framework [8].

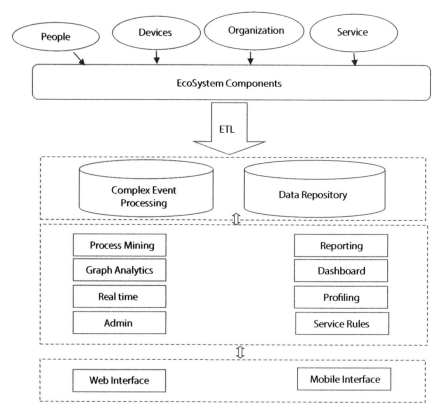

Figure 5.7 Ecosystem-based data analytics framework [19].

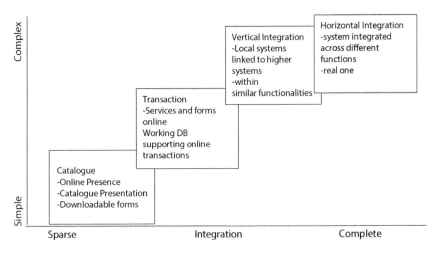

Figure 5.8 Four stage model of E-Governance [3].

vertical and horizontal integration of E-Governance applications. At the early catalogue stage, government is in the process of putting online presence for government in front of citizens.

At next transaction stage, services and form online with working database has been developed. Vertically, local systems are linked to higher systems. Horizontally, all projects/applications are integrated at different operations.

5.3.1   Smart City Features in India

In this section, areas of smart cities/towns are discussed. This part focuses on smart city dimension adopted by Indian government. The Indian government declared the list of 100 cities in year 2015 [61]. Various smart city features are also defined. The features are housing for all, preserving and development of open space, promoting transport connectivity to last mile of city, making citizen friendly governance, giving identity to city in terms of local cuisine, education, health, arts, crafts, textile, infrastructure, dairy and industries and also make area less vulnerable to natural disaster and cheap services. The features are described in Figure 5.9.

5.4   Proposed Smart Governance Framework

This section proposes the smart governance architectural framework that handles research issues raised in previous part of chapter. The framework comprises above discussed issues as per Figure 5.10. In this framework, an

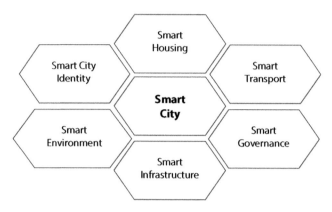

Figure 5.9 Smart city features/dimensions in India [61].

ICT layer is between data base and government. ICT layer helps government to take decisions to implement the E-Gov. Applications in various areas named as transport, scholarship distribution, direct benefit transfer (DBT), UIDAI, customs, goods and service tax (GST), passports, income tax payments/filings, GIS, land records, weather, eOffice, government data sharing, courts, police, ePorts, National knowledge Network (NKN), etc. A cloud computing or Blockchaining layer is added for high volume data set or high security purpose. The cloud environment provides user virtual server and space, RAM, CPU on need basis over internet with the help of virtual private network i.e. CISCO VPN Client. After connection, ready-made development environment using open source technology is available or may be created. The open source programming languages such as Java, PHP, Perl, Python etc. and open source based operating systems such as Linux and open source based databases such as MySQL, PostGreS, MongoDB, CouchDB, SQLite, MariaDB, open source web server Apache Tomcat, WebLogic, JBOSS, IIS can be used for development in cost effective manner. Mobile software development kit can be used to create development environment. The all the application can be hosted using secure protocol such as HTTPS. The Secure Websites, Mobile Applications, Application Program Interface (APIs), open data websites etc. can be developed for public usage.

The user interface provides actual government services in terms of websites, mobile applications, APIs and Web APIs. At this layer, common citizen accesses the government E-Services and performs tasks on need basis. At this layer, businesses also access the government services and perform tasks. Other stake holders of this layer are self-central/state government or vice versa. The various E-Gov. services are also started by government

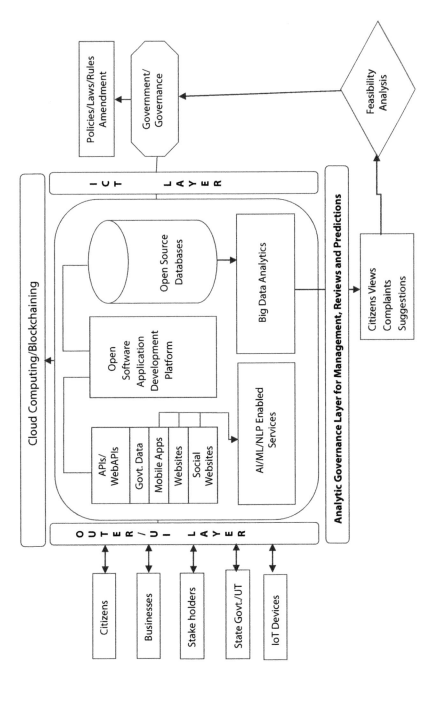

Figure 5.10 Proposed framework for smart governance applications.

for their employees in the form of Public Financial Management Systems (PFMS), eOffice, File Tracing System (FTS), etc. At this layer, common citizen can also participate in government policy making and amendment laws and give suggestions. The government websites and applications should be Artificial Intelligent using Machine Learning, Natural Language Processing (NLP), Deep Learning to give impression of individuality of citizens. The multilingual websites also play a major role for accessibility of information across nations where a lot of community peoples are living. The citizen should have the impression of that my information is secured in any way.

Though proposed framework compliances all the research issue, but still some barriers are in E-governance. Internet connectivity and speed is major challenges for successful E-Governance application implementation. Approximately 70% of populations are living in rural areas in India and so to access E-Government services; it requires stable and speedy internet connectivity. Another factor is education and Information Technology (IT) illiteracy. The literacy rate in different developing nations is as follows in Table 5.3.

The literacy rate by United Nations Educational, Scientific and Cultural Organization (UNESCO) French shows that adult literacy rate is lower than youth literacy rate so education and literacy rate of adults is a big barrier for adoption of E-Gov. services in India as well as developing nations. Power shortage and connectivity to rural areas is another barrier for E-Gov. application successful implementation. In developing nation, there is a gap in demand and supply of power and power connectivity in rural areas. Combating with large multilingual population with quality of

Table 5.3 Literacy rate comparison by UNESCO Data Source [62].

Country	Adult literacy rate	Youth literacy rate Ages 15–24
China	96.40%	99.70%
Sri Lanka	92.6%	98.80%
Myanmar	93.1%	96.3%
India	72.1%	95.2%
Nepal	64.70%	86.9%
Bangladesh	61.50%	83.2%
Pakistan	58.5%	74.8%

service is also the factor that affecting the effectiveness of E-Gov. applications in developing nations. Other major challenges are policy for E-Gov. application usage, legal liability, security/privacy of information, reliability to government, citizen participation for decision making through E-Gov. applications, and tendency to work in traditional environment. Baum and Maio [64] discussed that the traditional government can be transformed using four steps named as presence, interaction, transaction and transformation. All the government practices should be available over internet.

5.5   Results Discussion

In this part, we will discuss about the result of study. The study is divided into three steps: initial step, design development, and delivery stage.

5.5.1   Initial Stage

At this stage, we have found that Electronic governance, smart city governance evaluation indicators in Table 5.4.

Table 5.4 Electronic governance, smart city governance evaluation indicators.

Evaluation standard name	Key parameters	Types of indicator
Digial Service Standard Indian Government [63]	• No. of digital service provided by department against total number of services • No. of digital transactions in a given period of time against all potential transactions • Degree of coverage geographically • Other Key Parameter indicator (KPIs) such as turnaround time, cost of data collection, transport, storage and analysis	Quantitative (understanding, Accurate, Responsive, and Effective)

(Continued)

Table 5.4 Electronic governance, smart city governance evaluation indicators. (*Continued*)

Evaluation standard name	Key parameters	Types of indicator
Smart Governance (100 Indian cities named)	• Smart Housing for all • Smart Health • Smart Transport • Smart Infrastructure • Smart Environment • Smart Connectivity • Smart City Identity	Qualitative

5.5.2   Design, Development and Delivery Stage

At this stage, in design stage, functionality, user interaction and technology are considered. In development stage, Service development and service maintenance needs to be considered. Service development includes APIs, local language, documentation, user experience (UX), user interface (UI), etc. and maintenance includes change control, access control and performance monitoring. In Delivery stage, delivery channels and feedback handling needs to be considered.

5.6   Conclusion

This chapter studies the research area, dimensions and issues of E-governance and governance in digital smart city. This chapter proposes the framework of Smart digital governance applications in smart city where E-governance applications should adopt artificial intelligence, blockchain, data analytics techniques. Time to time applications should be modified after the customer feedback or compliant. Cloud based framework E-governance application have already been used, it is time to shift the E-governance application to Smart Governance AI, data science and blockchain based framework for more secure reason. E-governance/Smart City governance evaluation standard parameters are also discussed.

The E-Gov. application can be developed using open source technology based (Java, PHP, HTML, etc.) on service Oriented Architecture (SOA) configured at cloud environment having functionality based on Artificial Intelligence (AI), Natural Language Processing (NLP), Neural Network (NN), Machine Learning (ML), Internet of Things (IoT), Block Chain will help to enhance E-government application efficient implementation in cost effective manner and timely delivery of E-services to its citizens. The future trends are as follows in Table 5.5.

The future scope of E-Governance applications depends upon number of peoples accessing E-Governance online digital applications/services. E-Governance digital application/services adoption analysis has to be done on the basis of geographical divided citizens with different age groups and gender. E-Governance applications can be customized for physically disabled citizens. These E-services should be artificial intelligent to fulfill the needs of individual citizen. There should be one single platform or website having artificial intelligence techniques where website could self-explain the functionality, usage and benefits of using E-Services launched by Government of nation.

Table 5.5 E-Government/Smart Digital City Applications.

S. No.	E- Governance and Smart Digital City Applications
1.	Increasing customized web portals with platform independence with multilingual support
2.	Introduction of AI, ML, NLP in web applications to understand the citizen needs
3.	Data Analytics Techniques for predicting the trends and needs of citizens for decision making
4.	Parallel development of Mobile Applications of E-Gov. for anytime, anywhere access
5.	Standardization the policies and IT Laws
6.	Capacity Building and Content Handling
7.	Monitoring of E-Gov. applications accessibility/usage matrix
8.	Ensure the information security of citizens
9.	Awareness of Citizens with self-guided E-Gov. applications
10.	Increase in Common service centers across the nations

References

1. Chourabi, H. *et al.*, Understanding smart cities: an integrative framework, in: *45th Hawaii International Conference on System Science (HICSS)*, pp. 2289–2297, 2012.
2. Beniwal, V. and Sikka, V., E-Governance In India: Prospects and challenges. *Int. J. Comput. Commun. Technol.*, 4, 1–5, 2013.
3. Layne, K. and Lee, J., Developing fully functional E-government: A four stage model. *Gov. Inf. Q.*, 18, 122–136, 2001.
4. Odendaal, N., Information and communication technology and local governance: Understanding the difference between cities in developed and emerging economies. *Comput. Environ. Urban Syst.*, 27, 585–607, 2003.
5. Zouridis, S. and Thaens, M., E-Government: Towards a Public Administration Approach. *Asian J. Public Adm.*, 25, 159–183, 2003.
6. Michel, H., E-Administration E-Government, E-Governance and the learning city, A topology of citizenship management using ICTs. *Electron. J. e-Gov.*, 3, 213–218, 2015.
7. Caragliu, A., Del Bo, C., Nijkamp, P., Smart cities in Europe. *Proceedings to the 3rd Central European Conference on Regional Science*, Košice, Slovak Republic, pp. 45–59, 2009.
8. Mukherjee, K. and Sahoo, G., Cloud Computing: Future Framework for e-Governance. *Int. J. Comput. Appl.*, 7, 31–34, 2010.
9. Al-Shafi, S. and Weerakkody, V., Factors Affecting E-Government Adoption in the state of Qatar. *European and Mediterranean Conference on Information Systems*, pp. 1–10, 2010.
10. Batty, M., Axhausen, K.W., Giannotti, F., Pozdnoukhov, A., Bazzani, A., Wachowicz, M., Portugali, Y., Smart cities of the future. *Eur. Phys. J.*, 214, 481–518, 2012.
11. Yadav, N. and Singh, V., E-Governance: Past, Present and Future in India. *Int. J. Comput. Appl.*, 53, 36–48, 2012.
12. Joshi, A. and Tiwari, H., Security for E-governance. *J. Inf. Oper. Manag.*, 3, 1, 254, 2012.
13. Aazam, M., Khan, I., Alsaffar, A., Huh, E., Cloud of Things: Integrating Internet of Things and Cloud Computing and the Issues Involved. *11th International Bhurban Conference on Applied Sciences and Technology (IBCAST)*, pp. 414–419, 2014.
14. Lee, J. and Lee, H., Developing and validating a citizen-centric typology for smart city services. *Gov. Inf. Q.*, 31, supplement 1, S93–S105, 2014.
15. Morabito, V., *Big Data and Analytics for Government Innovation*, pp. 23–45, Springer International Publishing, Switzerland, 2015.
16. Santana, E.F., Chaves, Z., Gerosa, A., Kon, M., Milojicic, D.S., Software Platforms for smart cities: Concepts, requirements, challenges and a unified reference archtecture, Article in. *ACM Comput. Surv.*, 50, 6, 2–35, 2016.

17. Meijer, A.J. and Bolívar, M.P.R., Governing the smart city: A review of the literature on smart urban governance. *Int. Rev. Adm. Sci.*, 82, 2, 392–408, 2016.

18. Mehr, H., *Artificial Intelligence for Citizen Services and Government*, Ash Center for Democratic Governance and Innovation, 1–12, Harvard Kennnedy School, Cambridge, MA, 2017.

19. Shrivastava, S. and Pal, S., A Big Data Analytics Framework for Enterprise Service Ecosystems in an e-Governance Scenario. *ICEGOV*, 2017.

20. Mahdi, H., Miraz, M., Ali, M., Applications of Blockchain Technology beyond Cryptocurrency. *Ann. Emerg. Technol. Comput.*, International Association of Educators and Researchers, 2, 1–6, 2018.

21. Rao, L. and Rama Krishna, S., Challenges and future trends in e-Governance. *Int. J. Sci. Eng. Res.*, 4, 772–785, 2013.

22. Dutta, A. and Devi, M., e-Governance status in India. *Int. J. Comput. Sci. Eng.*, 3, 1–6, 2005.

23. https://www.nic.in/projects-all/; https://www.nic.in/about-us/.

24. Singh, P., Gupta, P., Jyoti, K., Nayyar, A., Research on auto-scaling of web applications in cloud: Survey, trends and future directions. *Scalable Comput.: Pract. Exp.*, 20, 2, 399–432, 2019.

25. Malik, P., Dhillon, P., Verma, P., Challenges and Future Prospects for E-Governance in India. *Int. J. Sci. Eng. Technol. Res.*, 3, 1964–1972, 2014.

26. Mergel, I., *Digital Service Teams, Challenges and Recommendations for Government, Using technology series*, IBM center for The Business of Government, University of Konstanz, 2017.

27. Munne, R., Big Data in the Public Sector, in: *New Horizons for a Data-Driven Economy*, 2016.

28. Wei, C. and Xiaofeng, The Mining Method of the Road Traffic Illegal Data Based on Rough Sets and Association Rules. *International Conference on Intelligent Computation Technology and Automation*, pp. 856–859, 2010.

29. Das, S. and Nayyar, A., Innovative Ideas to Manage Urban Traffic Congestion in Cognitive Cities, in: *Driving the Development, Management, and Sustainability of Cognitive Cities*, pp. 139–162, IGI Global, 2019.

30. Corrêa, A., Borba, C., Lins, D., Silva, D., Corrê, P., A Fuzzy Ontology-Driven Approach to Semantic Interoperability in e-Government Big Data. *Int. J. Soc. Sci. Humanity*, 5, 178–181, 2015.

31. Agarwal, S. and Sureka, A., Investigating the Potential of Aggregated Tweets as Surrogate Data for Forecasting Civil Protests. *Proceedings of the 3rd IKDD Conference on Data Science*, 2016.

32. Kumar, A., Sangwan, S.R., Nayyar, A., Multimedia social big data: Mining, in: *Multimedia Big Data Computing for IoT Applications*, pp. 289–321, Springer, Singapore, 2020.

33. Chen, M., Mao, S., Liu, Y., Big data: A survey. *Mobile Netw. Appl.*, 19, 171–209, 2014.

34. Rajagopalan, M.R. and Solaimurugan, V., Big Data Framework for National e-Governance Plan. *Eleventh International Conference on ICT and Knowledge Engineering*, pp. 978–983, 2013.

35. Agnihotri, N. and Sharma, A., Big Data Analysis and its need for effective E-Governance. *Int. J. Innov. Adv. Comput. Sci.*, 4, 219–224, 2015.

36. Akkaya, C., Wolf, P., Krcmar, H., Factors Influencing Citizen Adoption of E-Government Services: A cross-cultural comparison (Research in Progress). *IEEE 45th Hawaii International Conference on System Sciences*, 2012.

37. Sidek, Z., Hasimah, N., Teo, I., A Value of E-Service in Local Government: A Fuzzy Approach Evaluation. *Int. J. Comput. Eng. Res.*, 2, 1677–1681, 2007.

38. Nayyar, A., Rameshwar, R., Solanki, A., *Internet of Things (IoT) and the Digital Business Environment: A Standpoint Inclusive Cyber Space, Cyber Crimes, and Cybersecurity*, 2020.

39. Agarwal, S. and Sureka, A., Investigating the Role of Twitter in E-Governance by Extracting Information on Citizen Complaints and Grievances Reports. *International Conference on Big Data Analytics Lecture Notes in Computer Science*, vol. 10721, pp. 300–310, 2017.

40. Jain, R., Jain, N., Nayyar, A., Security and Privacy in Social Networks: Data and Structural Anonymity, in: *Handbook of Computer Networks and Cyber Security*, pp. 265–293, Springer, Cham, 2020.

41. Patil, P., Data Mining with Rough Set Using MapReduce. *Int. J. Innovative Res. Comput. Commun. Eng.*, 2, 6980–6986, 2014.

42. Nithya, P., Jeyarani, S., Kumar, P., Rough Sets for analyzing road traffic accidents. *Int. J. Comput. Eng. Appl.*, 12, 377–391, 2018.

43. Bentaher, A., Fouad, Y., Mahar, K., Online Incremental Rough Set Learning in Intelligent Traffic System. *Int. J. Adv. Comput. Sci. Appl.*, 9, 77–82, 2018.

44. Zhang, S., Yu, Y., Wang, Y., Zhang, W., Evaluation about the Performance of E-Government Based on Interval-Valued Intuitionistic Fuzzy Set, Hindawi Publishing Corporation. *Sci. World J.*, 2014, 1–10, 2014.

45. Singh, S. and Singh Karaulia, D., E-Governance: Information Security Issues. *International Conference on Computer Science and Information Technology, (ICCSIT'2011)*, Pattaya, 2011.

46. Syamsuddin, I. and Hwang, J., A new fuzzy MCDM framework to evaluate e-government security strategy. *4th International Conference on Application of Information and Communication Technologies*, IEEE, 2010.

47. Krishnamurthi, R., Nayyar, A., Solanki, A., *Innovation Opportunities through Internet of Things (IoT) for Smart Cities. Green and Smart Technologies for Smart Cities*, pp. 261–292, CRC Press, Boca Raton, FL, USA, 2019.

48. Wu, X., Zhu, X., Wu, G., Ding, W., Data Mining with Big Data. *IEEE Trans. Knowl. Data Eng.*, 26, 97–107, 2014.

49. Hou, H., The Application of blockchain technology in E-government in China. *Computer Communications and Networks 26th International Conference*, 2017.

50. Weigong, L., Meng, F., Zhang, C., Yuefei, L., Ning, C., Jiang, J., Research on Unified Architecture of IoT System. *IEEE International Conference on Computational Science and Engineering (CSE) and IEEE International Conference on Embedded and Ubiquitous Computing*, pp. 345–352, 2017.

51. Guinard, D. and Trifa, V., Interacting with the SOA-based Internet of things: Discovery, query, selection, and on-demand provisioning of Web services. *IEEE Trans. Serv. Comput.*, 3, 223–235, 2010.

52. Wei, Q., Jin, Z., Li, G., Li, L.X., Preliminary study of service discovery in Internet of things, Feasibility and limitation of SOA. *J. Front. Comput. Sci. Technol.*, 7, 97–113, 2013.

53. Xie, K., Chen, H., Li, C., PMDA, A Physical Model Driven Software Architecture for Internet of Things. *J. Comput. Re. Dev.*, 50, 1185–1197, 2013.

54. Mukhopadhyay, M., Pal, S., Nayyar, A., Pramanik, P.K.D., Dasgupta, N., Choudhury, P., Facial Emotion Detection to Assess Learner's State of Mind in an Online Learning System, in: *Proceedings of the 2020 5th International Conference on Intelligent Information Technology*, pp. 107–115, 2020.

55. Nayyar, A., *Handbook of Cloud Computing: Basic to Advance research on the concepts and design of Cloud Computing*, BPB Publications, New Delhi, India 2019.

56. Hashem I., T., Yaqoob, I., Anuar, N., Mokhtara, S., Gani, A., Khan, S., The rise of "Big Data" on cloud computing: Review and open research issues. *Article in Inf. Syst.*, 47, 98–115, 2014.

57. Tosh, D., Shetty, S., Liang, X., Charles, A., Kamhoua, K., Kwiat, A., Njilla, L., Security Implications of Blockchain Cloud with Analysis of Block Withholding Attack. *17th IEEE/ACM International Symposium on Cluster, Cloud and Grid Computing (CCGRID)*, 2017.

58. Kaur, A., Nayyar, A., Singh, P., Blockchain: A path to the future, in: *Cryptocurrencies and Blockchain Technology Applications*, pp. 25–42, 2020.

59. Singh, P., Nayyar, A., Kaur, A., Ghosh, U., Blockchain and Fog Based Architecture for Internet of Everything in Smart Cities. *Future Internet*, 12, 4, 61, 2020.

60. Hiller, J. and Bélange F. Hiller, S.J., *Privacy Strategies for Electronic Government*, E-Government Series, 200, 162–198, 2001.

61. http://smartcities.gov.in/content/innerpage/smart-city-features.php.

62. https://en.wikipedia.org/wiki/Literacy_in_India.

63. http://egovstandards.gov.in/sites/default/files/Digital%20Service%20Standard%2Version%201.0.pdf.

64. Baum, C. and Maio, A., *Gartner's Four Phases of E Government Model*, Gartner Group, Research Note, 12, 2000.

6

Revolutionizing Geriatric Design in Developing Countries: IoT-Enabled Smart Home Design for the Elderly

Shubhi Sonal* and Anupadma R.

School of Architecture, REVA University, Bangalore, India

Abstract

The research study emanates from concern for growing population of elderly in our cities who are forced to live alone without much assistance due to shrinking family size, intercity and international migration of their children in search of better opportunities and jobs. The study looks at middle class to upper middle-class elderly population aged 65 and above living in urban cities of India such as Bangalore. The research study stems from the idea that a smart city should have holistic concern for the health and quality of life for all sections of the society. While most smart city proposals usually cater to the young generation and their need for connectedness, there remains a scope for inclusion of IoT based technologies for development of smart and safe homes for the elderly. The project aims to create a design prototype of IoT enabled smart homes which can be adopted easily for cost effective construction of homes for the elderly. The first part of the study focuses on assessment of elderly behavior, socio cultural aspects and sustainable independent living requirements for elderly population in urban cities of India. The second part of the study will propose a Schematic design of an IoT enabled smart home for the elderly including architectural, technological and sustainability aspects. The chapter proposes nesting homes as a smart amalgamation of architectural as well as state of the art technological interventions. A framework for design and integrated health monitoring system based on internet of things is the main contribution of the study.

Keywords: Smart homes, geriatric design, Internet of Things, elderly behavior, architectural interventions, elderly living

---

Corresponding author: shubhi.sonal@reva.edu.in

Arun Solanki, Adarsh Kumar and Anand Nayyar (eds.) Digital Cities Roadmap: IoT-Based Architecture and Sustainable Buildings, (193–220) © 2021 Scrivener Publishing LLC

6.1   Introduction to Geriatric Design

Building or purchase of a home has been one of the prime targets of retirement planning for the middle-class Indian in urban areas. However, as age progresses, people often find themselves unable to continue living in their homes as they require constant assistance for their daily living activities, access to healthcare facilities and emergency assistance. Modern living in cities entails a forced seclusion of the elderly as the young and middle aged barely find time to cater to this section of our population. Most of the market economics is also driven by needs of the youth and hence the elderly people are left with few options when it comes to housing. Though we have examples of old age homes, assisted living facilities, etc. there continues to be a social stigma attached to these facilities and very few people with sufficient means look at these as viable options for their future. A vast gamut of elderly needs including social, cultural, economic, health and wellbeing, technology integration must be kept in mind to cater to their requirements.

Data from UNFPA 2020 [27] states that nearly 6.6% of India's population lies in the elderly category and the average life expectancy has increased to 70 years. As per Indian Census 2011, there are nearly 104 million elderly persons (aged 60 years or above) in India, out of which 53 million females and 51 million males. The life expectancy at birth during 2009–2013 was 69.3 for females as against 65.8 years for males. At the age of 60 and 70 years average remaining length of life was found to be about 18 years and less than 12 years, respectively. Over 71% of elderly population resides in rural areas while 29% reside in urban areas. Prevalence of heart diseases and other life-threatening conditions among elderly population was found to be much higher in urban areas than in rural parts. Furthermore, the most common disability among the aged persons was loco motor disability and visual disability, as reported by surveys carried out by Elderly India, 2016 [1]. Census data compiled in the draft of Revised Master Plan—2031 for Bangalore, shows that population of people above 60 in Bengaluru has been on a constant rise. Improved life expectancy is expected to project a demographic of 9% of total population (65–79 years age group) and 1.5% (80+ age group) by 2031 in Bangalore city [15]. In such a scenario, Geriatric design is a much-needed effort required to make Bangalore a better place to grow old.

Geriatric design is rooted in the philosophy of Universal design principles. Universal design is defined as the design of built and unbuilt environment such that it becomes easily usable by all to the greatest extent possible without the need for adaptation or specialized features. Some of the constituent principles of Universal design include Equitable Use, Flexibility,

Simplicity and intuitiveness, perceptible information, Tolerance for error and Size & space for approach. Universal design has several advantages from both the user's and developer's perspective. While the obvious advantage is provision of greater comfort and usability across various groups, Universal design can also add a competitive edge and add a unique selling point for the building project. Implementation of universal design principles demonstrates a sensitive approach towards the user groups and also ensures enough flexibility and adaptability towards future expansion.

The first principle of Universal design is "Equitable Use". Equitable use mandates that the design should be usable and marketable to people with diverse needs. The onset of old age often brings with it issues such as limited mobility, reduced vision, etc. Equitable design principle dictates that the design of the built environment should be such that there is no segregation or stigmatizing of the users. Furthermore, it also requires provisions for privacy, security and safety in an equitable manner for all sets of users. The principles of "Tolerance for error" and "low physical effort" are also major contributors towards design of geriatric use spaces. Tolerance for error aims at minimizing hazards and occurrence of accidents through the design of the built and unbuilt environment. Low physical effort mandates the usability of a space and its features with the minimum possible fatigues. Both these principles bear great significance when we think of living spaces for the elderly. A subset of Universal design philosophy is the concept of Barrier free design. It may be defined as the removal of any physical barriers from the built environment for users facing physical or mental challenges. Once again, independent functioning of the individual irrespective of physical or mental disabilities is the prime feature of barrier free design. Some of the basic initiatives required to ensure barrier free living environment for the elderly includes wheelchair accessible space, proper lighting, semi ambulatory services, focus on color, textures and materials for easy way finding, etc. In terms of building architecture, a barrier free built environment demands special consideration for dimensioning of building elements such as doorway width, corridor width, window heights, countertop height, etc. Larger building elements such as staircases and ramps also need to be designed in such a way that maneuvering them remains as effortless as possible for users from all categories. Toilets and kitchens need special emphasis in barrier free design as these are usually constricted spaces in conventional home designs. While all the aforementioned factors can help ease mobility within the house, an equal amount of emphasis is required to enhance visibility and lighting requirement for elderly users. Lighting is an element which can single handedly refine the health, mood and well-being of the elderly user group in senior living residences. Task lighting can enhance the experience that the elderly derives from day-to-day activities such as reading, crafting, etc. Furthermore, visual performance can also be an aid in ensuring safety for the senior residents.

One of the age friendly initiatives in the field of technology enabled geriatric design is the concept of IoT-enabled smart homes. Targeting the middle-class elderly population as its focus group, affordable housing retrofitted with critical social and health services bears the possibility of being a lifesaving initiative for the elderly. Also, simple architectural interventions such as providing a smooth textured and anti-slippery floor, tiny handy projections in the wall or in the furniture to balance, etc., can go a long way in making life easier for the elderly within their own homes. Recent literature in the field lists interventions for various spaces within the house such as seated workspace in kitchens, wheelchair friendly clearance spaces, ergonomic toilet seats, furniture, etc. Moreover, design of the macro scale community with green shared spaces can easily enhance the social quality of life for the elderly residents. At the community level, stipulated space for their daily workouts, food hubs and small-scale markets at the accessible limit can become active measures towards provision of a healthy, comfortable, and relaxed environment for the elderly.

6.1.1   Aim, Objectives, and Methodology

The study aims to propose a design prototype of IoT-enabled smart homes which can be adopted easily for cost effective construction of homes for the elderly. The prototype design may be utilized by individual homeowners, state housing boards, private developers, etc.

The objectives of the study are:

1. To study and design a cost-effective architectural module for elderly living which addresses their health, safety, and socio-cultural requirements.
2. To incorporate technology for health monitoring, safety, and communication solutions for elderly living.
3. To identify smart technologies that can facilitate energy efficient ease of living for the elderly.

The study roots itself in extensive secondary research on the available smart homes design for geriatric use around the world. A parallel study of assessment of needs of the elderly in the Indian context was carried out as an integral part of the study. The final proposal of IoT-enabled smart home design is an amalgamation of both architectural as well as technological inputs deemed necessary for comfortable geriatric living in the

Indian context. The study proposes a framework for architectural design and technological interventions along with a schematic design for a workable prototype.

6.1.2   Organization of Chapter

Section 6.2 focuses on the concept of smart homes in general and for senior living and the current scenario in India in the context of smart homes for the elderly. Section 6.3 is composed of detailed assessment of elderly behavior, socio cultural aspects and sustainable independent living requirements for elderly population in urban cities of India. A detailed framework for the study is also established in Section 6.3 with a step by step listing of the initiatives towards design of Smart homes for the elderly in the Indian context. The backdrop created in Section 6.3 becomes a firm base for proposing a Schematic design of an IoT-enabled smart home for the elderly including architectural, technological and sustainability aspects in Section 6.4. The final part of the chapter contains discussions about the proposed design of IoT-based smart homes for the elderly and their applications in the Indian scenario.

6.2   Background

6.2.1   Development of Smart Homes

One of the pioneering works in this area was the design of Smart Rooms implemented by the MIT Media Lab [2]. This has evolved from its initial design to its matured state of five networked smart rooms being further developed in the United States, Japan and the United Kingdom. According to De Silva *et al.* [4], there are three types of smart homes available for elderly. The first category supports detecting and recognizing their actions or by detecting their health conditions, with help of test beds. The second category involves storing and retrieving of multi-media captured within the smart home, in different levels from photos to experiences. But this typology may be sometimes seen as an intrusion into privacy of the individual and hence its acceptability remains to be seen. The third category is termed as supported surveillance, where the data captured in the environment is processed to obtain information that can help in raising alarms aimed at protection of the home and its residents from various extraneous threats such as burglaries, theft and natural disasters like flood etc. Various techniques including video, audio and multimodal based smart systems were employed to improve the accuracy of detection and tracking for the third category of smart homes. Vadakkepat *et al.* [5] as cited in De silva [3] addressed a scenario where robots are used to track and follow the elderly using multimodal techniques.

Video based Surveillance techniques including vision and head movement-based techniques are widely available in the home surveillance market. System setup with multiple movable and stationary cameras was employed and executed for human recognition and movement monitoring purpose by Vadakkepat *et al.* [5]. Sequencing the video clips based on the video surveillance to identify the routine event is necessary to predict and alert the unusual actions at site. But video-based surveillance has some shortfalls like occlusion, axis coverage of camera, etc., Hence, De Silva investigated on necessity and possibilities on usage of Audio and video based sensors for surveillance and fall detection, and progressed further to real-life data capture and analysis using multi-sensor integration. Multimedia sensors [3] were used by several researchers to study specific application-based targets.

Sensors installed in the homes can report in real time and store the data in offline memory for processing to address emergent situations in smart rooms. Mobile phone applications are widely available to control activities of a home from a remote location and to alert the user on unusual activities on the site [7]. However, existing infrastructure needs to be upgraded to install these systems in conventional homes.

6.2.2 Development of Smart Homes for Elderly

Smart homes for geriatric use are applications with demand levels growing at a very fast phase across the world. The innovative human detection and activity classification is required, several such techniques are currently being used for human detection using different sensory information. Detection of human presence is essential before processing the human activities like falling, standing, or walking, etc. [4]. The authors described an experiment that extends the distributive sensing approach to identify the three-dimensional location of an object in constant motion that can be applied to human activity detection in a smart home. In their study, they propose a novel system to measure balance or sway of a human. Aware Home Project is another such initiative for supporting elderly residents. Basic activities such as opening and closing of doors were recorded using switch-based sensors [6]. Vast research is currently being done in the field of energy efficient smart homes with aids such as smart switches and the same can be successfully deployed for geriatric house design as well [13].

Supporting healthcare in elderly homes based on daily routine, ambient assisted living (AAL) integrating Internet of things (IoT) was proposed in South Korea [8]. Preliminary prototype was developed an overview of developed by installing and integrating several sensors such as magnetic switches, infrared motion sensors and pressure sensitive mats to monitor the home environment and security in elderly homes. They proposed a four-tier alarm system based-on the severity of the detected anomalies. Another group of researchers studied the feasibility of integrating IoT with web-based services and cloud computing [9]. They installed actuators to control lights and fans as well as several sensors such as temperature, humidity, ambient light and proximity sensors to monitor home environment. Xu *et al.* [35] proposed the design and implementation of a mobile healthcare system (mHealth), particularly for wheelchair users. The design proposed a wearable HR and ECG sensor, which facilitates cardiovascular activity measurement along with mechanized systems installed in the wheelchair to monitor activity and detect falls in the elderly users. The researchers also developed an Android-based software interface to monitor and display the physiological signs as well as to control the home environment by activating the actuators. The software collaborates with a third-party service to send text messages and voice calls in case of an emergency. Similar studies were done across the globe for ambient living for elderly.

In an interesting study, Helal *et al.* [10] tested health platform technologies in two physical smart environments. Data from these employed physical layers was further analyzed to validate the lifestyle enhancement for individual with diabetes. Behr *et al.* [11] proposed and validated a model for employing lucrative technologies and neighborhood retrofit methods for low- to middle-income neighborhoods. Several research studies have proposed monitoring systems for psychological and neurological disorders in the elderly such as dementia, Alzheimer's syndrome, etc. Majumder *et al.* [12] introduced a smart home system which exploits the concept of Internet-of-Things and connects all sensors and systems of the home to facilitate remote surveillance of the occupant's health as well as the environment, safety and security of the home. Although several standalone systems such as vital sign monitoring, emergency call and reminding systems are available, a fully-fledged smart home is still far from the reality.

Focused research and development is required in this sector to develop a fully functional smart home. Some of the other important parameters to be looked into for geriatric design include energy-efficiency and low setup and maintenance cost. These factors are extremely important in order to make elderly living units truly sustainable for the user group. Low maintenance cost coupled with features promoting easy adaptability to support diverse lifestyles can increase the demand of geriatric homes. Today, technology has made it possible to integrate health monitoring systems into the built environment. Sensors and IoT-based technologies are fast replacing the need for human assistance and reliance on family for supporting the elderly in their daily activities. While technology as a paradigm needs to be seamlessly integrated with architectural design, focus on system reliability, privacy and data security, robustness of processing and prediction algorithms is also necessary to ensure that quality of life and privacy is not hampered in any way. Needless to add, all the above-mentioned interventions are highly dependent on seamless connectivity with minimal transmission delay. Access to high speed internet connectivity at affordable cost remains one of the biggest challenges in effective implementation of the smart home concept for the elderly population in developing countries such as India.

6.2.3   Indian Scenario

In India smart homes for the elderly is an emerging trend. Most of the options available in the market are international technology adopted homes which are found in urban areas. The adoption of technology led solutions often hinges on uninterrupted internet services and power supply which continue to be a challenge in the country. Furthermore, most of the solutions are tailored for a western lifestyle and detailed study of the lifestyle and behavior in the India context is not evidential. An understanding of the same can aid in development of architectural design that can customize the IoT-enabled smart homes to Indian conditions.

Senior living communities are a new concept for India [31]. A few senior living communities with homes designed for self-independent living are coming up in various parts of India in response to the changing social structure [32–34]. One of the successful examples of senior living community in the city of Bangalore is the Suvidha Retirement community [29] located on the outskirts of the city. Built in 2004, this assisted living facility was built on a plot of 30 acres and was designed by Architect Krishnarao Jaisim. A total of 200 cottages have been designed spread across two BHK and 3 BHK typologies. The age friendly design philosophy of the architect follows the mantra of "Active ageing", whereby walking tracks, long winding ramps and easy accessibility to cottages encourage the residents to lead an active lifestyle at the community. The dwelling units have compact living-dining cum kitchenettes along with private rooms as per the typology. An open layout plan with ample space for wheelchair access makes the cottages ideal for use by the elderly users.

Another example of senior living home is the Covai, Tapovan Solace homes [30] located in Mysore. Spread over 1.8 acres, the community houses 72 senior living homes. The facility offers homes across 3 BHK, 2 BHK and one-bedroom typologies. Once again open plan layouts are used to ensure easy access for wheelchair users. The building community seeks to enhance the internal ambience by use of large courtyards which are used as community spaces as well.

As seen in most of the best-case examples of senior living homes in India, we observe that most of the initiatives for easy senior living are implemented at the community level rather than at the dwelling unit level. In the case of both Suvidha and Tapovan homes, the community design offers the services of large multipurpose halls, dining facilities, recreational spaces and interaction nodes for the elderly residents. However, it may also be noted that most of the architects and builders shy away from providing differentiated design features for the homes. The various typologies of dwelling units observed in the case studies are not much different from typical dwelling units seen in housing communities built for generic use. Furthermore, inclusion of technological interventions to make assisted living easier is still quite rare in India. While IoT-based technologies in form of voice command enabled services for home automation are gaining traction in the regular housing market in Indian cities, design for senior living continues within the conventional framework.

6.3 Need for Smart Homes: An Assessment of Requirements for the Elderly-Activity Mapping

In a developing country such as India, there is a huge gap between volume of ageing population and the supply of elderly care facilities. On a familial level, most nuclear families struggle with establishing a balance between childcare and home care for the elderly. An increased stress on education coupled with globalization opportunities persuades people to move out of country for study, job and even permanent abode. In such a scenario, care for the elderly left behind in India is left to hired care workers who are often untrained for the job. Of late, many cases of abuse of invalid seniors have been reported in the media. Due to this crisis, many senior citizens have been reported to suffer from depression and other associated psychological ailments. Faced with an apathetic system and absolute lack of emergency medical and care facilities has indeed proved to be fatal and life threatening for many senior citizens [13].

Living in traditional houses usually suits the ethnicity and cultural lifestyle of the elderly. However, traditional house plans are often known to be inefficient for elderly use as represented by the numerous cases of spine and bone injury reported due to falls at home. In order to promote a safe and healthy lifestyle for the elderly, it is important to design a smart home specifically for their convenience. Smart homes can enhance their lifestyle, promote easy communication with their family and friends and relatives, monitor their health and support an independent lifestyle for the elderly [14].

6.3.1   Geriatric Smart Home Design: The Indian Context

Most of the research studies available in this discipline are rooted in the western world. Transplanting the same design into the Indian context carries the perils of overlooking the lifestyle preferences and socio-cultural ethos of the region. A lifestyle study of the Indian community is essential to develop a smart home prototype. It may be recalled at this point that most of the senior citizens in India at this point have spent the prime of their lives in the decades of 1970–1980s. Multifamily apartment living was quite a foreign concept in that era. Urban Middle class Indian homes were typified in plotted developments with reasonable amount of open space in form of internal courtyards, open verandas, open backyards, etc. where many domestic activities would be carried out. A close-knit community structure reinforced with active interaction at the community level was an important part of the Indian lifestyle and way of living. The advent of apartment living in urban areas has deprived Indian homes of the traditional interactive open spaces such as courtyards and verandahs, causing distress to the elderly who are forced to spend most of their day indoors owing to physical and health limitations. With this background, a study of spatially linked activities in a typical Indian home occupied by the elderly was carried out (Table 6.1).

6.3.2   Elderly Activity Mapping

A glance at the compilation above reflects that the living, dining, courtyard, bedroom, terrace, etc. are the primary zones in the house occupied by the elderly through the day. Unfortunately, modern compact living concepts do not allow for the benefits of the courtyard and terrace leading

Table 6.1 Elderly activity mapping source: authors (based on primary interviews).

Activity VS Spaces	Drawing room	Living	Dining	Pooja	Courtyard	Kitchen	Bedroom	Toilet	Balcony/Sit out	Backyard	Terrace	Out of home
On call Communication	★	★				★	★	★	★		★	
Washing					★	★		★				
Fresh up										★		
Drink	★	★			★	★	★		★			
Breakfast		★	★									
Lunch		★	★			★						
Dinner		★	★			★						
Snack	★	★	★			★			★			
Food preparation			★		★	★						
Walking/Exercise/Yoga												
YOGA/Exercise		★			★						★	
Cleaning	★	★	★		★	★	★	★		★	★	
Gardening									★	★	★	
Watching TV		★					★					

(Continued)

Table 6.1 Elderly Activity Mapping SOURCE: Authors (Based On Primary Interviews). (*Continued*)

Activity VS Spaces	Drawing room	Living	Dining	Pooja	Courtyard	Kitchen	Bedroom	Toilet	Balcony/Sit out	Backyard	Terrace	Out of home
Mobile/Ipad	★ ☆	★ ☆	★ ☆			★ ☆	★ ☆		★ ☆		★ ☆	
Relaxation	★ ☆		★ ☆		★ ☆		★ ☆		★ ☆		★ ☆	
Socializing with close circle	★ ☆	★										
Socializing with acquaintance		★ ☆		★ ☆	★ ☆							
Religious activity (indoor)		★ ☆			★ ☆							
Religious activity (outdoor)							★ ☆					
Nap time		★ ☆										
Bedtime		★ ☆					★ ☆					
Shopping (Small Retail)												★ ☆
Medical check												★ ☆

*Male ★
*Female ☆

to transferring of activities traditionally carried out in these spaces to the already overused living and dining spaces.

In addition to space preference for daily activities, old age also brings with itself limitations and issues in form of physical, emotional and communal factors which are necessary for a decent quality of life. A compilation of the issues faced by the elderly is given in Table 6.2 below.

From the point of view of architectural and space design, most of the issues listed above can be dealt with in varying measures using interventions at the community, residence, interior design, and furniture/fittings design level. At the community level, well designed barrier free landscape, ease of access to small retail, fall free walkways with support in form of

Table 6.2 Issues faced by the elderly in the Indian context.

Physical	Emotional/lifestyle related	Communal
Reduced mobility	Isolation/loneliness	Reduced interaction with friends and family
Difficulty in way finding	Technological challenge	Lack of social engagements
Loss of vision/hearing	Dietary preferences/ restrictions	
Poor memory	Reduced stamina to carry out daily chores	
Delayed reflex action	Low self esteem	
Poor motor control		
Physical weakness		
Urinary incontinence/ frequent trips to the washroom		
Reduced immunity/ increased susceptibility to infections and disease		
Obesity		

handrails and opportunity for intimate as well as community level social interaction can help make life better for the elderly. However, the major challenge lies in the design of the residence itself where space utilization and efficiency need to be balanced with the various requirements of the elderly.

6.3.3   Framework for Smart Homes for Elderly People

Review of literature as well as an analysis of issues and daily activities of the elderly in the Indian context [16] has given us a broad framework of inputs required for a schematic design of smart homes for the Indian geriatric population. The framework is represented in the diagram below—Figure 6.1.

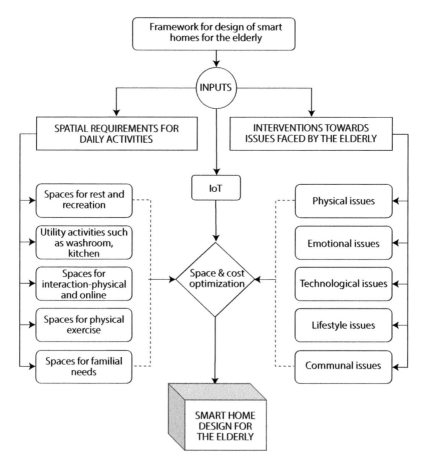

Figure 6.1 Framework for design of smart homes for the elderly.

6.3.4   Architectural Interventions: Spatial Requirements for Daily Activities

An analysis of daily activities of the elderly in the Indian context has suggested that the elderly spend most of their time during the day in the living dining area except when taking an afternoon nap. The living dining area in an Indian home is a space which has multiple uses as it transforms from a space to entertain guests to a space of personal relaxation with activities such as watching TV or for animated discussions within the family. The dining space in an Indian home is often the space where activities of the kitchen, family space and living space spill over as it becomes an informal version of the more formal living room. Literature suggests the provision of open plans as fit for elderly living to support ease of way finding and unobstructed and easy single directional movement as an intervention towards elderly mobility issues.

Based on the above a new scheme for home design is proposed. *Nesting home* is a new concept proposed in the specific context of elderly living rooted in the Indian socio-cultural setting. The nesting home is proposed as an open plan multipurpose space which has the advantages of both modularity and flexibility. The modularity feature can help in clustering of individual units to create a community of retirement homes with adequately designed open spaces and communal activity nodes.

The flexibility feature targets one of the most important issues of the Indian familial setting viz. the need for extra space and privacy for large extended family during certain times in the year. It has been observed that most elderly people in India are still highly connected and emotionally dependent on their family and kin and as such interactions with the family is an emotional as well as a spatial need of the elderly in the Indian context. Conversely, it is also true that most senior citizens find it difficult to maintain and negotiate large homes with multiple rooms on a day to day basis. This dilemma of space requirement can be easily resolved with the inbuilt flexibility feature of nesting homes.

A *nesting home* is visualized as a large single space open plan unit with minimal walls placed only for washrooms and utility space in the interest of privacy and hygiene. The rest of the house operates as one single space with minimal obstructions to movement. As per the requirement the large single space may be partitioned into private rooms to be of use when family visits or when guest are invited over to the house.

Another feature tailored to the Indian context would be the provision of open space within the house in form of well-lit atrium spaces with skylight feature above to ensure that the home is well lit and is culturally in sync with the requirements of Indian traditional living.

Some of the additional features of nesting homes which would customize them for geriatric use would include:

1. Anti-skid surfaces to avoid falls and accidents.
2. Use of minimal walls to keep the space free for movement.
3. Use of fixed furniture/furniture attached to the wall/floor surface to prevent accidents.
4. Provision of low height cabinetry, drawers and wardrobes to allow easy access for wheelchair users.
5. Safe kitchen with easy to maintain/self-cleansing surfaces and easy access storage spaces.
6. Provision of safety rails in areas such as kitchens, pooja, washrooms wherever there is frequent transition of postures due to nature of daily activities.
7. Provision of adequate natural light to aid in visibility without the use of artificial lights.
8. Energy saving components to minimize the heating/cooling loads within the home and to make the house easy to maintain.

6.3.5   Architectural Interventions to Address Issues Faced by Elderly People

The nesting homes will be designed with features that specifically address the issues faced by the elderly in the physical, lifestyle, emotional and communal realms. A brief compilation of the interventions is given in Table 6.3 below.

6.4   Schematic Design for a Nesting Home: IoT-Enabled Smart Home for Elderly People

6.4.1   IoT-Based Real Time Automation for Nesting Homes

One of the path breaking developments in the area of automated smart homes is the focus on real time monitoring and assessment as an alternative to human assisted geriatric care. Puri & Nayyar [18] propose a Novel Cost Effective cum Efficient home automation system implemented using an Android App titled "Smart Home Control". Such cost-effective mechanisms

Table 6.3 Nesting homes: interventions for issues faced by the elderly in the Indian context.

Nesting Homes: Interventions for Issues faced by the elderly in the Indian context					
Physical	Interventions	Emotional/lifestyle related/technological	Interventions	Communal	Interventions
Reduced mobility	Wheelchair friendly clearance/torque sensor	Isolation/loneliness	Voice assistance	Reduced interaction with friends and family	Social media or frequent calls/Communal spaces
Difficulty in way finding	Ultrasonic feet detector sensor	Technological challenge	User friendly app	Lack of social engagements	Community gathering spaces
Loss of vision/hearing	Torque sensor with vibration alert	Dietary preferences/restrictions	App to support and prompt		
Poor memory	Memory wall	Reduced stamina to carry out daily chores	Smart households		
Delayed reflex action	Anti-skid tiles and finishes; avoid loose furniture and furnishings				

(Continued)

Table 6.3 Nesting homes: interventions for issues faced by the elderly in the Indian context. (*Continued*)

Nesting Homes: Interventions for Issues faced by the elderly in the Indian context					
Physical	Interventions	Emotional/ lifestyle related/ technological	Interventions	Communal	Interventions
Poor motor control	Large sized handles and fittings				
Physical weakness	Height adjustment for cabinetry				
Urinary incontinence/ frequent trips to the washroom	Regular prompting device/alarm				
Reduced immunity/ increased susceptibility to infections and disease	Self-cleansing surfaces				
Obesity	Space for workout				

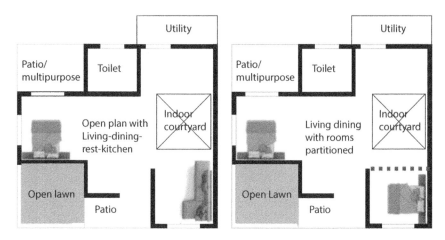

Figure 6.2 Schematic design for Nesting Homes.

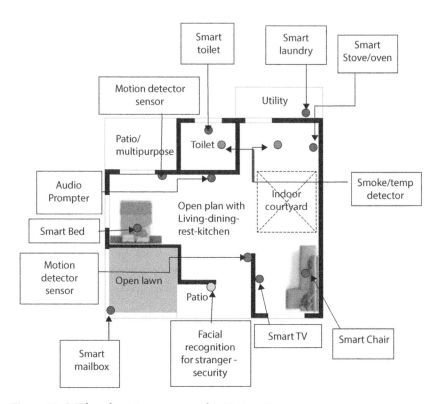

Figure 6.3 IoT-based provisions proposed in Nesting Homes.

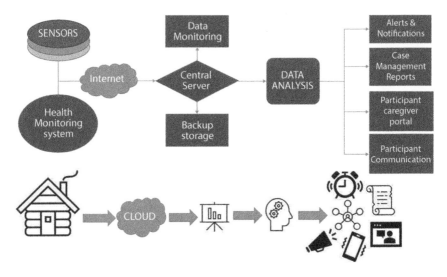

Figure 6.4 Comprehensive health monitoring system integrated in nesting homes.

can become the new ways of monitoring elderly health on a daily basis and can also assist in generating alarms and notifying health professional and family during medical emergencies. Most of the home automation systems rely on Bluetooth technology which can be easily integrated with the various sensors installed in the nesting homes prototype proposed here (Figures 6.2 & 6.3). The comprehensive health monitoring systems can help in generating case management reports and enable constant contact with the participant caregiver portals. Easy and quick communication enabled by real time systems can be an active tool towards securing health and longevity for the elderly population in developing countries such as India.

The IoT-based interventions may be considered to be a part of an integrated health monitoring system whereby data is collected and processed to activate a comprehensive system of elderly care. The nesting home in this case becomes an active tool towards monitoring and reporting on the health of its resident. The diagram below (Figure 6.4) gives a brief insight into the IoT-based health monitoring system that can be an active part of the smart home design.

6.4.2   Technological Components of Elderly Smart Homes

6.4.2.1   Sensors for Smart Home

Smart homes are the way to the future. Motion sensors are a popular tool in smart homes which allow the reduction of human interventions in monitoring the usage of space and to curb unwanted usage of lights, fans and electrical appliances. Energy efficient IoT, also refereed to Green IoT is being proposed to emphasize the energy efficiency component in Internet of things-based technologies [25]. Some of the applications of green IoT include services such as alerts on the usage of energy based on humidity and temperature sensors and connected to the air-conditioning systems at home. Remote controls, digital controls are employed in managing kitchen appliances and HVAC, Heating systems, video audio appliances. Smart home companies like NEST, ECOBEE and AUGUST are shaping future homes to deliver Smart living in the residential sector [23]. Occupancy Sensors can be installed in chair, bed, toilet seat to be set with their routine time coding and thus it can alarm/alert for assistance on their delayed routine [26].

Home security surveillance systems hold great assistive value for elderly residents. Video door entry system to warrant the strangers' entry and to give access to the visitors with remotely operated door access is one such feature that can be integrated into the smart Nesting homes. Use of robotics to reduce their workload is also advisable as a future intervention. Smart home functionalities can be extended or customized based on affordability, adaptability and user requirements.

6.4.2.2   Health Monitoring System

Wearable Watches, Wrist Bands and Chip implants are already launched by Google, Samsung, etc., which can track the daily routine, fitness care and alert critical situations and conditions [22]. Such interventions begin to acquire greater significance when we reimagine their application in the realm of elderly care and health monitoring [16, 17]. The sensors and software in such devices can collect vital data of the elderly user. Medical investigation document and reports from healthcare specialist's portal can also be linked for sending regular updates to their caregivers or family members who may be staying in different locations.

6.4.2.3   Network Devices

Network devices like Bluetooth, IR, ZigBee, Z-Wave, NFC, Wi-Fi can be used to connect the devices and to compute the data and send alerts [28]. IoT devices generate enormous amounts of data for ordered processing. Usually we imagine the use of these technologies based on cloud-based networks. However, the use of fog networking can improve the efficiency of these systems. Layering based on Fog computing is necessary to avoid false alarm rate reduction. Mobile-based Emergency help alert systems with usage of Fog computing technology can also access stored contact information for ambulance services, etc. [24]. Thus, fog computing system can be alternative to cloud as it gives individual attention to the sorted data.

6.4.2.4 Alerts

Reminders and notifications with human voice alerts like, Alexa, Siri, OK Google can be inbuilt into smart nesting homes as they can help in providing an interactive environment for the elderly. Alerts like reminders for mail, call, calendar events can also be set up as an integrated home alerts system. Security monitoring like water overflow, fire alerts are also important aspects from the point of view of day to day maintenance of home utilities. To make the alarm system more easily accessible, we can employ personal alarms using pendant or chain locket, pull cords, and button/ switches at respective accessible locations. These can also be programmed to pass on the alarm to an external response center in case of an emergency. Medical alerts like health summary data of the elderly can also be sent to their care givers, local guardian and their children staying away to for easy remote monitoring.

6.5 Worldwide Elderly Smart Homes

The function of smart homes could be largely extended to satisfy needs of older people, who seek to live as independently as they can in the comfort of their home. This is a manifestation of the multi-functionality of smart homes, which implies diversity as well as flexibility in functions. Numerous projects involving smart home technologies for older people have been launched worldwide, with a view to reducing the level of dependency and increasing the safety of older adults [14]. Elderly supportive smart home technologies have been set up worldwide, in view of reducing their dependency on others and to ensure their safety, security aspects. Some of the best case examples of the same include the Welfare Techno-house Project in Japan (1995), assisted interactive dwelling house in UK (1996), Aware Home in the US (1999), Health Integrated Smart Home Information System in France (2002), Tiger Place in the US (2003), Gator Tech Smart House in the US (2004) and ROBOCARE Domestic Environment in Italy (2007). These feedbacks received from these projects was analyzed and reported to have a positive impact on the physical and mental health of the geriatric users. The studies also reflected that smart monitoring systems can help in swift and easy detection of health issues thereby ensuring early medical care and solutions to aid the longevity and quality of life of the elderly users [21]. Outcomes from these smart home projects have been reported to be positive in extending the length of community residence, enhancing physical and mental health status, delaying the onset of serious health problems and reducing the strain on family and care givers [9]. With favorable findings on their effectiveness, smart home technologies have enabled of continuous monitoring, psycho-social benefits and overall sense of wellbeing for older adult users.

6.5.1   Challenges in Smart Elderly Homes

During initial stages of technology installation, it is common to find the elderly struggle with adapting to the gadgets. Such usage related issues including adaptability and continued usage of technology are inevitable for the older generation users. Regular practice and user-friendly design can help make the same easier for the elderly users. Sustainable usage is also an important point to be kept in mind in implementation of these smart technologies for domestic use.

There is a need to upgrade existing homes as well with new sensors, new interaction techniques using effective and ubiquitous computing techniques. Alongside, the social, environmental, and cultural context needs to be considered while customizing the same to the regional and local context. IoT-connected devices has many advantages and ease of usage, on the other hand it has few threats in terms of security issues [20].

One of the main limitations of such smart data collection and storage technologies is the threat posed to individual privacy. Since the data is stored online it increases the vulnerability of users to malicious acts such as Spying on daily movements and hacking into personal medical information. In most situations, users may not have the knowledge and expertise to appreciate the risks and protect themselves. This becomes a major limitation of the IoT-based devices. Manwaring & Clarke [19] have recorded that Australia proposes a 'Co-regulatory approach' which is a combined approach of robust efforts industry, government, and community input. It includes laws that create incentives for compliance and regulatory oversight by an independent and well-resourced protector or guardian. Furthermore, detailed survey and research is required in the field to ensure strengthened security and to make the technology viable and foolproof for use by the masses.

6.6   Conclusion and Future Scope

The schematic design and IoT-based system proposed above in form of *Nesting homes* can become an active prototype towards technology enabled elderly care in the Indian context. As the world embraces the idea of inclusive universal design principles, architectural design in developing countries also needs to adapt itself towards providing customized solutions for the needs of all sections of the demographic chain.

The elderly community can benefit vastly through the implementation of the smart home design as it would provide them with the liberty of independent living along with the assuredness of health monitoring and care during times of need. Overall, the nesting home design prototype can be an effective step towards improving the quality of life of the elderly in the country. From an economic point of view, early adoption of nesting home features can help save the unnecessary cost of moving or retrofitting usually required to make homes friendlier for geriatric use.

Development of cost-effective prototypes using low impact building materials and a renewed focus on life cycle cost optimization of nesting homes can be an important stream for future research in this field. Another challenge that the user group usually faces is an inherent hesitance to rely on technology and difficulties in operating mobile phone home automation apps. Future research in the direction of Elderly friendly user interface for the IoT-based apps and a sensitization programme among the user groups can help to bring the smart home technology into real world use and practice.

References

1. Elderly in India, Central Statistics Office, Ministry of Statistics and Programme Implementation, India, 2016, http://mospi.nic.in/sites/default/files/publication_reports/ElderlyinIndia_2016.pdf.
2. Pentland, A.P., Smart Rooms. *Sci. Am.*, 274, 4, 68–76, 1996.
3. De Silva, L.C., Audiovisual sensing of human movements for home-care and security in a smart environment. *Int. J. Smart Sens. Intell. Syst.*, 1, 1, 220–45, 2008, https://doi.org/10.21307/ijssis-2017-288.
4. De Silva, L.C., Morikawa, C., Petra, I.M., State of the art of smart homes. *Eng. Appl. Artif. Intell.*, 25, 7, 1313–1321, 2012, https://doi.org/10.1016/j.engappai.2012.05.002.
5. Vadakkepat, P., Lim, P., De Silva, L.C., Jing, L., Ling, L.L., Multimodal approach to human-face detection and tracking. *IEEE Trans. Ind. Electron.*, 55, 3, 1385–1393, 2008, https://doi.org/10.1109/TIE.2007.903993.

6. Abowd, G., Bobick, A., Essa, I., Mynatt, E., Rogers, W., The Aware Home: A living laboratory for technologies for successful aging, AAAI Technical Report WS-02-02, 2002, https://www.researchgate.net/publication/237132095_The_Aware_Home_A_living_laboratory_for_technologies_for_successful_aging.

7. Ogawa, M. and Togawa, T., Monitoring daily activities and behaviors at home by using brief sensors. *1st Annual International IEEE-EMBS Special Topic Conference on Microtechnologies in Medicine and Biology. Proceedings (Cat. No.00EX451)*, Lyon, France, pp. 611–614, 2000.

8. Choi, D., Choi, H., Shon, D., Future changes to smart home based on AAL healthcare service. *J. Asian Architect. Build. Eng.*, 18, 3, 190–199, 2019.

9. Wang, S., Skubic, M., Zhu, Y., Activity Density Map Visualization and Dissimilarity Comparison for Eldercare Monitoring. *IEEE Trans. Inf. Technol. Biomed.*, 16, 4, 607–614, 2012.

10. Helal, A., Cook, D.J., Schmalz, M., Smart home-based health platform for behavioral monitoring and alteration of diabetes patients. *J. Diabetes Sci. Technol.*, 3, 1, 141–148, 2009, https://doi.org/10.1177/193229680900300115.

11. Behr, R., Sciegaj, M., Walters, R., Bertoty, J., Dungan, R., Addressing the Housing Challenges of an Aging Population: Initiatives by Blueroof Technologies in McKeesport, Pennsylvania. *J. Archit. Eng.*, 17, 4, 162–169, 2011, https://ascelibrary.org/doi/pdf/10.1061/%28ASCE%29AE.1943-5568.0000033.

12. Majumder, S., Aghayi, E., Noferesti, M., Memarzadeh-Tehran, H., Mondal, T., Pang, Z., Deen, M.J., Smart Homes for Elderly Healthcare—Recent Advances and Research Challenges. *Sensors*, 17, 2496, 2017.

13. Yu, L., Research on smart homes for the elderly, School of Computer Science, University of Birmingham, UK, 2018, https://www.cs.bham.ac.uk/~rjh/courses/ResearchTopicsInHCI/2017-18/Coursework/yuliangye.pdf cited as on 15/07/2020.

14. Singh, D., Kropf, J., Hanke, S., Holzinger, A., Ambient Assisted Living Technologies from the Perspectives of Older People and Professionals, in: *Machine Learning and Knowledge Extraction, CD-MAKE 2017*, Lecture Notes in Computer Science, vol. 10410, A. Holzinger, P. Kieseberg, A. Tjoa, E. Weippl, (Eds.), Springer, Cham, https://doi.org/10.1007/978-3-319-66808-6_17, 2017.

15. *Long-term Care of Older Persons in India*, SDD-SPPS Project Working Papers Series, UNESCAP and SDD, Bangkok, 2016. https://www.unescap.org/sites/default/files/SDD%20Working%20Paper%20Ageing%20Long%20Term%20Care%20India%20v1-2.pdf cited as on 15/07/2020.

16. Gupta, R., Systems Perspective: Understanding Care Giving of the Elderly in India. *J. Health Care Women Int.*, 30, 12, 1040–56, 2009, https://doi.org/10.1080/07399330903199334.

17. Yu, J., An, N., Hassan, Md T., Kong, Q., A Pilot Study on a Smart Home for Elders Based on Continuous In-Home Unobtrusive Monitoring Technology. *HERD: Health Environments Research & Design Journal*, 12, 2, 206–219, 2019.

18. Puri, V. and Nayyar, A., Real time smart home automation based on PIC microcontroller, Bluetooth and Android technology, in: *2016 3rd International Conference on Computing for Sustainable Global Development (INDIACom)*, IEEE, pp. 1478–1484, 2016.

19. Manwaring, K. and Clarke, R., Are your devices spying on you? Australia's very small step to make the Internet of Things safer, The Conversation, Australia, 2020, https://theconversation.com/are-your-devices-spying-on-you-australias-very-small-step-to-make-the-internet-of-things-safer-145554.

20. Krishnamurthi, R., Nayyar, A., Solanki, A., *Innovation Opportunities through Internet of Things (IoT) for Smart Cities. Green and Smart Technologies for Smart Cities*, pp. 261–292, CRC Press, Boca Raton, FL, USA, 2019.

21. Le, Q., Nguyen, H.B., Barnett, T., Smart Homes for Older People: Positive Aging in a Digital World. *Future Internet*, 4, 607–617, 2012.

22. Nayyar, A. and Puri, V., Data glove: Internet of things (IoT) based smart wearable gadget. *J. Adv. Math. Comput. Sci.*, 15, 1–12, 2016.

23. Rathee, D., Ahuja, K., Nayyar, A., Sustainable future IoT services with touch-enabled handheld devices, in: *Security and Privacy of Electronic Healthcare Records: Concepts, Paradigms and Solutions*, p. 131, 2019.

24. Singh, S.P., Nayyar, A., Kumar, R., Sharma, A., Fog computing: from architecture to edge computing and big data processing. *J. Supercomput.*, 75, 4, 2070–2105, 2019.

25. Solanki, A. and Nayyar, A., Green internet of things (G-IoT): ICT technologies, principles, applications, projects, and challenges, in: *Handbook of Research on Big Data and the IoT*, pp. 379–405, IGI Global, USA, 2019.

26. Tan, H.C.C. and De Silva, L.C., Human activity recognition by head movement using Elman network and Neuro-Markovian hybrids. *Proceedings of Image and Vision Computing New Zealand (IVCNZ 2003)*, Massey University, Palmerston North, New Zealand, pp. 320–326, 2003.

27. *UNFPA India Data Overview*, United Nation population Fund, https://www.unfpa.org/data/IN, 2020.

28. Ullah, F., Al-Turjman, F., Nayyar, A., IoT-based green city architecture using secured and sustainable android services. *Environ. Technol. Innovation*, 20, 101091, 2020.

29. https://www.suvidha.co.in/ accessed on 13.09.2020.

30. https://www.covaicare.com/ accessed on 13.09.2020.

31. Roy, L.D., Forget Old-Age Homes, How India's Senior Citizens Are Giving Life A Golden Lining, Outlook Magazine, India, 13 May 2019, https://magazine.outlookindia.com/story/business-news-forget-old-age-homes-how-indias-senior-citizens-are-giving-life-a-golden-lining/301536 accessed on13.09.2020.

32. Yadav, S., *Why India's elderly are moving to retirement homes*, BBC Hindi, Bangalore, 5 July 2013, https://www.bbc.com/news/world-asia-india-23176206 accessed on 13.0.2020.

33. Sharma, A.K., Senior living societies a home away from home for elderly, Livemint, India, 12 November 2018, https://www.livemint.com/Money/ApoKwqu9CBJ4aZxX0gmh3M/Retirememt-homes-India-Senior-living-societies-a-home-away.html accessed on 13.09.2020.
34. Gupta, A., How retirement homes ensure care and comfort to members amid Covid-19, Hindustan times, India, May 20, 2020, https://www.hindustantimes.com/more-lifestyle/how-retirement-homes-ensure-care-and-comfort-to-members-amid-covid-19/story-2edeSnbammxYSO1N-TUmOKM.html accessed on 13.09.2020.
35. Xu, B., Xu, L., Cai, H., Jiang, L., Luo, Y., Gu, Y., The design of an m-Health monitoring system based on a cloud computing platform. *Enterp. Inf. Syst.*, 11, 1, 17–36, 2017.

7

Sustainable E-Infrastructure for Blockchain-Based Voting System

Mukta Goyal[1] and Adarsh Kumar[2]*

[1]Department of Computer Science and Engineering, Jaypee Institute of Information Technology, Noida, India
[2]Department of Systemics, School of Computer Science, University of Petroleum and Energy Studies, Dehradun, India

Abstract

Blockchain, a distributed ledger, is helpful in maintain data for immutable records. It is helpful for both data recording and updation. In this work, we have used blockchain technology to implement an electronic voting system. E-voting can change the way of voting that we did for decades. It can help Indian citizens to use their power of vote effectively and efficiently to create the government of India, now there is no reason for standing in such a large row, and waiting for your turn in the voting booth you can now vote from anywhere. Through this system, the Indian Government can organize the whole election over the digital platform. All the Election organized by the Election Commission of India would be created on the digital platform through DApp and Candidates can also file their nomination for any election they want then further Organizers have the right to approve or reject the request. The main feature of this system is that voters can cast their vote from anywhere in the world as this voting process goes digital and online the Voter from outside the country can also vote from wherever they are, it can tremendously increase the total voting percentages. As this E-voting is powered by Blockchain technology, so it is completely secure and authorizes the system and the most important features are that this system is Portable, Transparent, Reliable, Easy to Use, Trustable and Fast. This system is an initiative in the way of making Election system more secure and hassle free and transparent for everyone.

Keywords: Blockchain, e-voting, optimization, smart city, sustainable infrastructure

*Corresponding author: adarsh.kumar@ddn.upes.ac.in

Arun Solanki, Adarsh Kumar and Anand Nayyar (eds.) Digital Cities Roadmap: IoT-Based Architecture and Sustainable Buildings, (221–252) © 2021 Scrivener Publishing LLC

7.1　Introduction

Blockchain was employed for financial transactions and commerce, but now Blockchain finds its application in various regions be it governance, healthcare, banking system, etc. The main reason for this widespread use is the transparency that comes with it [1–6]. Being a decentralized system, it gives every participant the access to every transaction made. Ever since our country became a democratic country, voting has been done via conventional methods, mainly ballot paper based voting. A voter's participation is only limited to voting. once voted, he/she cannot verify if his/her vote has been tampered with. Also, with every system using a digital platform to enhance their work, it's time to conduct voting using digital means as well. However, security risks in digital methods are high. Voting requires a lot of confidential data, which can be at risk of a cyber attack on any digital platform. Here, blockchain can play an important role. Blockchain is a distributed ledger, based on the architecture of cryptocurrency. Since it is a decentralized system, it is difficult for any hacker to manipulate any data. A voter's participation does not just end at voting [7–12]. They can verify if their vote was recorded correctly or not. Since a copy of each transaction exists with every block. It becomes very difficult for anyone to manipulate any data. Every transaction is secured using a public and private key, reducing the risk of cyber attacks.

Voting has always been done using a centralized system in our country. A handful of people manage the decisions made by the entire country, who can be influenced to tamper the results. With the current voting system, the voters have no power to check its authenticity. We, as a voter, have no means to ensure that there was no malpractice in the system or if any extra, unfair votes were added [13, 14]. Problems encountered during the usual elections are as follows: It requires a lot of manual labor, in tallying the votes that makes the elections time consuming and prone to human error. It is difficult for people to live away from the address in their voter id, to vote. It is less cost effective as well. Extra, unfair votes can be added too as there is no proper authentication. EVM are not secure as Blockchain. Voting process takes too much time and that is inconvenient for people especially elder ones. It requires too much cost for arranging Booth camps over the entire country or states. Proxy voting is used during current voting systems that might be risky.

The problems that can be solved using blockchain based e-voting system are [15–22]:

- Accuracy: It is not possible for a vote to be altered, eliminated by anyone other than the voter.

- Democracy: It permits only eligible voters to vote, only once.
- Privacy: Each vote is converted into a hash to main privacy.
- Verifiability: Each transaction (vote) is verified by all the blocks.
- Resistance: No person can add unverified votes or stop anyone from going to the polling booth, as voting can be done from anywhere.
- Availability: Every poll has a time limit, and any voter can vote within the limit.

Estonia used an internet-based voting system from 2005 to 2014. It was the first country to implement a blockchain based voting system in their local municipal voting system in 2013 [7, 23–29]. The system used RSA-based encryption. The system provided end-to-end verification where not only the organizer, but the voter too could verify if his/her vote was recorded successfully or not. Anyone could verify the counts of vote due to the distributive ledger property of the system [7]. However it was easy to implement such a system in Estonia due to its small population. Another such implementation was Open Vote Network [8], which can be used for boardroom meetings. It is written as a smart contract using Ethereum and is a decentralized system and self-tallying [8], i.e., no third party is required to tally the number of votes. It ensures privacy to the voters. Digital Voting with the use of Blockchain Technology [1, 30–35] was proposed by a Plymouth University, United Kingdom team. With the help with this system a voter can go to a polling booth in his area and use it to cast his vote or he can do it using a web browser at home. A voting system requires three categories of participants: Organizers, Candidate and Voters. Each participant will use the system differently, hence will have different requirements. Organizers are the users who organize the elections or start the election by initializing the election with the opening of the candidate registration process and declare the election result date and voting date. Candidates are the users or stakeholder who can nominate themselves for the participate in the election by providing the information or details to the election committee or election organizer by sending the approval request to the election committee or election organizer. Then later-on, if everything is accurate as per requirements then the organizer will approve the request. After approval of the request the candidate is listed on the election poll [36–41]. Voter are the users or stakeholder who can cast the vote by authenticate themselves with their documents and then they are able to cast their vote to their nominated candidate in the election.

7.1.1   E-Voting Challenge

Traditional E-voting system may face following problems [42–49]:

- EVM are not secure as Blockchain.
- Voting process takes too much time and that is inconvenient for people especially elder ones.
- It requires too much cost for arranging a Booth camps over the entire country or states.
- Proxy Voting are used during current voting system that are might be risky. Decreasing amount of vote counts.
- It is too time consuming.
- No analytical data collected and manage after the election.

Blockchain technology can address problems seeing strategies mentioned in the section and earn more protected, simpler, and e-voting cheaper to execute. It's a new paradigm which could help form decentralized systems, which guarantee fault tolerance, availability, and the information integrity. Some say that "this blockchain technology is bringing the Web of significance: a brand fresh, distributed platform which may help us all over the area of business and alter the old arrangement of human affairs to the better" [50–55]. This technology intends to re-evaluate these systems. The blockchain systems have been shaped as unmanned methods of computers that can be used for documenting and supporting the pure trades. They comprise ledgers known as the blockchain. The documents around the blockchains are immutable.

This work is organized as follows. Section 7.2 presents the state-of-the art work associated with the proposed system development. Section 7.3 shows the system model and use case diagrams for E-voting system using blockchain technology. Section 7.4 shows the implementation aspects and results. Section 7.5 highlights blockchain creation and integration of smart contracts. Section 7.6 concludes the chapter with future scope.

7.2   Related Works

Blockchain is a technology which has emerged with this Bitcoin's look, which has included a new means of coping [15]. Dependent on the technique with the concept of Bitcoin's success, the procedure implemented in actions, whether private or governmental and was relied upon and obtained satisfaction and the assurance of consumers. The newspaper highlights the challenges ahead and chances in this Modern technology that's all set to create our electronic world. This newspaper has discussed blockchain engineering alongside a number of its significant benefits. The technology is advancing with a great deal of areas for businesses and various places and can be set to alter the planet's manner. Nonetheless, it isn't free of challenges, a number of them happen to be emphasized.

This paper addresses the shortcomings of keeping Aadhaar data at a database. Applying this technology the info would be saved in a fashion that was distributed [14, 56–58]. The taxpayer's information is made protected using the hash functions alter and to store the information. The machine is currently utilizing Ethereum contracts that are intelligent to make sure third parties get. Being a system 21 procured by functions which makes it tough to hack into misuse information that is personal and the systems. Blockchain is a decentralized ledger that guarantees protection, immutability, transparency, verifiability. Transactions are stored in cubes that are connected with since the hash of each block is a part of blocks hash the information of that hash, hash values called keys. SHA256 algorithm is utilized for creating these functions [59–63]. All these hashed information or messages are known as message digest. Because of hashing, the information can't be tampered as a small shift in the message results this is known as avalanche effect. Aadhar implementation utilizing the info in a system to blockchain stores procured by function. Aadhaar is an identification number issued from India's exceptional Identification Authority information is obtained by that. It's used to gather data about citizens of India. Aadhaar card is related to several services like bank accounts, sim cards, welfare strategies, etc., despite its own safety problems. If the machine gets hacked countless people's information may be endangered.

The Blockchain is an information institution improvement and a decentralized exchange grew for Bitcoin cryptographic money [13, 64–66]. A Blockchain is an open record everything considered, or a passed database of records or motorized occasions which have been executed and shared among shooting an interested party. A greater bit of those people who live in the structure's assertion certifies each exchange the network listing. The Blockchain contains a certain and clear listing of every exchange whenever made repressions. In this evaluation. In this examination, we have written a considered mapping study with the event's aim all simple research on progress. We will understand the stream research subjects, inconveniences and prospective headings with regard to Blockchain progression.

This paper focuses on a basic comparative study of Hyperledger fabric and Ethereum. It talks about different types of blockchain, consensus algorithms, Hyper ledger, Ethereum [16, 67–69]. The three main types of blockchain are public, federated or consortium and private. This paper focuses on a basic comparative study of Hyperledger fabric and Ethereum. It talks about different types of blockchain, consensus algorithms, Hyper ledger, Ethereum. The main difference between Ethereum and Hyperledger is the mode of operation. Ethereum is a permissionless, public or private blockchain whereas Hyperledger is permissioned and private. The consensus algorithm used in Ethereum is proof-of-work, where miners mine the blocks and the first miner to complete the computational task is awarded in terms of Ether. Hyperledger uses Practical Byzantine Fault Tolerance consensus mechanism and there are no cryptocurrency involved in it. Also, nothing is known about scalability of Hyperledger yet. On the other hand, Ethereum claims to be scalable, i.e, the number of data members can be increased anytime without affecting its functionality. However, the level upto which Ethereum is scalable is not known.

This paper presents a concept for a voting system based on blockchain. Voting has already been attracting the interest of research teams and authorities with work on the topic speaking to the consumer needs a system must meet [17]. For circumstances requirement identification goes farther than a straightforward narrative description of some pair of features. On the other hand reports refer to prerequisites since the record of laws pertaining to a voting process that is specific. Both sides appear to dismiss the simple fact that an online voting process is an information program with nonfunctional, in addition to operational requirements. They employed the Rational Software Development Procedure for introducing and identifying the needs a digital voting system must fulfil.

In their analysis, they've utilized Ethereum surroundings as the evolution platform [18]. In that the Ethereum system, all surgeries and all of the blocks are composed in the greatest series in exchange for a few Ethers. These are awarded as decoration to the miners, that implement these composing and validation surgeries, which can be expensive concerning computation time plus power. They have executed intelligent contracts, and which Rinkeby system, which includes over 1.5 million cubes and provides the consumers 20 imitation Ethers to invest during code analysing [70–73]. Blockchain turned into a domain that was dominant following Bitcoin's entry. Originally with passing moment just for trades but blockchain was believed, it's currently finding its programs in different fields. The usage of cryptography also it turned into a decentralized system which makes it a really secure method for various different implementations such as e-voting system. With a lot of vote misuse and privacy problems coming up with the present voting system, e-voting appears to be quite a fantastic solution with appropriate security steps being guaranteed by blockchain.

Also, with the support of e-voting, individuals that aren't currently available from the constituency may also vote from distant locations using their distinctive login credentials. This paper discusses about the very initial step towards voting that is stable based blockchain. This paper suggests a wise contract established e-voting system together with talking about a number of their present basic issues. They have utilized Ethereum to execute their voting strategy and have clarified in detail regarding their clever repayment and voting strategy.

In this project the program, the E-Voting App may be accessed with the internet browser which in our case will be Chrome using the MetaMask plugin or the command line interface [19]. In case the app using command line interface is accessed by the user he's greeted with the Nodejs console. The commands need to be typed in here. Else, the user interface can be utilized by the user. Web3.js is a selection of libraries which enable you to interact with a local or distant Ethereum node, using an HTTP, WebSocket or IPC connection. The voting contract created will be deployed over this blockchain. The config file controls this blockchain's configuration parameters. VoteEth utilized the intelligent contracts to maintain of the ballots and a record of each user from the system along with the data about them [74]. They utilized the smart contracts to attain access control. With the deployment of the machine onto the testnet for experiments revealed that the system can easily be set up and setup to utilize as a voting program for universities or other settings. In future work, they will investigate the possibility of developing an consensus algorithm to match for the varying demands of safety and also making the transaction processing by the machine more efficient.

7.3   System Design

This section explains the use cases designed for the proposed system. Figure 7.1 shows the organizer use case. In this use case, Blockchain and organizer are the actors and they interact with register, login, create Election, Transaction, View candidate request, approve request and add to election. Every organizer has to register, thereafter, he can login to the system and create election with specific dates and schedule. This portal gives the provision for candidate registration and approval. The registered candidate can vote after announcement of elections and through their voting login.

Figure 7.2 shows the candidate use case diagram. In this case, a candidate has to login after registration and respond to election queries and perform voting transactions after approval. Through request status use case,

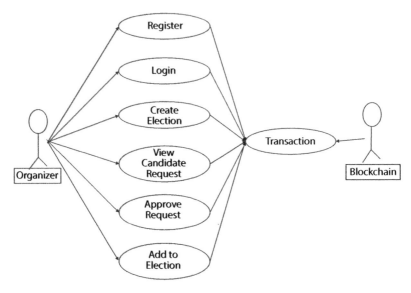

Figure 7.1 Organizer use case diagram.

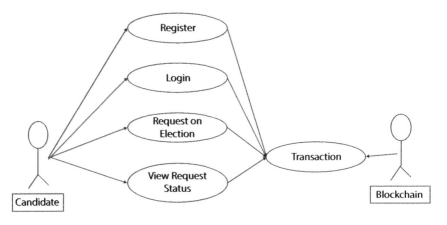

Figure 7.2 Candidate use case diagram.

candidate can make a request to election commission for adding his/her name in case it is absent from the list. The added name is allowed to vote in specified elections only. Thereafter, a new list is generated specifying the eligibility in elections.

Figure 7.3 shows the voter use case diagram. In this case, a candidate has to login after registration and respond to election queries and perform voting transactions after approval. Through request status use case, voter can make a request to election commission for adding his/her name in case it is absent from the list. The added name is allowed to vote in specified elections only. Thereafter, a new list is generated specifying the eligibility in elections.

Figure 7.4 shows the class diagram for complete E-voting system. In this case, the classes include voter, cast voter, candidate, voter profile, result and

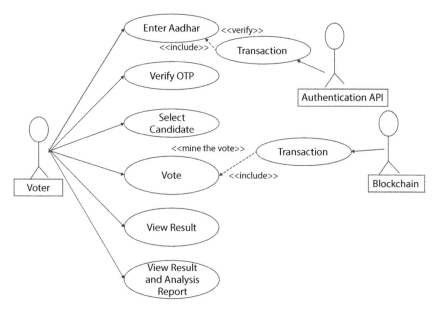

Figure 7.3 Voter use case diagram.

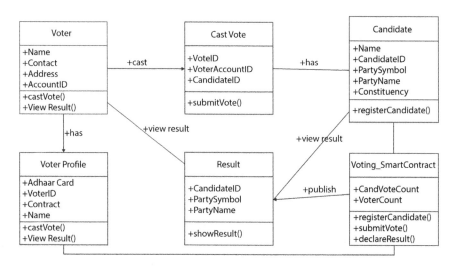

Figure 7.4 Class diagram for E-voting system.

voting smart contract. The role and functionalities of each of these class is understood. A voter can cast a vote. Create/update/change profile and see election results. Similarly, a candidate has the right to vote in election provided he is registered properly in the system and allowed to appear in election. Voting smart contract class is connected with candidate and vote classes, and result class to display the election outcomes.

7.4   Experimentation

This section explains the E-voting implementation and related details.

7.4.1   Software Requirements

Table 7.1 shows the software requirements for E-voting implementation.

7.4.2   Function Requirements

This section explains the non-functional requirements and related details.

Table 7.1 Software requirements.

Ganache	Allows user to set up a virtual blockchain to run tests and provides 10 addresses and hashes.
NodeJS v 8.9.4	It is an open source environment on JavaScript used to develop front-end of an application.
Truffle v 5.0.4	Truffle script lets you change the state as well as the address of a contract as you develop or perform transactions.
Solidity v 0.5.8	Solidity is a high level language that is used to implement smart contracts.
Remix	Remix is an Integrated development environment that's used to write, compile, run and test Solidity code.
Web3.js	Collection of libraries which lets the frontend to interact with the Ethereum Blockchain, including making transactions and calls to smart contracts.
Ethereum Virtual Machine	The Ethereum Virtual Machine (EVM) provides an environment to run smart contracts.

7.4.2.1   Election Organizer

Organizer Registration
Description: The Organizer should register itself.
Initial SBS Flow:

- The Organizer visit the WebApp by its link or install in the mobile as per requirement.
- Then Organizer click on the "Register as Election Organizer".
- The Organizer should register successfully.

Organize the Election
Description: The Organizer should able to organize the election by submitting the election information like type of election, date, time, etc.
Initial SBS Flow:

- In the WebApp the button called "Start Election" should available.
- By clicking it, Organizer have to login by its credentials.
- Then able to fill the form having information about the election that must organize.
- Then click on submit button to submit the form.
- Then the Election Scheduling should start working.

Approve the Nomination Request
Description: The Organizer should be able to approve the request of the candidate nomination which candidates have requested for their election event in Organizer's Dashboard.
Initial SBS Flow:

- In the Organizer Dashboard the request list is shown having the list of nomination candidates.
- For approving the candidate nomination, Organizer should click the Approve button on the right side of the request list.
- For rejecting the candidate nomination, Organizer should click the Reject button on the right side of the request list.

7.4.2.2   Candidate Registration

Description: The Candidate able to register.
Initial SBS Flow:

- The Candidate visit the WebApp by its link or install in the mobile as per requirement.
- Then Candidate click on the "Register as Election Candidate".
- The Candidate should register successfully by providing the Adhaar card and biometric authentication with OTP confirmation.
- After the Aadhaar verification, it must redirect to the next verification step i.e. Voter ID verification.

After successful verification of Voter ID the Candidate should register successfully.

7.4.2.3   Voter Registration Process

Description: The Voter able to register with its document and legitimate authentication.

Initial SBS Flow:

- The Voter visit the WebApp by its link or install in the mobile as per requirement.
- Then the Voter clicks on the "Register as Election Voter".
- The Voter should register successfully by providing the Adhaar card and biometric authentication with OTP confirmation.
- The after Aadhaar verification it must go on to the next verification step i.e. Voter ID verification.
- If everything goes well then voter can able to vote in the election.

Voting process

Description: The Voter able to vote in the election by selecting their favourable nominated candidate.

Initial SBS Flow:

- After the successful register and authentication, the voter must redirect to the election's candidate selection page.
- Then voter can choose the candidate form the list.
- Then after selecting the candidate, they must click the "Submit" button for casting the vote.

7.4.3 Common Functional Requirement for All Users

7.4.3.1 Result Display

Description: All the users can able to view the election result on the result date.
  Initial SBS Flow:

- The Users visit the WebApp by its link or install in the mobile as per requirement.
- Then the User Click on the "Result" button.
- Then they must be directed to the result page.

7.4.4 Non-Function Requirements

This section explains the functional requirements and related details.

7.4.4.1 Performance Requirement

The proposed implementation of our project will easy to use as the graphical user interface will be user friendly.

- The performance of the system is fast and accurate; only the transaction validation process is time consuming.
- Since it is a voting system, there will be a large number of transactions. So the system should be able to handle such a large number of transactions.

7.4.4.2 Security Requirement

The security factor is really high in this system as we are using the blockchain technology which is known for its security and privacy So, every data and transaction that is involved in this WebApp is completely secure because no one is controlling it, it is decentralized.

7.4.4.3 Usability Requirement

The system extends its limit not just for the election voting the user can also use this system for any kind of voting process from small scale to large scale i.e. this system can use from colleague level to the international level.

7.4.4.4   Availability Requirement

The system should always be available for access at 24/7 a week. As this system is Decentralize so there is no worry of availability of system access if any one fails to validate the transaction there are many other minors who are able to validate the transaction because in decentralize application everyone have the copy of ledger with them.

7.4.5   Implementation Details

Below are the implementation steps in detail:

- Set up an Ethereum network with a number of test nodes.
- Develop smart contracts using solidity language that would help in facilitating the election process digitally.

Various platform used in this work are explained as follows.

- *Solidity* is a high level language that is used to implement smart contracts.
- *Remix:* Remix is an Integrated development environment that's used to write, compile, run and test Solidity code.
- *The Ethereum Virtual Machine(EVM)* provides an environment to run smart contracts. After writing and compiling our smart contracts, we run our test blockchain and deploy these contracts onto the Blockchain which will be done via web3.js.
- *Web3.js* is a collection of libraries which lets the frontend to interact with the ethereum Blockchain, including making transactions and calls to smart contracts. It is a javascript API that allow you to perform actions like read, appending, create smart contracts, send transactions and hence Ether from one account to another. Then, we migrate the contract. *Migrations* is a Truffle script that lets you change the state as well as the address of a contract as you develop or perform transactions. After deploying the smart contract to the Blockchain, we will have to create an object of web3.0 with ReactJs on the browser.
- Next we will make the user-interface for the application to make it interactive for the end users using HTML, CSS, javascript framework—ReactJS.

- *ReactJS* basically is an open-source JavaScript framework developed by Facebook which is used for building frontend components. It's used for handling frontend for web applications. We can also create components that are reusable. It lets you update parts of the webpage without reloading the page.
- *Decentralized applications (DApps)* are applications that run on a Peer to Peer network and is not depended upon a single centralized system, and there is transparency of code. We deploy our smart contracts with Truffle which helps in better interaction and connection with the smart contract.

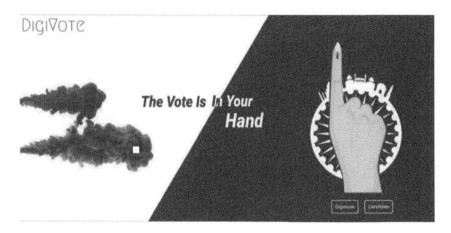

Figure 7.5 Home page.

Figure 7.6 Organizer registration.

Figure 7.5 to 7.11 show the implementation results and outcomes. Figure 7.5 shows the home page which is displayed when the application is executed. Figure 7.6 shows the organizer registration page where election commission can register in the system with image and mobile number. Figure 7.7 shows the next registration page where candidate has to provide more details for verification. Figures 7.8 and 7.9 show the subsequent pages where registration details are provided to confirm the candidature. Figure 7.9 shows the candidate details after registration completion. Figure 7.10 shows election options as per Indian scenario. Figure 7.11 shows the example of result.

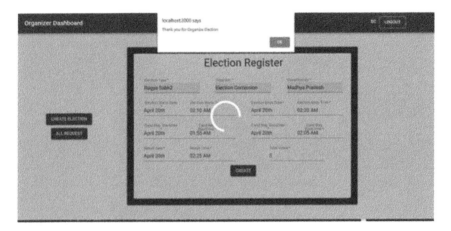

Figure 7.7 Organizer registration.

Figure 7.8 Candidate registration.

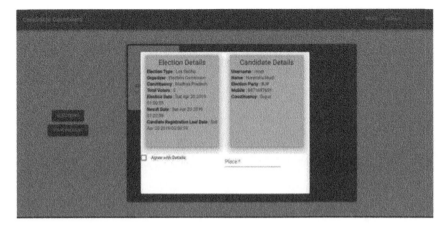

Figure 7.9 Candidate dashboard.

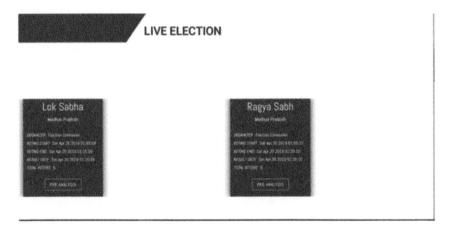

Figure 7.10 LIVE election section of HomePage.

7.5   Findings & Results

Here, we can say, with the amount of work done, that blockchain is reliable method to conduct online voting. If we follow the protocols of the Model results were convincing and accurate. For the different amount of error which was provided in the data Model accurately rejected the defected blocks and added the correct blocks of data in the chain. We also find out that during the initial feeding of the data, if correct public/private keys were not use, block were not included in the chain. Same is true for the

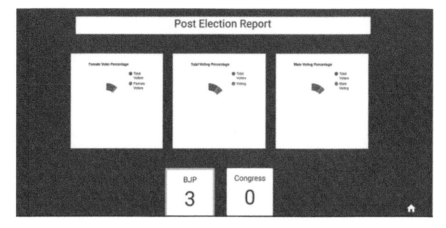

Figure 7.11 Election result.

incorrect sender and receiver addresses. All the test cases were passed by the model and faulty blocks were rejected We also made it clear that as currently only one system is mining the data, planning a systematic attack would be easier right now. Culprit can find out private or public key using various kinds of cyber attack and can hack the whole model if miners are not added.

Figure 7.12 shows the use of truffle environment to setup user account and use of existing account for the proposed system. Figure 7.13 shows

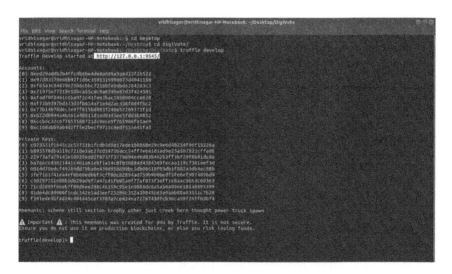

Figure 7.12 Truffle environment.

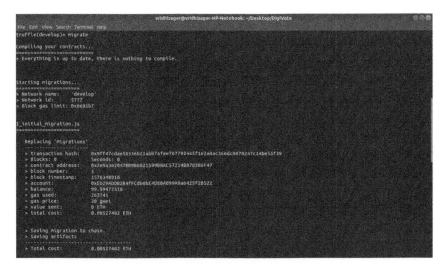

Figure 7.13 Migration of our contacts to our test environment.

the migration of smart contracts to test environment. It shows the use of blockchain creation and integration with developed environment. Figures 7.14 and 7.15 show the example of two logs. Figure 7.14 shows the log of election records created after smart contract integration. Similarly, Figure 7.15 shows the use of transaction log for admin. All these logs are helpful

Figure 7.14 Transaction Logs of user Election Contract.

Figure 7.15 Transaction logs of admin contract.

Figure 7.16 Smart contract deployed.

in keeping the records of transactions performed starting from creating the network to deploying and testing.

7.5.1   Smart Contract Deployment

In this work, Remix, a web browser-based IDE for Solidity smart contracts testing, is used to deploy and run the developed smart contract. Figure 7.16 shows the election smart contract deployed on Ethereum. Results show that there are multiple smart contracts designed and developed for proposed system. All of the smart contracts are successfully deployed with different parameters. Figure 7.17 shows the transaction in execution. Here, different values are tried to test the system functionality. It also shows that the smart contracts are well integrated and functional.

Figure 7.18 shows calling function to show aadhaar card. Here, only one aadhaar card is entered with number 5,192. Similarly, other testing scenarios can be executed. Tables 7.2, 7.3 and 7.4 show the various testing scenarios that are followed in this work to test the system functionality. Results show that the system is functional.

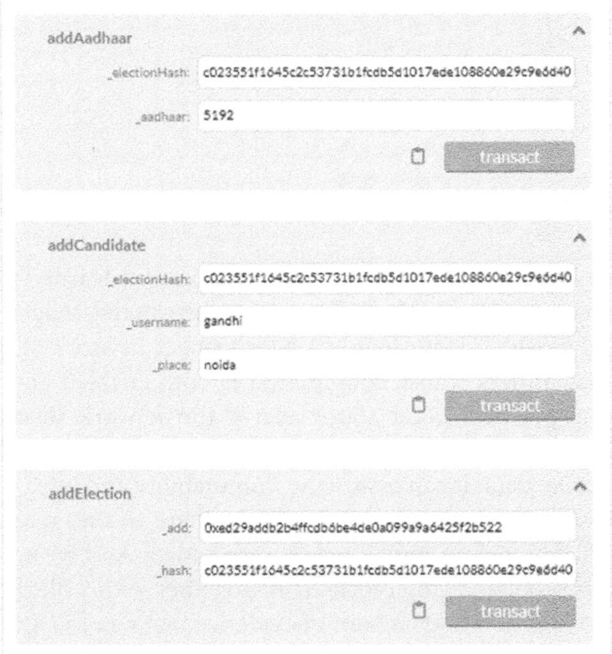

Figure 7.17   Adding credentials.

Figure 7.18 Check Aadhaar.

7.6 Conclusion and Future Scope

From all the literature study and implementation we learned how a distributed ledger works. A blockchain is a distributed ledger used for record-keeping, which is hosted on a peer-to-peer network of participating nodes and miners whose cooperation is both enabled and governed by a consensus protocol which states rules of the network. Blockchain has the potential of solving a lot of problems related to long term storage of publicly available data. It can assure the immutability and integrity of data. We, as a voter, have no means to ensure that there was no malpractice in the system or if any extra, unfair votes were added. And we are trying to overcome this problem using Blockchain. Together with a Blockchain network, Smart Contracts add a chain of evidence that comes from a history that cannot be altered.

Table 7.2 Testing the application.

Case Id	Input	Functionality	Expected output	Output	Pass or fail
1.	Open Webpage	Web Page should load	Home page should open	Interface Should open smoothly	Pass
2.	Candidate/ Organizer Signup Form	Registration of candidate/organizer	Data is stored and course graph selected according to the course choice of learner	Data is successfully stored and verified by the API	Pass
3.	Verify Voter ID	To verify whether a voter is valid or not	Should Verify Voter's Credentials and eligibility to vote	Verify the Voter ID entered by user	Pass
4.	Verify Aadhaar Card	To verify whether a person is eligible to participate in voting	Should let the user enter if he is eligible	User able to participate if the Aadhar is valid	Pass
5.	OTP verification	The Voter at the time of voting receives a OTP on his/her provided mobile number.	The Voter should receive the OTP on his/her mobile phone and he/she should be able to enter that OTP to cast their vote	OTP is received on the mobile number provided and the voter is able to cast the vote.	Pass

Table 7.3 Testing the application.

No.	Type of test	Will the test be performed?	Comments/explanations	Software component
1.	Requirements Testing	Yes	To make sure all the requirements are fulfilled to run a blockchain Environment	Windows, Lunix
2.	Unit Testing	Yes	Check for block size, chain size, data transmission, adding a Block	Ethereum Tester, Truffle
3.	Integration Testing	Yes	Deployment over different environment/systems	Windows, Linux
4.	Performance Testing	Yes	Checking the number of transactions and size of block also check for network latency, performance bottleneck	Ethereum Tester, Truffle, Ganache
5.	Peer/Node Testing	Yes	It is to check whether nodes are reaching consensus, if they don't where nodes are failing to do so	Linux Terminal, Ganache, Remix
6.	Compliance Testing	Yes	It is done to check whether our project meets the basic standard of any organization's norms	Linux Terminal, Ganache, Remix
7.	Security Testing	Yes	Check for any vulnerability to attacks. If the authorization system is robust and genuine	Ethereum, Ganache
8.	Load Testing		Load is an important parameter. Transactions/second will keep increasing, and testing for load is important	Ethereum Tester
9.	Volume Testing	Yes	Testing our project against a large volume of data	Ethereum Tester

Table 5.4 Testing the application.

Risk Id	Classification	Description	Mitigation plan
1.	Project purpose and need is not well defined.	Business delegates and the business logic is not well defined which can lead to the creation of faulty smart contracts.	Complete the business case and ensure purpose is well defined with all the constraints.
2.	Scalability issue	For implementing the system for a large population, scalability can be an issue.	Use Ethereum platform which claims to be scalable, although to what extent, is unknown.
3.	Confidentiality	Keeping the data of voters confidential	All votes are in the form of transactions and are converted into hashes to maintain confidentiality.
4.	Using Blockchain as Database	The more data we store in the blockchain the more transaction cost we have to give for mine that transaction	We can use the IPFS protocol for storing all the lengthy data.
5.	Public Blockchain	Our project is made on Ethereum Blockchain. So anyone in the world can participate as a miner in mining the blocks and validate the transactions.	We can make our own Blockchain Ledger exclusively for voting.

As this system is the prototype and it on its first stage, so there are several future enhancements that are needed that we suggest.

- As we can get the Overall data of Election so combining it with Machine Learning we can predict the result of future elections.

- More Options and Operations will be implemented and added to the creation of elections.
- More Operation and features will be added to the Organizer of the Election and Candidate of the Election.
- In future versions we can deploy this DApp to the private hybrid blockchain so that only reliable nodes or systems can participate in the mining of the Blocks.
- More Accuracy needed in Nomination Process or we can say that more Authentication is required.
- The Voter will be having its own personal Dashboard so he/she can manage its account.
- Try to make it simple and easy so that anyone can use it without any professional knowledge of Computers.

Acknowledgement

Thanks to Ayushi Jain (Roll. No. 9916103226), Ritika Singh (Roll. No. 9916103153) and Vridhi Sagar (Roll. No. 9916103029) for their contributions in this work.

References

1. Hall, D.L. and Llinas, J., An introduction to multisensor data fusion. *Proc. IEEE*, 85, 1, 6–23, 1997.
2. Liggins II, M., Hall, D., Llinas, J. (Eds.), *Handbook of multisensor data fusion: Theory and practice*, CRC Press, 2nd edition, 2017.
3. Yokoya, N., Grohnfeldt, C., Chanussot, J., Hyperspectral and multispectral data fusion: A comparative review of the recent literature. *IEEE Geosci. Remote Sens. Mag.*, 5, 2, 29–56, 2017.
4. Alam, F., Mehmood, R., Katib, I., Albogami, N.N., Albeshri, A., Data fusion and IoT for smart ubiquitous environments: A survey. *IEEE Access*, 5, 9533–9554, 2017.
5. Chen, F.C. and Jahanshahi, M.R., NB-CNN: Deep learning-based crack detection using convolutional neural network and Naïve Bayes data fusion. *IEEE Trans. Ind. Electron.*, 65, 5, 4392–4400, 2017.
6. Wang, M., Perera, C., Jayaraman, P.P., Zhang, M., Strazdins, P., Shyamsundar, R.K., Ranjan, R., City data fusion: Sensor data fusion in the internet of things. *Int. J. Distrib. Syst. Technol. (IJDST)*, 7, 1, 15–36, 2016.
7. Xiao, F., Multi-sensor data fusion based on the belief divergence measure of evidences and the belief entropy. *Inf. Fusion*, 46, 23–32, 2019.

8. Schmitt, M. and Zhu, X.X., Data fusion and remote sensing: An ever-growing relationship. *IEEE Geosci. Remote Sens. Mag.*, 4, 4, 6–23, 2016.

9. Smilde, A.K., Måge, I., Naes, T., Hankemeier, T., Lips, M.A., Kiers, H.A., Acar, E., Bro, R., Common and distinct components in data fusion. *J. Chemom.*, 31, 7, e2900, 2017.

10. T.P. Blackadar and D.P. Monahan, Versatile sensors with data fusion functionality, U.S. Patent 9,734,304, 2017.

11. Noack, B., Sijs, J., Reinhardt, M., Hanebeck, U.D., Decentralized data fusion with inverse covariance intersection. *Automatica*, 79, 35–41, 2017.

12. Zhou, D., Al-Durra, A., Gao, F., Ravey, A., Matraji, I., Simões, M.G., Online energy management strategy of fuel cell hybrid electric vehicles based on data fusion approach. *J. Power Sources*, 366, 278–291, 2017.

13. Rajguru, U.D., A review on challenges and opportunities in Blockchain Technology. *Int. J. Adv. Res. Dev.*, 3, 10, 122–127, 2018.

14. Gracia, S.J.B., Raghav, D., Santhoshkumar, R., Velprakash, B., February. Blockchain Based Aadhaar, in: *2019 3rd International Conference on Computing and Communications Technologies (ICCCT)*, IEEE, pp. 173–177, 2019.

15. Farah, N.A.A., Blockchain Technology: Classification, Opportunities, and Challenges. *Int. Res. J. Eng. Technol.*, 5, 5, 3423–3426, 2018.

16. Sajana, P., Sindhu, M., Sethumadhavan, M., On blockchain applications: Hyperledger fabric and ethereum. *Int. J. Pure Appl. Math.*, 118, 18, 2965–2970, 2018.

17. Ayed, A.B., A conceptual secure blockchain-based electronic voting system. *Int. J. Netw. Secur. Appl.*, 9, 3, 01–09, 2017.

18. Yavuz, E., Koç, A.K., Çabuk, U.C., Dalkılıç, G., March. Towards secure e-voting using ethereum blockchain, in: *2018 6th International Symposium on Digital Forensic and Security (ISDFS)*, IEEE, pp. 1–7, 2018.

19. Kumar, S., Darshini, N., Saxena, S., Hemavathi, P., Voteeth: An E-voting system using Blockchain. *Int. Res. J. Comput. Sci.*, 6, 06, 11–18, June 2019.

20. Kumar, A., Sharma, K., Singh, H., Naugriya, S.G., Gill, S.S., Buyya, R., A Drone-based Networked System and Methods for Combating Coronavirus Disease (COVID-19) Pandemic. *Future Gener. Comput. Syst., arXiv preprint arXiv:2006.06943*, 115, 1–9, 2020.

21. Kumar, A., Gopal, K., Aggarwal, A., Design and Analysis of Lightweight Trust Mechanism for Accessing Data in MANETs. *KSII Trans. Internet Inf. Syst.*, 8, 3, 1119−1143, 2014.

22. Kumar, A., Aggarwal, A., Gopal, K., A novel and efficient reader-to-reader and tag-to-tag anti-collision protocol. *IETE J. Res.*, 1–12, 2018.

23. Kumar, A., Rajalakshmi, K., Jain, S., Nayyar, A., Abouhawwash, M., A novel heuristic simulation-optimization method for critical infrastructure in smart transportation systems. *Int. J. Commun. Syst.*, 33, 11, e4397, 2020.

24. Kumar, A., Kumar Sharma, D., Nayyar, A., Singh, S., Yoon, B., Lightweight Proof of Game (LPoG): A Proof of Work (PoW)'s Extended Lightweight Consensus Algorithm for Wearable Kidneys. *Sensors*, 20, 10, 2868, 2020.

25. Kumar, A. and Aggarwal, A., Comparative Analysis of Elliptic Curve Cryptography Based Lightweight Authentication Protocols for RFID-Sensor Integrated MANETs, in: *International Conference on Intelligent Systems Design and Applications*, Springer, Cham, pp. 934–944, 2018.

26. Chugh, N., Kumar, A., Aggarwal, A., Availability Aspects Through Optimization Techniques Based Outlier Detection Mechanism in Wireless and Mobile Networks. *Int. J. Comput. Netw. Commun. (IJCNC)*, 10, 77–96, 10, 2018.

27. Kumar, A., Gopal, K., Aggarwal, A., A Novel Cross-Layer Network Architecture and Its Performance Analysis Using Mobile Ad Hoc Network Routing Protocol. *J. Adv. Comput. Netw.*, 1, 3, 208–212, 2013.

28. Kumar, A., Jain, S., Aggarwal, A., Comparative Analysis of Multi-round Cryptographic Primitives based Lightweight Authentication Protocols for RFID-Sensor Integrated MANETs. *J. Inf. Assur. Secur.*, 14, 1, 1–10, 2019.

29. Kumar, A. and Aggarwal, A., Analysis of DCNS anti-collision protocol with contiguous channel allocation, in: *2016 Ninth International Conference on Contemporary Computing (IC3)*, IEEE, pp. 1–7, 2016.

30. Kumar, A., Gopal, K., Aggarwal, A., Lightweight trust propagation scheme for resource constraint mobile ad-hoc networks (MANETs), in: *2013 Sixth International Conference on Contemporary Computing (IC3)*, IEEE, pp. 421–426, 2013.

31. Kumar, A. and Jain, S., Proof of Game (PoG): A Proof of Work (PoW)'s Extended Consensus Algorithm for Healthcare Application, in: *International Conference on Innovative Computing and Communications*, Springer, Singapore, pp. 23–36.

32. Manjulata, A.K., Survey on lightweight primitives and protocols for RFID in wireless sensor networks. *Int. J. Commun. Netw. Inf. Secur.*, 6, 1, 29, 2014.

33. Kumar, A., Gopal, K., Aggarwal, A., Outlier detection and treatment for lightweight mobile ad hoc networks, in: *International Conference on Heterogeneous Networking for Quality, Reliability, Security and Robustness*, Springer, Berlin, Heidelberg, pp. 750–763, 2013.

34. Kumar, A., Srikanth, P., Nayyar, A., Sharma, G., Krishnamurthi, R., Alazab, M., A Novel Simulated-Annealing Based Electric Bus System Design, Simulation, and Analysis for Dehradun Smart City. *IEEE Access*, 8, 89395–89424, 2020.

35. Gill, S.S., Chana, I., Singh, M., Buyya, R., RADAR: Self-configuring and self-healing in resource management for enhancing quality of cloud services. *Concurr. Comput.: Pract. E.*, 31, 1, e4834, 2019.

36. Kumar, A. and Jain, S., Proof of Game (PoG): A Game Theory Based Consensus Model, in: *International Conference on Sustainable Communication Networks and Application*, Springer, Cham, pp. 755–764, 2019.

37. Kumar, A., Krishnamurthi, R., Nayyar, A., Sharma, K., Grover, V., Hossain, E., A Novel Smart Healthcare Design, Simulation, and Implementation Using Healthcare 4.0 Processes. *IEEE Access*, 8, 118433–118471, 2020.

38. Chugh, N., Jain, S., Kumar, A., Aggarwal, A., Ahuja, N.J., An Improved Outlier Detection Mechanism for Hierarchical Key Management in Hierarchical Mobile Ad-hoc Networks (MANETs), *International Journal of Recent Technology and Engineering (IJRTE)*, 8, 3, 385–392, 2019.

39. Kumar, A. and Srikanth, P., A Decision-Based Multi-layered Outlier Detection System for Resource Constraint MANET, in: *International Conference on Innovative Computing and Communications*, Springer, Singapore, pp. 595–610.

40. Yánez, W., Mahmud, R., Bahsoon, R., Zhang, Y., Buyya, R., Data Allocation Mechanism for Internet-of-Things Systems With Blockchain. *IEEE Internet Things J.*, 7, 4, 3509–3522, 2020.

41. Kumar, A. and Sharma, D.K., An Optimized Multilayer Outlier Detection for Internet of Things (IoT) Network as Industry 4.0 Automation and Data Exchange, in: *International Conference on Innovative Computing and Communications*, Springer, Singapore, pp. 571–584.

42. Saharan, S., Somani, G., Gupta, G., Verma, R., Gaur, M.S., Buyya, R., QuickDedup: Efficient VM deduplication in cloud computing environments. *J. Parallel Distrib. Comput.*, 139, 18–31, 2020.

43. Kumar, A., Gopal, K., Aggarwal, A., Lightweight Trust Aggregation Through Lightweight Vibrations for Trust Accumulation in Resource Constraint Mobile Ad Hoc Networks (MANETs), in: *Proceedings of the Conference on Advances in Communication and Control Systems-2013*, Atlantis Press, 2013.

44. Kumar, A., Performance & probability analysis of Lightweight Identification Protocol, in: *2013 International Conference on Signal Processing and Communication (ICSC)*, IEEE, pp. 76–81, December 2013.

45. Singh, V., Aggarwal, A., Kumar, A., Sanwal, S., The Transition from Centralized (Subversion) VCS to Decentralized (Git) VCS: A Holistic Approach. *IUP J. Electr. Electron. Eng.*, 12, 1, 7–15, 2019.

46. Kumar, A., Gopal, K., Aggarwal, A., Cost and performance analysis of server-centric authentication protocol in supply chain management, in: *2014 IEEE International Symposium on Signal Processing and Information Technology (ISSPIT)*, IEEE, pp. 000269–000274, 2014.

47. Krishnamurthi, R. and Kumar, A., Modeling and Simulation for Industry 4.0, in: *A Roadmap to Industry 4.0: Smart Production, Sharp Business and Sustainable Development. Advances in Science, Technology & Innovation (IEREK Interdisciplinary Series for Sustainable Development)*, A. Nayyar, and A. Kumar, (Eds.), Springer, Cham 2020., https://doi.org/10.1007/978-3-030-14544-6_7.

48. Mara, G.C., Rathod, U., RG, S.R., Raghavendra, S., Buyya, R., Venugopal, K.R., Iyengar, S.S., Patnaik, L.M., CRUPA: Collusion resistant user revocable public auditing of shared data in cloud. *J. Cloud Comput.*, 9, 1, 1–18, 2020.

49. Chugh, N., Sharma, D.K., Singhal, R., Jain, S., Srikanth, P., Kumar, A., Aggarwal, A., Blockchain-based Decentralized Application (DApp) Design, Implementation, and Analysis With Healthcare 4.0 Trends, in: *Basic &*

Clinical Pharmacology & Toxicology, vol. 126, pp. 139–140, Wiley, 111 River St, Hoboken 07030-5774, NJ USA, 2020.

50. Kumar, A., Gopal, K., Aggarwal, A., August. Simulation and cost analysis of group authentication protocols, in: *2016 Ninth International Conference on Contemporary Computing (IC3)*, IEEE, pp. 1–7, 2016.

51. Kumar, A., Gopal, K., Aggarwal, A., A novel lightweight key management scheme for RFID-sensor integrated hierarchical MANET based on internet of things. *Int. J. Adv. Intell. Paradig.*, 9, 2–3, 220–245, 2017.

52. Hilman, M.H., Rodriguez, M.A., Buyya, R., Workflow-as-a-Service Cloud Platform and Deployment of Bioinformatics Workflow Applications, *arXiv preprint arXiv:2006.01957*, 2020.

53. Kumar, A. and Aggarwal, A., Efficient hierarchical threshold symmetric group key management protocol for mobile ad hoc networks, in: *International Conference on Contemporary Computing*, Springer, Berlin, Heidelberg, pp. 335–346, 2012.

54. Kumar, A., Gopal, K., Aggarwal, A., Simulation and analysis of authentication protocols for mobile Internet of Things (MIoT), in: *2014 International Conference on Parallel, Distributed and Grid Computing*, IEEE, pp. 423–428, 2014.

55. Ghosh, S., Ghosh, S.K., Buyya, R., MARIO: A spatio-temporal data mining framework on Google Cloud to explore mobility dynamics from taxi trajectories. *J. Netw. Comput. Appl.*, 164, 102692, 2020.

56. Kumar, A. and Aggarwal, A., Lightweight cryptographic primitives for mobile ad hoc networks, in: *International Conference on Security in Computer Networks and Distributed Systems*, Springer, Berlin, Heidelberg, pp. 240–251, 2012.

57. Gholipour, N., Arianyan, E., Buyya, R., A novel energy-aware resource management technique using joint VM and container consolidation approach for green computing in cloud data centers. *Simul. Model. Pract. Theory*, 104, 102127, 2020.

58. Razian, M., Fathian, M., Buyya, R., ARC: Anomaly-aware Robust Cloud-integrated IoT service composition based on uncertainty in advertised quality of service values. *J. Syst. Softw.*, 164, 110557, 2020.

59. Aujla, G.S., Singh, M., Bose, A., Kumar, N., Han, G., Buyya, R., BlockSDN: Blockchain-as-a-Service for Software Defined Networking in Smart City Applications. *IEEE Network*, 34, 2, 83–91, 2020.

60. Roy, D.G., Das, P., De, D., Buyya, R., QoS-aware secure transaction framework for internet of things using blockchain mechanism. *J. Netw. Comput. Appl.*, 144, 59–78, 2019.

61. Tuli, S., Mahmud, R., Tuli, S., Buyya, R., Fogbus: A blockchain-based lightweight framework for edge and fog computing. *J. Syst. Softw.*, 154, 22–36, 2019.

62. Roopa, M.S., Pattar, S., Buyya, R., Venugopal, K.R., Iyengar, S.S., Patnaik, L.M., Social Internet of Things (SIoT): Foundations, thrust areas, systematic review and future directions. *Comput. Commun.*, 139, 32–57, 2019.

63. Ilager, S., Wankar, R., Kune, R., Buyya, R., GPU PaaS Computation Model in Aneka Cloud Computing Environments. *Smart Data*, 1, 19–40, 2019.

64. Li, W., Cao, J., Hu, K., Xu, J., Buyya, R., A trust-based agent learning model for service composition in mobile cloud computing environments. *IEEE Access*, 7, 34207–34226, 2019.

65. Rodriguez, M.A., Kotagiri, R., Buyya, R., Detecting performance anomalies in scientific workflows using hierarchical temporal memory. *Future Gener. Comput. Syst.*, 88, 624–635, 2018.

66. Son, J. and Buyya, R., A taxonomy of software-defined networking (SDN)-enabled cloud computing. *ACM Comput. Surv. (CSUR)*, 51, 3, 1–36, 2018, 2018.

67. Sotiriadis, S., Bessis, N., Buyya, R., Self managed virtual machine scheduling in cloud systems. *Inf. Sci.*, 433, 381–400, 2018.

68. Sun, D., Yan, H., Gao, S., Liu, X., Buyya, R., Rethinking elastic online scheduling of big data streaming applications over high-velocity continuous data streams. *J. Supercomput.*, 74, 2, 615–636, 2018.

69. Mahmud, R., Koch, F.L., Buyya, R., Cloud-fog interoperability in IoT-enabled healthcare solutions, in: *Proceedings of the 19th International Conference on Distributed Computing and Networking*, pp. 1–10, 2018.

70. Kumar, A., Krishnamurthi, R., Nayyar, A., Luhach, A.K., Khan, M.S. and Singh, A., A Novel Software-Defined Drone Network (SDDN)-based Collision Avoidance Strategies for On-Road Traffic Monitoring and Management. *Vehicular Communications*, p. 100313, 2020.

71. Vora, J., Nayyar, A., Tanwar, S., Tyagi, S., Kumar, N., Obaidat, M.S., Rodrigues, J.J., BHEEM: A blockchain-based framework for securing electronic health records, in: *2018 IEEE Globecom Workshops (GC Wkshps)*, IEEE, pp. 1–6, 2018.

72. Balaji, B.S., Raja, P.V., Nayyar, A., Sanjeevikumar, P., Pandiyan, S., Enhancement of Security and Handling the Inconspicuousness in IoT Using a Simple Size Extensible Blockchain. *Energies*, 13, 7, 1–17, 1795.

73. Singh, P., Nayyar, A., Kaur, A., Ghosh, U., Blockchain and Fog Based Architecture for Internet of Everything in Smart Cities. *Future Internet*, 12, 4, 61, 2020.

74. Kaur, A., Nayyar, A., Singh, P., Blockchain: A Path to the Future, in: *Cryptocurrencies and Blockchain Technology Applications*, pp. 25–42, 2020.

8

Impact of IoT-Enabled Smart Cities:
A Systematic Review and Challenges

K. Rajkumar* and U. Hariharan

Department of Information Technology, Galgotias College of Engineering and Technology, Uttar Pradesh, India

Abstract

The rise of an intelligent home is an excellent idea in which the IoT is replacing conditions for individuals worldwide, a smart home occupied with devices that can communicate with one another, with individuals residing in the house and outside third parties. IoT built to include transmitting and sharing information across networks the need for human responsibility to protect. They could manage the distant locations, as information is frequently used and stored in the cloud. IoT opted to predict the small change in advance. The monetary part is the most significant benefit since that brand-new technology might change humans in the cost of checking and preserving provides. IoT can also help you obtain entirely new insights. Deliver the recent smart cities' challenges, the government is turning to IoT innovative developments to correct each smart existing facet. Several of the present IoT uses are town surveillance, traffic monitoring, smart parking, smart lighting, and waste management. In this particular chapter, you are going to read about the way the IoT influences specific areas and daily human life. It covers the role of 5G technologies in the IoT, along with Big data analysis. Additionally, the fundamentals of smart cities along with its challenges and solutions.

Keywords: IoT, smart cities, security system, smart home, 5G, big data analytics, cloud computing, WSN

Corresponding author: rajonline7@gmail.com

Arun Solanki, Adarsh Kumar and Anand Nayyar (eds.) Digital Cities Roadmap: IoT-Based Architecture and Sustainable Buildings, (253–292) © 2021 Scrivener Publishing LLC

8.1   Introduction

Because of the rapid development of the inhabitants in cities, substructure and treatments are required for neighborhood inhabitants' requirements. On this foundation, there's a remarkable boost for smartphones, actuators, for example, intelligent device or sensor, and digital devices that travel towards significant commercial growth of IoT. Meanwhile much equipment could connect and talk with each other on the web. Technical advances in Wireless Sensor Networks (WSN), Ubiquitous Computing (UC), and Machine to Machine (M2M) interaction could even strengthen IoT to advanced level [1, 2].

The Modern IoT model is governed by smart and automatic-configuring products associated with the worldwide community framework. Internet of Things is primarily deemed as actual clothes, widespread, with lesser storage space capacity and processing capability, to improve dependability, performance, and security of the smart neighborhood and its setups [3, 4]. Particular expertise and evaluation of the Internet of Things-based smart cites is carried out.

The global population will increase to 2.5 billion folks in another 20 years, with currently 7.9 billion to 9.8 billion in 2040, according to a new United Nations (UN) report presented these days. The global population projected for 2020 [1] emphasize as posted in the residence section in the United Nations Department of ESA (Economic and Social Affairs), offers the considerable introduction to worldwide industry patterns & possible customers [5] shown in Figure 8.1.

The evaluation realized the global inhabitants might touch the peak in 20th century conclusion, on the quality of close to eleven billion. Mainly, IoT is utilized in cities that are modern for several operations e.g., wired town, telicity, cybervillage, digital city, flexicurity, electronic city, smart cities, etc. [6–8]. In addition, different applications are made with the base foundation of IoT technologies, for example, IP digicams, smart wheelchairs, Web of Things (WoT), to blend the IoT with current net standards, booking designs that enhance the caliber of gathered up information about smart cities (PaaS) Platform as a service product mainly evolved from Internet of Things, routing-by-energy plus quality is linked by a website (REL) for communication protocol, orientation, Internet of Things-enabled inspection, decision (OODA and action), incorporated info systems that blend Internet of Things, creating data management, initial warning systems, as well cloud services, minimal energy Smart wellness monitoring (SWM), Sensor & realizing solutions, wellness tracking

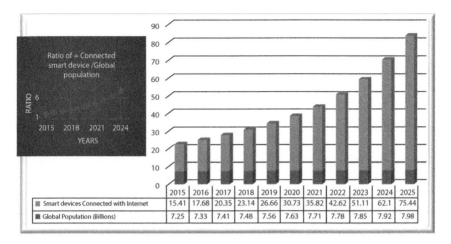

	2015	2016	2017	2018	2019	2020	2021	2022	2023	2024	2025
■ Smart devices Connected with Internet	15.41	17.68	20.35	23.14	26.66	30.73	35.82	42.62	51.11	62.1	75.44
■ Global Population (Billions)	7.25	7.33	7.41	7.48	7.56	7.63	7.71	7.78	7.85	7.92	7.98

Figure 8.1 Comparability in the middle of the approximated global population and the projected variety of sensible gadgets attached to the web: 2015–2020.

methods for locations, harm prediction version, power harvesters, buckling induced power harvesting systems, Wi-Fi-based Industrial networks and WSN in IoT, and medical group [9, 10]. Figure 8.2 shows the IoT-based interconnecting devices.

As a result of the quickly growing abilities of the IoT, it's poised to run as the critical component of sensible urban areas [11–13]. Within the last few years, there has been a surge of investigation focused on checking out the possibility of the renewable improvement by utilizing IoT in smart cities. This chapter is created to: Offer an ultra-modern launch to Internet of Things as a phrase for smart community related uses as well as engineering domains, talk about present advances, future trends, and also research gaps of Internet of Things enabled community, in addition, offer a literature study on building a well-performing Internet of things based monitoring system for real-time scenarios.

The chapter organized as follows: Section 8.2 discusses recent development in IoT application for the modern city, problems, and related solutions in modern smart cities application. Section 8.3 highlights classification of IoT based on smart cities, along with a survey on communication protocols for fulfilment of IoT-enabled smart city. Section 8.4 elaborates IoT 5-layer framework for smart city applications, and IoT computing paradigm for smart city applications. Section 8.5 discusses Research advancement and drawback on Smart Cities. Section 8.6 represents a summary of

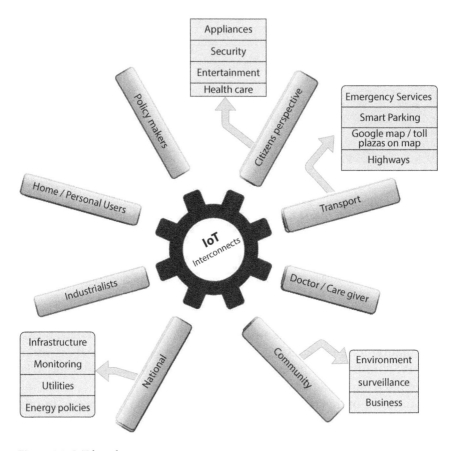

Figure 8.2 IoT-based interconnection.

smart cities and future research challenges and their guidelines, and finally the chapter concludes with future directions in section 8.7.

8.2   Recent Development in IoT Application for Modern City

Revolutionary technological advances and in mobility, building, manu-facturing, and energy, particularly eco-friendly innovations, change how individuals communicate with and form their environment. Engineering innovations are lighting the road to the long term, enabling us to picture towns where LED could illuminate wearables and traffic patterns point us to probably the closest medical center or maybe where city-sponsored bicycles share lanes with electric powered automobiles [14]. Brand new revolutionary suggestions interrupt older patterns, opening the door to energy-saving solutions and new thinking such as lean manufacturing or green roofing. Does it keep us on the shift and the correct path to alternative living.

'Smart City', among the visionary factors of the brand-new era community. The web is steadily changing our views regarding particular items like info and data. It's ready to alter the whole imagination of ours of contemporary city preparation and the idea of new towns. Let us start the drive by recognizing when a community is called a wise community and figure what are associated with the same. Hence, essentially, an intelligent community is a metropolitan area that uses various kinds of electric internet of things (IoT) sensors to gather information then make use of the information to control resources and assets virtually [15, 16]. It involves information collected from assets, devices, and citizens which is prepared as well as examined to watch as well as control site visitors and transportation methods, energy plant life, drinking water source networks, hospitals, libraries, schools, information systems, crime detection, waste management, along with other community services [17, 18].

IoT is helping cities link disparate energy, public service grids, and infrastructure. These smart cities create real-time aggregate information to control services and programs more effectively and gauge the impact instantly. Various applications of smart cities are shown in Figure 8.3.

8.2.1 IoT Potential Smart City Approach

Table 8.1 IoT applications for Smart City.

Smart power [31]	Intelligent buildings [30]	Smart water [24]	Smart transportation [20, 21]
• Smart metering • Demand effect as well as demand-side managing • Distribution hands-free operation	• Light command • Heating influence • Energy performance • Local power development • Privacy and Security management	• Pressure management • Predictive maintenance and remote control • Integrated platforms for drinking water control	• Vehicle-to-everything (V2X) • Managing the driver behavior • Mobile uses based upon receptive details

(Continued)

Table 8.1 IoT applications for Smart City. (*Continued*)

Smart power [31]	Intelligent buildings [30]	Smart water [24]	Smart transportation [20, 21]
• Distributed age group • Integration of renewables as well as decentralized power • Network keeping track of as well as control	• safety and comfort protection • Create a network for IoT-based integration of several solutions (materials, storage, renewable, mobility, safety, fire, plug loads, lighting, etc.) • Software: Efficiency, big data, and analytics, control and automation management	• Smart metering • water preservation and efficiency	• Traffic and also fleet keeping track of and control • Services for motorists & passengers based upon real- or near-real-time info • Integrating public transportation
Smart education [32]	Smart healthcare [19]	Smart physical safety/ security [22]	Smart waste [23]
• Flexible mastering within an active mastering atmosphere • Accessing planet type electronic articles on the internet utilizing collaborative solutions • Massive open online training course (MOOC)	• Adequate sanitation— Mitigation and disease control • Smart clinics • Real-time healthcare as well as for analytics • Remote health care and home-like monitoring • Electronic documents management	• Video surveillance, in addition to video clip analytics • Seamless interaction during human-made and natural disasters	• Waste Management • Wastewater remedy • City cleaning • Sorting of waste • Waste tracking

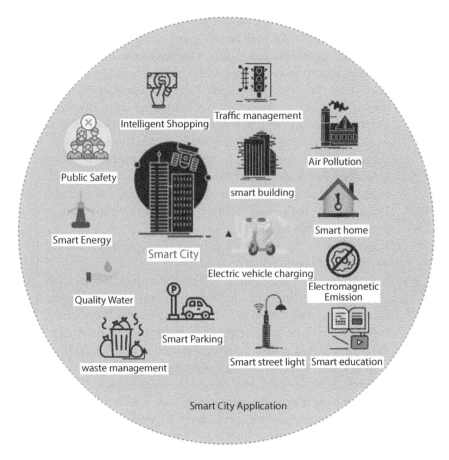

Figure 8.3 Applications of Smart City.

8.2.2   Problems and Related Solutions in Modern Smart Cities Application

Based on scientists, there are five significant demands for companies planning to produce sensible urban areas. They are: quality of the air, urban mobility, energy efficiency, data sharing, and security and safety—these are five of most asking for difficulties that crop up with urbanization [25].

- *Privacy and security within receptive details or even sharing the information:* When all the information is gathered and then analyzed inside one standard IoT wedge, the device could be put through many attacks [26] (e.g., Cross-site scripting, along with side-channel). Also, these kinds of devices are subject to essential vulnerabilities. Besides, this particular method's multitenancy may also draw out the protection problems and induce information leakage.

- *Wide-range services enhance citizens:* Some particular framework calls for the interactions between many embedded devices that are perhaps sent out over great area environments. Internet of Things systems offer an appropriate framework for analyzing and incorporate information receiving through various intelligent gadgets [27]. Nevertheless, suitable storage is required for the information and operational ability together at an excessive-rate, making distinctive challenges more challenging. Alternatively, the division of IoT products are able to affect the keeping track of points simply because the items ought to cope with the lag time related to dynamics and connectivity.

- *IoT sensors employed in smart cities:* The web of Things represents joining smart products like sensors and intelligent cars or trucks to networks, including the web. These units have grown to be an essential component of a smart city. Whereas shrewd communities has grown to be a fascinating setting for Internet of Things programs, the solutions have to recognized a secure, and scalable fashion allow for future economic development and tackle the present problems regarding heterogeneous IoT devices. Inadequate investment decision as well as high cost, high energy consumption and cybersecurity are included by these challenges. The IoT receptors are deployed as well as taken care of within their respective places to keep track of various phenomena as well as respond to adjustments inside the smart community environment. These reactions are improved to permit sensible urban areas to function successfully [28]. An easy use of IoT realizing is receptors prefer all those deployed within wise auto parking meters to observe auto parking bays offered within a community. Data gathered up by the receptors is transmitted and preserved centrally and outline 9 types of receptors that can provide telemetry within a smart community. Sensors are mentioned in Table 8.1. Besides the categories listed, different sensor types are usually connected with the smart city.

- *Extensive data:* Considering approximately fifty billion devices, it's undoubtedly required to consider transferring, recalling, and storing and analyzing such a massive amount of information created by the [29] Internet of Things framework will probably be several of the primary sources of big data.

- *Air pollution:* Air pollution is among the most serious problems in most cities, particularly in emerging nations. Bosch engineers created 'Climo'—a method for checking the weather and counteracting pollution. Climo collects and analyzes information relating to pollutant information, humidity as well as pollen concentration. Cities can use the data to introduce steps to enhance air quality, for example, altering traffic flows.

- *Challenge urban mobility:* More folks mean fuller streets as well as roads—there's a necessity for action with regards to urban mobility. Bosch's product portfolio probably includes intelligent mobility strategies and services. There are methods for connecting parking, electromobility, autonomous cars, along with multimodal transport. For instance, automobile owners don't need to waste time looking for parking areas due to Community-based-Parking (CBP). The automobile recognizes a parking area upon passes and approaches the information anonymously to other automobile owners close by via the cloud, making it possible for the driver to focus on crucial issues. Therefore, drivers looking for a free parking area are directed immediately to the next room with no loss of time. Folks parking rapidly in a multistory automobile park or some other free room don't need to operate many times across the block—roads clear, emissions sink. These new developments individuals can save gas, time, money, and above all, lower levels of stress [30, 31].

- *Challenges safety and protection:* Many people worry whenever they pick up about break-ins in their neighborhood or when they've to walk by themselves through the community park at night. Connected surveillance cameras can offer a deterrent against crime in both city life as well as the personal sphere. In the function of a catastrophe, the cameras also recognize where assistance is required. Nevertheless, it's not just the cameras, but also miniature sensors that play a role in giving increased security and safety: a motion sensor detects whether someone is tampering with doors or windows. All those looking to be accompanied virtually on the way of their back home can link up with their buddies with Bosch's Vivitar app. They can recognize the place of other user's apps at any time and find out whether they are going to arrive back home secure because of the GPS signal and also chat functionality [32].

- *Wisely combined:* Smart cities are a reality in numerous areas. Intelligence solutions can produce numerous small and significant improvements—but just as an entirety do, they lead to an intelligent city: Smart city means not just designing cities far more meaningful—both ecologically and economically—but above all, it implies individuals' daily lives are enhanced. The technologies which will resolve the difficulties of urbanization and infrastructure are available today. Therefore, the inhabitants of numerous towns can appreciate the benefits long into the future. With an extensive portfolio of intelligent city concept.

8.3   Classification of IoT-Based Smart Cities

Internet of Things-based intelligent city realization much depends on many short and also Broad range telecommunications protocols to transport information involving equipment & back up servers. Probably the most visible limited-range wireless solutions consist of ZigBee, Bluetooth, WiMAX, Wi-Fi, as well as IEEE 802.11p, that happen to be primarily utilized in sensible metering, e healthcare, along with vehicular reception. Wide-range solutions, for instance, GSM for Mobile Communication (Global Standard for Mobile) stereo program GPRS (General Packet Radio Service), and Long-term Evolution and Advanced-LTE (LTE/LTE-A) are usually employed. It includes V2I (vehicle to infrastructure), smart grid, mobile electronic healthcare, and infomercial expertise. Besides, LTE-M is viewed as being a (C-IoT) advancement of cellular internet of thing. The 3GPP (3rd Generation Partnership Project) idea boosts security, battery duration, and unit complexity [33]. In addition, important existing protocol, like the normalizing LoRaWAN protocol allows for smart cities programs and mainly guarantees interaction among a few operations. Furthermore, the Sigfox network is an ultra-narrow band wireless technology with a comprehensive star-based framework which provides a very expandable worldwide system designed to understanding smart city programs that incredibly consume less power. A survey on communication protocols for the fulfilment of the internet enables smart cities to be offered is shown in Table 8.2. This particular section provides a classification of IoT-based smart cities which organize a survey on foundation of current routing protocols, primary services suppliers, offered services, standardization efforts, network types, along with vital needs. An introduction to the invented smart city classification is depicted in Figure 8.4.

8.3.1 Program Developers

The researchers believed that the Smart City sector would develop to Thousands of enormous amounts of dollars by 2020, with an annual development of almost Intelligent Smart devices seventeen billion dollars. The Internet of Things is supported as a possible source of energy to boost service suppliers' earnings. The mass-market, global service providers have been begun checking out this particular novel cutting edge communication prototype. Internet service providers are AT&T, Telenor, Orange, NTT DOCOMO, Vodafone, Ericsson, Nokia, SK Telecom, Airtel, Reliance, and Telefonica, offering a variety of platforms and services for smart cities uses, including ITS (Intelligent Transportation System), logistics, e-healthcare, smart metering, and home automation.

8.3.2 Network Type

Internet of Things-based smart city programs depend on many communication topologies to do completely self-governing environment. The vein internet of things networks provide services over a minimal range, e.g., WLANs, BANs, (Body area network) and WPANs. Inside e-healthcare services, street lighting, and home automation are included in the application areas. On the other hand, uses including Intelligent transport service, m-healthcare, and garbage disposal choose WANs, MANs, and mobile communication networks. The above-listed communication protocols produce similar capabilities in terms of info, latency requirements, network coverage, size, and capability.

8.3.3 Activities of Standardization Bodies of Smart City

The extensive smart city programs did not merely expect complete range formation of several internet types of things systems but need a device instructs. Thus, many distinguished governances like IETF (Internet Engineering Task Force), 3GPP (Third Generation Partnership Project), European Telecommunications Standards Institute (ETSI), IEEE, machine to machine, as well as OPM (Open Mobile Alliance), remain

Table 8.2 A survey on communication protocols for fulfilment of IoT-enabled smart city [33–36].

Wireless communications protocol	Frequency	Data rate	Range	Latency	Power usage	Cost	Application
Z-wave	Sub GHz, 908.42 mHz	40 kbps	~100 feet	Low	Low	Moderate	smart lighting, thermostats and locks more
IEEE 802.15.4 (ZigBee)	2.5 GHz 915 mHz	256 kbps	40 to 110 m	15ms	Lower power Consumption	Moderate	Intelligent metering
Wireless HART	2.4 GHz	250 kb/s	~300 feet	46ms	Lower power Consumption	Moderate	Indoor e-healthcare offers a wireless protocol for the complete selection of process measurement, asset management, and control.
BLE/Bluetooth	2.4 GHz	1 to 3 Mbps	15 m	110ms	Lower power Consumption	Low	Interior e-healthcare
Wi-Fi	Sub GHz, 2.4 GHz 5 GHz, 802.11 n	0.1–55 Mbps, 6.8 Gbps	<300 feet	48ms	Average	Low	Smart Metering, Garbage Collection.

(*Continued*)

Table 8.2 A survey on communication protocols for fulfilment of IoT-enabled smart city [33–36]. (*Continued*)

Wireless communications protocol	Frequency	Data rate	Range	Latency	Power usage	Cost	Application
Weightless	Sub GHz	0.1–24 Mbps	<300 feet	40ms	Lower power Consumption	Low	Home automation system, Power management.
802.11p (WAVE)	5.8 to 5.95 GHz	6.5 Mbps	<3,000 feet	200ms	Low	High	infotainment, automation, safety-related, environment-related and mobility
IEEE 802.15.4	Sub GHz, 2.4 GHz	40–250 kbps	>100 sq. miles	10ms	Low	High	Industrial control and automation
DASH7 is an open-source protocol of LPWANs	433, 868, 915 mHz	55.5 kb/s, 200 kb/s	3,116 feet	15ms	Low	Moderate	operation of low rate wireless personal
6LoWPAN	2.4 GHz, 869, 914 mHz	256 kbps	>300 feet	Low	Low - latency	Moderate	Intelligent Transport System, (V2V/V2I), metering, logistics

(*Continued*)

Table 8.2 A survey on communication protocols for fulfilment of IoT-enabled smart city [33–36]. (*Continued*)

Wireless communications protocol	Frequency	Data rate	Range	Latency	Power usage	Cost	Application
LoRaWAN [56]	915, 780, 868, 433 mHz	56 kbps	2,000 to 5,000 m	Low	Low latency	Moderate	ITS, automation, Metering, Garbage Collection
GSM/GPRS	1,900, 180, 850, 900 mHz	73 to 384 kb/s	5,000 to 30,000 m	1.5 to 3 s	High	High	Smart Meters; Smart Home (Lighting)
2G/3G	Cellular Bands, 850 mHz	10 Mbps	5,000 to 30,000 m	100ms	High	High	Mobile operators, enterprises cities
Long Term Evolution and LTE-Advanced	2,500, 1,900, 800, 750, and 700 mHz	1 Gbps, 500 Mbps	5,000 to 30,000 m	5ms	High	High	Intelligent Transport System, smart metering m-healthcare

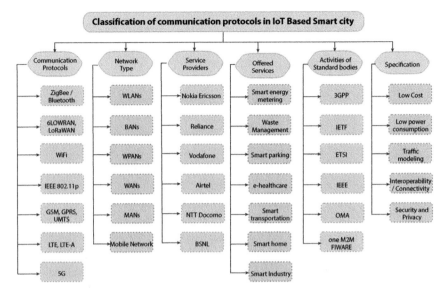

Figure 8.4 Classification of IoT-Based Smart Cities.

conscientiously intricate to create standards to allow for sensible cities uses over a big scale. This section covers the central standard bodies' main contributions and regular tasks for allowing smart city applications. The first Internet Engineering Task Force, working group (WG), 6LoWPAN, an identical method to handle things in tiny packets utilizing head density and neighboring detection SEO. Furthermore, the Routing Over Lossy and Low-power networks working group standardized Routing Protocol for Low Lossy and Power Networks for sensible IoT presents various uses in an intelligent city, therefore require quite a few requirements. For example, the Internet of Things-based results is likely low cost, shallow power usage, QoS, Broad coverage, improved flexibility, considerable security, secrecy, ultra-dense network, and different vendors city apps. Additionally, many Internet Engineering Task Force WGs, such as Device Identifier Composition Engine, are active in standardizing safety accounts, like TLS and Datagram Device Identifier Composition Engine (DTLS) internet of things products.

- *3GPP:* The new version release in 2013, (3GPP) third generation partnership project standardized narrowband IoT to offer much better network service for smart cities programs by further lowering the bandwidth to 200 kHz (up/downlink), decrease the throughput during a physical aid block amount, supporting substantial internet of things equipment, minimal energy usage, as well as improving extended coverage up to 22 dB [34]. The final effect, narrowband IoT, encounters the application requirements in the manufacturing, personal, and household domains. Furthermore, the Third Generation Partnership Project introduces lengthy discontinuous transmission (eDTX) or reception (eDRX) methods in Release thirteen to decrease energy usage and boost the unit running time.

- *ETSI:* ETSI seeks to provide cost-effective and interoperable solutions to allow for sensible city applications. The first machine to machine is the European Telecommunications Standards Institute's global effort in collaboration with the part research institutions like the Open Mobile Alliance, Broadband Forum, and the Continua to allow for the internet of things connectivity on a big scale. Lightweight Machine-to-Machine seeks to produce one horizontal platform for enabling interop among all applications through a decentralized data storage analysis in layer-3. Furthermore, smart city five-layer architecture is delivered by it, Specification, Application programming interface, privacy and protection solutions, and an Interop scheme for Intelligent smart city apps. So, the standardized application programming interface and open interfaces may be used within a few devices to allow an excess of IoT products to connect globally and with the master servers.

- *Institute of Electrical and Electronics Engineers, or IEEE:* The backdrop of sensible cities, IEEE mostly concentrates on search engine optimization of the atmospheric Interface for ultra-internet of things infrastructure. Moreover, it concentrates on using the sub 6.5 Gigahertz spectrum for the internet of things connected to several smart city applications [35].

- *Open mobile alliance:* Standardized the open mobile alliance Lightweight machine to machine (Open Mobile Alliance M2M/OPM Lightweight M2M) process for use limited resources exp Internet of things unit management for cellular networks and both sensors. OMALWM2M is situated in the unit end and provides a communication path between a Lightweight M2M customer and a Lightweight M2M server. Therefore, OPM Lightweight M2M is a compact, and lightweight protocol that's often employed together with the

(CoAP) Constrained Application Protocol and also provided an effective tool information model for the source constrained internet of things intelligent devices. Furthermore, it offers something for providers of services to implement devices to support corresponding sensible city apps.

8.3.4   Available Services

IoT provides many significant interest services in sensible neighbourhood's and enhances the quality of people's life and controls the smart city organization by decreasing the functional expenses [35]. IoT offering includes Intelligent lighting systems, water management, waste management. Consider the example, and the smart IoT structure may be a framework within workplaces, homes, and grid computing for distributing as well as Energy consumption. In mobile healthcare, the internet of thing products will be placed on the living or non-living things of individuals for keeping an eye on health parameters. For example, sugar level, pulse rate, and temperature, as well as provide opportunities for physicians to check the patients routinely. Besides, the urban internet of things can offer answers to manage road congestion or Traffic gridlock by checking traffic intensity working with either a global position system device in modern cars or maybe a wireless area network. The truck path could be enhanced in garbage collection depending on the ton level indication by wise waste containers. So, it will improve the quality of recycling by decreasing the price of collecting waste.

8.3.5   Specification

IoT offers various uses in an intelligent city, thus requires numerous requirements. For example, the Internet of Things-based solutions is likely to be the cost that is low, very low power usage, higher quality of service, broader coverage, improved flexibility, considerable security as well as privacy, ultra-dense deployments, and also multivendor interoperability. Many novel methods can be used, for example, congestion demonstrating the ability to show a crucial part in dealing with massive IoT traffic. Thus, rather than utilizing the conventional supply traffic modeling strategy wherein every IoT unit accesses the system separately to transmit and receive essential emails, an aggregated smart community modeling strategy must be typically suggested and used in Figure 8.4.

IoT offers various uses in an intelligent city and hence demands numerous specifications. For example, the Internet of Things-based solutions are shown in Figure 8.4 and give the detail on the classification of communication protocols in IoT-based Smart cities.

8.4   Impact of 5G Technology in IT, Big Data Analytics, and Cloud Computing

The modern IoT structure proceeds to generally be usually examined about the process to do sensible functionalities belonging in the latest previous [37]. Figure 8.5 presents a traditional approach. Know that the middleware levels possess an essential job within the framework. Middleware brings together standard abstraction systems & functionalities, packaging IoT infrastructure for consumers. Current scientific tests would like to offer an IoT middleware degree by way of a particular target about the enhanced resilience on the IoT structure as shown in Figure 8.5.

8.4.1   IoT Five-Layer Architecture for Smart City Applications

The comprehensive alternative for IoT sensible applications needs communication technologies, hardware, and different software to integrate several frameworks, services, components, and apps. Various functions are played by the solutions as well as offer abilities that run within different perspectives of the scenarios handled by sensible programs. Figure 8.6 depicts our recommended IoT Five-layer structure for Smart City, specifically the Sensing Layer (Get info offered by Sensor), Network Layer (Access and also transmit Information), Data Analyzing (Analyzing) and data Storage, Smart Cities design (Smart Industry version, wise health care version, smart towns, wise farming version), as well as Application Layer (Dedicated apps as well as Services) together with the improvement of IoT sensible uses [35–56]. We identify that many-layered architectures might be conceived, possessing inside brain various goal apps.

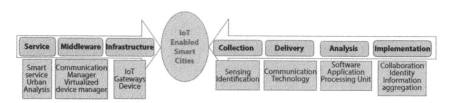

Figure 8.5 IoT-Enabled Smart Cities concerning technologies in IoT Five-layer Architecture.

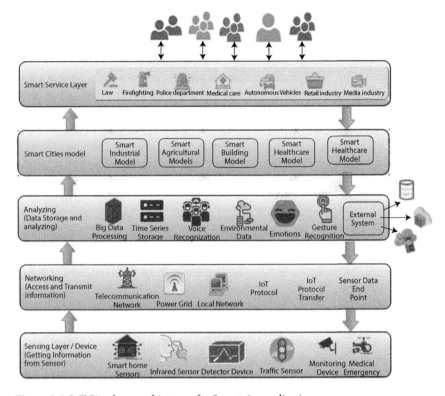

Figure 8.6 IoT Five-layer architecture for Smart city applications.

Nevertheless, the IoT Five-layer architecture structure for Smart City may be the outcome of equally analyzing the literature in the second section, aside from that in general performance evaluation research. Five-layer IoT smart city architecture [38], our 5-level leather explicitly offers assistance for incredibly sent out info managing abilities and separates physical and data-driven versions from system expertise. In addition, by clearly determining as well as sorting out areas that are logically certain of the data, model, and service layers, IoT Five-layer structure for Smart City helps the deployment of Internet of Things brilliant uses over numerous dispersed places within the mist, fog, then merely cloud. Coming from an application structure perspective, aspects of different amounts are used by providers—really encapsulated into Docker canisters having an uncovered API, for that reason, microservices. Parts within every amount perform as symbolic instances of different choices that may differ based upon attributes, prerequisites, and applications and users' limitations.

8.4.1.1   Sensing Layer (Get Information from Sensor)

Sensors, actuators, along with corresponding solutions—each wired as well as wireless—recoup most likely the lowest amount of the IoT structure. Products are receptors together with actuators, which position for IoT issues. Figure 8.6 depicts several instances of Layer a single portion, such as producing robots, with several receptors to take notice of the measures of theirs, and also sensors to management engines that produce them go based on various quantities of independence, each one swapping mail messages with a smart internet business plan via wired as well as wireless correspondence strategies.

8.4.1.2   Network Layer (Access and Also Transmit Information)

Collecting information from receptors, which makes it accessible to data management capabilities, getting instructions from application versions, and also delivering them to actuators need plenty of intermediate elements to get it done. Figure 8.6 depicts some significant types of generic particulars transportation works for realizing as well as actuation programs, for example, IoT process (e.g., MQTT [39]), which transmits information coming from IP talking products to put exactly where they're converted or even filtered possibly by additional elements of this particular level or perhaps by information managing components,

a) IoT processes translator (e.g., FIWARE internet of things agent) shifts info from the internet of thing process structure (e.g., Byte stream for Message Queuing Telemetry Transport (MQTT)) to its inner format within information control components (e.g., NGSI/JSON [40] for FIWARE) and also vice versa.

b) Sensor info endpoint (e.g., Chirp Stack [41]) transports, unpacks, and also decodes info for specific internet of thing wireless correspondence strategies such as LPWAN [56].

c) Device register offers with all the assortment of devices that are connected [49].

d) Data encryption and Authentication, Authorization, and Accounting (AAA) are pervasively needed for internet of thing communications and incorporated in Level two. A fundamental feature of information protection, as well as network/service control, is transversal features, as almost all layers pervasively needed them [50, 54, 55].

8.4.1.3   Data Storage and Analyzing

Each stage of just about any end-to-end Internet of things info flow has to deal with info in in-depth tactics, which are various, retrieving, distributing, transforming, like storing, and air filtering. Figure 8.6 depicts some significant types of generic details managing abilities, this kind of as:

a) Framework agent (e.g., FIWARE Orion [56]) for context info division and connected storage space process.
b) Bigdata pipeline (e.g., Apache Kafka [51]) for raw particulars division in addition to replication.
c) Bigdata processing (e.g., Apache Spark [52]) for processing a great deal of information.
d) Precious time sequence storage space (e.g., CrateDB [53]) for historic particulars.
e) Interfacing with outside techniques, just like weather forecasting services, online city traffic monitoring services together with databases.

8.4.1.4   Smart Cities Model (Smart Industry Model, Smart Healthcare Model, Smart Cities, Smart Agriculture Model)

Stand for application-specific versions for almost any kind of processing over info gathered up of receptors as well as exterior procedures surrounding an assortment of algorithms, formulas, approaches. Strategies that replace the info into info that client-side employ to change the globe in-depth tactics that come across the very best passions. For example, an intelligent sprinkler system application may use environmental information and soil, aside from that to weather prediction info, to nurture physical and also printer mastering clothes airers to compute when and how plenty of plants should be irrigated [42–44].

8.4.1.5   Application Layer (Dedicated Apps and Services)

Has answers that help support the interfaces and interact with clients-side of sensible programs. Graphical interfaces include this level, applications, and all services that provide visualization of sensor information, realizing in addition to actuation infrastructures, analyses, alternatives, and options, and directions to modify the express on the service. Figure 8.6 depicts four internet of things verticals as smart applications: sensible farming, smart city, smart healthcare, and the intelligence industry. IoT Five-layer structure for Smart City, depicted by Figure 8.6 comes with a high-level structural perspective of software, hardware, and communication components positioned into levels for facilitating technique style and advancement. Nevertheless, it does not indicate exactly where the components have to deployed, fog, i.e., or perhaps cloud within a usually sent out internet of things advanced program. When the end-to-end info flow is taking place within a smart system with receptors deployed within the part whose information is generally ready within cloud, deployment of architectural components is a complicated procedure that might differ based upon the attributes, prerequisites, and also limitations of applications and stakeholders.

8.4.2   IoT Computing Paradigm for Smart City Application

To offer a distinct method of the various deployment locations for architectural elements, classified into 5 stages, we created the idea of an internet of things computing continuum shown in Figure 8.7. Deployment locations are split up into stages (or) maybe deployment locations that might differ based on attributes of the current infrastructure, and also stretches the idea of the Internet of Things–fog–cloud Continuum [43]. Deployment architecture is an approach of formalizing the distributed infrastructure of Internet of Things methods and facilitating various deployment ideas because of the mapping between layered architectural elements into staged locations. Benefit to the article, it recognize 5 levels: Intelligent Smart Device Thing, Modern Computing Resource, Cloud Computing-Cloud, Fog Computing, And End User Interface Terminal. Represent application-specific models for just about any sort of processing over information gathered from different

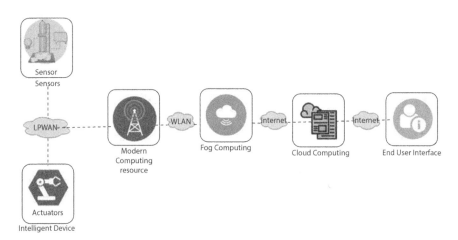

Figure 8.7 The IoT Computing paradigm for Smart City Application.

sensors and outside methods, encompassing an assortment of algorithms, equations, strategies & scenario that change the information into information that client side utilize to alter planet ways that meets the best interests of theirs. For instance, an intelligent irrigation program might make use of soil and environmental information, in addition to weather forecast info (external system), to nourish tangible and ML models to precisely calculate how and when much crops must be fertilization [44–46].

Intelligent Smart Device: It represents the point implemented by hardware systems, i.e., actuators and sensors that transforms analog to electronic signals and conduct necessary device-specific transformations, like calibration.

- *Modern Computing Resource (MIST):* Intelligent Sensor nodes are set up in the area and also play the job of radio gateways [40–56] in the context of low power wireless area network - or maybe related techniques—that assistance unit information interaction but additionally processing, like information aggregation. Mist nodes are near the equipment they assist and usually have moderate computing resources, like a Raspberry Pi.
- *Fog Computing:* Is installed in sheltered locations with a healthy energy source and also includes products like small servers, desktops, or laptops, that offer system reliability, resilience, robustness, as well as minimal latency for time-sensitive applications [42].
- *Cloud Computing:* private or public cloud host virtual machines and physical servers in a data center with lots of resources. There's a notice able rise in the processing power from Intelligent Smart Device Thing to Computing-cloud [43].
- *End-user Interface:* The end-users location interacts with an intelligent program linked to Cloud computing and Fog Computing in specific configurations.

The architecture, concentrating on 5-layers, determine end-to-end info course, beginning with information gathered by sensors around commands performed by actuators. These 5 stages may not be necessarily contained in all configuration scenarios. Instead, based on application characteristics, constraints, and requirements, Modern Computing Resource, Fog Computing, or Cloud Computing stages might not be present. Communication technologies between Intelligent Smart Device Thing and Modern Computing Resource are typically LPWAN (e.g., LoRaWAN), and between Modern Computing Resource and Fog Computing are WLAN (e.g., Wi-Fi) [47]. Figure 8.8 shows various mappings of the internet of things architecture into two deployment views or maybe configurations to make a distinct view of the various deployment locations for architectural elements and no Fog Computing—for intelligent agriculture and wise city scenarios. The end users implicitly represent the End-User Interface. Figure 8.8(a) Depicts a scenario associated with intelligent irrigation-based for a middle pivot that sprays water during a circular plot in which the Modern Computing Resource is positioned. Networking (access and transmit info) parts of the structure place in fog computing-Fog-placed in the farm office and data analyzing and data Storage, Model Layer, and Application Layer (Dedicated and service) layers are placed in the cloud computing. Figure 8.8(b) depicts a sprinkler irrigation scenario exactly where Modern Computing Resource Mist is situated on an eco-protected box in the industry. The farmer's option doesn't

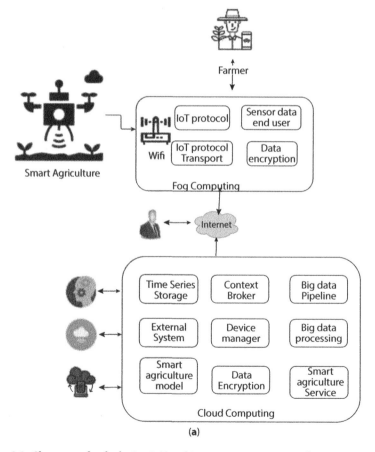

(a)

Figure 8.8 Clever uses for deploying IoT architecture components on distinct configurations IoT Five-layer architecture for Smart city applications. (a) Smart agriculture: 5-Layered approach (with fog Computing). *(Continued)*

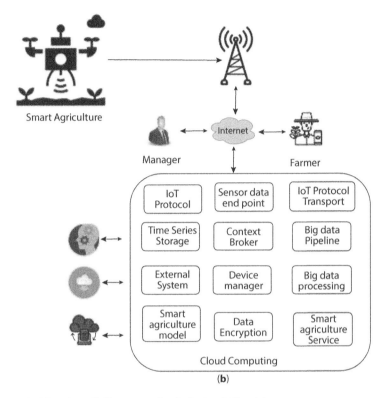

Smart Agriculture

Manager

Farmer

(b)

Figure 8.8 (Continued) Clever uses for deploying IoT architecture components on distinct configurations IoT Five-layer architecture for Smart city applications. (b) Smart agriculture: 4-Layered approach (with out fog Computing).   (*Continued*)

apply fog Computing, and thus all remaining elements are placed in Cloud Computing. Figures 8.8(c), (d) depict the same configurations for wise traffic management. In both instances, Modern Computing Resource Mist is situated inside a lamppost, whereas in Figure 8.8(c), Fog Computing is situated in an aggregation point (a point of presence of energy consuming) [48].

In Figure 8.8, even more areas out the mapping in between design and continuum with an intelligent irrigation situation of smart water management platform undertaking [33] and have a deployment put in place that merges aspects of the five amounts on IoT Five-layer system for Smart City. For this specific made simple case in point, the sensing (Device) Layer has the receptors (soil dampness sensor in addition to water station) and sensors (pump and sprinkler) in Intelligent Smart Device Thing & additionally a LoRaWAN network Gateway in Modern computing resource fog. Both stages are set up in the farm area. Networking (access and also transmit info) is deployed into the fog computing fog together with the

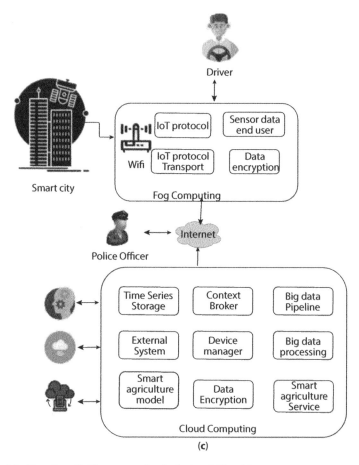

Figure 8.8 (Continued) Clever uses for deploying IoT architecture components on distinct configurations IoT Five-layer architecture for Smart city applications. (c) Smart city: 5-layred approach (with fog Computing). *(Continued)*

LoRaWAN server (actuators information endpoint), and also in the computing cloud with FIWARE IoT agent (internet of things protocol translator). Data are analyzed, and Data Storage is deployed solely in Cloud Computing, characterized by FIWARE ORION. Smart community style is deployed in Cloud Computing, represented by particular variations in sprinkler system preparation and efficiency. The program leading end-of Application Layer (dedicated together with the service) operates in the end User Interface (SWAMP program). Farm proprietors observe that through the smartphones of theirs. The application backend works within Cloud Computing, although not represented around Figure 8.9.

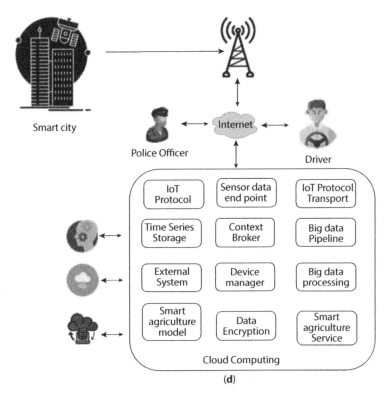

Figure 8.8 (Continued) Clever uses for deploying IoT architecture components on distinct configurations IoT Five-layer architecture for Smart city applications. (d) Smart city: 4-Layred approach (with out fog Computing).

Two vital observations might be turned on the subject of the scenario depicted within Figure 8.9. First, it is only one illustration and distinct technique of deploying architectural ingredients (IoT Five-layer system for Smart City layers) more than deployment places. For instance, in a situation where the farmers don't desire any on-premises infrastructure, Fog Computing disappears, and the LoRa WAN server might deploy in Cloud Computing. Second, a real wise irrigation application demands extra parts that aren't in Figure 8.9, which shows up in Figure 8.8 represented by generic functionality labels. By representing structure amounts and deployment phases separately and mapping one of the many other, obtain an adaptable mechanism for consideration on functionality and placement and keeping the capability to supply deployment ideas for internet of things wise uses for various applications. It believe it is a much more effective way when as opposed to mixture each problem in a single framework, similar to the main recommended by (Asif-Ur-Rahman *et al.*) for Intelligent health care apps [38–40].

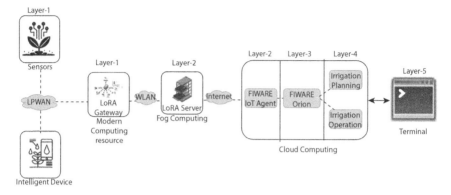

Figure 8.9 5-Layered IoT Architecture for Smart City Over the 5-Staged of Smart Irrigation Scenario.

8.5 Research Advancement and Drawback on Smart Cities

8.5.1 Integration of Cloud Computing in Smart Cities

Though the cloud computing mechanism ensures low and convenient costs to host huge details, incorporating the ways by IoT to understand the advantages linked to an intelligent community is a tremendous fight. Despite cloud computing solutions just lately seeing substantial improvements, the adoption of cloud computing intended on smart city incorporation may have many issues in open platforms, administration, also security [57]. These problems arise due to transferring the data and processing it through a firewall in cloud computing. An excellent cloud commercial agenda towards coping with cloud integration [58], safety, administration, and framework flexibility for smart city shows have been created. Moreover, the potential to change treatments founded on client endorsement may attract many customers to such telecommunications providers, thus producing increased revenue.

Additionally, cloud providers generate cash through info center adjacency by hosting their devices in many merchant facilities, offering them ease in offering services in many or perhaps actually varied geographical settings. Information integration smart community info encompasses various information formats working with an indefinite range of sensible items lodged throughout the community. Nevertheless, a smart community notion introduced a significant quantity of information through various resources; information integration in the smart community is a primary issue addressed [16]. In the latest post, a few technologies are united into the smart community, and they decrease the technological hurdles to deal with the info. Nevertheless, data quality is the more formidable difficulties founded in every info integration mechanism, especially if the info is incorrect, missing, do the wrong format, or partial [59].

8.5.2   Integration of Applications

The idea of intelligent society is linking different program domains to augment the overall performance of urbanized facilities. A smart lighting system could be incorporated with several comforts to offer enhanced solutions to cities. A sensible/smart traffic managing device is a promising framework that could easily be integrated into Sol Chip is an IoT system (SoLS) to produce an economical independent remedy. Moreover, the utilization of different atmosphere sensors (e.g., rain sensor, temperature sensor, moisture sensor, etc.) in a smart lighting system can be useful smart environmental methods. Extra exploration within linking sensible burning process with several applications can make a great deal a bit more affordable as well as cost-efficient urbanized services [60].

8.5.3   System Security

A smart lighting system can be a potential target for assailants due to the centralized management process of a smart lighting system provides permission to get into other interconnection services. Besides, threats can have an opportunity to use the confidential information from CC (Cloud Computing), which may end up in possible malicious attacks [61] even perhaps they may get the command of the whole smart lighting device of the neighbourhood, just in case they can exploit the basic safety mechanisms. Additionally, hackers can launch sensor-based attacks to influence a smart lighting system [16]. Hence, applying many protection mechanisms over SLS is a challenging investigation location for later on researchers. The encryption procedure within the protocols is not yet mature, or even well-defined, and critical management and revocation challenges are correctly addressed. Not safety, but furthermore, a privacy-preserving mechanism might be used in smart lighting systems to preserver the user secrecy [62]. As the end items are low-energy and cheap-cost devices, there be a continuous trade-off between security and efficiency. Robust protection systems in communication protocols can compromise the system's performance that improves the cost of setup. An addition hand, really improper implementation of the security mechanism can result in disastrous results. The mentioned issues need to be viewed, even though using a SLS. The overall summary of smart cities and future research challenges and their guidelines are given in Table 8.3.

8.6   Summary of Smart Cities and Future Research Challenges and Their Guidelines

Table 8.3 Summary of Smart cities and future research challenges and their guidelines.

Characteristics	Implementation	Pros	Investigation encounters	Essentials
Security	Smart Schools, Smart Health, Intelligent Transportation System (ITS).	Secure attack free execution setting to framework services	1. Absence of standardized protection techniques without hindering information integrity. 2. Safe integration and deployment of cloud-based expert services in the device and network ranges. 3. Sufficient earlier identification of each insider and outsider attack	Distinguishing of vulnerabilities in the community which can improve as vulnerable appearance for different malicious threats
Privacy	Smart healthcare, smart schools, Logistics, ITS.	Provides data Security and also user privacy within the range network	Promising users' anonymity on the Internet of Thing system for utilizing specific services	Pervasive net type with strong encryption and also cryptographic tools

(Continued)

Table 8.3 Summary of Smart cities and future research challenges and their guidelines. (*Continued*)

Characteristics	Implementation	Pros	Investigation encounters	Essentials
IoT sensors	Sensors enable online of Things by gathering the information for wiser decisions. Find out how TE Connectivity (TE) sensors are utilized in applications like consumer products, Industry 4.0, and health uses such as remote patient monitoring.	Collaboration with AI technology Security improvements it continues to improve our lives, make the internet smarter and better	1. (integrity)/Sensor information agreement 2. Information protection on the communication medium. 3. We have authorized a chance to access the sensor data.	1. Barcode number of sensors, humidity, temperature, location, timestamp High 2. Log documents in .csv or.log (high level of format) 3. Information can able kept in .log /.csv (high level of format)
Trust	The intelligent Transport system, electronic healthcare, smart schools, logistics	Makes certain users trust as well as belief that the desired services are free from vulnerabilities	1. Effective decentralized (TMS) trust management system 2. Smart trust analysis at the time of program unavailability and jeopardized internet of things network	Decentralized trust design staying away from one point of failure within the network range.

(*Continued*)

Table 8.3 Summary of Smart cities and future research challenges and their guidelines. (*Continued*)

Characteristics	Implementation	Pros	Investigation encounters	Essentials
Jeopardize management	indoor Electronic healthcare, ITS.	Makes specific Security protection by determining uncertain events & attacks on the internet of things network	1. Cheap-cost and effective risk management services to recognize newly emerged attacks effectively 2. Ultra-Efficient and fast threat choice mechanism to check determined attack.	1. Specific threat modeling to determine different attacks in the network 2. Point out the different risks areas through an asset-based attack and attacker actors modeling
Interoperability	ITS, personal electronic healthcare ecosystem, and smart home.	Provides a platform for two IoT devices from diverse domains to communicate	Incorporating products for seller locked in services	In general, centralized, supple, and wide-open research versions for products to incorporate as well as talk (e.g., Internet Protocols, Constrained Application Protocol)
Low-Cost communication and low power	smart meters, Intelligent Transport System, and electronic healthcare	Offers a broad range of uses in the internet of things based on smart cities if communication is the cheap cost	The best way to extend the power life of the internet things products?	Developments in wireless communication and microelectronics to offer inexpensive interaction and improved battery life.

(*Continued*)

Table 8.3 Summary of Smart cities and future research challenges and their guidelines. (*Continued*)

Characteristics	Implementation	Pros	Investigation encounters	Essentials
Extensive data or Big Data	ITS, e-healthcare, and Smart meters	Raises IoT system effectiveness by processing info that's helpful, displaying authenticated sources (e.g., examining visitors' info are in a position to take down traffic congestion processing.	1. Not enough appropriate tools to deal with the massively generated info 2. Safeguard of users' security and privacy 3. Significant centralized data acquisition as well as info	1. Cloud Storage (centralized data) large information processing centers 2. People attention to make use of resources in the internet of things network safely

(*Continued*)

Table 8.3 Summary of Smart cities and future research challenges and their guidelines. (*Continued*)

Characteristics	Implementation	Pros	Investigation encounters	Essentials
Cloud Computing	smart meters, Intelligent Transport System, and electronic healthcare	Offers a broad range of uses in the internet of things based smart city if communication is a cheap cost	1. Proprietary application programming interfaces for every cloud provider digital evidence in the cloud computing system. 2. The transient nature of information prevents verification of findings 3. Intruders can probably target pots which service logging infrastructure	Cloud services continue to be in its infancy. Of course, if cloud services had been attracting huge enterprise clients, they have to do much more than today to deal with data/application portability, federated scalable structure, full end-to-end interoperability, and security problems.
Connectivity	Waste management, ITS, e-healthcare, and smart industry	Ensures that IoT units can connect from different domains	How can you guarantee connectivity in a broad range of internet of things products during no correspondence networking as well as substantial mobility?	1. Effective use of spectrum for the internet of thing products to meet up. 2. Smart device use for every possible Transmission medium (example, LTE, WiMAX 3G, and WLAN, etc.) 3. Advancement of gossip-based algorithms to offer connectivity through the internet of things products lacks a correspondence network.

8.7   Conclusion and Future Direction

An intelligent community thought emerged as being an application program domain of the internet of things, among different principles that utilize ICT in citified environments, i.e., electronic community, smart cities, sustainable city, green city, etc. The smart cities stand out owing to its alternative vision, smart cities act as a composition of various other urban environmental management methods. In this chapter offered basics associated with intelligent town in terms of definitions, implications, and standards. Features and characteristics are discussed regularly to recognize the gist of the wise city notion. Going into much more technological detail, general design associated with a smart city is explained after reviewing suggested smart city framework. The smart city is a method that facilitates interoperability among different sub-methods to better the QoL of citified citizens. Henceforth, to accept the structure's value, the main parts that create a smart city are discussed elaborately. The survey determined that the smart city's realization depends on expedited information processing, ubiquitous accessibility, and platform cantered interoperability among products. Real-world implementations of sensible cities are provided towards the conclusion of the content and a few newer statistics. Although smart cities have turned into a buzzword in the contemporary world, it nevertheless faces several severe issues and challenges thanks to the prodigious data processing heterogeneity and demands of connected wise items. To improve the database and offer assistance for future investigation, we described several challenges are identified and possibilities for development.

Future directions for Smart cities related to Energy efficiency are:

- Energy-efficient mechanisms for software-defined Internet of things solutions, which can offer context-aware and scalable data and services.
- Directional power transmission from dedicated sources of energy for wireless energy transfer.
- Energy efficiency and intricacy of security protocols are vital features for the practical implementation of theirs in IoT; consequently, it's essential to explore robust security protocols for electricity-constrained IoT products.
- Fog computing can result in energy saving for nearly all of the IoT programs; thus, it's essential to learn fog products' electricity usage for IoT applications.

References

1. Solanki, A. and Nayyar, A., Green internet of things (G-IoT): ICT technologies, principles, applications, projects, and challenges, in: *Handbook of Research on Big Data and the IoT*, USA, pp. 379–405, IGI Global, 2019.
2. Batth, R.S., Nayyar, A., Nagpal, A., Internet of robotic things: driving intelligent robotics of future-concept, architecture, applications, and technologies, in: *2018 4th International Conference on Computing Sciences (ICCS)*, 2018, August, IEEE, pp. 151–160.
3. Rhee, S., Catalyzing the Internet of Things and smart cities: Global city teams challenge. *1st International Workshop on Science of Smart Citi Operations and Platforms*, 2016.
4. Nayyar, A. and Puri, V., Smart farming: IoT based smart sensors agriculture stick for live temperature and moisture monitoring using Arduino, cloud computing & solar technology, in: *Proc. of The International Conference on Communication and Computing Systems (ICCCS-2016)*, 2016, September, 9781315364094-121.
5. Kelaidonis, D., Vlacheas, P., Stavroulaki, V., Georgoulas, S., Moessner, K., Hashi, Y., Hashimoto, K., Miyake, Y., Yamada, K., Demestichas, P., Internet of Things framework for enabling services in smart cities. *Cloud Internet of Things Framework for Enabling Services in Smart Cities*, 163–191, 2017.
6. Angelakis, V. *et al.*, (Ed.), *Designing, developing, and facilitating smart cities: Urban design and IoT solutions*, Springer, Springer International Publishing Switzerland, 2017. https://doi.org/10.1007/978-3-319-44924-1_9, 2017.
7. Sotiriadis, S., Stravoskoufos, K., Petrakis, E.G.M., Future Internet systems design and implementation: Cloud and IoT services based on IoT-A and FIWARE, in: *Designing, developing, and facilitating smart cities: Urban design and IoT solutions*, V. Angelakis, *et al.* (Eds.), Springer, Springer International Publishing Switzerland, 2017. https://doi.org/10.1007/978-3-319-44924-1_10.
8. Krishnamurthi, R., Nayyar, A., Solanki, A., *Innovation Opportunities through Internet of Things (IoT) for Smart Cities. Green and Smart Technologies for Smart Cities*, pp. 261–292, CRC Press, Boca Raton, FL, USA, 2019.
9. Kumar, A., Sangwan, S.R., Nayyar, A., Multimedia social big data: Mining, in: *Multimedia Big Data Computing for IoT Applications*, pp. 289–321, Springer, Singapore, 2020.
10. Ghasempour, A., Optimum number of aggregators based on power consumption, cost, and network lifetime in advanced metering infrastructure architecture for smart grid Internet of Things. *13th IEEE Annual Consumer Communications & Networking Conference (CCNC)*, Las Vegas, NV, USA, 2016, https://doi.org/10.1109/CCNC.2016.7444787.
11. Khajenasiri, I., Estebsari, A., Verhelst, M., Gielen, G., A review on Internet of Things solutions for intelligent energy control in buildings for smart city applications. *Energy Procedia*, 111, 770–779, 2017.

12. Rathore, M.M., Ahmad, A., Paul, A., Rho, S., Urban planning and building smart cities based on the Internet of Things using big data analytics. *Comput. Networks*, 101, 63–80, 2016.
13. Ahmed, E., Yaqoob, I., Gani, A., Imran, M., Guizani, M., Internet of Things based smart environments: State of the art, taxonomy, and open research challenges. *IEEE Wireless Commun.*, 23, 5, 10–16, 2016.
14. Rathee, D., Ahuja, K., Nayyar, A., Sustainable future IoT services with touch-enabled handheld devices, in: *Security and Privacy of Electronic Healthcare Records: Concepts, Paradigms and Solutions*, p. 131, 2019.
15. Atzori, L., Iera, A., Morabito, G., The internet of things: A survey. *Comput. Networks*, 54, 2787–2805, 2010.
16. Ullah, F., Al-Turjman, F., Nayyar, A., IoT-based green city architecture using secured and sustainable android services. *Environ. Technol. Innovation*, 20, 101091, 2020. https://doi.org/10.1016/j.eti.2020.10109
17. Evangelos, A.K., Nikolaos, D.T., Anthony, C.B., Integrating RFIDs and smart objects into a Unified Internet of Things architecture. *Adv. Internet Things*, 1, 5–12, 2011. "Six Technologies with Potential Impacts on US Interests Out to 2025," Disruptive civil technologies, 2008.
18. Alamri, Ansari, W.S., Hassan, M.M., Hossain, M.S., Alelaiwi, A., Hossain, M.A., A survey on sensor-Cloud: Architecture, applications, and approaches. *Int. J. Distrib. Sens. Netw.*, 2013, 1–18, 2013.
19. Jain, R., Jain, N., Nayyar, A., Security and Privacy in Social Networks: Data and Structural Anonymity, in: *Handbook of Computer Networks and Cyber Security*, pp. 265–293, Springer, Cham, 2020.
20. Neyestani, N., Damavandi, M.Y., Shafie-khah, M., Catalão, J.P.S., Modeling the PEV traffic pattern in an urban environment with parking lots and charging stations. *PowerTech, 2015 IEEE Eindhoven*, Eindhoven, 20, pp. 1–6, 2015.
21. Yazdani-Damavandi, M., Moghaddam, M.P., Haghifam, M.R., Shafie-khah, M., Catalão, J.P.S., Modeling Operational Behavior of Plug-in Electric Vehicles' Parking Lot in Multienergy Systems. *IEEE Trans. Smart Grid*, 7, 124–135, 2016.
22. Nayyar, A., Rameshwar, R., Solanki, A., Internet of Things (IoT) and the Digital Business Environment: A Standpoint Inclusive Cyber Space, Cyber Crimes, and Cybersecurity. *The evaluation of Business in the Cyber age: Digital transformation, Treats and Security*, 1, 106–147, 2020.
23. Shafie-khah, M., Heydarian-Forushani, E., Golshan, M.E.H., Siano, P., Moghaddam, M.P., Sheikh-El-Eslami, M.K., Catalão, J.P.S., Optimal trading of plug-in electric vehicle aggregation agents in a market environment for sustainability. *Appl. Energy*, 162, 601–612, 15 January 2016.
24. Horizon 2020 work programme 2014–2015, Industrial leadership, Leadership in enabling and industrial technologies, in: *Information and Communication Technologies*, https://ec.europa.eu/programmes/horizon2020/en/h2020-section/leadership-enabling-and-industrial-technologies, 2014.

25. Ballon, P., Glidden, J., Kranas, P., Menychtas, A., Ruston, S., Van Der Graaf, S., Is there a need for a Cloud platform for European smart cities? *eChallenges e-2011 Conference Proceedings, IIMC International Information Management Corporation*, pp. 1–7, 2011.

26. Suciu, G., Vulpe, A., Halunga, S., Fratu, O., Todoran, G., Suciu, V., Smart cities built on resilient Cloud computing and secure Internet of Things. *19th International Conference on Control Systems and Computer Science (CSCS)*, pp. 513–518, 2013.

27. Petrolo, R., Mitton, N., Soldatos, J., Hauswirth, M., Schiele, G. et al., Integrating wireless sensor networks within a city Cloud. *Swansity workshop in Conjunction with IEEE SECON 2014*, 2014.

28. Chen, S.Y., Lai, C.F., Huang, Y.M., Jeng, Y.L., Intelligent home appliance recognition over IoT Cloud network. *Wireless Communications and Mobile Computing Conference (IWCMC)*, pp. 639–643, 2013.

29. Kaur, A., Singh, P., Nayyar, A., Fog Computing: Building a Road to IoT with Fog Analytics, in: *Fog Data Analytics for IoT Applications: Next Generation Process Model with State of the Art Technologies*, p. 59.

30. Ye, X. and Huang, J., A framework for Cloud-based smart home. *International Conference on Computer Science and Network Technology (ICCSNT)*, December 2011, vol. 2, pp. 894–897.

31. Martirano, L., A smart lighting control to save energy. *IEEE 6th International Conference on Intelligent Data Acquisition and Advanced Computing Systems (IDAACS)*, September 2011, vol. 1, pp. 132–138.

32. Castro, M., Jara, A., Skarmeta, A., Smart lighting solutions for smart cities. *27th International Conference on Advanced Information Networking and Applications Workshops*, March 2013, pp. 1374–1379.

33. Zanella, Bui, N., Castellani, A., Vangelista, L., Zorzi, M., Internet of Things for Smart Cities. *IEEE Internet Things J.*, 1, 1, 22–32, 2014.

34. Papadimitratos, P., De La Fortelle, A., Evenssen, K., Brignolo, R., Cosenza, S., Vehicular communication systems: Enabling technologies, applications, and future outlook on intelligent transportation. *IEEE Commun. Mag.*, 47, 11, 84–95, 2009.

35. Lee, S., Su, Y.-W., Shen, C.-C., A comparative study of wireless protocols: Bluetooth, uwb, zigbee, and Wi-Fi, in: *Industrial Electronics Society, 2007. IECON 2007, 33rd Annual Conference of the IEEE*, IEEE, pp. 46–51, 2007.

36. Lin, X., Adhikary, A., Wang, Y.-P.E., Random Access Preamble Design and Detection for 3GPP Narrowband IoT Systems. *IEEE Wireless Communications Letters, arXiv preprint arXiv:1605.05384*, 5, 640–643, 2016.

37. Kamienski, C., Soininen, J.-P., Taumberger, M., Dantas, R., Toscano, A., Salmon Cinotti, T., Filev Maia, R., Torre Neto, A., Smart Water Management Platform: IoT-Based Precision Irrigation for Agriculture. *Sensors*, 19, 276, 2019.

38. Omoniwa, B., Hussain, R., Javed, M.A., Bouk, S.H., Malik, S.A., Fog/Edge Computing-based IoT (FECIoT): Architecture, Applications, and Research Issues. *IEEE Internet Things J.*, 6, 4118–4149, 2019.

39. Khan, R., Khan, S.U., Zaheer, R., Khan, S., Future Internet: The Internet of Things Architecture, PossibleApplications and Key Challenges, in: *Proceedings of the IEEE 10th International Conference on Frontiers of Information Technology*, Islamabad, Pakistan, 17–19 December 2012.

40. Mashal, I., Alsaryrah, O., Chung, T.Y., Yang, C.Z., Kuo, W.H., Agrawal, D.P., Choices for interaction with things on internet and underlying issues. *Ad Hoc Netw.*, 28, 68–90, 2015.

41. Bellavista, P., Corradi, A., Foschini, L., Scotece, D., Differentiated Service/ Data Migration for Edge Services Leveraging Container Characteristics. *IEEE Access*, 7, 139746–139758, 2019.

42. Mekki, K., Bajic, E., Chaxel, F., Meyer, F., A comparative study of LPWAN technologies for large-scale IoT deployment. *ICT Express*, 5, 1–7, 2019.

43. Asif-Ur-Rahman, M., Afsana, F., Mahmud, M., Kaiser, M.S., Ahmed, M.R., Kaiwartya, O., James-Taylor, A., Toward a Heterogeneous Mist, Fog, and Cloud based Framework for the Internet of Healthcare Things. *IEEE Internet Things J.*, 6, 3, 4049–4062, 2019.

44. Open Mobile Alliance, NGSI Requirements, OMA-RD-NGSI-V1_0. Available online: http://www.openmobilealliance.org (accessed on 20 December 2019).

45. FIWARE Ultralight 2.0 Protocol. Available online: http://fiware-iotagent-ul. rtfd.io (accessed on 20 December 2019).

46. Gozalvez, J., New 3GPP standard for IoT. New #GPP standard for IoT, *IEEE Veh. Technol. Mag.*, 11, 14–20, 2016.

47. Sigfox, Available online: http://sigfox.com (accessed on 20 December 2019).33.LoRa Alliance. Available online: http://lora-alliance.org, (accessed on 20 December 2019).

48. ChirpStack, Available online: https://www.chirpstack.io (accessed on 16 December 2019).

49. Bittencourt, L., Immich, R., Sakellariou, R., Fonseca, N., Madeira, E., Curado, M., Villas, L., DaSilva, L., Lee, C., Rana, O., The Internet of Things, Fog and Cloud continuum: Integration and challenges. *Internet Things*, 3–4, 134–155, 2018.

50. Kamienski, C., Jentsch, M., Eisenhauer, M., Kiljander, J., Ferrera, E., Rosengren, P., Thestrup, J., Souto, E., Andrade, W., Sadok, D., Application Development for the Internet of Things: A Context-Aware Mixed Criticality Systems Development Platform. *Comput. Commun.*, 104, 1–16, 2017.

51. OASIS, MQTT Version 5.0.OASIS Committee Specification 02, May 2018. Available online: http://docs.oasis-open.org/mqtt/mqtt/v5.0/cs02/mqtt-v5.0-cs02.html (accessed on 17 September 2019).

52. FIWARE, Orion Context Broker. Available online: http://fiware-orion.rtfd.io (accessed on 20 December 2019).

53. Apache Kafka, Available online: http://kafka.apache.org (accessed on 20 December 2019).

54. Apache Spark, Available online: http://spark.apache.org (accessed on 20 December 2019).

55. CrateDB, Available online: http://crate.io (accessed on 20 December 2019).

56. Farrell, S., Low-Power Wide Area Network (LPWAN) Overview, in: *Internet RFC 8376*, Internet Engineering Task Force, Fremont, CA, USA, 2018.

57. Neirotti, P., De Marco, A., Cagliano, A.C., Mangano, G., Scorrano, F., Current trends in smart city initiatives: Some stylised facts. *Cities*, 38, 25–36, 2014.

58. Watteyne, T. and Pister, K.S., Smarter cities through standards-based wireless sensor networks. *IBM J. Res. Dev.*, 55, 1.2, 7–1, 2011.

59. Centenaro, M., Vangelista, L., Zanella, A., Zorzi, M., Long-range communications in unlicensed bands: The rising stars in the IoT and smart city scenarios. *IEEE Wireless Commun.*, 23, 5, 60–67, 2016.

60. Flowfence: Practical data protection for emerging IoT application frameworks, in: *25th USENIX Security Symposium (USENIX Security 16)*, USENIX Association, Austin, TX, 2016, [Online]. Available: https://www.usenix.org/conference/usenixsecurity16/technicalsessions/presentation/fernandes.

61. Sikder, A.K., Aksu, H., Uluagac, A.S., 6th sense: A context-aware sensor-based attack detector for smart devices, in: *26th USENIX Security Symposium (USENIX Security 17)*, USENIX Association, Vancouver, BC, pp. 397–414, 2017, [Online]. Available: https://www.usenix.org/conference/usenixsecurity17/technicalsessions/presentation/sikder.

62. Acar, A., Celik, Z.B., Aksu, H., Uluagac, A.S., McDaniel, P., Achieving secure and differentially private computations in multiparty settings, in: *IEEE Privacy-Aware Computing (PAC)*, 2017.

9

Indoor Air Quality (IAQ) in Green Buildings, a Pre-Requisite to Human Health and Well-Being

Ankita Banerjee*, N.P. Melkania and Ayushi Nain

Gautam Buddha University, Greater Noida, India

Abstract

Indoor Air Quality (IAQ) is one of the most important determining factors of human health as more than half of the air inhaled by a person during his/her lifetime is at home. Prominent air pollutants found indoors are Volatile Organic Compounds (VOCs), Particulate Matter (PM), Carbon monoxide (CO), Lead (Pb), Oxides of Nitrogen (NOx), and Asbestos. These pollutants are well-known causative agents of allergies, hypersensitivity, lung infections, and Sick Building Syndrome (SBS). Several forms of these pollutants are reported to be carcinogenic too. Primary sources of emissions are ordinarily from building materials, paints, furniture, Environmental Tobacco Smoke (ETS), and other secondary pollutants. Indoor air pollution exacerbates due to inadequate ventilation, air distribution inefficiency, and improper air intake location. Smart and sustainable approaches to green building construction should incorporate IAQ as a critical component of building design. Usage of low-VOC emitting building materials, interior components, and paints needs to be emphasized to create a wholesome indoor environment. Strategies for ample ventilation, efficient distribution of fresh air supply, properly designed Heating, Ventilation, and Air Conditioning (HVAC) systems along with indoor air pollution control measures should be imperative to a healthy home or workspace. At a reasonable energy cost, maintaining good IAQ is incorporated by notable green-building certification systems like LEED and GRIHA. These rating agencies have included IAQ and human well-being as one of the central principles of green buildings' evaluation. A better perception of how the IAQ affects us, and compliance of Green Building certification is, an urgent requirement for a better and healthier lifestyle.

*Corresponding author: ankita3221@gmail.com

Arun Solanki, Adarsh Kumar and Anand Nayyar (eds.) Digital Cities Roadmap: IoT-Based Architecture and Sustainable Buildings, (293–318) © 2021 Scrivener Publishing LLC

Keywords: Indoor Air Quality (IAQ), green buildings, Volatile Organic Compounds (VOCs), Particulate Matter (PM), Sick Building Syndrome (SBS), Ozone (O_3)

9.1　Introduction

The characteristics of the air present in and around buildings and building structures is known as the indoor air quality (IAQ). It has a primary influence on the healthfulness and well-being of the building inhabitants.

Historically, healthy IAQ and proper ventilation have been determinants of hygiene since the dawn of human awareness concerning pollution and its detriments to health. With more advances in studies and research, by the 18th century, it was clear that polluted enclosures, small and unventilated places had stale or 'bad' air that was harmful to the health of human beings. The presence of odors and the absence of fresh air sources were regarded as the benchmark for IAQ before the advent of scientific progress [1].

There has been a significant shift in the global economy from primary and secondary sectors to service and knowledge-based sectors, that essentially take place in indoor environments [2]. It is imperative to comprehend the influence of the indoor environment better, as not only is it our living space but also the workspace of millions. In the present scenario, studies have proven the direct bearing of IAQ on the healthfulness of inhabitants. Studies conducted in the developing countries highlight the prevalence of unvented fossil fuel burning that cause heavily polluted indoor environments. Health ailments like Chronic Obstructive Pulmonary Disease (COPD), Acute Respiratory Infections (ARI), and lung cancers have often been attributed to polluted indoor environments in developing nations. Meanwhile, the developed countries have already faced the challenges of low IAQ and are now moving towards novel diseases. Allergies, hypersensitivity, Sick Building Syndrome (SBS), Legionnaire's disease, Multiple Chemical Sensitivity (MCS) as well as ARI have taken over the developed regions due to highly insulated spaces, devoid of natural ventilation.

Poor IAQ could be as a result of organic pollutants, synthetic building materials as well as biological contaminants. With increasing consciousness and better knowledge about common indoor pollutants, the risks of health impacts can be minimized. Studies on sustainable building designs have proven that technologies and strategies can create a favorable environment for occupant's performance, comfort, and healthfulness [3, 44, 46].

As advances are being made in building design and efficiency, the need for a healthy living space becomes all the more imperative [4, 42].

Since the inception of green building certification programs, air quality has been considered one of the default elements. Indoor air quality as a parameter is currently included, in some measure in various certification schemes worldwide. However, standardized information on the number of credits addressing IAQ that are to be employed during the certification method and, if awarded, whether this would considerably improve the IAQ remains unanswered. The average contribution of the credits specified for IAQ from various green building programs is 7.5%. It could vary from about 3 to 11%, based on an evaluation of 55 green building certifications from 30 different countries [5]. This insignificant percentage of credits allotted to IAQ might pose a challenge to the builders for considering it as an incentive to be accomplished.

Different inorganic gases, volatile organic chemicals (VOCs), particulate matter (PM), microbes, and their spores are released and suspended in the indoor air and are inhaled by building occupants leading to health impacts. Green buildings could lead to better occupant satisfaction in terms of health and well-being. Various studies provide insights into the impact green buildings can have on the health of occupants [35]. One such study on the comparison of green and conventional hospital buildings showed reduced mortality rates and lower bloodstream infection rates. It also lowered medicine intake in green hospital buildings; some of the impacts could be attributed to better IAQ.

Section 9.2 of this chapter discusses the commonly encountered indoor air pollutants often responsible for a poor IAQ. Commonly encountered indoor air pollutants like carbon monoxide (CO), particulate matter (PM), volatile organic compounds (VOCs), asbestos, environmental tobacco smoke (ETS), lead (Pb), nitrogen dioxide (NO_2), ozone (O_3), and biological pollutants along with the impact they have on human health are discussed in Sections 9.2.1 through 9.2.9. The possible health ailments related to these indoor air contaminants are discussed in Section 9.3. The symptomatic exposure-related characterization of building-related illnesses like sick building syndrome (SBS), acute and chronic impacts is also addressed in Sections 9.3.1 through 9.3.3, respectively. Under Section 9.4, different strategies are discussed that describe the efficient ways and methods that are successfully used or can be useful in green buildings for maintaining a healthy IAQ. Section 9.5 concludes the chapter with future scope.

9.2 Pollutants Responsible for Poor IAQ

Various indoor sources are responsible for the release of gaseous or particular pollutants that lead to a poor IAQ (Table 9.1). Inadequate ventilation could also increase the pollutant levels indoors by lowering dilution levels, and low levels of incoming outdoor air prevent the escape of pollutants from living spaces. High temperatures and moisture levels could also alter the concentration of some indoor pollutants.

Pollutants responsible for impacting health in indoor environments can be of chemical or biological origin. Many of the contaminants could cause temporary symptoms like irritation and allergies, while some carcinogenic compounds are responsible for deleterious impacts.

Some of the commonly encountered indoor air pollutants, their sources, and their effects on human health and well-being have been explored in the subsequent sections.

9.2.1 Volatile Organic Compounds (VOCs)

Volatile Organic Compounds (VOCs) are a group of organic compounds with a vapor pressure of 0.01 kPa or more at 20 °C. These compounds can

Table 9.1 Sources of indoor air pollution.

Sources	Example
Building materials	Asbestos, cement, paints, adhesives, lacquers, varnish
Furnishings	Carpet, flooring, upholstery, pressed wood products
Fuel combustion	Vented or unvented cooktops, heaters
Tobacco containing products	Cigars, cigarettes, *beedis*, tobacco in *hookahs*
Central heating/cooling/ Humidification system	Cooling towers, HVAC systems, humidifiers
Household cleaning, maintenance, and personal care products	Pesticides, disinfectants, cosmetics, room fresheners, polishes
Outdoor sources	Radon, outdoor air pollution

be emitted from varied indoor sources like furnishings, building materials, cleaning, and consumer products, tobacco smoke, outdoor air presence, and from chemical reactions indoors [34, 45]. These pollutants could also enter into the indoor living environment from attached buildings or garages. Some typical symptoms pertaining to VOCs exposure are shown in Figure 9.1. Indoor air typically comprises many VOCs, and the concentrations can often be higher than outdoor spaces. Formaldehyde and BTEX (Benzene, Toluene, Ethylbenzene, and Xylene) are examples of some common indoor VOCs. The VOCs may be odorous compounds, and some of them are known or suspected causative agents of a variety of short-term as well as long-term adverse health impacts [6].

Organic chemicals are used mainly as the ingredients of sundry household products. Paints, varnish, and wax carry organic solvents, as does the variety of disinfecting, cleaning, and degreasing agents, cosmetic products, as well as art supplies. Fuels also are organic constituents. Such organic products are capable of releasing its constituent organic compounds while in use, and, to some extent, when stored.

A study conducted by USEPA in 1985 found the levels of a dozen organic contaminants to be 2 to 5 times higher in buildings than outside.

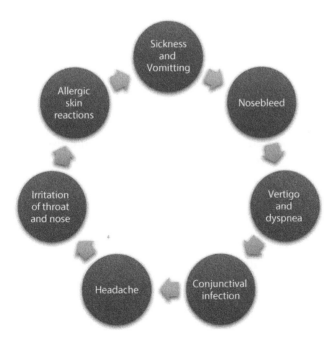

Figure 9.1 Common symptoms of VOC exposure.

The pollutant levels were higher indoors regardless of the location of the houses, be it in rural or industrial-urban localities. It indicates that people could expose themselves and others in their vicinity to the high levels of organic chemical pollutants while using specific products. High concentrations of the organic pollutants could also persist in the air long after the product's use was complete.

Health impacts: Potential adverse health impacts from VOC exposure may include a sense of unpleasant odors, irritation of mucous membrane, and aggravation of asthma [43]. The systemic impacts can consist of fatigue and strain in concentration. Toxic and chronic effects like carcinogenicity is also a possibility [7]. Some commonly found VOCs in the indoor environment are human (benzene) or animal (chloroform) carcinogens. Certain VOCs are also known to be genotoxic.

9.2.2   Particulate Matter (PM)

Particulate matter (PM) can be dry solids or liquid suspensions. Smoke, dust, fume, and mists are examples of different forms of particulates. Dust consists of solid particles ranging in size from 0.1 to 100 μm, whereas smoke particles are typically 0.25 μm, while fumes are generally 0.1 μm or less in diameter. Mists are fine droplets of liquid in suspended air. Solid particles with significantly greater length than their diameter are known as fibers, such as asbestos, synthetic mineral and vitreous fibers, and refractory ceramic fibers. Aerosols of microbial, plant, or animal origin, also known as bioaerosols, are of particular concern to human health. Bioaerosols could range from 0.5 to 30 μm in diameter.

Health impacts: The airborne particulate matter can cause diverse health effects depending upon various factors, such as dimension, dose, and durability of the particles as well as the toxicity of its material constituent. Particles in the respirable range can vary in size from 4 to 10 μm. The time limit for which the particle could exist inside our bodies is its 'durability'. The dosage of particulate exposure and its durability are responsible for the toxicity it can cause. In certain instances, even low exposures could lead up to detrimental health impacts, while higher exposures may not always have adverse consequences on building occupants' health. Particles smaller than 2 μm are of particular concern. The larger particles measuring from 8 to 10 μm in diameter are separated and retained by the upper respiratory tract. The intermediate-sized particles are deposited primarily in the lung airways, where they can be cleared-out by swallowing or coughing out.

Less than 50% of particulates inhaled settles down in the respiratory tract. The submicron particulates can infiltrate more profoundly into the lungs, but much quantity of these particles can also be exhaled [7].

9.2.3 Asbestos

Asbestos is a naturally-occurring mineral fiber that occurs in rocks and soil. This material fiber is known for being tensile and heat resistant and has been used in various construction materials for insulation purposes and as fire-retardant material. Asbestos finds uses in a wide range of manufactured materials like roofing materials, coating materials, tiles, and other building components. High airborne asbestos concentrations could occur when the asbestos-containing building components are disturbed due to sanding, cutting, or other revamping works. Attempts to remove asbestos-containing materials without proper precautions can release the fibers into the indoor air, increasing the asbestos levels and causing an unhealthy environment. Asbestos was a prevalent building material for constructions done before the 1970s. It usually does not cause any respiratory hazard except in cases where individuals actively disturb it while doing routine maintenance and construction work.

Health impacts: Diseases like asbestosis or silicosis may occur on inhalation of the asbestos fibers. The asbestos fibers on inhalation cause scarring of the lungs leading to symptoms like dyspnea and cough. Such illnesses require chronic exposures of at least 10 to 20 years to develop and, thus, are rare in homes or workspace environments [7].

9.2.4 Carbon Monoxide (CO)

Carbon monoxide (CO) gas is difficult to detect as it is colorless and odorless. Carbon monoxide gas gets produced on the incomplete combustion of hydrocarbons. One is unable to recognize its inhalation, which could even be fatal as it is an asphyxiant. Inhalation of carbon monoxide induces headache as hemoglobin in our blood has a high affinity for carbon monoxide (about 240 times higher than for oxygen). Due to this affinity of the carbon monoxide molecules, there is a deleterious shift in the blood's oxygen dissociation curve. Carbon monoxide is known to inhibit the transport of oxygen in the blood by forming a compound called carboxyhemoglobin that inhibits the cytochrome oxidase enzyme. Cobb and Etzel have suggested that carbon monoxide poisoning inside homes represented a significant preventable disease.

Familiar indoor sources that emit carbon monoxide include stove-tops, kerosene lanterns, water heaters, mainstream, and sidestream smoke from tobacco-containing products, furnaces, and unvented or improperly vented sources of combustion [8]. Carbon monoxide emanating from automobiles can enter a building that has air intake situated at street level or nearby garages and carry them to the indoor environment. Improper use of portable generators is another growing issue that can release carbon monoxide gas. The air contaminated with carbon monoxide may also directly enter the building if the indoor air is at a negative atmospheric pressure relative to the outdoor atmosphere. Generally, carbon monoxide levels in homes rarely cross the 5-ppm mark. In samples collected from randomly selected households, 10 percent failed a back-drafting test; in such conditions, carbon monoxide sources may contribute to considerably high emissions levels.

Health impacts: The high affinity of carbon monoxide for blood hemo-globin could result in intoxication, further causing tissue hypoxia, and impacting multiple organ systems. Fatigue, chest pain in people suffering from heart disease, headache, vertigo, memory impairment, tinnitus, and nausea are other frequent symptoms resulting from chronic carbon monoxide poisoning [7, 9].

9.2.5   Environmental Tobacco Smoke (ETS)

There has been a remarkable increase in the importance of environmental tobacco smoke (ETS) as a pollution source in indoor air, especially in developing countries. The ETS is an aggregate of particulate and gaseous pollutants that primarily emanate from cigarettes, cigars, pipe, and beedi smoking. Various ETS components are respirable suspended particles, nitrogen oxides, nicotine, acrolein, and nitroso compounds. The average long-term concentrations of suspended particulate matter in indoor environments is much higher in smokers' homes than in non-smokers' homes. Exposures to ETS can lead to lower respiratory tract related illnesses in infants and the incidence of chronic respiratory symptoms in adults. Non-smokers are also vulnerable to exposure to ETS at smoker-homes. Thus, public health risk of lung cancers associated with ETS exposure is potentially high. The smoke emanating from cigarettes, pipes, and cigars comprises of more than 3,800 different substances. Airborne particulate matter is reportedly 2–3 times higher in smokers' homes. Exposures to ETS may occur at home, workplace, relatives' homes, and other public places.

The ETS is a significant source of particulates and consists of the mainstream smoke exhaled by the smoker as well as the sidestream smoke emitted from the burning tobacco. It has been seen that about 70 to 90% of the smoke could emanate from the sidestream smoke. The sidestream smoke is known to have chemical constituents slightly different than that of the mainstream smoke. Over 4,700 types of compounds have been identified from tobacco smoke, including notable human toxins and carcinogens, like nicotine, carbon monoxide, formaldehyde, ammonia, nitrosamines, and benzo(a)pyrene, various heavy metals, benzene, and aromatic amines.

Health impacts: From the studies conducted inside residences and offices where tobacco-smoking was allowed, ETS has been perceived as a significant source of a variety of gases and particulates. ETS is known to induce lung cancers, respiratory infections, asthma exacerbation, middle ear effusion, as well as causing low birth weight in children. The USEPA classifies ETA as a known human carcinogen. It could also lead to headaches, irritation, and heart diseases [7].

9.2.6 Biological Pollutants

Indoor air pollutants of biological origin (bio-aerosols) can be derived from a host of organisms and their cellular components. These are the airborne substances generated by bacteria, viruses, fungi, algae, protozoa, mites, insects, plants, as well as their by-products. In indoor environments, locations that provide optimum nutrition, humidity, and temperature may become the hot-bed for microbial proliferation. Various building components and materials may provide suitable conditions for such agents to effectively thrive, grow, and spread to other parts of the building. A humidifier or an air cooler is one such example where all the conditions are ideal for microbe growth (like *Legionella*) and dissemination. For microbes to be pathogenic, the bioaerosols must be transported to the building occupants in sufficient doses. Bioaerosols can impact occupant health through several mechanisms like allergy, infection, or toxic reactions depending upon the type of organism, the exposure dose, and the susceptibility of the individual.

Water pipelines in the buildings are a significant source of microbe proliferation. Several instances of legionellosis have resulted from subjection to potable water pipelines. Water drainage systems are well-established sources of infective aerosols. Building inhabitants themselves are an essential root of infectious bioaerosols in indoor environments. Infected individuals can disperse virulent particles and aerosols by talking, sneezing, coughing, or even through flaking of skin lesions. Larger airborne droplets could transmit infectious particles to those in close proximity to the patient, while smaller droplets could remain airborne for even large distances [7].

Health impacts: The presence of biological pollutants in the indoor air is capable of causing allergic or infective building-related illnesses. Viable microbes cause infection, while non-viable particles may promote an allergic immunological response. The microorganisms that are known causative agents of diseases in healthcare facilities include bacterial pathogens of the genus *Mycobacterium*, *Legionella*, and *Pseudomonas*, fungal pathogens like *Fusarium* and *Aspergillus*, and protozoan pathogens like *Acanthamoeba*, *Cryptosporidium*, and *Giardia*.

Fungal pathogens: The exposure to fungal spores, fragments of fungal hyphae, or secondary metabolites, from an indoor environment could lead to respiratory issues ranging from allergic responses (like asthma, rhinitis, hypersensitivity, and pneumonitis) to diseases of infectious nature like blastomycosis, aspergillosis, and histoplasmosis. Besides acute toxicosis, various forms of cancers are attributed to respiratory exposures of mycotoxins [10]. Sufficient literature provides backing to the association between moisture indicators in homes and related symptoms like wheezing or coughing. The filamentous fungi reproduce through spore formations and are known as molds. Mold spores can range from 2 to 10 μm in diameter. These spores disperse readily through water droplets and airflow and remain airborne for long periods. Symptoms suggesting irritant and toxigenic responses from mold-spore exposure indoors could range from mild to extreme. Molds are capable of producing more than 300 different toxins (mycotoxins). Mycotoxins are associated with actively proliferating fungal colonies and spores, and are not gaseous. The natural by-products of microbial metabolism, produced by actively growing organisms are known as microbial volatile organic compounds (MVOCs). These compounds are known to cause headaches and a feeling of nausea and uneasiness in building occupants [7].

Viral pathogens: Viruses can easily spread from infected persons but cannot proliferate outside a host cell. Thus, viruses do not reproduce in building components or structures but can be disseminated throughout buildings via airflow and air ducts. The spread of viruses from person-to-person is widespread. In an instance, most of the passengers inside an airline contracted influenza from being exposed to a single acutely ill passenger [11].

In this example, the plane was parked on the runway for a few hours, with the air-ventilation turned off. A type of coronavirus causes severe acute respiratory syndrome (SARS). The scientific community earlier assumed that SARS resulted from droplet transmission. However, an apartment building outbreak established the airborne mode of communication for this particular disease (in this case, it most likely disseminated from the bathroom drain) [7].

9.2.7   Lead (Pb)

Lead (Pb) is a heavy metal that has been recognized as a harmful environmental pollutant for a long time. Lead is particularly toxic for children as their rapidly growing bodies can accumulate more lead than adults. The brain and the nervous system of children are also more responsive to the damaging effects of lead. Toddlers and young children also tend to place their hands or other objects into their mouths that may contain lead-dust, thereby being more exposed to the metal. Children can also get exposed to lead from eating and drinking food or water that is contaminated by lead or from dishes or tumblers that might contain lead. Inhalation of lead dust from chipping of lead-based paint, dust from lead-contaminated soil, or playing with toys coated with lead paint can also result in harmful impacts. Before lead was known to be toxic, it was used extensively in paints, automobile fuel, pipelines, and in a variety of other products.

The chipping of lead-based paint is a crucial source of lead exposure. The process of removal of lead-based paint, if conducted improperly by methods like sanding, scraping, or open-flame burning, can lead to harmful levels lead-particles in the indoor air. High airborne lead concentrations can also result from intrusion of outdoor dust laden with lead particles, like contaminated soil. Lead particles can also get generated from indoor activities like and stained-glass making and soldering [12].

Health impacts: Exposure to lead is proven to cause severe consequences on the health of children. Higher exposure levels can attack the brain as well as the central nervous system, causing convulsions, coma, and in extreme cases, even death. Survivors of acute lead poisoning often suffer from mental retardation or are impacted by several behavioral disorders. Low concentrations of lead exposure, causing no obvious external symptoms, can induce a gamut of injuries across several organ systems. Lead can immensely impact children's brain development, leading to lower intelligence quotient (IQ), behavioral changes, like reduction in attention span, increased anti-social behavior, and low educational attainment. Health ailments like renal impairment, anemia, hypertension, and immunotoxicity can also result from lead exposures. Neurological and behavioral impacts of lead are often irreversible. There are no known 'safe' concentrations for lead in human blood, as even concentrations below 5 µg/dl may be associated with impaired intelligence and behavioral development in children along with various learning difficulties. As the lead concentrations increase, the severity and range of symptoms and impacts also keep on increasing [13].

9.2.8   Nitrogen Dioxide (NO$_2$)

The most commonly encountered oxide of nitrogen is nitrogen dioxide gas. It is a pungent, corrosive gas, with a perceived odor threshold between 0.1 and 0.4 ppm. It is orange-brown in color but appears yellowish or colorless at lower concentrations. Nitrogen dioxide is a pollutant and causes respiratory effects in humans at high concentrations. Stovetops are one of the significant sources of emission of nitrogen dioxide gas inside buildings. High nitrogen dioxide concentrations are often linked to the usage of candles and mosquito coils, unvented and vented combustion appliances with defective installations, welding, and also from environmental tobacco smoke (ETS).

Sources that generate carbon monoxide gas can also give rise to nitric oxide (NO) and nitrogen dioxide (NO$_2$) gas as well. Provisions of underground or attached garages near homes can also increase indoor levels of nitrogen dioxide gas. An unvented gas stove could contribute approximately 0.025 ppm of nitrogen dioxide inside the living spaces of homes. Peak levels of nitrogen dioxide may reach up to 0.2 to 0.4 ppm during cooking activities. Various epidemiological studies have tested the hypothesis that exposure to an indoor concentration of nitrogen dioxide damages health, but findings have not been remarkably consistent. However, since gas appliances are widely in use, and short-term exposures can be high (2 to 3 mg/m^3), it is, thus, a pollutant of concern in the indoor environment. The exchange rate between the indoor and outdoor air also affects the nitrogen dioxide levels inside buildings. Indoor concentrations can vary widely depending on indoor sources, air circulation within and in-between the rooms, building characteristics, types of furnishing material, and the rate of reactive decay from interior surfaces [9]. The indoor concentration of nitrogen dioxide often exceeds the ambient levels due to the presence of a strong indoor source and a trend towards energy-efficient homes with reduced ventilation mechanisms. The usage of unvented indoor combustion seldom observes concentrations to induce acute toxicity as its quantity is insufficient. Chronic effects like pulmonary disorders, from exposure to combinations of low-level combustion products, are, however, possible [7].

Health impacts: Commonly observed symptoms related to nitrogen dioxide exposure are lung function deterioration, increased airway reactivity, and increased susceptibility to infections. Continued high exposure can be a contributing factor to the development of acute or chronic bronchitis. Nitrogen dioxide has low water solubility and thus can be inhaled deep into the lungs, where it can cause a delayed inflammatory response. Higher airway resistance has been reported at concentrations of 1.5 to 2 ppm. Nitrogen dioxide also is registered as potentially carcinogenic due to its property of free radical production. At high concentrations, nitrogen dioxide can cause lung damage and may inflict indirect health impacts by enhancing the susceptibility to respiratory infections [7].

9.2.9   Ozone (O$_3$)

Ozone (O$_3$) gas is a respiratory irritant that can alter humans' pulmonary functioning at concentrations as low as 0.12 ppm. Ozone-induced reactions impact the indoor air quality since they give rise to secondary pollutants, mainly aldehydes that are known irritants and odorous compounds [36]. The concentration of ozone in indoor air leads to total ozone exposure, and the reactions caused by indoor ozone can give rise to submicron particles contributing to the total particulate exposure. Ozone exposures of 60 to 80 ppb can induce inflammatory responses, increased airway responsiveness, as well as broncho-constriction.

Ozone gas emits from electrical or coronal discharge from office equipment, like laser printers and photocopy machines. Ozone gas can form when ozone-generating devices (portable air cleaners and ionizers) are being used indoors [14]. Indoor ozone concentrations can be highly variable, depending upon the outdoor concentrations, air exchange rate, and indoor sources, varying significantly, hourly as well as seasonally. The half-life of an ozone molecule is between 7 and 10 min, which is also determined by ozone removal through air turbulence. Reactions between other indoor pollutants and ozone gas are favorable thermodynamically, but the rate of reaction is slow in the majority of cases. Indoor ozone adversely affects health [15]. It can also give rise to stable reaction products, which could be more of an irritant than their precursors [16]. The reaction products could be respiratory irritants having chronic toxicity as well as carcinogenicity [15].

Health impacts: Ozone inhalation can damage the lungs. A low amount of ozone exposure can be responsible for throat irritation and cough, chest pain, and shortness of breath. Ozone is capable of worsening chronic respiratory illnesses like asthma and compromises the ability to resist respiratory infections. Susceptibility to ozone varies from person to person. People suffering from respiratory issues, as well as healthy people, could experience problems in breathing while exposed to ozone concentrations.

9.3   Health Impacts of Poor IAQ

As it has been established in the preceding sections, pollutants can be significant determinants of the IAQ of buildings. Various symptoms of exposure to the individual pollutants overlap and are not often easy to attribute to a pollutant group. Specific names are collectively used to relate the impacts due to such unhealthy indoor surroundings like building-related illness (BRI) and sick building syndrome (SBS). Sick building syndrome is a familiar occurrence and is often talked about nowadays. It has been explained in detail in the subsequent sections. Similarly, illnesses related to indoor air exposure could be from long-term (chronic) pollutant exposures in low doses or short-term (acute) exposures in high doses. The human health symptoms pertaining to such chronic or acute exposures differ considerably and have been described in detail.

9.3.1   Sick Building Syndrome (SBS)

Sick building syndrome (SBS) describes several adverse impacts on the health of the 'sick' building occupants like headache, mucosal irritation, fatigue, occasional lower respiratory-tract infections, nausea, and various other symptoms. There is a need for consensus on a working definition for sick building syndrome. It has been defined as a severe discomfort in the form of eye, nose, or throat irritation. Other symptoms may include headaches, sore throat, feeling of fatigue, mild neurotoxic symptoms, skin allergies, and nausea. The sick building occupants often complain about odors that may persist for more than two weeks, while a large percentage of complainants report instant relief upon exiting the building premises [33].

The high prevalence of health issues in office-workers is a typical sign of SBS. The widespread occurrence of such building-related symptoms has elicited the World Health Organization (WHO) to categorize SBS under various heads like sensory eye, nose or throat irritation, skin irritation, neurotoxic symptoms, or complaints of odors. Sick building syndrome is characterized by the lack of common physical signs and clinical result anomalies. The term 'non-specifics' is employed at times to show that the symptomatic patterns reported by affected building occupants are not consonant with any particular disease. Supplementary signs of SBS could include nosebleeds, tightness of chest, or fever. Researchers have tried correlating SBS symptoms with low neurological and physiological performances also. In controlled studies, SBS symptoms have been shown to induce a reduction in the performance of susceptible individuals [7].

9.3.2   Acute Impacts

Specific health issues may appear right after exposure or on continued exposure to any pollutant. Health impacts like headache, dizziness, fatigue, irritation of eye, nose, and throat may be regarded as common symptoms. Such instantaneous effects are often short-lived and usually treatable. The treatment often lies in eliminating the patient's exposure to the pollution source if it is identifiable. Susceptibility to certain indoor air pollutants can aggravate symptoms of certain diseases, like asthma. The probability of immediate responses to air pollutants can depend on various determinants, including the age and presence of other pre-existing medical infirmities. In some instances, one's reaction to a contaminant may rely on individual responsiveness, which can vary significantly from person-to-person. Few individuals can also get sensitized to chemical or biological pollutants after recurrent or high doses of exposures.

Several immediate impacts of exposure to indoor air pollutants are related to the common cold and other viral diseases. Therefore, it is often difficult to ascertain if the symptoms are specifically due to indoor air pollution exposure. Thus, it is imperative to pay heed to the time and place where the symptoms befall. For instance, if the signs decline or go away in a short while when the person is away from the space, effort should be made to recognize indoor pollution sources that might be possible causes. Some impacts might worsen by a reduced supply of outdoor air inlet or the heating, cooling, or humid conditions prevailing inside the buildings.

A biological standard for an acute response to low indoor VOC levels is based on three mechanisms: sensory perception of the surroundings, weak inflammatory reaction, and environmental stress response [17]. An expanding body of literature efficiently reviews the techniques for estimating VOCs' effects on nasal and ocular mucosa. Low, sub-threshold concentrations of various VOCs, as observed in different contaminated indoor environments, could add to the sensory impact, producing significant sensory irritation [7, 37].

9.3.3   Chronic Impacts

Chronic impacts are the health effects that might appear after years of exposure to a pollutant or occur only after long and recurring periods of exposure. These impacts could be fatal and include certain respiratory diseases, heart diseases, and even cancers. It is wise to try to improve the IAQ at homes even when the indications are not detectable. The pollutants commonly encountered indoors can induce many hazardous health outcomes, but there is uncertainty concerning the ambient levels or period of exposure that causes specific health issues. It has also been observed that people respond quite differently to exposure to indoor air pollutants. Further investigation is required to understand the health outcomes after exposure to average and high concentrations of contaminants occurring for short periods in indoor spaces.

Theoretical risk assessment researches suggest that risk from chronic VOC exposures from indoor environments is more significant than that associated with outdoor air exposure. Exposures to gaseous oxides of nitrogen (NO_x), sulfur dioxide (SO_2), and ozone (O_3) in residential and commercial buildings are of significant concern as it could potentially cause acute and chronic respiratory impacts on exposed individuals. People with pre-existing pulmonary disorders are particularly vulnerable to such exposure [7].

9.4   Strategies to Maintain a Healthy Indoor Environment in Green Buildings

'Green Buildings' are the fabrications planned explicitly for the efficiency in the use of energy, water, and materials, ensuring sustainability while maximizing occupant comfort. The United States Environmental Protection Agency (USEPA) defines green buildings as structures that utilize resource-efficient processes and are environmentally responsible throughout the building's life cycle [18]. Recent years have seen some green building certification programs that strive for a healthy indoor environmental quality (IEQ) inside buildings, ensuring the well-being of building occupants [19, 38–40]. The IAQ, along with other factors like lighting, acoustics, ergonomics, and temperature, are considered for creating a healthy IEQ.

Particulate or dust control strategies incorporate source reduction or elimination, acceptable housekeeping practices, dilution of indoor air contaminants through ventilation, and enhanced air filtration [32]. Control at the source is the generally preferred method for particulate control. An overview of commonly encountered strategies for maintaining a healthy IAQ in Green Buildings has been depicted in Figure 9.2. The combustion appliances used at homes must be adequately vented and adequately maintained. If there is an issue of dust exposure, the dust type must be identified to create a suitable intervention strategy. Wet mopping and the use of high-efficiency vacuum cleaners can be considered. Under construction spaces or areas undergoing renovation or refurbishing should be appropriately isolated from occupied spaces to limit dust and other contaminants' transport. Eliminating vehicles with diesel-powered engines and generators near buildings can reduce the entry of suspended particulate matter.

Environmental tobacco smoke (ETS) control can be achieved practically through regulatory mandates on the practice of tobacco smoking in indoor spaces. Many countries have enacted laws to regulate tobacco smoking in public spaces, like public buildings and workplaces. In areas where smoking is allowed, appropriate dilution and proper ventilation measures should be used for ETS control [20]. Studies have indicated that very high ventilation rates might be necessary to reduce secondhand smoke to low-risk levels. Management of ETS in indoor environments can be undertaken using separate ventilated spaces with exhaust, where no other work activities would occur concurrently with smoking. These smoking-lounges

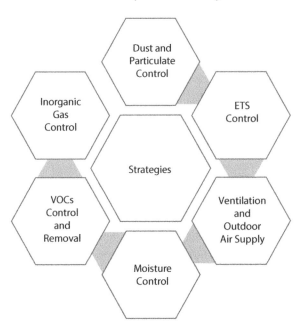

Figure 9.2 Various strategies for maintaining healthy IAQ in Green Buildings.

should be kept under a negative atmospheric pressure corresponding to the adjacent indoor areas [7].

Strategies like source reduction or elimination, provision of exhaust, atmospheric pressure control, and general dilution by ventilation are usually applied to control the inorganic gaseous pollutants. The reaction by-products of primary indoor air pollutants can be reduced using carbon-filters in spots where outdoor ozone concentration generally approximates or surpasses ambient levels. Gaseous pollutants with relatively higher molecular mass can be captured using activated carbon or alumina pellets infused with potassium permanganate crystals.

The methods applicable for controlling organic gaseous pollutants could be the source and ventilation control and excluding gas infiltration using filters. The source control measures for volatile organic compounds (VOCs) involve limiting or removing the emission sources. For example, avoidance of cooktops for use in space heating, a challenge encountered in low-income urban homes. Limiting automobile parking in and around building air intake spaces can also help control infiltration. VOCs' source control should always be the primary consideration but is not always practicable, especially where contaminant sources are diverse, as observed in new buildings where the building-components and the furnishings may be the primary contributors to the pollutant load. Control of ventilation helps bring clean air into the living area or directly exhaust the air pollutants at the generation source.

Based on the different pathogen sources, a wide range of bioaerosol exposure control strategies can be designed. The methods are based on adequate ventilation, provisions for exhaust, disinfection procedures, filtration, and source control, including regular cleaning and proper working of the HVAC system [31, 41]. Generally, in hot and humid climates occurrence of molds is commonly encountered. Hence, controlling moisture is crucial for preventing the growth of molds. Monitoring indoor relative humidity decreases dew-point, which results in moisture cumulation in the building contents and materials. For safe environmental and operational regulation of building water systems, ASHRAE Guideline 12 is followed, which also helps minimize the risk of Legionnaires' disease [7].

Experiences in engineering and field studies have indicated that a supply of outdoor air of approximately 10 L/s per person is suitable to provide satisfactory perceived air quality in indoor environments. In contrast, lower air supply rates could lead to increased signs of developing sick building syndrome (SBS) [21].

In buildings relying on natural ventilation for cooling, the floor-to-ceiling height often increases well beyond the regular 2.5 to 3.2 m. Higher ceilings allow warm air and contaminants to rise above the room's occupied areas, as observed in buildings constructed before air-conditioning was available. The air is then exhausted from the ceiling zone, and the relatively cooler outdoor air reaches towards the rooms' occupied areas. Thus, a range of floor-to-ceiling displacement airflow is advisable when using natural ventilation.

Energy efficiency is a chief aspect of green buildings, but energy-efficient strategies can often lead to lower ventilation rates, leading to an unhealthy IAQ. Some energy-efficient strategies that may lead to poor IAQ are summarized in Table 9.2. It is thus desirable that air quality improvement strategies take into account the energy efficiency of buildings and vice versa [22, 27, 39].

For overcoming the poor air quality and ensure energy efficiency, building standards also consider such parameters to address both issues. The ANSI/ASHRAE/USGBC/IES Standard 189.1-2014 contains the necessary pre-requisites for increasing the environmental as well as wellness accomplishments of green buildings [23]. ANSI/ASHRAE Standard 62.2-2016 contains guidelines for achieving ventilation and an agreeable IAQ in homes [24]. Important building rating systems like LEED 2009 for New Construction and Major Renovations Rating System [25] and ANSI/GBI 01-2010 Green Building Assessment Protocol for Commercial Building, also contain several strategies addressing the indoor air quality [26, 27, 29, 30]. Table 9.3 discusses a list of various energy-efficient strategies for achieving an improved IAQ in green buildings.

As described in Table 9.3, it is discernable that the maintenance of good IAQ strategy in buildings can often lead to less efficiency in energy use [28]. Thus, it becomes all the more critical in maintaining a delicate

Table 9.2 The relationship between energy-efficient strategies for Green Buildings and the challenges they pose on IAQ.

Energy efficient strategy	Challenges on IAQ
Increase in thermal insulation	May increase condensation in buildings that may lead to the growth of biological contaminants
Reduction in the outdoor air inlet	May increase the concentration of pollutants from indoor sources
Increase of cooling efficiency	May increase humidity levels inducing the growth of biological contaminants

Table 9.3 Strategies for improving IAQ in an energy-efficient manner.

Strategy	Impact on IAQ
Envelope design and construction for improved moisture management	Reduces microbe growth potential, thereby lowering bioaerosol concentrations.
Source control of contaminants	Significantly lowers inorganic and organic pollutants.
Integrated pest management	Reduces allergen and irritant exposures associated with pests and use of pesticides.
Heat recovery ventilation	Maintains outdoor air supply providing adequate ventilation indoors.
Demand controlled ventilation	Enables low-ventilation rates at low occupancies through sensor use.
Economizer operation	Cooling through outdoor air supply instead of mechanical cooling. It can reduce moisture-related impacts on IAQ.
Dedicated outdoor air systems	Easy to clean, control, and condition the outdoor air.
Displacement ventilation	Less outdoor air supply with improved IAQ in the occupant breathing zone.
Task ventilation or occupant control	Less outdoor air supply with improved IAQ in occupant breathing zone with provisions of individual control.
Natural/hybrid ventilation	More outdoor air supply provision for cooling purposes reduces problems associated with moisture build-up in mechanical cooling devices.
Envelope tightness	Low infiltration of outdoor air with provision of moisture and pollutant management.

(*Continued*)

Table 9.3 Strategies for improving IAQ in an energy-efficient manner. (*Continued*)

Strategy	Impact on IAQ
Air distribution system tightness	Contributes to good IAQ in buildings where ductwork is in unconditioned space.
More efficient particle filtration	Clean air supply devoid of particulates with regular filter maintenance.
Gaseous air cleaning; lower ventilation rates	Less outdoor air supply with better IAQ.
Source control and lower ventilation	Source characterization for indoor air pollutants and low supply of outdoor air for better IAQ management.

balance between the two aspects. Both energy and healthcare can prove costly in the long run, so the development of efficient air ventilation or cleaning strategies along with energy-saving modes can prove beneficial.

9.5   Conclusion and Future Scope

So far, it has been observed that the IAQ of a building determines various health ailments, chronic as well as acute, that we commonly come across. Often the reasons for our illnesses are unknown and undetermined, especially when it has origins in our homes or workspaces where the majority of our life is spent. Construction of buildings and spaces should be done responsibly to take into account all such factors that can have a bearing on our health and well-being. As green and sustainable building construction methods are getting adopted by more people, the building certification and rating agencies give more weightage to air quality parameters. Green construction should also be delved into, such that the entire value chain of material to the built-home produces minimum emission of pollutants and harmful emissions. As energy efficiency is already a much-researched aspect of sustainable buildings, the shift towards renewables should also be undertaken to further the efficiency and reduce emissions to a minimum.

A need for some practical research in developing countries on the possible pollutant impacts can provide a broader scope for further developing strategies. Ultimately, good air quality can impact our healthfulness, productivity, and mental well-being, leading up to an economy with lesser disease burden.

References

1. Sundell, J., On the History of Indoor Air Quality and Health. *Indoor Air*, 14, Suppl 7, 51–58, 2004.
2. Haynes, B.P., The impact of office layout on productivity. *J. Facil. Manag.*, 6, 189–201, 2008.
3. Romm, J. and Browning, W., *Greening the Building and the Bottom Line—Increasing productivity through energy-efficient design*, Rocky Mountain Institute, U.S.A., 1994.
4. Al Horr, Y., Arif, M., Kaushik, A., Mazroei, A., Katafygiotou, M., Elsarrag, E., Occupant productivity and office indoor environment quality: A review of the literature. *Build. Environ.*, 105, 369–389, 2016.
5. Wei, W., Ramalho, O., Mandin, C., Indoor air quality requirements in green building certifications. *Build. Environ.*, 92, 10–19, 2015.
6. Wang, X.M., Sheng, G.Y., Fu, J.M., Chan, C.Y., Lee, S.C., Chan, L.Y., Urban roadside aromatic hydrocarbons in three cities of the Pearl River Delta, People's Republic of China. *Atmos. Environ.*, 36, 5141–5148, 2002.
7. ASHRAE, American Society of Heating, Refrigerating and Air-Conditioning Engineers, *2009 Ashrae Handbook: Fundamentals*, ASHRAE, Atlanta, GA, 2009.
8. Cobb, N. and Etzel, R.A., Unintentional Carbon Monoxide—Related Deaths in the United States, 1979 Through 1988. *JAMA*, 266, 5, 659–663, 1991.
9. WHO, World Health Organization, *WHO Guidelines for Indoor Air Quality: Selected pollutants*, WHO Regional Office for Europe, Copenhagen, 2010.
10. Levetin, E., Shaughnessy, R., Fisher, E. *et al.*, Indoor air quality in schools: Exposure to fungal allergens. *Aerobiologia*, 11, 27–34, 1995.
11. Michael, R.M., Thomas, R.B., Harold, S.M., Gary, R.N., Alan, P.K., Donald, G.R., An outbreak of influenza aboard a commercial airliner. *Am. J. Epidemiol.*, 110, 1, 1–6, July 1979.
12. U.S. EPA, *Integrated Science Assessment (ISA) for Lead (Third External Review Draft, Nov 2012)*, U.S. Environmental Protection Agency, Washington, DC, EPA/600/R-10/075C, 2012.
13. Agency for Toxic Substances and Disease Registry (ATSDR), *Toxicological Profile for Lead*, U.S. Department of Health and Human Services, Public Health Service, Atlanta, GA, 2020.

14. Eric, J.E. and Mark, F.B., Effect of an Ozone-Generating Air-Purifying Device on Reducing Concentrations of Formaldehyde in Air. *Appl. Occup. Environ. Hyg.*, 9, 2, 139–146, 1994.

15. Weschler, C.J., Ozone in the indoor environment: Concentration and chemistry. *Indoor Air*, 10, 269–288, 2000.

16. Weschler, C.J. and Shields, H.C., The influence of ventilation on reactions among indoor air pollutants: Modeling and experimental observations. *Indoor Air*, 10, 92–100, 2000.

17. EPA (2016). US Environmental Protection Agency Definition of Green Building. Available: https://archive.epa.gov/greenbuilding/web/html/about.html

18. Mølhave, L., Volatile organic compounds, indoor air quality and health. *Indoor Air*, 1, 4, 357–376, 1991.

19. Steinemann, A., Wargocki, P., Rismanchi, B., Ten questions concerning green buildings and indoor air quality. *Build. Environ.*, 112, 351–358, 2016. https://doi.org/10.1016/j.buildenv.2016.11.010

20. Repace, J. and Lowery, A.H., A quantitative estimate of nonsmokers' lung cancer risk from passive smoking. *Environ. Int.*, 11, 3–22, 1985.

21. Seppänen, O.A., Fisk, W.J., Mendell, M.J., Association of ventilation rates and CO_2-concentrations with health and other responses in commercial and institutional buildings. *Int. J. Indoor Air Qual. Clim.*, 9, 252–274, 1999.

22. Persily, A.K. and Emmerich, S.J., Indoor air quality in sustainable, energy efficient buildings. *HVAC&R Res.*, 18, 1–2, 4–20, 2012.

23. ASHRAE, *ANSI/ASHRAE/USGBC/IES Standard 189.1-2009, standard for the design of high-performance green buildings*, American Society of Heating, Refrigerating, and Air-Conditioning Engineers, Inc., Atlanta, GA, 2009.

24. ASHRAE, *ANSI/ASHRAE Standard 62.2-2016 Ventilation and acceptable indoor air quality in residential buildings*, American Society of Heating, Refrigeration, and Air-Conditioning Engineers, Inc., Atlanta, GA, 2016.

25. USGBC, *LEED 2009 for new construction and major renovations rating system*, U.S. Green Building Council, Washington, D.C., 2009.

26. GBI, *ANSI/GBI 01-2010, green building assessment protocol for commercial buildings*, Green Building Initiative, Portland, OR, 2010.

27. Xiong, Y., Krogmann, U., Mainelis, G., Rodenburg, L.A., Andrews, C.J., Indoor air quality in green buildings: A case-study in a residential high-rise building in the northeastern United States. *J. Environ. Sci. Health, Part A: Tox./Hazard. Subst. Environ. Eng.*, 50, 3, 225–242, 2015.

28. Rameshwar, R., Solanki, A., Nayyar, A., Mahapatra, B., Green and smart buildings: A key to sustainable global solutions, in: *Green Building Management and Smart Automation*, pp. 146–163, IGI Global, 2020. http://doi:10.4018/978-1-5225-9754-4.ch007

29. Allen, J.G., MacNaughton, P., Cedeño Laurent, J.G., Flanigan, S.S., Eitland, E.S., Spengler, J.D., Green Buildings and Health. *Curr. Environ. Health Rep.*, 2, 3, 250–258, 2015.

30. Altomonte, S. and Schiavon, S., Occupant satisfaction in LEED and non-LEED certified buildings. *Build. Environ.*, 68, 66–76, 2013.
31. ASHRAE, *ASHRAE Position Document on Filtration and Air Cleaning*, American Society for Heating, Refrigeration and Air-Conditioning Engineers, Atlanta, GA, 2015.
32. Carrer, P., Wargocki, P., Fanetti, A., Bischof, W., Fernandes, E.D.O., Hartmann, T., Kephalopulos, S., Palkonen, S., Seppänen, O., What does the scientific literature tell us about the ventilation–health relationship in public and residential buildings? *Build. Environ.*, 94, 273–286, 2015.
33. Cecchi, T., Identification of representative pollutants in multiple locations of an Italian school using solid phase micro extraction technique. *Build. Environ.*, 82, 655–665, 2014.
34. Cheng, M., Galbally, I.E., Molloy, S.B., Selleck, P.W., Keywood, M.D., Lawson, S.J., Powell, J.C., Gillett, R.W., Dunne, E., Factors controlling volatile organic compounds in dwellings in Melbourne, Australia. *Indoor Air*, 26, 2, 219–30, 2015.
35. Colton, M.D., MacNaughton, P., Vallarino, J., Kane, J., Bennett-Fripp, M., Spengler, J.D., Adamkiewicz, G., Indoor air quality in green vs conventional multifamily low-income housing. *Environ. Sci. Technol.*, 48, 14, 7833–7841, 2014.
36. Darling, E.K., Cros, C.J., Wargocki, P., Kolarik, J., Morrison, G.C., Corsi, R.L., Impacts of a clay plaster on indoor air quality assessed using chemical and sensory measurements. *Build. Environ.*, 57, 370–376, 2012.
37. Gabb, H.A. and Blake, C., An informatics approach to evaluating combined chemical exposures from consumer products: A case study of asthma-associated chemicals and potential endocrine disruptors. *Environ. Health Perspect.*, 124, 8, 1155–1165, 2016.
38. Garland, E., Steenburgh, E.T., Sanchez, S.H., Geevarughese, A., Bluestone, L., Rothenberg, L., Rialdi, A., Foley, M., Impact of LEED-certified affordable housing on asthma in the South Bronx. *Prog. Community Health Partnersh.: Research, Education, and Action*, 7, 1, 29–37, 2013.
39. Gou, Z., Prasad, D., Lau, S.S.Y., Are green buildings more satisfactory and comfortable? *Habitat Int.*, 39, 156–161, 2013.
40. Hedge, A., Miller, L., Dorsey, J.A., Occupant comfort and health in green and conventional university buildings. *Work*, 49, 3, 363–372, 2014.
41. Kibert, C.J., *Sustainable Construction: Green Building Design and Delivery*, 4th Edition, John Wiley & Sons, United States, 2016.
42. Liang, H.H., Chen, C.P., Hwang, R.L., Shih, W.M., Lo, S.C., Liao, H.Y., Satisfaction of occupants toward indoor environment quality of certified green office buildings in Taiwan. *Build. Environ.*, 72, 232–242, 2014.
43. Liu, C., Zhang, Y., Benning, J.L., Little, J.C., The effect of ventilation on indoor exposure to semivolatile organic compounds. *Indoor Air*, 25, 3, 285–296, 2015.

44. Newsham, G.R., Birt, B.J., Arsenault, C., Thompson, A.J.L., Veitch, J.A., Mancini, S., Galasiu, A.D., Gover, B.N., Macdonald, I.A., Burns, G.J., Do "green" buildings have better indoor environments? New evidence. *Build. Res. Inf.*, 41, 4, 415–434, 2013.
45. Steinemann, A., Volatile emissions from common consumer products. *Air Qual. Atmos. Health*, 8, 3, 273–281, 2015.
46. Thiel, C.L., Needy, K.L., Ries, R., Hupp, D., Bilec, M.M., Building design and performance: A comparative longitudinal assessment of a Children's hospital. *Build. Environ.*, 78, 130–136, 2014.

10

An Era of Internet of Things Leads to Smart Cities Initiatives Towards Urbanization

Pooja Choudhary[1,2]*, Lava Bhargava[1], Ashok Kumar Suhag[3], Manju Choudhary[1,2] and Satendra Singh[4]

[1]Department of Electronics and Communication Engineering, MNIT, Jaipur, India
[2]Department of Electronics and Communication Engineering, Swami Keshvanand Institute of Technology Management and Gramothan, Jaipur, India
[3]Department of Electronics and Communication Engineering, BML Munjal University, Gurgaon, India
[4]Department of Mechanical Engineering, Vivekananda Global University, Jaipur, India

Abstract

As urbanization is proliferating over the last few years there is an indispensable need for intelligent technology, digital surrounding, smart governance, and a sustainable environment to improve the quality of human life. As an outcome of the knowledge-based economy and accelerated development of technology Smart city is a combination of internet, network, sensors, etc. For implementing all the applications an emerging technology Internet of Things (IoT) acts as a backbone or one can say IoT is reaching urban living. The features and devices of smart cities are becoming smarter. The parameters like urban sustainability, infrastructure efficiency, and economic growth can be improved by the intervention of IoT. The aim of this chapter is to provide a comprehensive view of smart cities, its concepts, components and emergence. The table mentioned represents the established relationships between various sectors of industries and its services. Further in chapter the impact of smart cities on areas of science, technology, and society is illustrated. The focus is given to key applications, technologies and challenges related to IoT which are used in smart cities. The perceived concept of the smart city initiative

---

**Corresponding author*: poojachoudhary87@gmail.com

Arun Solanki, Adarsh Kumar and Anand Nayyar (eds.) Digital Cities Roadmap: IoT-Based Architecture and Sustainable Buildings, (319–350) © 2021 Scrivener Publishing LLC

will always remain critical for development and sustainability. The Future city is Smart and Economical.

Keywords: Smart cities, IoT, ICT, sustainability, smart building, smart healthcare, communication technologies

10.1 Introduction: Emergence of a Smart City Concept

Rapidly increasing global population will be about 15 billion people with nearly 75% of those pertaining to urban cities. As such, there are many consequences like water scarcity, traffic deadlock, elevated pollution, cleanliness, infrastructure, security issues, bad governance, poor public health care system, and increased resource consumption. But globalization and technology are becoming boundary-less, where everything is digitized. People are getting connected through the internet [1]. All smart electronics systems are connected to the internet. People are finding innovative and advantageous systems to connect. To eradicate the above-mentioned issues, the key is a Smart city, which is intelligent and connected. It is a place where devices and systems can communicate either with the people living in city or from outside. It is growing in terms of scope and capabilities. A smart city is a perfect framework composed of information and communication technologies (ICT) to develop, deploy and promote optimized efficiency and sustainability with enhancing the quality of life in each urban conglomeration. In the ICT framework data is transmitted through wireless technology and cloud from the intelligent network connected to objects and machines. These cities are flexible, greener, safer, faster, and friendlier. ICT with emerging technology Internet of Things (IoT) makes cities more flexible, responsive, and efficient. It is a place where public services and resources for inhabitants are translated from digital technologies. To eradicate issues raised by rapidly growing population and urbanization, the natural strategy is the development of smart cities [2].

Due to huge diversity around the globe specifications for driving growth, ensuring quality, efficiency, and safety are provided by International Organization for Standardization. All these standards play a vital role in the development and building. IEEE has developed its standards and different components for smart cities. For monitoring technical and functional performance indicators are provided in standards. These standards also mention how to tackle climate change in smart cities. An example of such a standard is ISO 37120 defining 100 cite performances.

With the help of information and communication technologies (ICTs) in an innovative city, there is an improvement in the quality, efficiency of operations and their related services [3]. With respect to various aspects such as economic, social, and environmental the needs of future and present generations are ensured perfectly.

The concept of Smart cities has emerged for planning of urban cities and its valid reasons are like-

    I. Creation and protection of jobs.
    II. Smart enriched educational opportunities.
    III. Functioning infrastructure at affordable prices.
    IV. Right conditions for prosperous economy and social equality.
    V. Sustainability regarding energy efficiency, environmental pollution, and resources.
    VI. Working mobility system with factors such as public security, health care, disaster management and social stability.
    VII. Offering good governance, telecommunication platforms, clean-air, innovative and attractive conditions for new businesses and scientific community.

The city which interacts continuously, acknowledges the needs and demands, fetches live data from sensors and acts on them and alters its functioning and behavior accordingly. Practical use of Information and communication technologies (ICT) most effectively IoT make city smart and intelligent in dealing with its resources [4].

10.2   Components of Smart City

Figure 10.1 shows the components and themes of a smart city. The figure represents nine potential components of a smart city and four themes. Component comprises of smart infrastructures, technologies, education, governance, citizens, health care, transportation, buildings, and energy.

The level of components depends on the framework of smart cities [5]. Figure 10.1 also shows the core themes of the smart city. The society theme presents the people of city. Economic theme denotes job and economic growth. The environment theme signifies cleanliness, greenness, and resource availability for future generations. The indicators of good

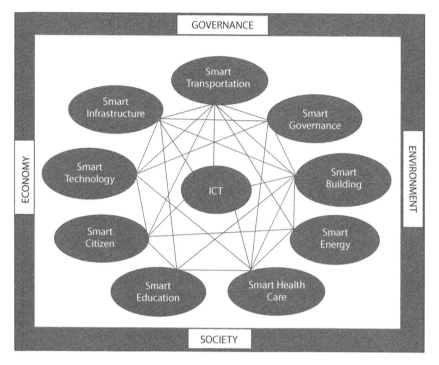

Figure 10.1 Components and themes of a Smart City.

governance in smart cities are flexibility, good policies, and the ability to administer. The main characteristic of smart cities includes urbanization, standard of living, smartness, and sustainability.

Emotional, empathy, and financial wellness of people of that smart city all these aspects measure the quality of life. Urbanization includes technology, governance, economics, and infrastructure. The idea and aim is to improve all the issues related to city and its people. Smart infrastructure, smart buildings, smart energy, smart governance, and smart health care are associated with the sustainability of smart cities [6].

ICT acts as the mind of a smart city. With rapid advancement in infrastructure, the demand for ICT is also increasing. All the information and fast communication between different devices and systems are secured and communicated through ICT mode. ICT thereby helps to reduce resource consumption, pollution, and congestion. All the components are stuck together to the ICT infrastructure forming a bigger framework.

The number of smart cities facilities required can be calculated as follows:

$$Fn = Pn \left(\frac{Pr}{Year} \right) \left(\frac{1\ Year}{D\ Days} \right) \left(\frac{1\ Hour}{C} \right) \left(\frac{1\ Day}{H\ hours} \right)$$

Where, Fn is number of facilities, Pn is population of the city in million, Pr is rate/person/year, C is customers/hour, D is for Days/year and H is hours/day.

10.2.1 Smart Infrastructure

Smart city is not just trend it's a futuristic vision. It is referred to as a physical component and an integral part of a smart city. It includes services related to physical, electrical, or digital and these services are the backbone of a smart city. All these services are critical. The common appearance of the city must be clean and organized. To maintain such an appearance city must follow smart infrastructure guidelines [7]. The main facilities of the city are waste management, office space, street lighting system, water, and power supply systems, digital library, internet, and economic systems, etc. For example, if the bandwidth of the internet is 300 Mbps then each and every inhabitant of the city must get the same speed. So all these issues are handle by ICT which makes the infrastructure "SMART". ICT has many factors associated like performance, availability; its information system is service-oriented and can be fetched from anywhere. So, these aspects make physical infrastructure smart, flexible, efficient and fault-tolerant. Smart infrastructure provides foundations to all the key elements related to city such as smart economy, smart living, smart governance and smart citizen and smart buildings. These elements are highly context specific and their nature is estimated by cities development.

Applications related to smart infrastructure provides bases for innovations which will help in efficient growth and preferable handling of resources. This can be understood with the help of an example; data gathered by smart mobility can be useful and informative for transport network as well as for apps managing them.

10.2.2 Smart Building

Smart foundations are need of smart cities. It is part of infrastructure or can act as an independent component for smart cities. Structures which are connected with sensor networks that can easily monitor, track, use real time data, and interact with other devices or structures all belongs to category of smart buildings. The information retrieved from the outside world and use at an appropriate place of requirement. For example, if it's raining outside smart windows will alert the housemates and if clothes are hanging outside then shade will automatically protect the clothes from getting wet. Another example can be a smart panel that will use ambient energy from surrounding for lighting the houses. In a smart building, everything like software, hardware, sensors, actuators, and smart appliances are connected to one another for different operations and controlling purposes.

Figure 10.2 shows smart building concept. Smart buildings can reduce the use of resources and energy and it can adapt sustainable structures. The reduced cost, high efficiency, low cost, great management systems, and data-driven decision are key advantages of smart buildings [8]. By gathering data and making adjustments rapidly gives greater efficiency at operational areas. Systems like fire protection, lighting, ventilation, surveillance are separately operated in buildings but in smart buildings all these systems are connected with each other through IoT. These systems basically have a centralized control. If sensors detect any movement in empty house or offices then the slight movement information can be forwarded to owner of house this will reduce the chances of theft. Bringing all the technologies like edge computing at one platform can keep data at one place for faster analysis, feedback and rapid decision-making. An ample number of data is generated, this generated data is an asset as it will tell us how the smart building performed and where are its gains and losses. By applying machine learning, artificial intelligence to generated data it will provide a strong foundation for next building

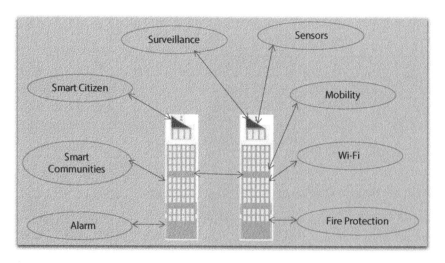

Figure 10.2 Smart building.

and measures to be taken for various issues. Smart buildings will give rise to smart communities and eventually smart cities.

10.2.3   Smart Transportation

Transportation systems such as railways, airline transport, road transport, and water transport have lived for a long time. These are operating independently, each having their specific time, type, and route. Due to which global usage became a very difficult task. Digital technologies are rigorously transforming vehicles and the way of interacting with them. This type of transportation is called as intelligent transportation systems (ITS). It is the heart of smart cities. ITS keeps people safe and secure on city roads, bridges, and tunnels systems. Real-time traveler systems, traffic signal systems, traffic and transport management are examples of ITS. It includes various types of communication i.e. between vehicles and locations. All sorts of transportation systems like rail, water, air, and road are covered by ITS and can interact with each other through ICT. ICT processes all the data in real-time. Intercity railway networks, airway hubs, protected cycle routes; pedestrian paths, etc. are made possible only by smart transportation system. Passengers can complete their journey at low cost, can choose the fastest route, and can select different options for transportation [9]. Using apps in mobile phones to hire a cab, share live location and driver's information with others to keep track of the movement is an excellent example of smart transportation technology. Nowadays drivers are using app, adopting smart technologies which have the ability to manage traffic flow on highways and inside city so that they can avoid traffic congestion and their journey can become smooth and hassle-free. Further, a novel heuristic simulation–optimization method is used for resolving issues related to the complicated transportation network and heavy traffic conditions. The method is based on genetic algorithms and annealing strategies which will provide the improved quality of service. For faster routes in small networks, an improvement of 3.4% minimum and 16.2% maximum is observed by implementing this method. The approach stated also improves the critical infrastructure monitoring performance [10]. For next generation transportation system is electric energy based vehicles. Simulation-optimization approach is used for integrating, analyzing and evaluating the feasibility of battery-operated electric bus system. The aim of this method is to optimize the battery consumption, IoT performance and efficiency [11].

Figure 10.3 depicts smart building framework. Due to poor traffic monitoring systems road accidents are increasing which results in loss of lives

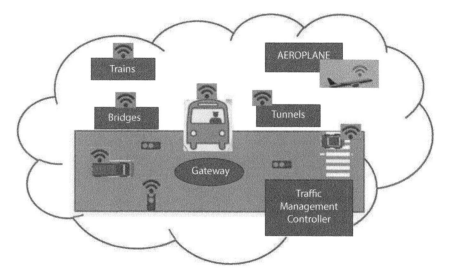

Figure 10.3 Smart building framework.

as well as economic resources. To reduce road accidents many rules, regulations, and fines are imposed by the Saudi Ministry and also introduced a system named SAHER. But the drivers always found ways to deceive the system. So, Unmanned Aerial Vehicle (UAV) based on 5G technology is implemented for surveillance of traffic. This system overcame the limitations of the existing scenario and the number of accidents falls to a significant number [12]. The range of technologies that rely on information can transform transportation networks into smart ones and transition towards the sustainable development of smart cities.

10.2.4 Smart Energy

Energy is a quantitative property that transfers from one object to another to perform. The law of conservation of energy states that "energy can neither be created nor be destroyed but can be converted from one form to another". Kinetic energy, potential energy, thermal energy, and chemical energy are various parts of energy. Fossil fuels are decreasing day by day, available resources will get exhausted so there is a huge demand to shift to new energy sources. There are various ambient energy sources available in environment like solar energy, wind energy, sustainable energy sources [13]. Green energies like solar and wind has a very minimal negative impact. There is one more concept i.e. Zero energy systems in these systems the net energy created and the net energy consumed are of the same quantity. The smart energy concept is very broad and has immense capability to reduce energy consumption, its cost-effective, energy-efficient, low carbon generation systems, and renewable. A smart grid is an excellent example of smart energy. The grid system has important aspects like production and distribution of electricity. Distribution and production control are done efficiently by the smart grid system by proper utilization of ICT [14]. The information infrastructure is the basic core of smart energy. ICT is used for controlling, operating, storing, optimizing, and smart metering all the factors associated with smart energy systems.

10.2.5 Smart Health Care

With the new generation of information technologies smart healthcare has come to fore. Due to the digital revolution, traditional health care system is in a great position to take full advantage. The use of ICT and IoT bring multi-level change in medical system, making the health care system smart,

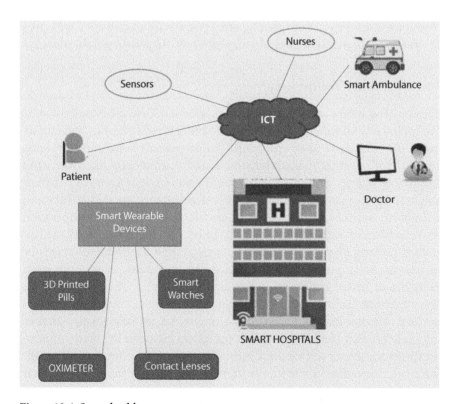

Figure 10.4 Smart health care systems.

efficient, convenient, and more personalized. It is a technology that leads to better diagnostics, improved patient care, effective surgical processes, improved treatment, and enhanced devices. Smart health care system uses technology such as wearable devices and IoT which has access to the information, connectivity to materials and hospitals related and manage and respond to the medical ecosystem [15].

The system consists of multiple participants such as doctors, patients, hospitals, research institutes. The smart hospitals have various tools and mechanisms for treatment and operations such as accessing real-time data of patients through ICT. Doctors, nurses can access the data and give their valuable opinion to save the patient's life. The best example is telemedicine. It uses ICT for clinical health care at remote locations where good health care services are not accessible. It is a new era of healthcare named as Smart Health.

Individual or patient can use Smart wearable devices these devices will help them to access their fitness and health status without any professional help [16]. These devices help them to check blood and glucose level, temperature etc. Such equipment's are boon to diabetic, heart patient. Nowadays these devices are gaining great popularity among all. Figure 10.4 shows idea of smart health care system with few the smart wearable devices.

10.2.6   Smart Technology

The key for better designs, implementation and effective operation is Technology. Components of smart cities comprise of buildings, infrastructures, physical structures, electronics, information technology, software, hardware all together make it happen. Smart technologies like Green and Renewable energy resources, sustainable resource management, sustainable transport system, communication infrastructure, social network and state-of-art technologies makes city smarter. The design and operation must be blended optimally for the city to be sustainable for years. As science is making progress, technology is becoming accessible to everyone in society. Solar power, wind power, green and clean energy are good examples of smart technologies. Sustainable and smart transport systems are important technologies which can reduce traffic congestion, greenhouse emissions, and prove beneficial for citizens, passengers and drivers. Internet, Wi-Fi, Bluetooth, and fiber optics are included in smart communication technology so that basic services can be used from home like calling a cab. Nowadays, society is moving towards a cashless system so near field communications are best utilized [17]. With the integration of computations, networking, communication mechanisms and physical entities services are becoming smart and efficient. Their utilities can be achieved in smart cities.

State-of-art technologies like smart cards, electronic cards can be used to make city smart. These cards embedded with a unique identifier that allows accessing its services to users in one login. Smart city is covered with objects which are connected to each other. For connecting the various objects IoT system came out as a winner. Data, people, processes, and things are basic blocks of IoT. Smart city is connected with these blocks to provide services.

Latest technologies like Blockchain, Fog Computing, Cloud Computing, and Big Data are utilized to solve the issues raised by IoT or for advancement in services. Cloud computing solves the problems of storage and processing of data. Fog computing is an extension of cloud computing it reduces the network traffic and processing time of data. Blockchain technology is a chain of blocks as transactions grow chain also grows. Security is the main concern in smart cities as it highly enhanced using this technology. It provides protection against attacks. So, Blockchain and Fog based architecture Network (BFAN) provides a secure architecture for applications used in smart cities [18]. This architecture provides on-demand services reduces latency and energy and provides enhanced security features.

10.2.7   Smart Citizen

Citizens are the most vital and integral part of the system. A citizen is who obeys all the laws, respect the constitution, and have civic sense. Smart city initiatives were taken just as the indicator of a developed economy. When citizens upgrade and update themselves country becomes a successfully developed country. Traditionally public participated in institutional planning but with the digitization of world people became proactive with new sense of responsibility to communicate and represent themselves with one another and with government or agencies. Ideas, projects suggested by inhabitants are usually implemented in the city [19]. Issues and problems of society can be solved and citizens can implement their prototypes in different domains. Citizens must be aware of their roles in society. There is always a strong relationship between people and their environment so the city create stronger bond between available resources, technology, and services. Smart cities are based on smart communities whose citizen plays active role in operation of society and designs. Citizens are stakeholders in smart cities and right to information has broadened with the vast development in ICTs which increases the interaction and networking among various communities and groups of society thus contributing more knowledge and information. This will directly affect the decision making processes at the community level [20]. There will be positive development in community which will empower the individual and groups.

10.2.8 Smart Governance

Governance using ICT is used for exchanging information, communicating with people, integrating with various systems within the government and outside. Technology is being used to support and enhance planning and decision-making steps taken by the government. It will help in improving the traditional system and transform the agenda. To strengthen e-governance, citizen participation and public welfare are main pillars due to this system becomes transparent, well-structured and well informed. Information will be accessible to all [21]. The improvement in government and governance systems can definitely transform the face of the city. Suggestions, grievances to government can easily be shared thorough web portals, online forums, and mobile apps. For example, RTI act in INDIA was passed to empower ordinary citizen but earlier RTI application was posted thorough post but now process made simpler and quicker with the help of RTI website. Likewise corruption and bribe information can be reported through websites and apps. Public participation is main feature of smart governance. Voice of their opinions, ideas, schemes, innovation and feedback must be directly communicated to government [22].

There are many challenges faced by government such as:

a. *Funding:* Huge funding and investment is required for infrastructure development.
b. *Lack of interest:* In many activities government don't include public, and sometimes due to security reasons there is always a distance, so it creates lack of interest.
c. *Illiteracy:* To acquire all the benefits of e-governance basic knowledge of computers is must. Rural areas, tribal areas and communities don't have access to computers.

10.2.9 Smart Education

Basic element of development is education. Educated citizens have tendency of development for living and quality of life. Present education system is not sufficient for smart cities. So, model of new learning adapted by new generations is Smart Education [23]. It is a framework where learning can happen anytime anywhere. Technology opened the door for many interactive tools, engaging teaching techniques so that learning can be encouraged and students can relate to real world. Digital and tech-centric behavior helps to acquire skills including effectively communication, innovative thinking and teamwork.

Many portals in India are associated with such smart education like NPTEL, SWAYAM, e-Pathshala. MHRD and the government are playing a vital role in improving education systems with the help of new technologies. Smart education is a common platform where students, teachers, and administration are integrated. The new education system provides a holistic approach to learning so that students can use technology and become fully prepared for a world where adaptability is a crucial component. Various learning methods like virtual classrooms, virtual learning, smartphones, are used by teachers so that they can help students to gain more knowledge.

In the COVID-19 pandemic due to the smart education system the majority of students are connected with schools, colleges through virtual classrooms and other platforms. They are getting their education and gaining learning out of it.

The changes that will take place in education system of smart cities are:

1. Real time knowledge and learning.
2. Emphasis on hands-on practice rather than more theoretical knowledge.
3. Equal opportunity for every student.
4. Interactive, collaborative and visual mode teaching style.
5. Emphasis on student's interests and learning preferences so that they can achieve their full potential.
6. Responsible students who contribute towards development of their community and as a whole society.

10.3   Role of IoT in Smart Cities

Smart cars, smart devices, smartphones, smart roads, smart education the whole Smart world have been adopted for many years. Achieving the goal of the smart world has brought many research communities and technologies together. IoT is the perfect candidate and technically it acts as a backbone of smart cities. It bridges the gap between real-world processes and their information systems. IoT pertains to a set of technologies that are sensing, collecting, and assessing the data collected through a wireless and wired network. These technologies are based on communication protocols having capability of self-configuring and infrastructure that is dynamic [24]. It is a platform where devices are becoming smart, data is processed intelligently and information is communicated effectively. Cutting edge technology like IoT acts as a driving force in transforming the urban cities into smart cities. In a smart city, all the data is collected through sensors and powerful analysis is done to automate various services of the city for optimizing resources, reducing cost for sustainable development of city.

Due to the scarcity of resources, it is crucially important to use advanced technology to tackle issues of society. The innovative architectural framework and concepts of IoT are adopted to intelligently utilize space and resources. It also fulfills the aim of increasing connectivity between inhabitants and the government.

With the technical support from IoT, the key features of Smart city i.e. intelligence, automation, and interconnectedness can be achieved easily. With the increase in scope and capabilities of technologies, IoT is having an impact on everything from lighting to the flow of traffic.

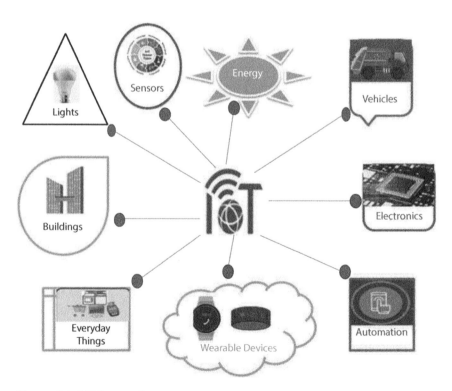

Figure 10.5 IoT framework.

Figure 10.5 represents IoT framework of smart cities which includes electronics, sensors, vehicles, weather forecasting, wearable devices, buildings, lights, streets, energy system, etc. IoT ensures communication with each system and application providing complete reliability, flexibility, security in services. IoT framework keeps track of various tasks such as monitoring, pollution control, tracking, automation, management location detection, etc. through ICT.

The concept of integration of smart technology with the city can achieve various important goals such as improving quality of life, enhancing infrastructure, reduce crime rates and traffic congestion, reduce cost, optimizing energy which helps to build a green city and brings sustainability and pleasant living environment for the people [25].

10.3.1   Intent of IoT Adoption in Smart Cities

Its purpose is to make cities connected, smart, co-related, co-operative, and participative as whole community. The governing bodies must focus mainly on citizens who can adopt and implement technology willingly. Its success will depend mainly on technology, society and humans.

The following dimensions allow the smooth adoption of IoT:

   a) *Focus-Citizen Centric:* IoT should solve the real-life problems of inhabitants. Urbanization, economic growth, and enhanced infrastructure goal must be fulfilled.
   b) *Secure and Robust solutions:* Security and privacy must be primary concerns around technology. The system must be robust to acquire a suitable solution [26].
   c) *Participation:* Participation will increase as citizens will be provided with ownership of services, which will accelerate the new jobs.
   d) *Educational Opportunities:* IoT should enrich the educational opportunities for children and adults.
   e) *Ease of Use and experience:* IoT technologies should be easily understandable, solutions to problems must enhance the user experience. Poor experience crate poor satisfaction, low social acceptability.

10.3.2   IoT-Supported Communication Technologies

Protocols of communication are the inseparable segment of IoT systems [27]. The defined protocols enable network connectivity between devices.

Data can be easily exchanged over the network. The different wireless technologies are described below can be used in various applications depending on the parameters such as frequency, data rate, etc. Figure 10.6 represents various types of communication technologies.

a) *Wi-Fi*

It is basically part of Local Area Network (LAN) protocols. MAC and PHY protocols should be set for implementing the Wi-Fi Wireless local area network (WLAN). It is mostly used in wireless networks and accessing the internet without wires. IEEE 802.11 is a cluster of various communication protocols such as 802.11a, 802.11b, 802.11g, 802.11n, 802.11ac, 802.11ad. 802.11a and 802.11ac operates at frequency of 5GHz, 802.11b and 802.11g operates at 2.4 GHz whereas 802.11n operates at frequency of 24./5 GHz and 802.11ad operates at 2.4/5/60 GHz. These provide bit rates from 1 Mbps to 7 Gbps. These communication standards have a range of order from 5 to 140 m. Energy consumption and cost are very high for these standards. In Smart cities many services and devices are connected with each other

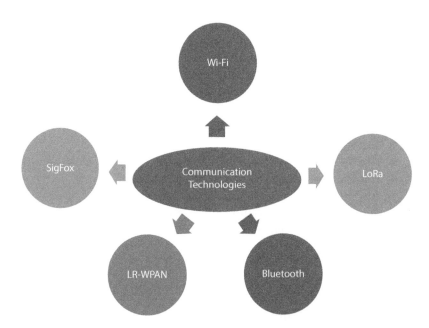

Figure 10.6 Communication technologies.

through Wi-Fi so data can be easily processed and transmitted [28].

b) *Bluetooth*

It is the IEEE 802.15.1 standard. It is a short range protocol; the range is approximately 8–10 m. Bluetooth is basically used as wireless communication for transmission of data in between two devices. It acts a personal area network. Its operating frequency is 2.4 GHz. Bit rate for transmission of data is 1Mbps to 24Mbps. Nowadays various IoT approaches for Bluetooth low-energy (BLE). It is suitable for long distance communication.

c) *LoRaWAN- LoRa*

It is developed for long-range communications. It can easily enable IoT applications. Its range is from 15–20 km. It defines the upper layers of the network. This wireless technology has low power consumption and secured data transmission. It operates at frequency of 868 and 900 MHz ISM Bands with bit ranges from 0.3 to 50 kbps. Smart city services like alarm systems, health and energy monitoring system, transportation, etc, are using LoRa standards for seamless integration among devices. Chirp Spread Spectrum used as modulation system. Star-based topology is used by network which can serves as end-points, and gateways for IoT devices [29]. The technology is deployed by telecom operators because of its advantages which include bi-directional communications, tracking, security and localization.

d) *LR-WPAN*

LR-WPAN stands for a Low-rate Wireless Personal Area network. Technical grade for LR-WPAN is IEEE 802.15.4. It is a base for Zigbee and 6LoWPAN. It operates at frequency of 868/915 and 2.4 GHz. Bit rates ranges from 40 to 250 kbps. Star, tree, and mesh topologies are supported by LR-WPAN. MAC and PHY sub layer defines the specifications. For smart health sensors communicate with medical devices using technology of WPAN (ZigBee, 6LoWPAN). These sensors measure various parameters such as temperature, blood pressure, PH and so on.

e) *SigFox*

It is based on Narrowband technology with Binary phase-shift keying BPSK transmission method. The carrier phase is changed for encoding of data in a small portion of spectrum. Its application cost is very low. It operates at frequency of 868/915 and 2.4 GHz. The technology deploys efficient, low throughput communication by restricting the number of antennas. By doing so, 1,000 times less antennas and base stations are required as compared to cellular networks. Network connected to SigFox in smart cities can easily access the management interface service through which it can enable temperature settings, signal quality and volume of exchanged data.

10.4 Sectors, Services Related and Principal Issues for IoT Technologies

Emerging concept in market is smart city and its important part is future infrastructure. Different services are associated with IoT technologies which brings pleasing and feasible environment for residents of smart city. To set up such environment various sectors and industries are collaborating and bringing the future concept of smart cities. For this concept to be implemented different technological issues are also taken into consideration. Table 10.1 summarizes the sectors providing the services to smart city with core issues related with IoT Technologies.

10.5 Impact of Smart Cities

With the capability to manage, monitor, analyze and measure city needs, services and utilities today's cities have earned to be called "SMART". With achieving all the capabilities smart cities have a huge impact on science, technology, and society.

10.5.1 Smart City Impact on Science and Technology

Science mostly deals with innovations and new ideas. New challenges faced are mostly dealt with science innovations. The solution to real-life problems is mostly imparted by new ideas conceived by science [42]. Smart technologies and methodologies can easily overcome the problem.

Table 10.1 Sectors, services and principal issues of IoT technologies.

Sectors	Services	Principal issues
Energy	Channeling and distribution of energy	a) Communication protocols, b) Potential Market in IoT technologies, c) important parts and components of systems, d) complex energy architectures and monitoring, e) Modeling and analytical technologies for the performance
	Uniform energy distribution system—Manage, optimize and reduce [30]	
	Management and optimization of energy—Smart building	
Architecture and smart building	Building—Automation, management	a) Different architectures with different IoT and WSN Technologies, b) Communication protocols, c) Automation and service scenarios, d) predicting energy consumption and efficiency, e) Real time monitoring, control and management, f) remote and control management control system, g) Utilization of resources consumed in buildings
	Control and management of optimization technology for smart building [31]	
Automation and System	Smart building automation technology [32]	a) Control services-autonomous or remote, b) Sensing technologies, c) Management system, d) Open architecture framework
	Home automation [33]	
Automation and transportation	Parking system [34]	a) Management systems for transportation vehicles, b) Wireless technologies required for devices, c) connection of mobile device with vehicles
	Vehicles telematics [35]	

(Continued)

Table 10.1 Sectors, services and principal issues of IoT technologies. (*Continued*)

Sectors	Services	Principal issues
Security	Home Security [36]	a) Privacy protection, b) data sharing, c) IoT technologies providing support for communication models (video and voice), d) Different modeling architectures, e) communication standards
	Security of children and elderly [37]	
	information security	
Health care and monitoring	Smart hospitals [38]	a) Extended market using healthcare IoT Technologies, b) Data protection and privacy, c) Tracking of medical team and facilities, d) requirement of healthcare equipment, services for maintenance of medical record.
	Smart health care	
Smart home	Sensor communication [39]	a) Energy usage and optimization, b) Background server technology, c) cloud computing services, d) recognizing speech and images, e) service platform (single or multiple), f) interfacing between different networks
	Controlling Platform	
	Framework	
	Wired and Wireless network [40]	
Intelligent home appliances	smart care	a) security, b) sensing technology and measurement device, c) information exchange (users and objects), d) home network and firewalls
	home appliances— security technology [41]	
	intelligent IP imagining devices	

Whenever there is any progress technology it is directly related to progress in science. Advancement is need of the hour so machine learning, artificial intelligence with IoT must be associated with Smart cities. Smart cities must generate new thinking about enabling new technologies and becoming smarter.

10.5.2   Smart City Impact on Competitiveness

New problems will always generate innovation and new concepts. The new concepts will be implemented and bring a revolutionary change in the system. Smart cities are competitive in nature. Smart cities adopt new IoT technologies such as smart infrastructure, smarty transport, smart health, and smart energy meter, etc. There is always competition between technologies [43]. Smart cities always acquire new and advanced technologies. So that IoT has to fight for its place in a smart city. Many cities are competing to provide improved living conditions, environmental conditions, and economic stability. Due to competitiveness, smart cities will be connected to smart applications will discover new services.

10.5.3   Smart City Impact on Society

In smart city things are connected with each other, data is exchanged over the network. All the services and facilities will be developed and accessible to each to make sure that everyone is accommodated. Form traditional city model i.e. more ethics and policies to govern are drawn to regulate smart cities [44]. IoT includes smart sensors and other devices. For example from sensor data is collected from a weather forecast system. The analyzed data can be used to manage traffic, reduce pollution, enhanced infrastructure, and keep citizens safe and clean with the help of IoT. There is a huge impact on society as everything is connected with IoT. The creation of a smart city is a gradual process technological awareness and literacy rate should be high. This leads to improved essence of life and sustainability.

10.5.4   Smart City Impact on Optimization and Management

In smart cities, one window service is provided for all the utilities. For managing assets and monitoring life availability of IoT is very important. All the valuable comprehensions on urban life and livability parameters are gained by gathering and analyzing data. There will be intelligent services with a proactive response. Audit and build capacity will help to manage efficiently. Solutions will be implemented with business process mapping

[45]. City surveillance used for security which will maintain the privacy of the citizens. Water, electricity, gas, and connectivity will be managed and optimized efficiently.

10.5.5   Smart City for Sustainable Development

Smart cities have huge contribution towards urban sustainability by using ICT. Sustainability in reference to smart cities are concept related to green buildings, recyclability reusability, water pollution control system, connectivity, maintenance and management system which includes smart citizen and smart governance system [46]. Basically, all this is dependent on internet based solutions. Data gathered is analyzed accordingly improve the performance and management. Services to citizens are given by mobile applications and these applications make daily routine very convenient. According to sustainable services, privacy and security are primary concern which must be maintained at any cost. But cloning of software is severe threat which may breach the privacy and security of applications. So IoT-enable green city architecture can be used for clone detection together with deep learning approach [47]. So, to make a sustainable environment around work has to be done on real life problems.

Various goals can be achieved with sustainability such as:

- Enhanced quality of life
- Economic growth with more job opportunities
- Smart health care system with proper access of social and community services.
- Efficient basic services
- Reduced environmental issues
- Good Governance ensuring equitable policies.

With smart solutions quality of live can be strengthened which is important factor for sustainable development.

10.6   Key Applications of IoT in Smart Cities

The most effective parameter of smart cities is IoT. Public resources can be optimized by the efficient use of IoT. The key aim of IoT is to provide easy access to resources so that surveillance, power, water, electricity, gas, and connectivity can be achieved. Transparency is increased in smart cities with the application of IoT. Figure 10.7 displays the applications of IoT.

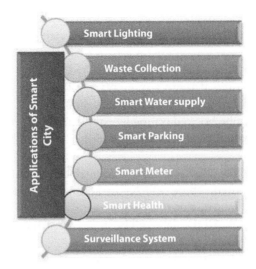

Figure 10.7 Applications of IoT.

A few IoT-based applications implemented in smart cities are listed below:

a) *Smart Lighting:* LDR, luminance sensors, PIR sensors for motion detection together forms an automated lighting system. As per the needs of streets, lights will glow and dimming will be controlled. The solar panel can be used for charging or giving power to sensors so net zero poles can be created [48].

b) *Waste Collection:* This system will be useful for the environment. There will be ultrasonic sensors or level sensors for measuring the level of waste in bins [49]. When the threshold level is reached, the notification on the mobile phone will be received by a waste collector person or in the office thorough cloud. The notification can be received at different stages like the bin is 50% full; a bin is 75% full or empties the bin. The design of waste collection systems depends on the need for location in the city. It will be an efficient waste collection system with reduced operational costs in comparison to traditional waste collection system.

c) *Smart Water Supply:* The fully automated system will help in proper distribution and monitoring of water supply in the locality. SCADA and pressure sensors are used for monitoring. The leakage and water spilling is also detected by the system.

d) *Smart Parking:* Vehicles can be tracked, parking spaces can be monitored if there any empty parking spaces available driver will be notified beforehand about the space location and it can be booked online by payment. The system is useful where vehicle density is high [50].

e) *Smart Meter:* Distribution of water, electricity, and gas will be automated. There will be an automated meter reading system, even the threshold value can be notified to the customer if set. All the data will be in real-time mode.

f) *Smart Environment Monitoring:* Monitoring of environmental health can be done through different sensors namely humidity, pressure, etc. Many parameters like air quality, pollution level can be checked continuously and information can be given to inhabitants of that area.

g) *Smart Health:* Wearable devices and sensors like heart rate measuring sensor, temperature, etc. will screen the person continuously and health can be monitored. These devices are attached to hospitals and health care services [51].

h) *Surveillance Systems:* Security and privacy are the main concerns of smart cities. Through cameras, the whole city can be monitored. Data received will be helpful in detecting crime and curbing it [52]. The security system must be enhanced with the privacy of citizens that must be taken care of side by side.

i) *Drones:* In technological context drones are unmanned air vehicles (UAV) which can be operated remotely or can be controlled through software. Smart city is based on integration of ICT with latest technologies. UAVs will play a key role in future of smart cities. With the smart use of technology city can achieve ideal environmental conditions, traffic monitoring, surveillance, security and surveying for monitoring development work on daily basis. UAV can gather data, analyze and deliver highly accurate and detailed data.

Drones can enhance security and run essential services like delivering packages, monitoring, medical and firefighting [53]. But there are challenges associated are that in densely populated areas safety, security and privacy are main concern issues.

10.7   Challenges

10.7.1   Smart City Design Challenges

Challenges associated with smart cities are very diverse and complex in nature as shown in Figure 10.8. There are many governing factors such as government policies, communities, environment, and the major part is played by economy. Cost, carbon emission, operation efficiency, safety, security, reliability, waste collection, etc. are design challenges associated with smart city. Among all challenges cost is most important. Cost includes NRE cost and operational costs are main components of cost. The former is a one-time it is basically the design cost and for maintaining the city operational cost is required. Cost optimization is one of the challenging tasks [54].

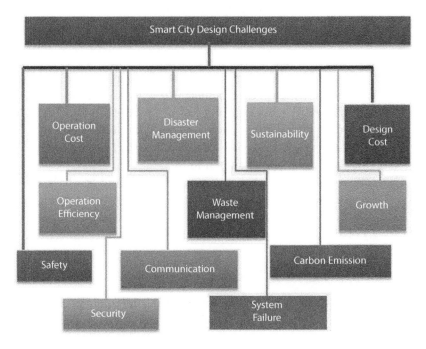

Figure 10.8 Smart city design challenges.

Efficiency and cost are indirectly related to each other, if operational efficiency increases the cost gets reduced in the long run and this improves the sustainability of the city. Population growth must be at a controlled rate in the smart cities for long term sustainability. Also, there must be a reduction in carbon emission and waste produced to increase efficiency and reducing operational costs. Natural disasters and failures such as power failure also fail components of smart cities. The city must quickly recover from such disasters and failures. Sensors and ICT are strong pillars of a city. So, by accumulating data from sensors and storing it at secure place requires large space [55]. The security of data is an important design parameter. By using surveillance cameras safety of citizens can enhance but there are other factors like fire, theft, kidnapping, etc. should be considered. So, there is increase in budget due to public safety which is the most critical design challenge for smart cities.

10.7.2   Challenges Raised by Smart Cities

IoT is a new sensation which faces many challenges. Few are listed below:

    i. *Data Exchange:* Due to large networks and complex system data commutation is a very tedious task.
    ii. *Privacy:* Real-time data is received from sensors. Live locations, posts on social sites can easily retrieve. So it's essential to take appropriate privacy precautions.
    iii. *Safety and Security:* It is the critical feature that must be provided by IoT. The system is subject to many attacks so it must be protected from leakage of data.
    iv. *Reliability:* If a vehicle is moving so the communication system is not reliable to provide exact and correct information. This causes reliability issues in IoT.
    v. *Network Security:* Data is received through wired or wireless transmission from sensors. The network must be so strong that it can handle huge data without deteriorating the quality of any data loss [56].

10.7.3   Challenges of IoT Technologies in Smart Cities

The most tedious task is collecting, monitoring, and analyzing real-time data. But IoT-based smart cities make quick and efficient decisions in a meaningful way [57]. From the urbanism perspective, there are lots of challenges that will be taken in to account.

Dynamic Elements:
Enhancing the standard of living is the main aim of smart cities, urbanization, and IoT. Future of connectivity is the Internet and IoT will provide the main framework for solving real-life problems of cities. So, weather, demographic, and traffic information are the main categories to get information for designing and planning smart cities. So the information collected through sensors are analyzed and categorized accordingly. In traditional cities mainly composed of static elements like roads. On the other hand, elements that react with real-time data are dynamic elements and smart cities are using dynamic elements. Real-time information is managed by IoT [58]. For example, according to weather conditions smart roads color will change so that drivers can see the road clearly. Traffic information is real-time is boon for today's cities. Using dynamic elements urban space is becoming very attractive for citizens.

Privacy:
The real-time data stored can jeopardize privacy. Due to the internet live location of people, their personal space is visible to everyone. This harms the privacy of an individual. So urbanization must consider this as a critical parameter in designing and only specific data must be provided about people.

Social Equity:
Urbanization must provide social equity. There are many social problems in society, so there must be an optimal distribution of services according to the requirement [59]. By analyzing real-time information the target groups or areas can be identified and urban designers can plan accordingly. For e.g. If in an area there are a majority of elderly, children and specially-abled people so to such sensitive groups extra care must be given in terms of safety or space.

Social Equality:
In smart cities, the services should be provided equally to every citizen without regard to social status. For e.g. Public security must be provided to every citizen. By giving public safety the crime rate will be reduced simultaneously. The speed of internet must be equally distributed in each area. For providing such services the most difficult task is to change the infrastructure or an area of people living [60]. By collecting data of people, services the best possible solution can be given to various groups of people in cities and without interference, emergency services can be commuted in IoT-based cities.

10.8   Conclusion

A smart city is a system of various services connected with each other. To flourish a city all its components, key factors, technologies used need to work together like a machine. IoT is turning the traditional cities into smart city which in turn moving towards urbanization. Availability in real-time data, integrity for reliability, confidentiality for collected data, and accountability for responsibility and actions are four objectives that integrate solutions. A smart city framework composed of ICT can address challenges related to urbanization by developing, deploying, and promoting sustainability. By using wireless networks and cloud data from sensors are transmitted and received using an intelligent network of objects and machines. In this chapter, we have discussed the concept, motivation and main agenda of developing smart cities. The related key components are outlined. Functional blocks like sensing, identification, actuation, communication, and management together form an IoT system. The IoT system is explained with the perspective of smart cities. Devices become intelligent and these devices give initiative for urbanization. With the tabular view, various sectors of technology, related services, and core issues related are highlighted. Chapter focus on the applications which are connecting IoT to cities services like waste management, smart meter, and traffic congestion improves the quality of life. At last challenges are discussed related to Smart Cities, Urbanization, and IoT. These challenges can give direction for research. Smart cities with high efficiency, the reduced cost will always provide long term sustainability for systems. The evaluation of the chapter is that IoT technologies with smart city concepts provide urban development which will improve the standard of living.

Acknowledgements

This work is supported by Visvesvaraya Ph.D. Scheme, Meity, Govt. of India. MEITY-PHD-2950.

References

1. Stojkoska, B.L.R. and Trivodaliev, K.V., A review of Internet of Things for smart home: Challenges and solutions. *J. Cleaner Prod.*, 140, 1454–1464, 2017.
2. Bahrainy, H. and Bakhtiar, A., Urban Design Definition, Knowledge Base and Principles, in: *Toward an Integrative Theory of Urban Design*, pp. 5–28, Springer, Cham, 2016.

3. Bibri, S.E. and Krogstie, J., Smart sustainable cities of the future: An extensive interdisciplinary literature review. *Sustain. Cities Soc.*, 31, 183–212, 2017.

4. Mueller, J., Lu, H., Chirkin, A., Klein, B., Schmitt, G., Citizen Design Science: A strategy for crowd-creative urban design. *Cities*, 72, 181–188, 2018.

5. Anthopoulos, L.G. and Vakali, A., Urban planning and smart cities: Interrelations and reciprocities, in: *The Future Internet Assembly*, pp. 178–189, Springer, Berlin, Heidelberg, 2012, May.

6. Hui, T.K., Sherratt, R.S., Sánchez, D.D., Major requirements for building Smart Homes in Smart Cities based on Internet of Things technologies. *Future Gener. Comput. Syst.*, 76, 358–369, 2017.

7. Angelidou, M., Smart cities: A conjuncture of four forces. *Cities*, 47, 95–106, 2015.

8. Solanki, A. and Nayyar, A., Green internet of things (G-IoT): ICT technologies, principles, applications, projects, and challenges, in: *Handbook of Research on Big Data and the IoT*, pp. 379–405, IGI Global, USA, 2019.

9. Xu, H., Lin, J., Yu, W., Smart Transportation Systems: Architecture, Enabling Technologies, and Open Issues, in: *Secure and Trustworthy Transportation Cyber-Physical Systems*, pp. 23–49, Springer, Singapore, 2017.

10. Kumar, A., Rajalakshmi, K., Jain, S., Nayyar, A., Abouhawwash, M., A novel heuristic simulation–optimization method for critical infrastructure in smart transportation systems. *Int. J. Commun. Syst.*, 33, e4397, 2020.

11. Kumar, A., Srikanth, P., Nayyar, A., Sharma, G., Krishnamurthi, R., Alazab, M., A Novel Simulated-Annealing Based Electric Bus System Design, Simulation, and Analysis for Dehradun Smart City. *IEEE Access*, 8, 89395–89424, 2020.

12. Khan, N.A., Jhanjhi, N.Z., Brohi, S.N., Usmani, R.S.A., Nayyar, A., Smart traffic monitoring system using Unmanned Aerial Vehicles (UAVs). *Comput. Commun.*, 157, 434–443, 2020.

13. Choudhary, P., Bhargava, L., Singh, V., Choudhary, M., Kumar Suhag, A., A survey—Energy harvesting sources and techniques for internet of things devices. *Mater. Today: Proc.*, 30, 52–56, 2020.

14. Minoli, D., Sohraby, K., Occhiogrosso, B., IoT considerations, requirements, and architectures for smart buildings—Energy optimization and next-generation building management systems. *IEEE Internet Things J.*, 4, 1, 269–283, 2017.

15. Rathee, D., Ahuja, K., Nayyar, A., Sustainable future IoT services with touch-enabled handheld devices, in: *Security and Privacy of Electronic Healthcare Records: Concepts, Paradigms and Solutions*, p. 131, 2019.

16. Demirkan, H., A smart healthcare systems framework. *It Prof.*, 15, 5, 38–45, 2013.

17. Krishnamurthi, R., Nayyar, A., Solanki, A., Innovation Opportunities through Internet of Things (IoT) for Smart Cities, in: *Green and Smart Technologies for Smart Cities*, pp. 261–292, CRC Press, Boca Raton, FL, USA, 2019.

18. Singh, P., Nayyar, A., Kaur, A., Ghosh, U., Blockchain and Fog Based Architecture for Internet of Everything in Smart Cities. *Future Internet*, 12, 4, 61, 2020.
19. Peltan, T., Smart Cities as complexity management, in: *2015 Smart Cities Symposium Prague (SCSP)*, 2015, June, IEEE, pp. 1–5.
20. Kannan, K.P., India's labour question is also a social question: inequalizing growth and increasing social equality under neoliberal economic regimes. *J. Soc. Econ. Dev.*, 19, 2, 263–282, 2017.
21. Guevara, M.M. and López, E.M.C., The urban public space and design as tools to promote social interaction. *Blucher Design Proceedings*, vol. 8(2), pp. 296–301, 2016.
22. Meijer, A. and Bolívar, M.P.R., Governing the smart city: a review of the literature on smart urban governance. *Int. Rev. Adm. Sci.*, 82, 2, 392–408, 2016.
23. Zhu, Z.T., Yu, M.H., Riezebos, P., A research framework of smart education. *Smart Learn. Environ.*, 3, 1, 4, 2016.
24. Zanella, A., Bui, N., Castellani, A., Vangelista, L., Zorzi, M., Internet of things for smart cities. *IEEE Internet Things J.*, 1, 1, 22–32, 2014.
25. Harrison, C., Eckman, B., Hamilton, R., Hartswick, P., Kalagnanam, J., Paraszczak, J., Williams, P., Foundations for smarter cities. *IBM J. Res. Dev.*, 54, 4, 1–16, 2010.
26. Ammar, M., Russello, G., Crispo, B., Internet of Things: A survey on the security of IoT frameworks. *J. Inf. Secur. Appl.*, 38, 8–27, 2018.
27. Arasteh, H., Hosseinnezhad, V., Loia, V., Tommasetti, A., Troisi, O., Shafie-khah, M., Siano, P., Iot-based smart cities: A survey, in: *2016 IEEE 16th International Conference on Environment and Electrical Engineering (EEEIC)*, 2016, June, IEEE, pp. 1–6.
28. Nolan, K.E., Guibene, W., Kelly, M.Y., An evaluation of low power wide area network technologies for the Internet of Things, in: *2016 international wireless communications and mobile computing conference (IWCMC)*, 2016, September, IEEE, pp. 439–444.
29. Augustin, A., Yi, J., Clausen, T., & Townsley, W. M., A study of LoRa: Long range & low power networks for the internet of things. *Sensors*, 16, 9, 1466, 2016.
30. Ejaz, W., Naeem, M., Shahid, A., Anpalagan, A., Jo, M., Efficient energy management for the internet of things in smart cities. *IEEE Commun. Mag.*, 55, 1, 84–91, 2017.
31. Coates, A., Hammoudeh, M., Holmes, K.G., Internet of things for buildings monitoring: Experiences and challenges, in: *Proceedings of the International Conference on Future Networks and Distributed Systems*, 2017, July.
32. Smirek, L., Zimmermann, G., Beigl, M., Just a smart home or your smart home—A framework for personalized user interfaces based on eclipse smart home and universal remote console. *Procedia Comput. Sci.*, 98, 107–116, 2016.
33. Han, D.M. and Lim, J.H., Smart home energy management system using IEEE 802.15. 4 and Zigbee. *IEEE Trans. Consum. Electron.*, 56, 3, 1403–1410, 2010.

34. Khanna, A. and Anand, R., IoT based smart parking system, in: *2016 International Conference on Internet of Things and Applications (IoTA)*, 2016, January, IEEE, pp. 266–270.

35. Xu, H., Lin, J., Yu, W., Smart Transportation Systems: Architecture, Enabling Technologies, and Open Issues, in: *Secure and Trustworthy Transportation Cyber-Physical Systems*, pp. 23–49, Springer, Singapore, 2017.

36. Bassi, A. and Horn, G., *Internet of Things in 2020: A Roadmap for the Future*, vol. 22, pp. 97–114, European Commission: Information Society and Media, Brussels, 2008.

37. Lohan, E.S., Kauppinen, T., Debnath, S.B.C., A survey of people movement analytics studies in the context of smart cities, in: *2016 19th Conference of Open Innovations Association (FRUCT)*, 2016, November, IEEE, pp. 151–158.

38. Pramanik, M.I., Lau, R.Y., Demirkan, H., Azad, M.A.K., Smart health: Big data enabled health paradigm within smart cities. *Expert Syst. Appl.*, 87, 370–383, 2017.

39. Ko, J., Lee, B.B., Lee, K., Hong, S.G., Kim, N., Paek, J., Sensor virtualization module: Virtualizing IoT devices on mobile smartphones for effective sensor data management. *Int. J. Distrib. Sens. Netw.*, 11, 10, 730762, 2015.

40. Kamalinejad, P., Mahapatra, C., Sheng, Z., Mirabbasi, S., Leung, V.C., Guan, Y.L., Wireless energy harvesting for the Internet of Things. *IEEE Commun. Mag.*, 53, 6, 102–108, 2015.

41. Wlodarczak, P., Smart Cities—Enabling Technologies for Future Living, in: *City Networks*, pp. 1–16, Springer, Cham, 2017.

42. Chourabi, H., Nam, T., Walker, S., Gil-Garcia, J.R., Mellouli, S., Nahon, K., Scholl, H.J., Understanding smart cities: An integrative framework, in: *2012 45th Hawaii International Conference on System Sciences*, 2012, January, IEEE, pp. 2289–2297.

43. Borgia, E., The Internet of Things vision: Key features, applications and open issues. *Comput. Commun.*, 54, 1–31, 2014.

44. Kakarontzas, G., Anthopoulos, L., Chatzakou, D., Vakali, A., A conceptual enterprise architecture framework for smart cities: A survey based approach. *2014 11th International Conference on e-Business (ICE-B)*, Vienna, pp. 47–54, 2014.

45. Minoli, D., Sohraby, K., Occhiogrosso, B., IoT considerations, requirements, and architectures for smart buildings—Energy optimization and next-generation building management systems. *IEEE Internet Things J.*, 4, 1, 269–283, 2017.

46. Sterbenz, J.P., Smart city and IoT resilience, survivability, and disruption tolerance: Challenges, modelling, and a survey of research opportunities, in: *2017 9th International Workshop on Resilient Networks Design and Modeling (RNDM)*, 2017, September, IEEE, pp. 1–6.

47. Ullah, F., Al-Turjman, F., Nayyar, A., IoT-based green city architecture using secured and sustainable android services. *Environ. Technol. Innov.*, 20, 101091, 2020.

48. Castro, M., Jara, A.J., Skarmeta, A.F., Smart lighting solutions for smart cities, in: *2013 27th International Conference on Advanced Information Networking and Applications Workshops*, 2013, March, IEEE, pp. 1374–1379.

49. Patil, M.V. and Gajbhiye, S.M., A review on internet of things based garbage bins detection systems. *Int. J. Sci. Res.*, 6, 1699–1702, 2017.

50. Ankitha, S., Nayana, K.B., Shravya, S.R., Jain, L., Smart city initiative: Traffic and waste management, in: *2017 2nd IEEE International Conference on Recent Trends in Electronics, Information & Communication Technology (RTEICT)*, 2017, May, IEEE, pp. 1227–1231.

51. Dawid, H., Decker, R., Hermann, T., Jahnke, H., Klat, W., König, R., Stummer, C., Management science in the era of smart consumer products: Challenges and research perspectives. *Cent. Eur. J. Oper. Res.*, 25, 1, 203–230, 2017.

52. Mohanty, S.P., A secure digital camera architecture for integrated real-time digital rights management. *J. Syst. Architect.*, 55, 10–12, 468–480, 2009.

53. Nayyar, A., Jain, R., Mahapatra, B., Singh, A., Cyber security challenges for smart cities, in: *Driving the Development, Management, and Sustainability of Cognitive Cities*, pp. 27–54, IGI Global, USA, 2019.

54. Kitchin, R. and Dodge, M., The (in) security of smart cities: Vulnerabilities, risks, mitigation, and prevention. *J. Urban Technol.*, 26, 2, 47–65, 2019.

55. Samuel, S.S.I., A review of connectivity challenges in IoT-smart home, in: *2016 3rd MEC International Conference on Big Data and Smart City (ICBDSC)*, 2016, March, IEEE, pp. 1–4.

56. Braun, T., Fung, B.C., Iqbal, F., Shah, B., Security and privacy challenges in smart cities. *Sustain. Cities Soc.*, 39, 499–507, 2018.

57. Mehmood, Y., Ahmad, F., Yaqoob, I., Adnane, A., Imran, M., Guizani, S., Internet-of-things-based smart cities: Recent advances and challenges. *IEEE Commun. Mag.*, 55, 9, 16–24, 2017.

58. Praharaj, S., Han, J.H., Hawken, S., Urban innovation through policy integration: Critical perspectives from 100 smart cities mission in India. *City Cult. Soc.*, 12, 35–43, 2018.

59. Pereira, G.V., Parycek, P., Falco, E., Kleinhans, R., Smart governance in the context of smart cities: A literature review. *Inf. Polity*, 23, 2, 143–162, 2018.

60. Nesti, G., Mainstreaming gender equality in smart cities: Theoretical, methodological and empirical challenge. *Inf. Polity*, 24, 3, 289–304, 2019.

Trip-I-Plan: A Mobile Application for Task Scheduling in Smart City's Sustainable Infrastructure

**Rajalakshmi Krishnamurthi[1]*, Dhanalekshmi Gopinathan[1]
and Adarsh Kumar[2]**

[1]Department of Computer Science and Engineering, Jaypee Institute of Information Technology, Noida, India
[2]School of Computer Science, University of Petroleum and Energy Studies, Dehradun, India

Abstract

In recent years, smart city concept focusing towards tourism industry is highly boosted by a variety of information & communication technology (ICT). Commercially, there exists a wide range of mobile applications available for end users to plan their travel itinerary. However, there are several gaps in existing mobile applications like, not adaptable to every city's sustainable infrastructure, confined method of trip booking, only static trip tasks scheduling is possible, and lack of dynamic geo-location-based task rescheduling. In this chapter, firstly, the smart city concept, various applications of smart city intervened by IoT, mobile computing technologies are addressed. The primary focus is to explore the smart tourism application under smart city concept. Secondly, the mobile application based approach and its various opportunities to enhance the growth of smart city's citizen planning and boosting the growth of smart sustainable infrastructure through smart tourism is explored. Here, the comparative study of exiting trip planner mobile application of task scheduling towards smart tourism is presented. Finally, to overcome several existing disadvantages of trip planner mobile application, a comprehensive, automatically task rescheduling for mobile application is proposed.

*Corresponding author: k.rajalakshmi@jiit.ac.in

Arun Solanki, Adarsh Kumar and Anand Nayyar (eds.) Digital Cities Roadmap: IoT-Based Architecture and Sustainable Buildings, (351–378) © 2021 Scrivener Publishing LLC

Keywords: Smart city, smart tourism, trip planner task scheduling, mobile application, geo-location, Information & Communication Technology

11.1   Introduction

The term smart city first originated in the 1990s. During that time, the main focus was on utilizing the information and communication technologies (ICT) with respect to modern infrastructures on cities. In a current scenario, a smart city is defined as a sustainable city that uses information and communication technologies (ICT) to improve the quality of life of people. A smart city is comprised of different areas locations in a city which use electronic data collection through sensors located in various infrastructures to supply real time information about the operation of the main cities. The real time information includes energy, transportation, supply of water, sewage, waste management, enforcement of law and information communication, etc. Information and communication (ICT) technology platforms analyze the data collected from different sensors which allows the decision makers to optimize the efficiency and pliability of services and operations by allowing them to operate remotely. It also allows connecting and communicating with stakeholders including citizens, companies, institutions and civic organizations. There are variants of definitions can be found in the literature. Some of them are listed below.

Smart cities were defined as "the effective integration of physical, digital and human systems in the built environment to deliver a sustainable, prosperous and inclusive future for its citizens" (BSI 2014) [1]. Harrison *et al.* [2] defined smart city as a city which links the physical, IT, social and business infrastructure to control collective intelligence of the city. Marsal-Llacuna [3] defined smart cities as the initiatives effort to improve quality of life in urban area by using data, information and information technologies (IT) by providing more efficient services to citizens thereby monitoring and optimizing existing infrastructure, increasing collaboration among public and private sectors to encourage innovative business models.

In today's scenario, a lot of things related to travel have been made easier by online services like TripAdvisor, Ibibo, MakeMyTrip, TripIt, and Google Trips. These online web services can be integrated into smart city concept. But these applications are helpful to only limited extent of the smart city service users, such as not having to actually go to the ticket counters for booking or booking through an agent [4, 5]. But one has to still plan their visit, make hotel reservations, book cabs, etc. Even planning a stress-free holiday requires some stressing over important details, negotiating deals, planning itinerary, etc. There are a few services that require you to input your date of arrival and departure and destination and choose from some predetermined travel plans, like the ones offered by the likes of offline players such as Thomas Cook Travels, DPauls Travels, etc. But none of these services (individually or combined) provide user with the option to choose their places of interest within a city or state or country and have an itinerary that is built around these choices and according to their convenience and choice [6, 7].

This chapter presents mobile application for trip planner named "Trip-I-Plan", which can tackle some of the above discussed specific gaps in the tourism industry under smart city concept. The app focuses on scheduling the activities slated for the day by the user and also tries to reschedule them by dividing the tasks as important and non-important [8]. Free slots are found and then according to the duration and nature of the task, it is rescheduled automatically by the mobile application for smart city environment. The best possible solutions are computed using various scheduling algorithms and also different permutations and combinations to provide the best possible solution or to provide the top solutions [9, 10].

The key contributions of this work are:

- There are many task rescheduling and task managing applications, but none provide comprehensive rescheduling.
- The app should make it possible for the user to just open it and enter, control and change most of the details with the least amount of effort.
- Since the app includes multiple functionalities, it is essential to make the UI (User Interface) simple, easy to understand, fluid, logical and fast.
- How to make it a multiple user platform with interactions between them that involves minimal effort.
- To cover maximum types of tasks and possibilities.
- Making the app as autonomous as possible, so that the app is itself able to infer which tasks have been missed and which are to rescheduled.

11.2   Smart City and IoT

Internet of things (IoT) has grabbed the attention of humans in a very short span of time due to its easiness in understanding and also its implementation. It has significantly indulged in various areas of human work and personal lives. IoT has been used in the houses of every human and due to its increasing demand, the new houses or cities that are building have smart devices inbuilt that helps human in living an easy and stress-free life. Application of IoT with the context of urbanization is a major aspect for the governments to take good care of public affairs and also it is a good investment to earn for the government. Smart city mainly means to have a better life and better usage of resources and providing better facilities for the citizens, with low cost so that they can use various facilities. These devices help in providing transparency to the citizens of what they are using and how much they are using so they can pay for only those resources which they use. These provide various services like transport, parking, maintenance, garbage collection, hospitals and schools. And this helps in creating awareness between the citizens about the public administration that plays an important role for healthy and good surroundings to live.

The general framework building is a very complex work for the IoT as it has very large varieties of devices, various technologies and the services that are involved in the system. Zanella *et al.* [14] in their paper had categorized the urban IoT system with the domain of specific application, these urban IoT provide a helping hand in the creation of smart city. The smart city aims at giving the most of communication and resources techniques for the citizens. They give the information about the architecture, protocols and technologies of Urban IoT. The most of the smart cities are having a structure that is centralized, and also have heterogeneous and dense sets of devices that helps in communication and also for controlling the center. The main characteristic of technologies is its capabilities of integrating the various technologies together and make use of it. Another characteristic includes the data collection process which helps in creating an awareness between the citizens and also helps in making people participate in urban city making.

The urban IoT system has various different components like the web services that are used for the IoT services to make and for this the various protocols are used in the various networks. In the IoT domain, there are various standards that are in a way of recognition but the main standard used is the IETF standards. As the IEFT standards are royalty free and open to use. The link layer technologies and devices are also a part of the structures. Chourabi *et al.* [15] and Yao [46] described that there are eight factors that are the major aspects in a IoT urban city making and they are the organization, management, technology, policy context, governance, economy, communities and people, policy context, natural environment and building infrastructure. Every infrastructure has these factors as their basic and that helps in making the government to work quickly and in examining the work. The agenda of smart city and also the practical implications of the government are outlined by the directions that are laid by the framework. This helps in comparing and assessing the smart cities and how they are working and implementing the devices.

The factors are basically of two types and they are classified as outer factors and the inner factors. The outer factors include the people and communities, governance, economy, infrastructure, and natural environment. The inner factors are the policy, management and technology. These helps in creating a healthy environment that included the smart city and homes. In making these smart cities and houses the sensors and other devices like actuators are used, and these devices provide convenient services but these services are somehow limited to certain points due to their regular exposer to the environment. These limitations intend to product failures, and these failures include the devices failure, hardware limitation or due to battery drainage. And for these faulty problems the methods used for finding the failure are proposed by many scholars.

Choi *et al.* [16] proposed a method that can detect the fault in the IoT devices. In their presented method two phases are there, first is the pre-computation phase: in this the computation of the transition probability and sensor correlation can be calculated before. And in the second phase the real time phase, the faults in the transition and sensor correlation helps in finding the faults. And after these phases the detection is done and by this the sensor data is analyzed, during this analysis the IoT devices that area new or missing are found by comparing the problematic context. They compared the data of various fault types and with different datasets. They discuss the four parameters, and they are first is multi-user cases are used, multi-fault is used to understand the case study, different parameters and their impact on the method and also the security is expanded. It detects the faults with high accuracy to the internet and provide their data to derive actionable insights in its own or through connected objects.

IoT comprises of network of smart devices which can send and receive information, analyze the data and make wise decision based on the obtained data. It makes the physical objects to smart objects by making use of the underlying technologies like embedded devices, communication technologies, sensor networks and internet protocols and applications.

The interconnected devices will keep on sharing information globally over the Internet. This effort develops a pervasive computing environment. IoT is applied in many domains including healthcare, transportation, environmental monitoring, personal and social, smart city, industrial control, and many more. Many industries like retail, manufacturing, health care, transportation and logistics, government sector, energy sector are widely using IoT.

The objective of Smart city enhanced by IoT is to understand consumer needs in real time, become more responsive, improve machine and system quality on the fly, streamline operations and discover innovative ways to operate as part of their digital transformation efforts. The IoT has many benefits like efficient resource management, enhanced productivity, and increased quality-of-life for human populations [1, 47, 48]. IoT is key enabler for smart environments such as smart homes, smart health, smart cities and smart factories. The flexible layered architecture is required as the backbone of IoT as it is dealing with heterogeneous connected devices. The next section discusses the architecture components of IoT.

Architectural components of IoT: IoT architecture components include a collection of physical objects, sensors, cloud services, developers, actuators, communication layers, users, business layers, and IoT protocols. The requirement of IoT system architecture is that it should bridge the gap between the physical and virtual worlds. The IoT ecosystem includes the integration of all the services and tools to deliver a complete solution. In general, every IoT system comprises four components regardless of any use case are the devices, connectivity, platform and an application. These four components are the main foundations of the every IoT solution since they add the sensors and actuators, add connectivity to the cloud, and implementing "things" so that its properties or abilities can be programmatically manipulated. There is no single consensus agreed for IoT architecture universally since each user or organization has different requirements. The basic IoT architecture can be viewed as a three-level architecture. Application layer is also considered as the business layer. It is implemented on the top of the network layer. Data received from the network layer is used by this layer to provide services to the application users. Network layer manages the connectivity between the smart things, network devices and servers. This layer also transmits and processes the sensor data. Perception layer precepts data from the environment through the sensors. Figure 11.1 below depicts basic architecture for IoT-based Smart City and Smart Tourism.

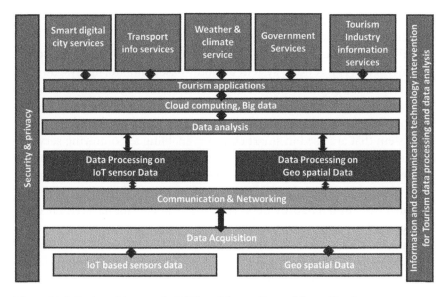

Figure 11.1 Basic architecture for IoT-based Smart City and Smart Tourism.

11.3   Mobile Computing for Smart City

The emergence of the smart cities, always provided services that are enhanced to the citizens. The data that we get from the sensor nodes and by monitoring the sensitive events that are on the large areas like the services that are helpful in making the dynamic actuation and also helps in providing the reporting of the real time. There are challenges that are to be addressed so that the heterogeneity of the various monitoring systems is to be in the large-scale area when there is coordination lack. The information exchange that is placed between the infrastructures that are inter-dependent so that it can be used for preventing the incidents. So, to overcome these challenges research has been done to provide solutions so that the smart city can be migrated on the cloud so that it can also uses the benefits of cloud.

The emergence of the smart cities in the whole world, the various services are needed and these services helps in providing the protection to the citizens. In these the supervisory systems are deployed so that they can make use of mobile sensors. The threats that are new can be resolved, and for resolving the systems new methods like cloud integration of devices is proposed. For monitoring the large area which are under the threat are using the entities that helps in preventing a protection from the malicious activities that are targeting the cities.

In literature, different systems are proposed and one of them is proposed by Dhief *et al.* [17]. A novel system of cloud-based monitoring system that helps in providing global monitoring services by using the set of sensors that helps in deploying the different systems that supervise is proposed. Authors designed and supported in developing the cloud-based monitoring system that are used in smart cities for enabling a monitoring services that are large scale and are based on a fixed set and also the mobile sensors that we get from different providers. The usage of virtualization of sensors helps in providing techniques that helps in enabling a multi usage that is provided from different providers. That can help in enabling a remote configuration of the sensors with the help of cloud breakers and also providing an efficient scheduling.

The cloud-based smart city has some requirements and those are, global monitoring service, sensor utilization, scalability privacy of sensing data and sensors reconfiguration [45]. The architecture they proposed have three layers that helps in providing global monitoring service and these layers are, physical supervisory system or provider, broker of virtual sensors, logical supervisory systems. An example for this can be taken as real time data used for parking allotment in smart cities with the use of IoT devices. The parking systems in the smart cities needed the cloud systems and for this the real time storing of data is useful. And for the real time monitoring of data sets is possible due to the moving of datasets and all the second to second information on the cloud without any delay. For this a hierarchical approach can be used that helps in getting free parking in the smart city very conveniently.

The hierarchical approach of smart city has two different levels the first level includes the algorithm to check for the nearest parks available and at the second level the checks whether the place is available for car parking. This hierarchical approach is more time and energy efficient as compared to non-hierarchical approach. Jin *et al.* [18] provides a framework for complete urbanization of information system with the sensory levels and also with the networking support structure that helps in data management and also in the cloud-based integration of the services that are there in the smart cities and systems. It also helps in providing a transformational part of the cyber physical system. The applications that are within the urban environment and these are grouped on the basis of the impact areas. The effects on transport, citizens and services. For these specific application domains are identified and these are used for utilizing the smart city structure of IoT framework.

IoT is introduced with the help of three different domains and these are cloud-centric IoT, network-centric IoT and data-centric IoT with respect to the communication, computation requirement and management of smart city development. The network architecture for the smart cities and they are of two main design approaches that are used for the network architecture [19]. These two main designs are, first is a clean-slate approach and second is an evolutionary approach. The evolutionary approach helps in making incremental changes so that the current network architecture can be reuse as many components as possible by the existing networking solutions. But the clean slate approach helps to redesign the network being constrained by the current structure. There are four most common architectures of networks for making smart city domain and these are: first is the ubiquitous network, second is autonomous network, third is service-oriented and last is the application layer overlay network architecture.

The application of task schedulers in any activity has a primary role. Various algorithms are applied in the process to achieve maximum speed and efficiency [1]. With the advent of artificial intelligence, neural networks can be used to learn from certain task scheduling situations and then testing them on future tasks by following the predictions [2]. This process is repeated to improve accuracy and speed. Such a heavy application can be offloaded completely or partially so that heavy computations are performed on offsite servers. The existing idea works better based on connectivity to mobile devices that can offer speed and reliability. We can even combine heuristic and metaheuristic optimization techniques like genetic algorithm which can be applied to find a general solution of this problem that result in an effective scheduling of tasks [3]. This technique is particularly helpful in tackling multiple tasks at the same time.

With multi-task scheduling comes the problem of handling them at the same time in real-time [15]. The solution can be found in multi-core processor systems which have the ability to tackle this problem [16]. Effective distribution of tasks while using minimal resources can be achieved here by taking help from some efficient methods, discussed earlier. But in the process of increasing power of computation, the battery life takes a huge impact. Battery life is an important aspect while discussing mobile devices. A method which finds middle ground between efficiency and speed is required so that the whole purpose of mobile devices is not destroyed [17, 18].

Since many applications are already using cloud-based data centers, concepts like virtual machines will only become more popular and require better development and understanding. The data center should be able to correctly analyze the requirements of the task, allot it resources accordingly and allocate it to a machine. Most applications use FCFS scheduling algorithm to schedule tasks [20]. The algorithm in effect works well in most situations but requires some additional parameters that provide hints about resource requirements so that server can quickly detect the task category and allot it the resources easily and effectively, while using minimal memory and time.

The primary problem is to find a method that schedules tasks effectively, allocates it resources effectively and complete the task successfully, while using minimum power, CPU strength and should work on any device [15]. With all this also comes the problem of security and reliability. By reading the literature, we can infer that artificial intelligence and cloud servers will play a major role in this field and its development is required to move forward. The power and number of cloud data servers will increase, thus decreasing the current dependency on the native processing capabilities of the mobile devices.

11.4   Smart City and its Applications

The few popular applications of smart city concept include city traffic monitoring, smart lighting, air quality monitoring, and smart tourism. This section elaborates each of these applications in detail.

11.4.1   Traffic Monitoring

Recently, traffic congestion on the roads, unsuitable scheduling allocation of traffic signals and traffic accidents have become bigger issues for the cities. A Smart Traffic Management System plays an important role in urban traffic management, especially in densely populated urban areas. An IoT-based smart traffic signal control system can address vehicle traffic problems such as congestion at crossroads or on the highways. An intelligent IoT-based traffic signal monitoring system utilizing smart algorithms becomes the need of the hour to reduce heavy traffic flow by allowing a large chunk of vehicles to cross through the traffic signal.

Traffic monitoring system can (i) track the vehicles with the help of sensors, (ii) Count the number of vehicles passing through the signals, (iii) RFID tags and readers can track the vehicles in order to control traffic congestion at signals and (iv), trace a stolen vehicle or clear traffic for emergency vehicles.

Nagamode and Rajbhoj [11] proposed an IoT-based traffic monitoring and controlling system based on priority. The design includes ultrasonic sensors equipped for real-time traffic monitoring that detects traffic level status at an intersection. These sensors are placed at roadside for monitoring traffic levels. Depending on the particular distance gap, these levels are categorised as low, medium, and high. The sensed data is then sent to controller unit and transfer through Wi-Fi module to the web server for detecting traffic levels. Detecting high level traffic in a lane, the controller provides more signal timings to pass the vehicles, while for a low-level traffic in a lane lessens the signal timings. Thereby giving priority to emergency vehicle at a high traffic level. The information regarding the traffic levels, timestamps and date is then sent to server of authorized open source for further analytics.

11.4.2 Smart Lighting

The smart lighting system in smart city environment is an autonomous and efficient system which is achieved by the use of IoT technology. The objective is to obtain a smart lighting management system since, the lighting system in a smart city consumes more energy than other parts of a city, it needs to be integrated with advanced sensors and communication channels.

Different IoT communication protocols, devices and sensors manages the Smart Lighting System in a centralized or distributed way. The goal of the smart lighting includes the energy consumption control in various institutions like home, offices and streets and to provide efficient illumination system and to avoid wastage of electricity in the smart city environment. Sikder *et al.* [12] provided an an overview of smart lighting system in the smart city environment. Smart Lighting system makes use of multiple sensors such as motion sensor, light sensor, fog sensor which adjust the on/off time depending on the presence of human. The smart lighting system includes three basic components such as

(i) Lamp unit which contains multiple sensors and controllers connected to it. It gathers data from motion and light sensors and communicates with each other and control unit. The main characteristic features of lamp unit are to include lamps which provides energy efficiency and easy maintenance. It should include necessary and sufficient sensors which is capable of controlling the system automatically with an intelligent on–off scheme to reduce the consumption of the power usage. Moreover, it should be efficient enough to handle various conditions in a centralized or distributed system.

(ii)   Local Control Unit which collects data from the lamp units via ZigBee, 6LoWPAN, Bluetooth, etc., and transmits to the control center.

(iii)   Control Center is responsible to collect the data from the local control unit and stores it into on a server on the cloud. It is then analyzing this data and actions are taken to control the overall operation of the smart lighting system.

The IoT-enabled Smart Lighting system can reduce power consumption up to 33.33% [12] as compared to conventional lighting system both indoor and outdoor environment.

11.4.3   Air Quality Monitoring

Air pollution is a most dangerous and severe, causing climate change and life-threatening diseases like other type of pollutants such as water, soil, thermal, and noise. The air quality can be monitored real time by integrating the IoT platform since these technologies can automatically transmit, process and analyze the data. Hence, merging these technologies provide great advantage to improve the air quality. The general design idea of the air quality monitoring is as follows:

Air quality sensors are installed in the designated area on the top of buildings, residential areas, and industrial areas. The sensors sense the level of the dust particles, carbon dioxide, carbon monoxide, nitrogen dioxide and sulfur dioxide present in the air. It is then transmitting this information via gateway to the microcontroller connected to it. The microcontroller which is responsible to control the sensor network. The microcontroller collects data from the sensors and sends to the cloud for analyzing the data. The analyzed observations are then transmitted to the applications which are installed on the smart devices. Jo et al. [13] proposed a device called Smart air to monitor the indoor air quality which transmits the real time data using IoT sensor network to the web server on the cloud computing platform. The webserver then analyses the data and issues a mobile alert to the users about the air quality so that the concerned party can take required actions. Smart air is equipped with different sensors such as laser dust sensor, a volatile organic compound sensor, a carbon monoxide sensor, a carbon dioxide sensor and a temperature and humidity sensor.

The indoor air quality monitoring generally comprises of various phases which includes

- Data perception—performed in hardware level through sensors. The data is collected from different sensors.
- Processing phase—performed in both hardware and software level. The data is collected and subsequently sent to the server for storage and processing. This phase also provides notifications for enhanced data visualization and analytics.

The air quality data supports the health professionals to make decision on medical diagnostics end. Furthermore, it will be possible to associate patient diseases with their ecological conditions.

11.5   Smart Tourism in Smart City

The current growth towards smart tourism in urban areas intervene with prospective development in industrial sector as well as revenue generation through government strategies [21]. The major strategies include integration of information communication technology with cognitive economy models that enhance the urban city planning, management and services. The strategy targets to converge three major factors such as industry, information technology and smart city-based tourism. Integrated and intellectual connection through social networking and media are consider as influential factors towards achieving the goal of smart tourism [23, 24]. Some of the smart tourism schemes are listed below

- Advanced Traveller Information Systems (ATIS)
- Advanced Vehicle Control Systems (AVCS)
- Advanced Vehicle Parking systems (AVPS)
- Advanced Commercial Vehicle Operation (ACVO)
- Electronic Toll Charge Collection Systems (ETCCS).

Smart technology includes development of urban and upgrading of industries also. In this context, smart tourism is further enhanced with the emerging technologies such as IoT, Mobile computing, Cloud computing, Big Data and Artificial Intelligence [22]. Table 11.1 below lists popular smart tourism scheme across world.

Here, discussion on the issues related to tourism industry is essential. To enrich travelling experience and travellers on demand decision making capability is one of the key challenges that smart tourism need to address

Table 11.1 Smart Tourism place and details.

Place	Organization	Programme	Concept
Singapore	Intelligent Nation 2015	Digital Concierge Program	Anytime and Anywhere tourism information through Interactive Mobile Tourism service for visitors.
Korea	Ubiquitous City	I-Tour Seoul	Mobile computing-based 24 × 7 Tourism Service
Colorado	Steam Boat Ski	RFID-based Guest Tracking System	RFID-based wrist band for Guests
Pennsylvania	Mountain Resort	Intelligence Tour Guide System	RFID-based wrist band for Guests
Belgium	TagTag City Program	Intelligence Tour Guide System	RFID-based wrist band for Guests
London	City Tourism	Intelligence Tour Guide System	RFID-based wrist band for Guests
China	Smart Tourist Service Center	IoT, cloud, mobile computing technologies	Tourism information services based on IoT enabled sensing using wireless and adhoc device network.

[25, 26]. The travel destination culture, socio interacting with locals and residence well-beings directly impact on the growth of the city economy and tourism industry. The entire urban life sustainability is directly proportional to the growth of the citizen well-beings and overall sustainable city development. Handling the over crowdedness in the city due to tourist is the next level of issues. There is need to improve quality of local residence and identifying methods for improving interaction between local habitants with tourist visitors also play major role towards growth of tourism industry.

Smart tourism concept involves amalgamation of tourism and ICT that represents the transformation and enhancement of tourism industry through the emerging technology such as IoT, Cloud, Mobile, and big data and Artificial Intelligence [27]. Technology intervention of Smart tourism involves three major processes namely data collection, data analysis and decision making. First, the collection of data through various front of tourism components includes local citizens, local governs, infrastructures of destination, visitors, destination sites, medical & emergency systems, climate & weather system, accommodation & food delivery systems and intermittent financial systems. Secondly, analysis of the tourists to get insight about the visitor, travel requirements, and enhancing travel experiences. By this way of analysis, the smart tourism provides job opportunities and economic boost up for the local citizens, enrich visitor travel experiences and sustainable economy growth for smart tourism industry. Third, the decision making through several interactive and readily available services at various application level such as transport services, accommodation and food services, emergency and medical services, destination attraction information services, money handling & banking services. Figure 11.2 below, depicts the influence of smart city components and smart tourism industry with each other.

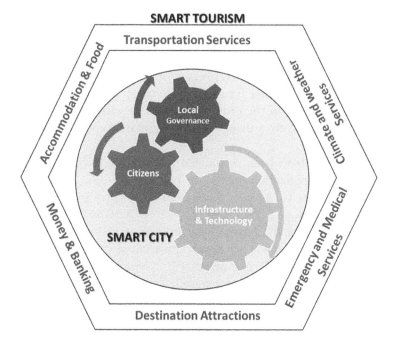

Figure 11.2 Smart city and smart tourism components.

11.6   Mobile Computing-Based Smart Tourism

Trip planner application development for tourism industry has been widely research in recent years due to intervention of ICT technologies such as IoT, Mobile, Cloud, Data analytics and Big Data systems [28, 29]. Among the communication technologies, the mobile-based trip planner applications are commonly used due to flexibility, simplicity, mobility and cost-effective solution. Figure 11.3 below depicts basic flow of mobile application-based trip planner. There exists tremendous increase day by day in information generation and dissemination regarding tourism and trip planning for online information services through various technologies such as mobile devices, social media & networking sites and IoT-based services.

There are basically three types of popular trip planning namely (i) individual trip planning, (ii) family trip planning and (iii) group trip planning [30–33]. The individual trip planning involves business or official travel that include business meetings, conference and training programs across countries. The need for such travellers involves business class stay, food and traveling requirements. The family trip planning involves limited members belong to within family. The needs for such trip include family-oriented staying, medical facilities, transport facilities and the trip planner should adapt to the personalization for respective family. The group trip planner usually involves guided travel assistance, with larger number of people in a group. The group trip may have individual from specific country, cultural background and native language speaking individuals. So, the trip planner for such group trip planning should involve specific requirements to the group. It further requires intragroup interaction & communication using efficient human computer application interfaces.

Several studies have been conducted in literature towards developing effective mobile application-based trip planner [34–37]. The commonly used techniques are (i) Activity theory, (ii) diary entry theory, (iii) Semi structured Interview and (iv) Emergent Themes Activity. The activity theory involves study of the tourist behaviour in terms of communicating with peer tourists, following rules and regulation in trip, meeting individual requirements, and effective usage of ICT-based information services. The diary entry theory system for mobile application-based trip planner involves answering to predefined set of question asked during certain period of the trip. This involves forced standard questions and answering format for all types of tourists. The diary entry includes details such as date

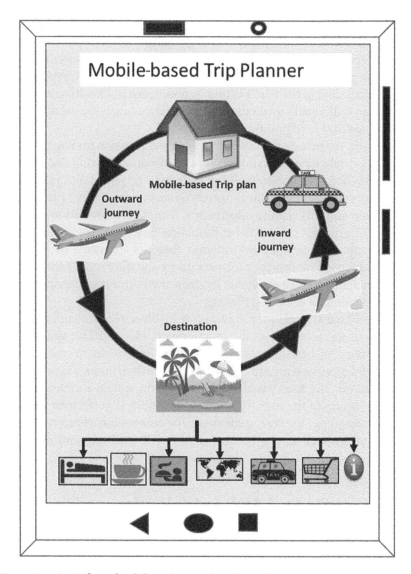

Figure 11.3 Basic flow of mobile application-based trip planner.

& time, duration of trip, information obtained, tourists experience during trip, etc. Semi structured interview involves in-depth analysis of tourist's requirement and understanding traveler specific needs. This involves specific information about individual tourists, travel plan, participation of tourist in interaction with others. The tourists are required to provide description about their plans, and various traveling methods adopted to search and provide information through online travel applications and services. The emergent theme activity involves building effective relationships among other tourists, practicing and adherence to the travel policies of individual during the trip. Further, traveler physical health conditions, monitoring individual's medicine intakes, behavior analysis, social interaction and avoidance, responding are performed.

Generally, the mobile devices are widely used platform for trip planning due to its portability and flexible ways of information sharing and dissemination [38–40]. The mobile applications involve travel details in three different information presentations namely (i) short information, (ii) detailed information and (iii) visiting information. The short information includes single page graphics and visual information based on user interest and requirements. The detailed information provides extensive background details and related reports for each user query and interests. Visiting information includes the details about location travel timings, transportation details and opening & closing timings.

Mobile-based trip planner application involves recommendation system to meet the tourist's specific requirements [41–43]. This system performs ranking of best destination as per the individual necessity. Such recommendation systems are of two types namely (i) user-based and (ii) content-based. The user-based recommendation system focuses on personalized desires of the user. The ranking of results is performed and best fitting output as per users are generated. The content-based recommendation system focuses on providing system-based attributes and measurements for ranking different results for each destination.

11.7   Case Study: A Mobile Application for Trip Planner Task Scheduling in Smart City's Sustainable Infrastructure

The app has been developed for android currently using technologies such as Java, SQL, JSON, etc. The app sends request to the Apache server, which in turn forwards it to NetBeans and SQL. The SQL returns the data in JSON to NetBeans which further passes it onto Apache. All the data is maintained on a central server and each user has a unique identification [44]. The app is unique in the sense that it provides one-stop travel solutions along with a task manager, scheduler and rescheduler. The app uses geo-location to pick up the current location of the user and understands

Table 11.2 Comparative analysis of various trip planner mobile applications.

App name	Purpose	Activity scheduler	Data input	New task input	Editing/updating of details	Tack rescheduling	Personalization & optimization
TRIPOTO	Hotel booking & social media app for travel packages	Not present, direct package booking	Automated through choices like dropdown menu	No	Hotel Booking cannot be changed	No	No
TRIP IT	An app that organizes all travel plan at one place	Present but the activities are handled manually	Manual and all the activities have to be planned from outside the app	Present by separate emails re sent to the servers for each task to be added in the list	No (only cancellation of the task functionality is there)	No	No
GOOGLE TRIP TRAVEL	App that keep all reservation at one place and provide suggestion	Present by the activities are suggested through Gmail or other Google accounts	Automated and with the app through choices provided to the user	Yes	Yes	No	No

(Continued)

Table 11.2 Comparative analysis of various trip planner mobile applications. (*Continued*)

App name	Purpose	Activity scheduler	Data input	New task input	Editing/updating of details	Tack rescheduling	Personalization & optimization
GOIBIBO	App that provide booking for transport & accommodation	No	Automated and within the app through choices	No	Details can be changed later	No	No
TRIP PLANNER: TRAVEL APP INDIA	Official app of incredible India	Present but have to choose from present package and their respective option	Has information about hotels, transport, etc. but booking functionality not provided	Present but choices are to be made from the corresponding packages	No	No	No
TRIP-I-PLAN (proposed app)	An one step app for all the bookings related to stay & transport and preparing scheduler for the same	Present and activities have to be chosen by the user	Automated through choices from the list etc. within the app	Yes	Yes (by going to the scheduler part)	Yes	Yes

whether the task was successful or missed. If missed, it provides the option for rescheduling the task. It can also find common free slots between two users and suggest rescheduling timings, thus reducing user-based inputs and efforts. It also provides customizable reminders to the user as an added functionality to make the app even more comprehensive. Table 11.2 presents the comparison of various trip planner mobile applications.

11.7.1   System Interfaces and User Interfaces

The proposed system is accessed in the mode of an application because of the android studio platform used in the project. In order to use our project or software, one should have a mobile device so that he/she can install the .apk file and can use the various functionalities of the project. Table 11.3 given below depicts the various user interface interaction during task scheduling and travel planning.

Figure 11.4 below illustrates the user interfaces for travel booking and task scheduling. The application can quickly add new locations to your itinerary to remember them later. Further, user can View task information and receive notification if anything happens. Geotagging is used in task creation of hotel and flights. Scheduling meeting and places of interest at the destination according to date and time is possible through this application. However, there are certain constraints faced. Like various integration problems during implementation [45]. The functioning of the app is dependent on the Internet connectivity and bandwidth issues. Figure 11.4 below depicts the user interfaces and task scheduling designed for the proposed mobile app.

11.8   Experimentation and Results Discussion

The functional requirements for implementing the application are as follows. Android studio is required for writing the code in JAVA to manipulate the functioning of the application. Further, NetBeans and MySQL are required to maintain the database. Apache creation is required for establishing the connection between database and applications. Users have to manually input the information for login/signup.

The logical database requirements are installation of NetBeans and MySQL in the operating system. Next is to insert relevant tables in the database created for task scheduling. All group data is exported/imported in MySQL and communicates to the application through apache creation, retrieving data in json format. Then, data is exported from apache to the

Table 11.3 List of user interfaces for the proposed mobile app.

Main Page (login/signup)	For maintaining the authenticity and to provide uniqueness to any user, we provide the functionality of login/signup through this page.
Main Page (task scheduling)	Here, user will be provided with his/her own dashboard including the functionality of add task, view task, view meeting and then logout at last.
Add task page	Here it provides the functionality of adding various task like scheduling hotel booking, flight booking, meeting scheduling and other services by taking source and destination.
View task page	Here it shows all the scheduled tasks.
View meeting page	Here it shows all the scheduled meetings along with time and place.
Scheduling page	Here on taking the date of travel of the user, he/she can schedule their task like hotel booking, flight booking, scheduling meeting, etc.
About	Details about the app & services and developer of the project.

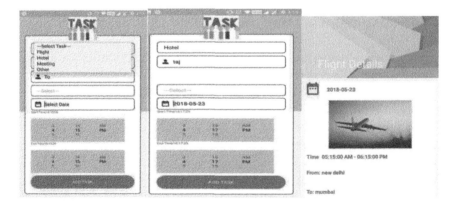

Figure 11.4 User interfaces for travel booking and task scheduling.

app in the form of json files. All the data entered by the user is maintained in MySQL database.

There are a lot of task scheduling and task managing apps, but none of them provide a comprehensive and to an extent, automatically-assisted rescheduling function. The most used scheduling algorithm for this purpose is FCFS (First Come First Serve) as it makes scheduling tasks easier and less complex. It is a rather compact app at less than 8 MB for the functionality it provides. Since most of the data is being stored on the server side, the app works at a faster rate. The meeting reschedule functionality which works with registered users, provides a unique proposition in the market. The rescheduling functionality uses an almost artificial intelligence like approach that helps it to reduce the efforts from the user.

Under the apportioning of requirements, after successfully entering the source and destination, a list of hotels is fetched for the user at the destination for selection purpose. Also, the implementation of the scheduler module is complete based on FCFS where the user can schedule his/her task. The app is operational for hotel booking, flight booking and scheduling meeting and the task.

The app is unique in the sense that it provides one-stop travel solutions along with a task manager, scheduler and rescheduler. The app uses geo-location to pick up the current location of the user and understands whether the task was successful or missed. If missed, it provides the option for rescheduling the task. It can also find common free slots between two users and suggest rescheduling timings, thus reducing user-based inputs and efforts. It also provides customizable reminders to the user as an added functionality to make the app even more comprehensive.

11.9   Conclusion and Future Scope

This chapter proposes an easy to use and understand mobile application which works as a one-stop solution for travel related needs in a smart city environment. The proposed mobile application Trip-I-Plan, includes meeting reschedule that scans the common free slots to suggest rescheduling timings. The app works well as such with minimal lag and displays all tasks in an easy to read and natural format of lists, from where further editing can be done. The app uses artificial intelligence to tackle the trip planning, cancellation and rescheduling aspects. The mobile application can be further bettered by using neural networks to learn from cases and then they test them out in the real world by predicting the cases. As the future scope, the proposed meeting reschedule can be extended to outside users as well and also include rescheduling between multiple users at the same time. A layer of multiple encryption technologies can be used to better the security robustness of the application. Before someone initiates rescheduling, an OTP can be sent to the other user to accept the initiation of this process. Different task scheduling algorithms like SJFS (Shortest Job First Seek) can be used with artificial intelligence in such a way that the app suggests when to schedule the task based on the user previous activities, location, preferences, etc.

References

1. Gomez, C., Paradells, J., Bormann, C., Crowcroft, J., From 6LoWPAN to 6Lo: Expanding the universe of IPv6-supported technologies for the Internet of Things. *IEEE Commun. Mag.*, 55, 12, 148–155, 2017.
2. Harrison, C., Eckman, B., Hamilton, R., Hartswick, P., Kalagnanam, J., Paraszczak, J., Williams, P., Foundations for smarter cities. *IBM J. Res. Dev.*, 54, 4, 1–16, 2010.
3. Marsal-Llacuna, M.L., Colomer-Llinàs, J., Meléndez-Frigola, J., Lessons in urban monitoring taken from sustainable and livable cities to better address the Smart Cities initiative. *Technol. Forecasting Social Change*, 90, 611–622, 2015.
4. Gavalas, D., Konstantopoulos, C., Mastakas, K., Pantziou, G., Mobile recommender systems in tourism. *J. Netw. Comput. Appl.*, 39, 319–333, 2014.
5. Garcia, A., Arbelaitz, O., Linaza, M.T., Vansteenwegen, P., Souffriau, W., Personalized tourist route generation, in: *International Conference on Web Engineering*, Springer, Berlin, Heidelberg, pp. 486–497, 2010.
6. Borràs, J., Moreno, A., Valls, A., Intelligent tourism recommender systems: A survey. *Expert Syst. Appl.*, 41, 16, 7370–7389, 2014.
7. Gavalas, D., Kasapakis, V., Konstantopoulos, C., Pantziou, G., Vathis, N., Zaroliagis, C., The eCOMPASS multimodal tourist tour planner. *Expert Syst. Appl.*, 42, 21, 7303–7316, 2015.
8. Buhalis, D. and Amaranggana, A., Smart tourism destinations enhancing tourism experience through personalisation of services, in: *Information and Communication Technologies in Tourism*, pp. 377–389, Springer, Cham, 2015.
9. Gavalas, D., Konstantopoulos, C., Mastakas, K., Pantziou, G., A survey on algorithmic approaches for solving tourist trip design problems. *J. Heuristics*, 20, 3, 291–328, 2014.
10. Abbaspour, R.A. and Samadzadegan, F., Time-dependent personal tour planning and scheduling in metropolises. *Expert Syst. Appl.*, 38, 10, 12439–12452, 2011.
11. Nagmode, V.S. and Rajbhoj, S.M., An IoT platform for vehicle traffic monitoring system and controlling system based on priority, in: *2017 International*

Conference on Computing, Communication, Control and Automation (ICCUBEA), 2017, August, IEEE, pp. 1–5.

12. Sikder, A.K., Acar, A., Aksu, H., Uluagac, A.S., Akkaya, K., Conti, M., IoT-enabled smart lighting systems for smart cities, in: *2018 IEEE 8th Annual Computing and Communication Workshop and Conference (CCWC)*, IEEE, pp. 639–645, 2018.

13. Jo, J., Jo, B., Kim, J., Kim, S., Han, W., Development of an IoT-based indoor air quality monitoring platform. *J. Sens.*, 2020, 1–14, 2020.

14. Zanella, A., Bui, N., Castellani, A., Vangelista, L., Zorzi, M., Internet of things for smart cities. *IEEE Internet Things J.*, 1, 1, 22–32, 2014.

15. Chourabi, H., Nam, T., Walker, S., Gil-Garcia, J.R., Mellouli, S., Nahon, K., Scholl, H.J., Understanding smart cities: An integrative framework, in: *2012 45th Hawaii International Conference on System Sciences*, 2012, January, IEEE, pp. 2289–2297.

16. Choi, J., Jeoung, H., Kim, J., Ko, Y., Jung, W., Kim, H., Kim, J., Detecting and identifying faulty IoT devices in smart home with context extraction, in: *2018 48th Annual IEEE/IFIP International Conference on Dependable Systems and Networks (DSN)*, 2018, June, IEEE, pp. 610–621.

17. Dhief, Y.B., Djemaiel, Y., Rekhis, S., Boudriga, N., Cloud-based global monitoring system for smart cities, in: *2018 32nd International Conference on Advanced Information Networking and Applications Workshops (WAINA)*, 2018, May, IEEE, pp. 307–312.

18. Jin, J., Gubbi, J., Marusic, S., Palaniswami, M., An information framework for creating a smart city through internet of things. *IEEE Internet Things J.*, 1, 2, 112–121, 2014.

19. Kizilkaya, B., Caglar, M., Al-Turjman, F., Ever, E., An intelligent car park management system: Hierarchical placement algorithm based on nearest location, in: *2018 32nd International Conference on Advanced Information Networking and Applications Workshops (WAINA)*, 2018, May, IEEE, pp. 597–602.

20. Thu, M.Y., Htun, W., Aung, Y.L., Shwe, P.E.E., Tun, N.M., Smart air quality monitoring system with LoRaWAN, in: *2018 IEEE International Conference on Internet of Things and Intelligence System (IoTAIS)*, 2018, November, IEEE, pp. 10–15.

21. Guo, Y., Liu, H., Chai, Y., The embedding convergence of smart cities and tourism internet of things in China: An advance perspective. *Adv. Hosp. Tour. Res. (AHTR)*, 2, 1, 54–69, 2014.

22. Zhang, L. and Sun, X., Designing a trip planner application for groups: Exploring group tourists? Trip planning requirements, in: *Proceedings of the 2016 CHI Conference Extended Abstracts on Human Factors in Computing Systems*, 2016, May, pp. 1329–1336.

23. Ahmed, A., Mehdi, M.R., Ngoduy, D., Abbas, M., Evaluation of accuracy of advanced traveler information and commuter behavior in a developing country. *Travel Behav. Soc.*, 15, 63–73, 2019.

24. Salvucci, D.L., Kline, M.J., Humphreys, E., U.S. Patent No. 10,692,374, U.S. Patent and Trademark Office, Washington, DC, 2020.

25. Amrani, A., Pasini, K., Khouadjia, M., Predictive Multimodal Trip Planner: A New Generation of Urban Routing Services, in: *TRANSITDATA2019 5th International Workshop and Symposium*, 2019, July.

26. Alghamdi, H., Zhu, S., El Saddik, A., E-tourism: Mobile dynamic trip planner, in: *2016 IEEE International Symposium on Multimedia (ISM)*, 2016, December, IEEE, pp. 185–188.

27. Yin, C., Xiong, Z., Chen, H., Wang, J., Cooper, D., David, B., A literature survey on smart cities. *Sci. China Inform. Sci.*, 58, 10, 1–18, 2015.

28. Bifulco, F., Tregua, M., Amitrano, C.C., D'Auria, A., ICT and sustainability in smart cities management. *Int. J. Public Sect. Manag. Public Sec. Manag.*, 29, 132–147, 2016.

29. Krishnamurthi, R., Nayyar, A., Solanki, A., Innovation Opportunities through Internet of Things (IoT) for Smart Cities, in: *Green and Smart Technologies for Smart Cities*, pp. 261–292, CRC Press, Boca Raton, FL, USA, 2019.

30. Lee, P., Hunter, W.C., Chung, N., Smart Tourism City: Developments and Transformations. *Sustainability*, 12, 10, 3958, 2020.

31. Femenia-Serra, F., Perles-Ribes, J.F., Ivars-Baidal, J.A., Smart destinations and tech-savvy millennial tourists: Hype versus reality. *Tour. Rev.*, 74, 63–81, 2019.

32. Ivars-Baidal, J. A., Hernández, M. G. and Mendoza de Miguel, S. "Integrating Overtourism in the Smart Tourism Cities Agenda", e-Review of Tourism Research (eRTR), 17, No. 2, 2019.

33. Kumar, A., Rajalakshmi, K., Jain, S., Nayyar, A., Abouhawwash, M., A novel heuristic simulation–optimization method for critical infrastructure in smart transportation systems. *Int. J. Commun. Syst.*, 33, e4397, 30, 2020.

34. Ahvenniemi, H., Huovila, A., Pinto-Seppä, I., Airaksinen, M., What are the differences between sustainable and smart cities? *Cities*, 60, 234–245, 2017.

35. Um, T. and Chung, N., Does smart tourism technology matter? Lessons from three smart tourism cities in South Korea. *Asia Pac. J. Tour. Res.*, 1–19, 2019.

36. Allam, Z. and Jones, D.S., On the coronavirus (COVID-19) outbreak and the smart city network: Universal data sharing standards coupled with artificial intelligence (AI) to benefit urban health monitoring and management. *Healthcare*, 8, 46, 2020.

37. Perles Ribes, J.F. and Ivars-Baidal, J., Smart sustainability: A new perspective in the sustainable tourism debate. *REsponse: Investigaciones Regionales*, 42, 151–170, 2018.

38. Basiri, M., Azim, A.Z., Farrokhi, M., Smart city solution for sustainable urban development. *Eur. J. Sustain. Dev.*, 6, 71–84, 2017.

39. Qin, Y., Analysis of Key Elements for Smart Tourist City Construction with G1-Entrophy Methods. *Rev. Fac. Ing.*, 32, 759–763, 2017.

40. Garau-Vadell, J.B., Gutierrez-Taño, D., Diaz-Armas, R., Economic crisis and residents' perception of the impacts of tourism in mass tourism destinations. *J. Dest. Mark. Manage.*, 7, 68–75, 2018.
41. Chung, N., Han, H., Joun, Y., Tourists' intention to visit a destination: The role of augmented reality (AR) application for a heritage site. *Comput. Human Behav.*, 50, 588–599, 2015.
42. Lee, H., Jung, T.H., Tom Dieck, M.C., Chung, N., Experiencing immersive virtual reality in museums. *Inf. Manag.*, 57, 5, 103229, 2020.
43. Kumar, A., Krishnamurthi, R., Nayyar, A., Sharma, K., Grover, V., Hossain, E., A Novel Smart Healthcare Design, Simulation, and Implementation Using Healthcare 4.0 Processes. *IEEE Access*, 8, 118433–118471, 2020.
44. Prusty, V., Rath, A., Rout, K.K., Mishra, S., Development of an IoT-Based Tourism Guide System, in: *Advances in Intelligent Computing and Communication*, pp. 495–503, Springer, Singapore, 2020.
45. Expósito, A., Mancini, S., Brito, J., Moreno, J.A., A fuzzy GRASP for the tourist trip design with clustered POIs. *Expert Syst. Appl.*, 127, 210–227, 2019.
46. Yao, G., A Study on the Construction Framework of Intelligent Tourism. *J. Nanjing Univ. Posts Telecommun. (Social Sci.)*, 14, 2, 13–16, 2012.
47. Wen, W., Xu, C., Li, X., Design and Implementation of Tourism Commodities Traceability System Based on Internet of Things. *Sci. Technol. Manag.*, 9, 116–120, 2013.
48. Qin, S., Man, J., Wang, X., Li, C., Dong, H., Ge, X., Applying big data analytics to monitor tourist flow for the scenic area operation management. *Discrete Dyn. Nat. Soc.*, 2019, 1–11, 2019.

Smart Health Monitoring for Elderly Care in Indoor Environments

Sonia[1]* and Tushar Semwal[2]

[1]*National Institute of Technology Delhi, New Delhi, India*
[2]*The University of Edinburgh, Edinburgh, United Kingdom*

Abstract

Within chaos created all around because of the ongoing pandemic, elders are at a high risk of health issues. Living independently and away from your family members, it becomes even more difficult for them to manage all the tasks. Considering the age and health wellness, elders tend to forget things. For example, one might forget to turn off the water tap which can lead to water wastage, electricity wastage, etc. So, the need of an hour is to make a sustainable environment to stop wastage of resource along with monitoring elders' health. On sensing abnormality, in either case, the concerned person can be contacted by raising the alarm. Also, being social distancing as a new norm, this chapter discusses how technology has emerged as a great help to understand, analyze and conclude from the data received from the living spaces of human beings. This is helpful to encourage the concept of sustainability and gather information about human health. The chapter also discusses the various technologies that are being used by researchers to measure indoor environmental quality, human health, and wellbeing, along with case studies and real-life examples. The chapter focuses on heterogeneous sensors which can be used in smart homes to sense various aspects of human beings. In the latter half of the chapter, applications being developed by researchers into this vital domain are discussed.

Keywords: Smart homes, health monitoring, IoT, sensors, indoor environment, activity recognition, independent living

---

Corresponding author: sonia@nitdelhi.ac.in

Arun Solanki, Adarsh Kumar and Anand Nayyar (eds.) Digital Cities Roadmap: IoT-Based Architecture and Sustainable Buildings, (379–400) © 2021 Scrivener Publishing LLC

12.1   Introduction

With the growing immigration of the young generation towards better career opportunities, elders are left to care by themselves. This issue is of grave concern, especially in countries with less population. This further gives rise to issues such as depression, loneliness which requires a regular check of their health status even from a distance. For example, one fine morning, an elderly person realized that the refrigerator is indicating that it is time to stock some fruits and milk, air conditioner is suggesting that it is time for service. Gas is left on and also water has been running for the last hour. Alternatively, in the worst case, an elderly person falls off the bed or slips while taking a bath. Now, the question arises: How can an elderly person manage by themselves in such scenarios? If not, then how can this information be sent to his/her relative or the concerned caregiver? Imagine, in the situations mentioned above, there is someone who can either give a helping hand or at least send an emergency message to the concerned person. The correct information provided at the right instant of time can prove to be life-saving. Can technology help? If yes, then how? Can sensing help to optimize resources and reduce wastage? These questions will be answered in this chapter. Technology plays a crucial role to support the self-sufficient living of elders and their caregivers. For obvious reasons, the environmental quality of the residing space affects their health. With the growing population of people in the age group above 55 years and busy lifestyle of the working generation, it has become challenging to provide constant care to the geriatrics. The older people are often left unattended and expected to cope with the daily routine as described earlier. Such a group of the population suffer from symptoms affecting memory, thinking and social abilities such that it severely interferes with their everyday life. Critical information provided at the time of need proves to be a life-saviour in many situations. Especially in the case of diseases such as dementia, information received at an early stage can help to prevent future complexities. The need of the day is to use technologies to unobtrusively monitor the health and wellbeing of indoor environments where such a group of the population inhabits. With the advent of the Internet of Things (IoT), the homes can be integrated with sensors and notification systems which can continuously monitor the activities of the elderly people. The information collected can then be transferred to the cloud systems for further analysis and study, thereby creating a connected smart environment. Principal activities include fall detection, heart rate, respiration cycles, physical movement, reminders, resource optimization and theft protection. These activities can be captured with the help of sensors either embedded in the living space of the human being or in the form of a wearable. Section 12.2 details sensors and their usage. Figures 12.1 and 12.2 show two scenarios, one where an elderly person A is living independently and being monitored by sensors continuously via sensor data, sensory data, information about his health status reaches to his respective caregiver, so this makes both A and his caregiver happy. They are delighted because on-time correct information provided to the caregiver helps him to take care of person A, which in turn keeps person A healthy and happy. However, in the second situation, an elderly person B is living independently and is sad and lying quietly on bed. There are no sensors to monitor the health status of person B. Therefore, a caregiver has to make a guess or wait for the call from person B to provide appropriate help. In this scenario, if a person is so unwell and not able to make a call, then this can be life-threatening. This example clarifies the usefulness and importance of technology to support the independent living of elders.

Where the living environments are embodied by intelligence to investigate the data and make decisions, then such living spaces can be called smart spaces. Further, each of such smart spaces can then be interconnected to provide a global view of the health status of a community of older adults. This ecosystem helps in delivering advanced analytic capabilities. This chapter discusses the various technologies that are being used by researchers to measure indoor environmental quality, human health,

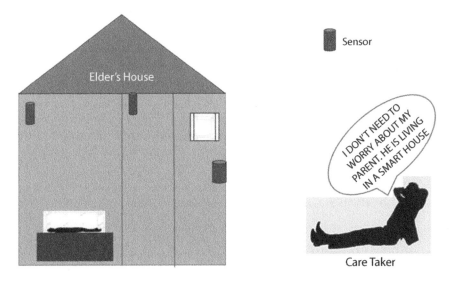

Figure 12.1 Elderly living in a smart home independently and a happy care taker.

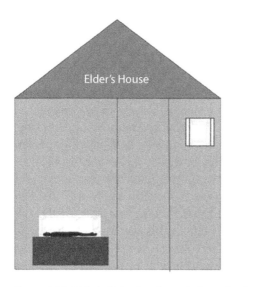

Care Taker

Figure 12.2 Elderly living in a home independently and a sad care taker.

and wellbeing along with case studies and real-life examples. We will first describe the different sensors that can be used for applications to monitor human health in an indoor environment. Real-world case study and their results are also discussed in the following sections.

During this on-going pandemic, our elders are at high risk. So, it becomes more important to keep a regular check on their health status. With the bliss of technology, it is possible even from distant places. Different sensors can be used in multi-ways to execute this task. In the next section, we will discuss various sensors and human traits that are sensed using sensors to monitor his/her health status. With the increasing demand for resources, it is high time that we should focus on sustainability. From the perspective of elders' health, one might suffer from multiple diseases. When a person is ill, he/she forgets certain things which lead to wastage of resources. With the bliss of intelligence embedded in the living area of human beings, such activities can be sensed and stopped. This helps to build sustainability buildings in this era of the Internet of things.

12.2   Sensors

The sensor can be defined as a device which detects or measures a physical property and records, indicates, or otherwise responds to it [29]. Since this chapter is focused on the health monitoring of elders, there should be some traits of human beings which can be captured by sensors.

12.2.1   Human Traits

Human beings possess some traits which can be sensed [44] and further analyzed to monitor their health which can be described as following.

1. Human Presence. This trait is being used to answer questions such as: Is there a human being? Was a human being present in the washroom yesterday at 10.00 PM? Did anyone enter the kitchen yesterday? Some of the most common sensors that are being used to sense the human presence are Pyro Infrared (PIR) sensor, vibration sensor, camera, etc. From a health perspective detection of human presence is important to track his/her last activity.

2. Identity (fingerprint). Identification of a person becomes crucial when it comes to the health domain to answer questions such as who consumed medicine? Who fell down? Who went to the hospital for a check-up? Identification can be extended to track a person. Some of the sensors which can be used to identify a human being are a camera, fingerprint sensor, etc.

3. Heartbeat is one of the traits that has been highly exploited by researchers to continuously monitor his/her health status. Heartbeat has been used to predict heart failures [23], predict unusual sleep patterns [17, 20], etc. Heartbeat can be captured with the help of a heartbeat sensor [26]. Most commonly, a heart rate sensor is used in wearable devices [14].

4. Blood Pressure. Fluctuations in blood pressure is an indication of many onset diseases, so sensing blood pressure and predicting abnormalities can be a life saver. This can be measured with the help of a pulse sensor [5].

5. Weight. In the era of fitness conscious people, weight is an important factor that draws everyone's attention. Sudden increase or decrease in weight can be an indication of abnormalities ahead such as thyroid level [48], diabetes [47], cancer [16], etc. This trait can easily be measured with the help of weighing cells.

6. Shape. The shape of a human being is one of the traits of a human being that differentiate him from other living beings. The appearance of a human being is one of the first things that specify humans' health conditions. This can be captured

with the help of ultrasonic imaging sensors [11], vision-based sensors [7], etc.

7. Gait. Injuries or body unbalancing can be identified by capturing the gait of a human being. It is a dynamic trait of a human being because it is only available when a human being voluntarily moves. It can be captured in the form of sound and vibration, i.e. with the help ultrasonic sensors and vibration sensors [9, 15].

As human beings, themselves possess multiple traits that can be sensed which makes it easier to monitor their health status. In the following section, we will discuss various sensors in detail, along with their application concerning human health.

12.2.2   Sensors Description

Sensors can be broadly classified into two categories, as shown in Figure 12.3:

– Passive sensors
– Active Sensors
• Passive sensors. A device which takes an input from the environment in any form and responds to that is known as passive sensors. In other words, passive sensors rely on the environment for their output [29]. For example, Passive Infra-Red sensors, camera.

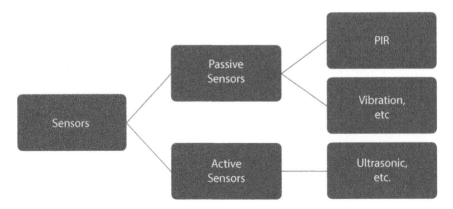

Figure 12.3 Classification of sensors.

- Active sensors. A device which sends some energy in the environment and based on the changes received, it gives output [29]. For example, X-ray sensors, Ultrasonic sensor.

12.2.2.1 Passive Sensors

1. Pyro-Infrared (PIR) Sensor. PIR sensor is most commonly used to sense the presence of human beings. It is a binary sensor that outputs 0 or 1 to indicate absence or presence of a human being. PIR is a low cost, low power sensor which is commonly used for human presence detection [4] [12], alarming systems [30] and human localization [28]. However, this sensor is not able to differentiate human beings from other living beings.
2. Temperature Sensor. This sensor notifies with the value of indoor environment temperature. This sensor can be used to monitor activities such as cooking, temperature of the drinking water and to measure body temperature as well. This also notifies if temperature rises or lowers down below the comfort level of a human being and can be controlled (in case of a sick person).
3. Smoke Sensor. Consider a scenario, where a person having dementia entered into the kitchen and lit the gas stove to cook, forgot to stop the burner after cooking and went outside the kitchen and got involved in other activities. This can be hazardous if not controlled. This situation can be controlled by raising a fire alarm which senses the smoke and temperature. Thus, are the importance of smoke sensor and temperature sensor.
4. Water Sensor. Water sensor can be used to measure the water level. This is useful to notify a person whether drinking water is available or not nearby a patient. This can also be used to notify when to empty the urine pouch of a bedridden patient.
5. Camera. Vision-based sensors are very handy when someone needs to be monitored continuously. However, one of the drawbacks of this sensor is that it works only for well-lit areas. It can also hamper the privacy concerns of a human being. This is why cameras are generally avoided in smart home scenarios.

6. Humidity Sensor. This sensor is generally used to monitor the quality of the indoor environment by measuring the humidity of the space. If humidity is above or low than a specified level then it can cause skin allergies, restlessness, etc.

7. Magnetometer. This sensor can be used to find the orientation and used in robots. So, in case of assisted living where robots assist a human being can be used.

8. Gyroscope is used for the gait detection of a human being. It can be used to monitor the walking, running and exercise patterns which contribute to human health.

9. GPS. This sensor is used to track the position of a human being which is necessary to track the trajectory, movements of a human being.

10. Vibration Sensor. Vibration sensor output depends on the amount of pressure put on the sensor. This sensor is used to find abnormalities in the gait pattern. This sensor is infrastructure dependent and is a costly affair if implemented from scratch.

11. Gas Sensor. To monitor the air quality of a living space can be monitored with the help of gas sensors. This sensor measures the level of CO_2, CO, O_2, etc. in the living area of a human being. This can raise alarm when levels of gases are above or below a certain level.

12.2.2.2   Active Sensors

1. Ultrasonic Sensor. Ultrasonic sensors emulate ultrasonic waves in the environment. Based on the energy difference between transmitted waves and reflected waves calculations are performed. This sensor is used for ultrasonic imaging to monitor the health status of a human being [45].

2. Laser Sensor. Laser is one of the most commonly used techniques used in the medical field and even used for surgeries.

3. Infra-red Sensor (light sensor). IR sensor is used to detect various activities of a human being in smart spaces such as location. Sensor list is not limited to the list above mentioned. With the advent of technology new sensors are being invented, new sensors are being introduced by researchers to enhance the research in the domain of smart homes [44], health monitoring [28], gait pattern analysis [36], etc.

12.2.3   Sensing Challenges

By now, we have understood that there are a variety of sensors that can be embedded in the living space of human beings and can sense various traits of human beings but is it that simple? Human beings are the most dynamic creatures that make the sensing task too challenging. Some of the challenges can be listed as:

1. Environmental Noise: Environment noise affects the sensing of sensors such as sounds in the environment affect ultrasonic sensors. Some other noises that are added from the environment are because of thermal noise, light, etc.

2. Variation in environment: Sensors are embedded in the environment and are affected by the variation in the environment. Environment variations such as temperature, humidity, living space layout, positioning of household items, rain, light intensity etc. Dynamic environment adds uncertainty to the data.

3. Appearance variability: Human beings can add variability to their appearance by having different clothing and are capable of possessing different pauses. This presents a number of challenges in front of researchers especially during identification, localization, etc.

4. Active deception: Human beings are smart enough to deceive hardware. He knows the ways to escape from sensors or fool sensors. This makes it even more challenging to collect data of activities of human beings.

5. Unpredictable changes: In the real scenario, it is not always possible that whatever is predicted using sensory data will happen. Not-Predicted events might happen such as sudden changes in heartbeat, entry of guests, etc. How technology handles challenges presented by not-predicted events.

12.3   Internet of Things and Connected Systems

The Internet of Things (IoT) is new paradigm which refers to a network of sensors, and actuators embedded on to physical objects such as walls of a smart home. IoT enables the sensors to not only just collect data but also to share the information generally with a central computing server. Sharing of data is crucial to perform advanced analytics to detect patterns, for example, symptoms of dementia in a human. Two IoTs deployed in geographically separate regions can also share information to produce better analytics, giving rise to connected systems. A typical IoT includes a sensing device, a communication module, central server to collect data, and finally an analytics and visualization software running on the server. IoT is a backbone of any smart-health monitoring system. Once the sensors have been selected based on the application, they can be connected on to a network, to gather information and extract meaningful information.

An IoT has three major components as described below:

1. Data Acquisition: Acquiring data is a primary and significant part of any IoT. Using different kinds of sensors such as temperature, heartbeat, and PIR, can help in sampling the data about a human user.
2. Data Communication: These components are responsible for transmitting the sampled data from sensors to a cloud or a data center. Communication devices such as Zigbee, Bluetooth, Wi-Fi, and LoRaWAN are commonly used for sharing the data. Mobile ad hoc networks have also been used to serve as a network for IoT [24, 25, 35].
3. Cloud Processing: Cloud processing has three distinct units—storage, analytic, and visualization. The main task of this component is to provide a long-term storage of health data. This large data can then be later accessed or queried to do further analysis. Analytic involves prognostic modeling of data generally using statistical or machine learning techniques. Visualization is a primary requirement for any IoT system. Visualization allows data to be presented in a human understandable manner.

Data collection is not the only feature of an IoT. Since the data an IoT generate is sensitive, privacy and security is a crucial part any IoT system. Research on privacy and security in IoT becoming an attractive scope for the academicians and professionals since it decides the applicability and acceptance of human beings. Privacy is of utmost importance in IoT. Secure cloud frameworks have been proposed to use sensitive health data [27]. Conventional cloud-based IoT architectures are more prone to privacy and security issues due to a single point of failure such as the central server. If the server gets compromised, user information will be leaked. Hence, to avoid this issue, decentralized and distributed architectures are also gaining importance [38]. Fog computing for IoT is also gaining interest from

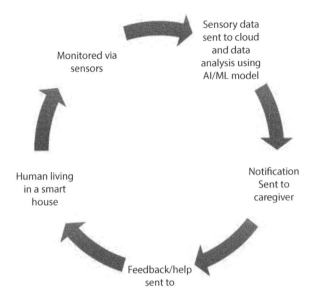

Figure 12.4 Smart health monitoring cycle.

researchers. Fog computing brings computations closer to the edge devices and thus happens on fog servers physically located near to the edge device [41]. Fog computing enables faster computation and reduces delays in communication and are particularly useful when robots and wearable devices are part of the IoT network [6, 31]. Finally, efforts to make the environment sustainable and reduce wastage also form a significant area of research [42].

At this point, we are aware of sensors and their usage, data collection, analysing data. Figure 12.4 shows a cycle of overall process. As explained in the figure, first sensors are embedded in the living space to gather data for different activities of human being. This data is then pushed to the cloud for further processing. Depending on the results obtained, notification is sent to the caregiver. Based on the notification received caregiver either sends feedback to the resident or sends him required help. Thus, health of human being is monitored.

12.4 Applications

Researchers are actively working in the domain of human healthcare. Some of the applications that are worth mentioning can be listed as:

1. Wearable Technology: In the recent past, with the recent development in the domain of designing and developing

wearable technology to monitor human health, has grabbed scientist attention. Over the period, the wearable devices are progressing with the continuous advancement of miniature bio-sensing devices, communication technology, microelectronics which makes scientists to believe that this technology can potentially transform the future in a better way. This can enhance health management by monitoring the health of a human being ubiquitously. Wearable devices have small sensors such as accelerometer, gyroscope, GPS, communications modules and processing capabilities. Thus, this technology can facilitate human being by providing low-cost wearable unobtrusive solutions to monitor human health status for continuous all-day and any-place health, mental and also activities of a human being can be tracked. Pantelopoulos and Bourbakis [33] had presented have presented a survey of the wearable devices being used by researchers over the period of time. Some of the work that has been done using wearable devices to monitor human health is presented in [3, 19, 22, 32, 43].

2. Mobile Applications: With the increasing needs for communication technology, mobile has become a necessity for everyone. Independent of their age, everyone owns a mobile. Researchers took this as an opportunity. A number of applications have been developed so far to track human health [21]. Though mobile has raised lots of questions over the privacy of user's data but health works are showing enthusiasm towards the usage of mobile applications. Mobile apps are being used for helping patients to recover from depression, monitor their exercise routine, monitor their diet habits, to directly communicate with doctors, etc.

3. Home device automation: Automating devices is a feature that has been added to the concept of smart houses to add comfort to human lives [2]. This includes switching on and off of Air conditioners, humidifier, washing machines, lights, fans, microwave, refrigerator, etc. This saves lots of human energy by shedding off the work tension from human brains. It is an important feature to enhance the independent living of elders because they tend to forget things. If washing machine is left unattended, it can autonomously switch off after completing the scheduled task.

4. Health and wellness detection using ambient sensors: Lots of research has already been done and still continuing to

detect health and wellness using ambient sensors. Ambient sensors are preferred over other technology such as wearable because they do not need human attention for their working. Some of the researches such as dementia detection [8], depression detection [40], activity monitoring [46], medication monitoring [40] are remarkable in this domain.

5. Chat-bots: In the times of independent livings, elders feel lonely. They need someone who can listen to them, talk to them and answer their queries. Lack of communication among people often leads to depression which can be fatal. To resolve this issues chat-bots were introduced to talk to people and to reply their queries. Along with talking, chat-bots are also used to track the talking pattern of a human being. With technical enhancements chat-bots can now predict weather a person is suffering or going to suffer from depression [37].

6. Assisted living: In assisted living, robots are designed to help human to complete his/her tasks. This includes cleaning robot. In this scenario robots can also sense human needs based on their gestures and complete the required task [1, 50].

7. Mood dependent Light automation: When a person is living alone, going through rough patch of life, having heavy work load, having hormonal changes, taking heavy dose of medicines, feeling sick or had arguments with someone he might have bad mood which affect his health. Depending on the mood, he might feel to have different light conditions. So, if a person's mood can be sensed autonomously and lights are adjusted accordingly, he can feel nice in the provided ambiance [18].

8. Analysis of sleep patterns: Sleep pattern dictates the health conditions of human beings. It is important to record the sleeping hours and quality of sleep. Sleep pattern analysis has been used to detect various diseases such as heart health and wellness, depression [10], etc.

9. Detection of early symptoms of dementia: Early detection of symptoms of dementia has proved to be life saviour. This can be done by monitoring the daily routine of a human being. The activities are being monitored to analyze the missing activities, repeated activities, random behavior of human being over a period of time. Researchers working in this domain have attained a good accuracy [39].

10. Abnormality detection using gait analysis: Walking pattern of a human being does tell about injuries, a human might have, body imbalance issues, health fitness, probable injuries in future [36].

11. Depression detection: When a person is depressed, it reflects in its activities and words he uses to communicate. Monitoring activities and tracing his/her talking patterns can help a depressed person to recover [28].

12.5   Case Study

Scenario: Consider a scenario, where you have a group of 50 elderly people who are of age equal to or above 60. To support their independent living an old age house is allocated individually. Architecture of all houses follows the same pattern. It is not possible to dedicate a caretaker for each individual because that is a cost intensive task. It has been assumed that they follow a routine to carry their daily activities. As it has been mentioned earlier that every person is living independently which implies that they have to carry out their routine tasks by themselves. Considering age as an important factor, it can be concluded that elders are more prone to diseases, sudden falls, forgetting things, etc. If a person suddenly falls down and he is not able to get up without any help or need emergency medical care then how that can be possible in the situations mentioned above. Similarly, if a person forgets to take his/her medication or showing some early symptoms of onset disease, then how to remind an elderly person who is living independently. Now, given this scenario where we have to support independent living of elders along with continuous monitoring of their health status. This statement raises multiple prompt questions that need to be discussed in detail to find out the solution to the mentioned problem. In the scope of this chapter we are considering two cases to discuss which are mentioned as following:

12.5.1   Case 1

A person named Mr. Gupta, aged 65, living independently, in flat 65C, is carrying his household works following his daily routine. One fine morning, after doing his breakfast he is going to have a bath. Suddenly, when he is heading towards the washroom, there is water spilling on the floor because of which he slipped over water and fell down. He has severe injury with his hip bone and unable to get up by himself. He immediately requires medical help.

12.5.2 Case 2

A lady named Mrs. Peter, aged 75, living in flat 89D, is living independently but is suffering from anxiety issues. For her anxiety issues she is on medication prescribed by a doctor. Over a period of time she seems to forget things such as going to the kitchen and forgets to cook, doesn't remember to take medicines, and sometimes takes double doses of medicine. From the description provided, it is evident that she is having early symptoms of dementia. But who is observing her routine to monitor her health status is a question to be answered?

12.5.3 Challenges Involved

Some of the common questions that arises for both the cases which are within the scope of this chapter can be listed as:

1. How to collect the data?
2. Which sensors to choose?
3. To whom and when to send the data?
4. How to analyze the data to find abnormality?
5. What is the accuracy of the result calculated?

12.5.4 Possible Solution

In this chapter, so far, we have discussed different types of sensors and their usages. So, sensors can be embedded in the old age houses of elders which can capture the different activities of human beings which can be logged with time. For example, PIR sensors, Vibration sensor, water sensor, temperature sensor, humidity sensor, etc, can be used to check human presence, walking style, running tap, AC condition, humidity level respectively. However, in this scenario vision sensors cannot be used to respect the privacy concerns of human beings. So, to ensure to capture all the activities of human beings old-age houses were embedded with 25 heterogeneous sensors at different places of the target living space similar to one described by Sharma and Ghose [39]. The activities that are majorly captured are human presence at different locations, sleeping, cooking, eating, medication routine, bathing, fall detection, washing clothes, talking, etc.

For case 1, fall detection is required, which further dependent human presence detection and his falling [34]. Therefore, as described by Yazar et al. [49] in this can be done by using vibration sensor and PIR sensor. To detect fall detection, the first step is to detect whether a human was present in that area or not which can be captured with the help of a PIR sensor. Once human presence is confirmed then the next step is to detect fall which can be detected by vibration sensors.

Or, if a human is wearing a smart wearable device [13], then fall detection can be detected with the help of an inbuilt accelerometer and gyroscope.

From the above discussion, it can be concluded that to detect the fall of Mr. Gupta, data which is required is only for the time span of incidence. However, this is not true for every incident like for case 2. For case 2, Only one incidence of forgetting things cannot confirm the symptoms of dementia. This requires logging of activity data of human beings over a period of time as described by Sharma and Ghose [39]. Unlike case 1, in this case instead of data of only one activity, data is required for all the activities. Once we have data of all the activities, it can be analyzed whether all the activities are performed as per daily routine or not. If not, then which activities are being missed, which activities are repeated and what is the frequency of such incidences. This analysis is helpful to conclude if Mrs. Peter is having symptoms of dementia or not.

In both cases 1 and 2, data of different activities is being captured via sensors. As sensors cannot perform analysis of data or they cannot speak and give information to someone that something wrong has happened. So, what to do next with the sensors data?

In this era of Internet of things, sensory data can be sent to clouds. Now the question arises: How much data to be sent to the cloud? Should all data be sent to the cloud directly? Or there should be processing locally and sent to the cloud only when abnormality is detected? This is again dependent on the application to be built to assist human being in an indoor scenario. For example, if only fall detection is to be detected like as in case 1, then in that case, first data should be processed locally. In other words when a sensor value is observed above a threshold (which is sensor dependent), then data should be sent to the cloud. However, in case 2 the data should be continuously sent to the cloud unlike case 1. This is because, in case 2, abnormalities cannot be observed by just looking at the sensory value or its threshold. As explained in Ref. [39], to find the early symptoms of dementia a machine learning model need to be trained and explored.

Now, by now, it has been discussed that sensors can be embedded in the living space of an elderly person to support their independent living. By analyzing the sensory data obtained, health status of a person can be monitored from distant.

Once, abnormality has been detected, notification is pushed to the caregivers. Now, depending on the severity of notification, either help or medical help is provided to the resident. In case of medical field, it is believed that motive is not to detect a sick person as a healthy person.

12.6 Conclusion

Being a dynamic creature, it is difficult to make a fool proof system that can sense human presence and his activities under all conditions. Despite of the mentioned fact, lots of research has already been done and still progressing in this vital domain. By monitoring human activities using embedded sensor, human health can be monitored. Also, by analyzing the data received via different sensors abnormalities at the various locations inside a house can be notified. These notifications are proved significantly useful to optimize the resource utilization and thereby support the sustainability. However, challenges mentioned in the section 3 of the chapter give the scopes for future research.

12.7 Discussion

Because of ongoing pandemic and vulnerable health conditions, it becomes more important to take care of elders. In this chapter, we discussed about, how the independent living of elders can be supported by monitoring their health status from distant. In Section 12.2, different sensors along with their usages are discussed. Following which challenges involved in the domain of smart health monitoring has been explained. This chapter also discussed about various applications towards which researchers have contributed to support digital health and wellness detection. In the latter part of the chapter, case study is included and explained in detail. Since this field is a mature field of research and still growing in multiple research directions, this chapter is limited to discussion of sensors and their roles to monitor human health in an indoor scenario.

References

1. Abtoy, A., Touhafi, A., Tahiri, A. *et al.*, Ambient assisted living system's models and architectures: A survey of the state of the art. *J. King Saud Univ.— Comp. Info. Sci.*, 32, 1, 1–10, 2020.
2. Alam, T., Salem, A.A., Alsharif, A.O., Alhujaili, A.M., Smart Home Automation Towards the Development of Smart Cities. *Comput. Sci. Inf. Technol.*, 1, 1, 2020.
3. Aliverti, A., Wearable technology: Role in respiratory health and disease. *Breathe*, 13, 2, e27–e36, 2017.
4. Andrews, J., Kowsika, M., Vakil, A., Li, J., A motion induced passive infrared (PIR) sensor for stationary human occupancy detection, in: *2020 IEEE/ION*

Position, Location and Navigation Symposium (PLANS), IEEE, pp. 1295–1304, 2020.

5. Baek, H.J., Chung, G.S., Kim, K.K., Park, K.S., A smart health monitoring chair for nonintrusive measurement of biological signals. *IEEE Trans. Inf. Technol. Biomed.*, 16, 1, 150–158, 2011.

6. Batth, R.S., Nayyar, A., Nagpal, A., Internet of robotic things: Driving intelligent robotics of future-concept, architecture, applications and technologies, in: *2018 4th International Conference on Computing Sciences (ICCS)*, IEEE, pp. 151–160, 2018.

7. Cao, S., *Applying Multimodal Sensing to Human Motion Tracking in Mobile Systems*, Ph.D. thesis, Purdue University Graduate School, Purdue, USA, 2020.

8. Chalmers, C., Fergus, P., Montanez, C.A.C., Sikdar, S., Ball, F., Kendall, B., Detecting activities of daily living and routine behaviours in dementia patients living alone using smart meter load disaggregation. *IEEE Trans. Emerging Top. Comput.*, 2020.

9. Chen, Y.Z., Chia, C.H., Wu, Y., Chia, T.L., The gait analysis system based on the first-person video for applications on home health care, in: *Twelfth International Conference on Digital Image Processing (ICDIP 2020)*, vol. 11519, International Society for Optics and Photonics, p. 115191C, 2020.

10. Cox, R.C. and Olatunji, B.O., Sleep in the anxiety-related disorders: A meta-analysis of subjective and objective research. *Sleep Med. Rev.*, 51, 101282, 2020.

11. Damarla, T., Mehmood, A., Sabatier, J., Detection of people and animals using non-imaging sensors, in: *14th International Conference on Information Fusion*, IEEE, pp. 1–8, 2011.

12. De, P., Chatterjee, A., Rakshit, A., PIR sensor based aal tool for human movement detection: Modified mcp based dictionary learning approach. *IEEE Trans. Instrum. Meas.*, 69, 10, 7377–7385, 2020.

13. Delahoz, Y.S. and Labrador, M.A., Survey on fall detection and fall prevention using wearable and external sensors. *Sensors*, 14, 10, 19806–19842, 2014.

14. El-Amrawy, F. and Nounou, M.I., Are currently available wearable devices for activity tracking and heart rate monitoring accurate, precise, and medically beneficial? *Healthc. Inform. Res.*, 21, 4, 315–320, 2015.

15. Gao, S., Chen, J.-L., Dai, Y.-N., Wang, R., Kang, S.-B., Xu, L.-J., Piezoelectric-based insole force sensing for gait analysis in the Internet of health things. *IEEE Consum. Electron. Mag.*, 10, 1, 39–44, 2021.

16. Guo, Y., Warren Andersen, S., Shu, X.O., Michailidou, K., Bolla, M.K., Wang, Q., Garcia-Closas, M., Milne, R.L., Schmidt, M.K., Chang-Claude, J. *et al.*, Genetically predicted body mass index and breast cancer risk: Mendelian randomization analyses of data from 145,000 women of European descent. *PLoS Med.*, 13, 8, e1002105, 2016.

17. Hajihashemi, Z. and Popescu, M., Detection of abnormal sensor patterns in eldercare, in: *2013 E-Health and Bioengineering Conference (EHB)*, IEEE, pp. 1–4, 2013.

18. S.W. Harel and U. Zevulun, Optimization of an automation setting through selective feedback, US Patent App. 16/213,759, Jun 11 2020.
19. Huifeng, W., Kadry, S.N., Raj, E.D., Continuous health monitoring of sports person using IoT devices based wearable technology. *Comput. Commun.*, 160, 588–595, 2020.
20. D.N. Jensen, L.L. Ruetz, C.R. Condie, Y.K. Cho, U. Strobel, S. Davie, Method and apparatus for monitoring heart rate and abnormal respiration, US Patent 6,752,765, Jun 22 2004.
21. Kerst, A., Zielasek, J., Gaebel, W., Smartphone applications for depression: A systematic literature review and a survey of health care professionals' attitudes to- wards their use in clinical practice. *Eur. Arch. Psychiatry Clin. Neurosci.*, 270, 2, 139–152, 2020.
22. Krey, M., Wearable device technology in healthcare—Exploring constraining and enabling factors, in: *Fourth International Congress on Information and Communication Technology*, Springer, pp. 1–13, 2020.
23. M.W. Kroll and K. Bradley, System and method for evaluating risk of mortality due to congestive heart failure using physiologic sensors, US Patent 6,645,153, Nov 11 2003.
24. Kumar, A., Gopal, K., Aggarwal, A., Novel trusted hierarchy construction for RFID sensor-based manets using eccs. *ETRI J.*, 37, 1, 186–196, 2015.
25. Kumar, A., Gopal, K., Aggarwal, A., A novel lightweight key management scheme for RFID-sensor integrated hierarchical Manet based on Internet of Things. *Int. J. Adv. Intell. Paradig.*, 9, 2–3, 220–245, 2017.
26. Kwak, Y.H., Kim, W., Park, K.B., Kim, K., Seo, S., Flexible heartbeat sensor for wearable device. *Biosens. Bioelectron.*, 94, 250–255, 2017.
27. Li, M., Yu, S., Zheng, Y., Ren, K., Lou, W., Scalable and secure sharing of personal health records in cloud computing using attribute-based encryption. *IEEE Trans. Parallel Distrib. Syst.*, 24, 1, 131–143, 2012.
28. Liu, X., Yang, T., Tang, S., Guo, P., Niu, J., From relative azimuth to absolute location: Pushing the limit of PIR sensor based localization, in: *Proceedings of the 26th Annual International Conference on Mobile Computing and Networking*, pp. 1–14, 2020.
29. Murphy, R.R., *Introduction to AI robotics*, MIT Press, USA, 2019.
30. R.M. Mysell, Monitoring device, US Patent 10,650,649, May 12 2020.
31. Nayyar, A. and Puri, V., Data glove: Internet of things (IoT) based smart wearable gadget. *J. Adv. Math. Comput. Sci.*, 15, 1–12, 2016.
32. Pakhomov, S.V., Thuras, P.D., Finzel, R., Eppel, J., Kotlyar, M., Using consumer-wearable technology for remote assessment of physiological response to stress in the naturalistic environment. *Plos One*, 15, 3, e0229942, 2020.
33. Pantelopoulos, A. and Bourbakis, N.G., A survey on wearable sensor-based systems for health monitoring and prognosis. *IEEE Trans. Syst. Man Cybern. Part C (Appl. Rev.)*, 40, 1, 1–12, 2009.
34. Popescu, M., Hotrabhavananda, B., Moore, M., Skubic, M., Vampiran automatic fall detection system using a vertical PIR sensor array, in: *2012 6th*

International Conference on Pervasive Computing Technologies for Healthcare (PervasiveHealth) and Workshops, IEEE, pp. 163–166, 2012.

35. Puri, V. and Nayyar, A., Real time smart home automation based on PIC microcontroller, Bluetooth and Android technology, in: *2016 3rd International Conference on Computing for Sustainable Global Development (INDIACom)*, IEEE, pp. 1478–1484, 2016.

36. Qiu, S., Wang, Z., Zhao, H., Liu, L., Li, J., Jiang, Y., Fortino, G., Body sensor network-based robust gait analysis: Toward clinical and at home use. *IEEE Sens. J.*, 19, 19, 8393–8401, 2018.

37. Reis, L., Maier, C., Mattke, J., Weitzel, T., Chatbots in healthcare: Status quo, application scenarios for physicians and patients and future directions, in: *ECIS*, 2020.

38. Semwal, T. and Nair, S.B., Agpi: Agents on raspberry pi. *Electronics*, 5, 4, 72, 2016.

39. Sharma, S. and Ghose, A., Unobtrusive and pervasive monitoring of geriatric subjects for early screening of mild cognitive impairment, in: *2018 IEEE International Conference on Pervasive Computing and Communications Workshops (PerCom Workshops)*, IEEE, pp. 179–184, 2018.

40. Silvera-Tawil, D., Hussain, M.S., Li, J., Emerging technologies for precision health: An insight into sensing technologies for health and wellbeing. *Smart Health*, 15, 100100, 2020.

41. Singh, S.P., Nayyar, A., Kumar, R., Sharma, A., Fog computing: From architecture to edge computing and big data processing. *J. Supercomput.*, 75, 4, 2070–2105, 2019.

42. Solanki, A. and Nayyar, A., Green Internet of Things (G-IoT): ICT technologies, principles, applications, projects, and challenges, in: *Handbook of Research on Big Data and the IoT*, pp. 379–405, IGI Global Hershey, PA, USA, 2019.

43. Sultan, N., Reflective thoughts on the potential and challenges of wearable technology for healthcare provision and medical education. *Int. J. Inf. Manage.*, 35, 5, 521–526, 2015.

44. Teixeira, T., Dublon, G., Savvides, A., A survey of human-sensing: Methods for detecting presence, count, location, track, and identity. *ACM Comput. Surv.*, 5, 1, 59–69, 2010.

45. Tripathi, A.M., Baruah, R.D., Nair, S.B. *et al.*, Ultrasonic sensor-based human detector using one-class classifiers, in: *2015 IEEE International Conference on Evolving and Adaptive Intelligent Systems (EAIS)*, IEEE, pp. 1–6, 2015.

46. VandeWeerd, C., Yalcin, A., Aden-Buie, G., Wang, Y., Roberts, M., Mahser, N., Fnu, C., Fabiano, D., Homesense: Design of an ambient home health and wellness monitoring platform for older adults. *Health Technol.*, 10, 1–19, 2020.

47. Watts, N.B., Spanheimer, R.G., DiGirolamo, M., Gebhart, S.S., Musey, V.C., Siddiq, Y.K., Phillips, L.S., Prediction of glucose response to weight loss in

patients with non-insulin-dependent diabetes mellitus. *Arch. Intern. Med.*, 150, 4, 803–806, 1990.

48. Yadav, D.C. and Pal, S., To generate an ensemble model for women thyroid prediction using data mining techniques. *Asian Pac. J. Cancer Prev.: APJCP*, 20, 4, 1275, 2019.

49. Yazar, A., Erden, F., Cetin, A.E., Multi-sensor ambient assisted living system for fall detection, in: *Proceedings of the IEEE International Conference on Acoustics, Speech, and Signal Processing (ICASSP'14)*, pp. 1–3, 2014.

50. Zimmerman, S., Sloane, P.D., Katz, P.R., Kunze, M., O'Neil, K., Resnick, B., The need to include assisted living in responding to the covid-19 pandemic. *J. Am. Med. Dir. Assoc.*, 21, 5, 572–575, 2020.

A Comprehensive Study of IoT Security Risks in Building a Secure Smart City

Akansha Bhargava[1]*, Gauri Salunkhe[1], Sushant Bhargava[2]
and Prerna Goswami[1]

[1]Department of General Engineering, Institute of Chemical Technology,
Matunga, Mumbai, India
[2]Godrej & Boyce Manufacturing Company Ltd., Mumbai, India

Abstract

The Internet of Things (IoT) is capable of assimilating a variety of heterogeneous systems, by facilitating seamless access and communication amongst an expansive range of devices, people and their environment making it the key feature in developing the idea of Smart Cities. The advancement of technology and deployment of a plethora of digital devices across the city will also require resilience of the services provided and also the security of data. As the number of IoT devices increases, the data generated will also escalate which will require more efficient and sophisticated algorithms to handle the big data, so that optimized decisions could be made. Interdisciplinary components and integrative arrangements in the IoT system have instigated new security challenges. Present day security solutions are not effective in providing the solution and to meet up the requirements of heavy computation and communication load for IoT devices and are not capable of detecting zero-day attacks. Hence, perpetuating the security demand in a comprehensive IoT system is strenuous. A compendious solution is required to deal with the security issues. The objective of this chapter is to present a holistic review of ML/DL algorithms which can be deployed to improve security solutions. This chapter delineates aforesaid challenges on technology's implementation and standardization, a brief overview of existing IoT architectures, enabling technologies and also explores the prospects of ML/DL methodologies that can be implemented on IoT platform to maintain an admissible level of services, security and privacy issues, aiming to enhance the overall experience of Smart Cities.

*Corresponding author: minidimi@gmail.com

Arun Solanki, Adarsh Kumar and Anand Nayyar (eds.) Digital Cities Roadmap: IoT-Based Architecture and Sustainable Buildings, (401–448) © 2021 Scrivener Publishing LLC

Keywords: IoT architecture, machine learning, security, privacy, smart cities, service management, attacks

13.1   Introduction

The Internet of Things (IoT) has unfolded a new world of possibilities where humans can communicate with the physical devices seamlessly and can evoke their ideas to the "things" around. These interconnected devices are capable of providing breakthrough and intuitive services. As shown in Figure 13.1, IoT has found its way in copious applications, e.g., remote monitoring, smart homes, smart vehicles, healthcare, parking areas and many more, and is pivoting a significant role in building Smart Cities. These emerging technologies also poses threat to the environment as they emit lot of hazardous pollutants and are depleting natural resources. Solanki and Nayyar [1] proposed a green technology for IoT systems which could be a potential solution for above listed issues. Apart from environmental threats, IoT ecosystem still has many flaws to implement it in full-fledged manner, although, ease of use is becoming simpler for humans, but many of these services necessitate end users to disclose

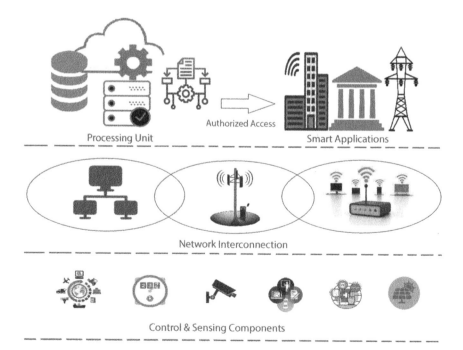

Figure 13.1 IoT for smart city.

private information to provide customized solutions. Mandating security is of prime importance. Unfortunately, many of the commercial products available today are not capable of providing adequate mechanisms. IoT environment consists of integrative positioning making it challenging to maintain the security needs. Many services call for having an app installed on the system to give a seamless service but these apps can easily get cloned. Ullah *et al.* [2] proposed has proposed a deep learning based model to find the cloned apps. Numerous data is being generated by these interconnected devices, making it impossible to manage in regards to assimilating with Confidentiality, Integrity and Availability (CIA triad), fundamental principles of information security [3]. As most of the IoT devices are implemented in an unfortified surrounding leaving them vulnerable to physical attacks, where an interloper can retrieve personal data by physically accessing it [4]. One will also have to note that IoT systems do need a built in security to ensure proper safety against breeches in an unattended environment [5]. In 2016, the world faced the most intense security attack, Mirai, which used IoT botnets to hamper the services; it exploited the login information and became the largest DDoS attack [6].

Deploying complex security measures in IoT devices is strenuous owing to the limited power resources availability [7]. Also, if a mechanism has been designed for a particular type of attack it cannot circumvent the zero-day attacks. Hence, laying down security methods on IoT devices would require conservational analytics methods and should work on cross platforms [8]. Additionally, discerning which technique to implement to protect IoT systems is tedious because of interconnected and interdisciplinary devices [7]. IoT systems available today cannot assure a secured network and are prone to malware attacks, which will lead to vulnerable "Smart City". Ml/DL methods are vigorous methods to identify anomalous behavior. Entire system data can be converged and inspected beforehand to look for any malicious activity. As ML/DL methods learn from the previous samples, they are capable of perceiving unknown threats.

The principal contribution of this chapter is collocated as follows:

Part 1: Smart City model with reference to IoT is discussed. This part gives an exhaustive overview of different vulnerabilities associated with different layers of the system. Main objective is to emphasize the challenges linked to achieve a secured environment for Smart City. This will assist researchers to design efficient IDS that can apprehend the attacks or threats linked to each layer.

Part 2: This part illustrates the potential attacks that can hinder the proper functioning of the ecosystem. An exhaustive list of vulnerabilities and threats is provided to identify the area of concern. An in-depth discussion of ML and DL methodologies for securing IoT devices coupled with insights on their working proposition, implementation and advantages. This will further help the researchers to address the security issues in an effective manner.

Part 3: This part recognizes probable methodologies that can be implemented to overcome the challenges. It also discussed past work conducted on designing IDS based on ML/DL technologies and the lack of available datasets for IoT specific devices. Details on available IoT datasets in conjunction with their respective issues/limitations have been captured in the section. And, at last the future work that uses integration of different technologies to assure complete security.

13.1.1   Organization of the Chapter

The chapter delves into the concerns related to privacy and security of IoT systems deployed to form a smart city. An exhaustive survey has been done to categorize the security elements and to determine open threats associated with implementing security practice in each layer of IoT architecture.

The main aim of this chapter is to provide the prospects in the field of IoT attacks and vulnerabilities and to explore the solutions to address the challenges. The chapter is organized as follows: Section 13.2 talks about the related works in the field of security and privacy. Section 13.3 highlights architecture of IoT as per smart city and discusses various threats and possible attacks associated with every layer of IoT. Section 13.4 provides an overview of security pre-requisites of the IoT environment. Section 13.5 gives an introduction to security areas Section 13.6 gives a comprehensive discussion of possible attack surfaces and threats. In Section 13.7, review of ML/DL algorithms is provided and their applications in IoT security are also discussed. In Section 13.8 immediate challenges present to deploy the advanced techniques are enlisted. Section 13.9 gives a brief review of emerging security measures that can be implemented with the ML/DL to provide promising security, and finally, the chapter is concluded in Section 13.10.

13.2   Related Works

This section presents a brief overview of the latest research done in the field of "Smart Cities" empowered by IoT. Many researchers have discussed various concerns and challenges in mitigating issues related to security and privacy.

Data is a key factor to devise the IDS system and considering the life cycle of data plays an important role to outline the security measures of data in three dimensions, a secured and low weight encryption is the requirement to protect the data from forensic or legal challenges [9]. IoT devices are heterogeneous in nature with limited resources, with the expectation of intelligence from these devices and having an open source to patch in the updates makes it challenging to deploy security on a common platform [8].

Diverse nature of IoT device makes them more susceptible to attacks. They don't have any proper authentication methodologies, inappropriate encryption techniques and firmware, almost nil physical security, apprehensive network services and protocols. Yavuz *et al.* [10] proposed a deep learning based method to detect routing attacks, authors have used Contiki-RPL to simulate the attacks and RPL protocols, IRAD dataset was used to train the deep neural network. However, only three types of attacks (decreased rank, hello flood and version number modification) attacks were detected.

Fog-based model, "ELM-based Semi-supervised Fuzzy C-Means (EFSCM)" has been implemented which is based on semi supervised learning to detect the attack. Model is first trained by labeled data and then is employed to train an unlabeled set which will return a matrix with membership degree for the entire dataset. This way data can be clustered according to the class they belong to and hence the data that is not labeled can be also detected. Distributed attacks were detected in real time using the EFSCM method [11].

Intrusion detection method was proposed by Zhang *et al.* [12] based on combining an improved genetic algorithm and deep belief network where GA makes a number of iterations to generate a best fitting model and this model is then used by DBN to detect the intrusion, DBN improved the efficiency of detection and also reduced the overall complexity of the system. Authors used NSL-KDD dataset for the simulation and to train the model.

To deploy IoT for "Smart Cities", an architecture was proposed by Greenstein *et al.* [13] based on SDN, but the complete realization of SDN is not possible in the suggested architecture as IoT devices have constrained supplies. This led to IoT end nodes becoming more vulnerable to various attacks.

Any IoT node connected in the system should be able to prove its identification and ownership, since the ownership of devices change, as the device moves from retailer to consumer or if it's being resold or is stolen. Hence a dynamic response to revoke or change the authority of IoT devices becomes necessary. To address this issue use of Blockchain was suggested [14]. Most of the IoT devices use public links to connect the users and the nodes, which are highly prone to get attacked by the intruders. A deep learning-block chain-based model is proposed by Ferrag and Maglaras [15], where authors had implemented RNN to discern attacks of network layer to find the hoax transactions in smart grid and have used blockchain to develop the trust amongst nodes. The proposed Intrusion detection system (IDS) was developed using CICIDS2017 dataset. However, to implement such IDS on resource constrained nodes are challenging.

Trust based system, for e-governance utilizing blockchain and AI was proposed by Yang *et al.* [16] to achieve significant lucidity amongst end users and the business providers. It is decentralized system to provide secured transactions which can be implemented at four layers (physical, communication, security and database) of the IoT system. Validation and analysis of system is proposed before deploying the system. With every new day intruders are devising new threats and are challenging the existing security system, the data coming out of various sensors is high dimension; hence having a regularization technique for detecting the threats is the need of hour. A concise survey is done for various DL techniques that can be implemented on Cyber-Physical Systems (CPS) by Wickramasinghe *et al.* [17].

Static and adaptive methodologies, state-of-the-art to detect and prevent CPS for various layers of CPS, are introduced by Shafique *et al.* [18], where the paper also discussed vulnerable surfaces of ML algorithms and have opened new research questions of the data security at inference phase and how can the identification of strongly correlated data be done. Kumar *et al.* [19] discussed various attacks associated with Narrow-band IoT such as; node failure attack, battery drainage attack etc. are discussed. NB-IoT security is also reviewed and an analysis is done on layer wise threats. The research also threw some light on healthcare and agriculture related security concerns. Alaba *et al.* [20] focused on heterogeneity of IoT environments and vulnerabilities associated with them. A comprehensive research has been done and state-of-art threats deployments at different application side, such as, smart grid, surroundings and healthcare has been discussed. Furthermore, some architecture (SDN, Service-oriented-architecture) that can be deployed to secure the IoT framework are also discussed. Ezeme *et al.* [21] surveyed security threats of IoT environment based upon the centralized and distributed frame. Some of the existing solutions are also discussed, moreover key requirements for security based on privacy and trust of IoT nodes is discussed.

Hassija *et al.* [22] presented a gives a comprehensive survey on security threats at different layers of IoT with the solution to implement any of the upcoming technologies, such as blockchain, fog computation, ML or Edge computation to make the IoT system secure or to mitigate the vulnerabilities. Moreover the survey also presented the issues related to implement these technologies. Hamad *et al.* [23] focused on energy constrained devices and issues related to secure them. However, this survey gives an exhaustive review of potential ML/DL methodologies that can be implemented to provide a cutting-edge technique for securing IoT devices. This survey identifies challenges associated with "Smart City", various attacks related to every layer of the system and the future directions to overcome them. The research also compares various datasets present today for training the IDS and the issues related to them.

13.3 Overview of IoT System in Smart Cities

A framework, principally constitute of "Information and Communication Technologies" (ICT), to expand, deploy, and stimulate unremitting establishment of urbanization challenges.

Major proportion of ICT architecture is fundamentally an ingenious network of inter-linked machines and humans that communicate using wireless medium such as traffic lights accepting data from car sensors to automatically control traffic in real time or garbage bins transmitting information about the garbage pick-up time rather than having a scheduled time. Societies can ameliorate smart energy distribution, waste management, improved air index, enriched human life and many more by utilizing IoT. Moreover, these services should also be capable of generating revenue [24]. The prospects of smart cities are pretty-much boundless, and the development of Smart cities will open myriad of opportunities for individuals. Also, IoT devices can also help in tracking the fitness of individuals [25].

IoT transforms an ordinary device into a smart device by employing technology on it and automating every single thing [26]. It becomes instrumental to implement an accurate system owing to the extensive applications that will capacitate the concept of "Smart City" by connecting every smart object [27]. However, as the number IoT devices will increase they will become more susceptible to attacks and threats. Almost 90%

unstructured big Data will be generated from these devices [28]. Nayyar *et al.* [29] discussed different modules constituting smart city and the security configuration that needs to be placed for proper functioning of all the components.

Unavailability of advanced and modern encryption techniques, improper security architecture for low-end devices and absence of physical protection will risk the productivity and sustainability of smart ecosystem. Attackers are jeopardizing the services by engineering new attacks by finding loopholes in the system and bringing all the services to standstill. They are capable of causing a worldwide panic just by manipulating data from the sensors.

This segment gives a critique of the IoT system deployed to make "Smart Cities". The section renders comprehensive insights on the deployment of IoT enabled solutions to build smart cities. A critical aspect of potential security threats and vulnerabilities associated with an IoT-enabled smart city has further been elaborated in the section. Different layers of Smart city are prone to different attacks and specific solutions are required to tackle these issues. However, in particular, this section is to elaborate the aspects of IoT systems that are vulnerable to security threats.

Figure 13.2 depicts an overview of IoT layers and respective threats associated with them.

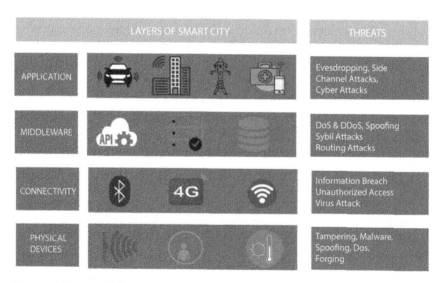

Figure 13.2 Potential threats in Smart City.

13.3.1   Physical Devices

This layer can also be called a sensing layer [27], involving all the physical sensors capable of comprehending variations in its surroundings. Sensors and actuators form the principle modules that will sense and collect the information about the changes and possibly be intelligent to process any significant changes or execute any required action. Sensors can also send the data to the cloud over a connected network for accumulated processing and storing.

IoT sensors are power hungry devices and have limited resources [30], making it difficult to upgrade the firmware and installing updated security protocols, which can affect their proper functioning if a malicious node is connected or an eavesdropper is sniffing the data as no proper security measures are available at this level. Being in the close vicinity of the system attackers can gain absolute control of the devices and can manipulate them. They can change the firmware or replace the nodes with malicious ones to eavesdrop the information or an absolute lockdown of services can occur by confiscating the communication devices.

The following threats and vulnerabilities are encountered at the physical layer.

- Physically tampered nodes will stop working and will not be available to transmit the data.
- IoT end nodes are vulnerable to physical attacks and an attacker can gain unauthorized access.
- Malware nodes can get connected and spoofed in the information or can upload faulty data in the system.
- Resource unavailability and bandwidth inaccessibility can cause some nodes to deliberately stop transmission of data.
- Denial of Service (DoS), where bandwidth is overloaded by malicious requests and resources are made unavailable to end users.
- Blocking and forging in transmission of the data.

13.3.2   Connectivity

Heterogeneous devices are connected in a collaborative manner in the IoT system to provide intelligent services [26]. Adopting a particular connectivity technology is a challenge in an IoT platform as the devices have limited resources and low storage capacity [31]. Sensors deployed must be able to work under constrained resources and in noisy communication channels [26]. Hence, determining the satisfactory solution while deploying sensors in a particular project incorporates finding tradeoffs between low power channels, routing protocols and energy efficient technology. Communication and connectivity is delivered by Network Layer.

The following threats and vulnerabilities are encountered at the Network layer.

- Information breaching can occur in an un-trusted framework.
- DoS or Distributed Denial of Service (DDoS), due to compromised network,
- Unauthorized access in the network by a malevolent access of public and private keys.
- Trojan or other software viruses' attacks.

13.3.3   Middleware

Middleware aims to obscure the intricacies at system level, and by helping software developers to emphasize exclusively on application level [32]. Apparently, data and information are forwarded to and fro between end user and system with the help of this layer [33] to provide seamless service amongst heterogeneous devices. Light and energy efficient schemes must be deployed at IoT nodes for safe configuration of application maintenance.

The following threats and vulnerabilities are encountered at Middleware.

- Unaccredited admittance in the authorized network.
- Leakage of information to un-trusted services.
- Fake or disguised gateways by attackers to impersonate IoT devices and nodes.
- DoS or DDoS attacks by over flooding the bandwidth.
- Routing attacks, like spoofing, Sybil, etc.

13.3.4   Human Interaction

IoT has found various applications, and when we talk about "Smart Cities", the IoT system is becoming a key factor in making things intelligent e.g., smart healthcare, smart transportation, smart agriculture, smart grid, smart supply chain and many more will constitute an easier and flexible lifestyle for humans. The objective of this level is to make use of the data apprehended, communicated and explored at lower levels to enhance societal and community growth. Any attack in this layer will directly hamper the individuals, many times it can be life threatening e.g., if attackers take control over the smart car, they can easily take control of the speed of the car or the airbag systems which could be lethal for the person.

The following threats and vulnerabilities are encountered at Human Interaction

- IoT devices are connected over the web; malicious software can slip in through the client side.
- Access information can be passed on to attackers by eavesdropping into the device.
- Remote configuration unavailability.
- Failure of devices leading to mismanagement.

13.4   IoT Security Prerequisite

Systems deploying IoT devices manage a large proportion of information which is sensitive and is vulnerable to various attacks. This has attracted perpetrators to attack the system and steal the sensitive information or completely shut off the system by gaining access to it. An intruder can launch attack through any compromised node or network, every device connected in the infrastructure could lead to risking the personal information. As IoT devices work in an unattended environment and with their capability to make autonomous decision the threat risk will multifold.

Complex embedded circuitry to give interoperability among heterogeneous IoT framework may add more vulnerability [34]. Smart city evolution will collect much personal information of the individuals which can be manipulated in various ways. Researchers will have to ensure that the data is protected from end-to-end in every domain.

At a wide spread, security prerequisites can be categorized as follows:

Confidentiality ensures information flow is not obstructed by intruders and end-devices are not corrupted or vulnerable to attacks which could lead to stealing of credentials or personal data. This ascertains that information can solely be accessed by the intended users and no un-authorized access is possible in the system [34]. E-commerce customers, when make a transaction on an online portal need to know that their credentials and personal information will not be leaked to perpetrators for any kind of misuse and is protected from unauthorized access. IoT systems can save the data locally (edge nodes) or can send it to the cloud. Now to ensure the security it becomes important to implement mechanisms that can secure the sensitive particulars and depending upon the sensitivity of information these measures can be designed.

Integrity ensures that data is received in true from and is not corrupted in any way. It becomes really important to know the origination and authenticity of the data to build the trust between the nodes. Entire information is original and is not compromised by active attacks. Banking sector, for example customers want to know all the information related to their account is correct and their account balance is not meddled.

IoT framework makes it more vulnerable to being attacked at various layers which could affect the integrity, hence authentication is very important e.g., In the perceptions layer, an intruder, if connected a fake node claiming to be the authentic one, could lead to potential damage of the entire ecosystem impacting the integrity. There are various IoT-based applications that carry critical information which if compromised can be life threatening. Sometimes anomalistic data could also occur because of server crash or any non-human involvement, hence having a backup plan to comprehend integrity is necessary.

Availability ensures that system is available, assets and resources are usable when an authorized person accesses them. For many IoT systems like, military services and healthcare systems it becomes of utmost importance that services are available the entire time. DoS, DDoS, flooding and many other active attacks can lead to resource unavailability. Apart from these threats, hardware/software failure can also jeopardize the availability. DoS or DDoS attacks have caused serious problems in past as well, where the entire network went down as the bandwidth was saturated by false traffic. As we talk about cloud services, they work on sharing of physical devices by implementing a logical virtualization to share resources amongst users, hence the issue becomes more prominent and frequent in cloud services hampering not just the intended organization but others too if cloud resources are being shared. Attacks can be launched on anywhere from application layer to network layer [35].

Authorization necessitates identification of access rights of all the individual users of a particular IoT system. The end user could be a person, device or an organization. Whenever a particular user asks for any data it should be only delivered if that user is an authorized to access it or in a broad way any action in the system should be taken by the authorized request specifically. Granting access and deploying an access control not just for humans but the machines (physical devices) is a challenging task [20], moreover handling of such huge data coming from heterogeneous sensors and delivering it to only authorized customer would need advanced technologies.

Authentication is a mechanism of validating and substantiating the identity of things present in the system. Every individual device connected in an IoT system should be able to confirm and ensure its identity before processing any communication. Authentication can be applied at every layer of IoT architecture and can be achieved by various ways such as token based (OAuth2 protocol or open ID), context (physical or behavioral) or identity based. Depending upon the IoT system, authentication methodologies change like a robust system would need a robust validation system.

Non-repudiation gives an irrefutable evidence of the rationality and validity of the data. It provides the origin records which can be used for verification in the situations where validation is not possible otherwise. This factor becomes important when payments are done online and both the alliances are not able to repudiate the transactions done.

Privacy confirms the protection of personal data of the users. IoT has gained applications in various sectors and is prevailing in diverse areas, such as smart grid, smart homes, supply chain, governance and many more. For all the applications, IoT devices involved are saving the personal data of the individuals in regards to their movements, daily routines and associations with others sometimes with consent and many times without. Securing and protecting the private information is the basic demand of the consumer.

Trust is a mechanism to give a measurement of how much an IoT device can be trusted as we know heterogeneous devices are connected in the IoT environment and multiple sensors to number of actuators, which raises a question, whether a particular node can be trusted or not. Developing a trust mechanism plays an important role in manifesting a secured and reliable system.

13.5 IoT Security Areas

IoT systems are vulnerable at various sections and where ML/DL methodologies can be predominantly applied to mitigate these attacks,

13.5.1 Anomaly Detection

This area deals with the finding anomalies by discerning certain pattern of the data, whenever an abnormal activity occurs, say credit card swindling or a sudden spike in energy at midnight which will give an unexpected behavior. Hence, anomalies are the pattern in the dataset which apparently do not follow normal behavior. Having a well-defined boundary for normal and abnormal pattern is very important as it keeps on changing for different attacks and with time something normal today can be abnormal in future. Real time situations are difficult to deal with as the traffic generated is huge and attackers are dynamic in engineering attacks. Moreover, availability of proper dataset for training and testing is also an issue.

Depending upon the area of anomaly generated, it can be categorized as point, contextual and collective anomaly. If only a single instance shows an abnormal pattern it is called as point, when abnormality is in a particular context then it can be said as context and if group of instances behaves in anomalous way then it is a collective anomaly.

13.5.2   Host-Based IDS (HIDS)

They monitor the individual hosts to look out for any outliers in the characteristics of the network traffic. They administer the information collected from host devices and are capable of conforming which user/processor intricate the malicious activity. HIDS utilizes a "digital inventory" of the data with their feature sets to store the individual files which is saved offline on a platform which is read-only and can be made available on request.

HIDS consumes more energy and resources and they cannot prevent DDoS attacks. When implemented on client–server platform they even build-up traffic obstruction in the network [36].

13.5.3   Network-Based IDS (NIDS)

These devices are aptly placed across the network to examine the traffic of the devices. They detect the anomalous traffic traversing the network in an indiscriminative manner. NIDS are passive devices and can be either software-based or a hardware system. They work by attaching themselves to diverse network platforms like FDDI, fast Ethernet and many more first by listening onto the network and then reporting to any anomalous behavior to NIDS management system. Network packets are being perceived at either host or router, all the data packets are inspected and any abnormal activity is recorded.

13.5.4   Malware Detection

A mechanism to ascertain and safeguard the system against any malware attacks such as Trojan horse, spyware, worms and others. The detection systems are available for gateways, mobile devices and workstations to prevent them from any sort of malware attack. These systems generally run the whole time, can be implemented for centralized systems and are employ signature-based detections. With the automated detection systems, they many times give false alarms as they work by analogizing network traffic to already learned patterns of malicious activities.

Conventionally, static and dynamic evaluation is two variants of malware detection. When a binary form is directly inspected, they are called as static and when binary files after execution are being monitored, they are called as dynamic.

13.5.5   Ransomware Detection

It is a process to discern the ransomware attacks and to protect the system from such attacks. In these types of attacks functionality of the entire system is disabled by either encrypting the system or infecting it. The intruder asks some kind of ransom to provide the access again to the system. Usual anti-virus cannot give the protection against the zero day or new ransomwares which implement new technologies to infect the system. Research is going on to devise and Ransomware- DS that will be able to give the complete protection.

13.5.6   Intruder Detection

It is a tool to intuit intruders trying to breach the system. IDS will raise a flag when someone tries to break-in to the network giving exact information of the transgression.

Intruder detection combines authentication and authorization to defend the system. They are capable of gathering information and establishing pattern from it to define if an intrusion has happened based on the abnormal patterns detected in the system. Intruders can be classified as Masquerader (someone trying to gain unauthorized access), Misfeasor (Someone trying to access the privileged data which is not meant for his level) and Clandestine (Someone who can control the system from being audited).

13.5.7   Botnet Detection

A detection scheme to protect the system against remotely controlled attacks, where large number of client device are being influenced by a remote server. The devices under attack are called as bots or zombies.

Bots are used to generate DDoS attacks as they are distributed in nature and can self-infect. Botnet detection can be classified as active, where the malware infecting the system is captured and deactivated and passive, in which the traffic is analyzed to know the infected system. Various researches have been done on detecting botnet, based on traffic analysis of the network. Zhao *et al.* [37] used have used ML to detect the botnet by analyzing the incoming network traffic, as the network traffic analysis can be done on encrypted packets.

13.6   IoT Security Threats

IoT works in a disparate environment to provide a coherent experience to its users. Demanding an exhaustive security need in both cyber and physical states [38, 39]. The developed and advanced cipher codes are difficult to deploy in the small and limited memory IoT devices [40]. A comprehensive solution is required to meet the desired security measures, as the physical devices are in un-attended environment, the end user must also get notification if the devices are being tampered. Every new day the attackers are coming up with more sophisticated attacks so it becomes essential to deploy a system that can learn and detect these zero-day attacks. Based on attack surfaces IoT threats can be classified into cyber and physical threats. Figure 13.3 shows the prospective role of ML/DL in securing Smart City.

Cyber threats are categorized as passive and active threats.

13.6.1   Passive Threats

In this threat, the attacker will eavesdrop and contemplate the data, by doing so; they are collecting data and making use of confidential information [41]. In this eavesdropper will snoop in the data and can also track the whereabouts of the device by knowing the communication channel [42, 43]. Various attacks are listed in Table 13.1 with their descriptions. Although, intruder is not harming users directly but they can sell the acquired data into black-market which then can be potentially used to harm the system. Table 13.1 lists various threats and their descriptions.

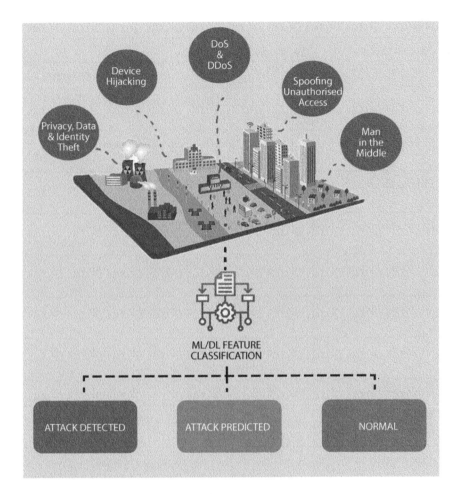

Figure 13.3 ML/DL in securing Smart City.

13.6.2   Active Threats

In this threat, the invaders are defter in attacking the system, as they not only steal the information but they also alter the operation of the IoT system [41]. The attacker can completely take hold by generating one or sequence of attacks. These types of attack can potentially be misused causing direct infliction to target victims. They are more harmful and can even cause threat to one's life. e.g., a perpetrator can gain the access to someone's

Table 13.1 Passive threats.

Passive threats	Description
Device monitoring	Infiltration of the activity and data of the computer.
Network spying	Observing the data being transferred over the network.
Wiretapping	Intercepting the phone lines and listening in a clandestine manner.
Port scouring	Scanning for the open ports to tap the information and activities.
Idle scanning	A TCP port scan method, intruders send hoax packets to the computer to find accessible services.
Keystroke capturing	Monitoring software to capture the keystroke of the legitimate users.
Web scraping	Extraction of data from the programs intended to be read by humans.
Backdoor	Circumventing the regular authentication process and gaining access of the devices.
Eavesdropping	Covertly listening to the private communications.
Vulnerabilities	Exploiting fragile points of systems to attack and stealing information.
Typo-squatting	A version of cyber-squatting where similar domain names are being used to do the fraud. It completely exploits the error in typing URL by a user.

pacemaker making it to malfunction and eventually causing harm. Table 13.2 lists various active attacks with the description.

13.7   Review of ML/DL Application in IoT Security

The upcoming trends of IoT will have an extensive commercial, financial and social percussion on our lives. The engaging nodes comprising the IoT system have limited resources, making them defenseless to innumerable cyber-physical attacks. With regard to this, substantial attempts to tackle

Table 13.2 Active attacks.

Active threats	Description
Brute force attacks	Acquiring access to the devices by cracking passwords, as most of the users keep the default passwords on their devices.
Cross-site scripting	Running the malicious script on the webpage of clients and sneaking the sensitive information.
Denial-of-service attacks (DoS)	Making the services unavailable to the authorized users and crashing the network with malicious traffic.
Email spoofing	Deceiving the users by sending forged emails to steal the information and duping them to download malevolent codes into their systems.
Man-in-the-middle	Perpetrator intercepting users traffic and placing himself in the middle of conversation, to eavesdrop or to steal the credentials.
Smurf attack	Obscuring the computer services by misusing the vulnerabilities of IP and ICMP. Intruder amplifies the attack over an unsecured network.
Zero-day exploit	A flaw in the software which is not known to the developer or end user that can be potentially exploited by the intruder to attack the system.
Malicious code	A harmful web-script that can give access to the intruder breaching the entire system and exposing all the confidential data.
SQL injection	A kind of vector attack which uses hostile SQL script to control the backend database which can lead to unauthorized access to various files.
Trojan horses	A type of malevolent software which could look legit but can completely take over the devices once installed. They are capable of damaging, stealing and interrupting the network.

(Continued)

Table 13.2 Active attacks. (*Continued*)

Active threats	Description
Ransomware	The attacker encrypts the user's file and then asks for some kind of ransom to give a decryption file.
Whaling attack	It is a type of phishing attack, which aims to target high level executives of an organization or high profile individual to gain access to sensitive data.
Privilege escalation	The intruder exploits the weakness of the system to attack the users and then eventually escalate to other users in the system. Escalation could be horizontal (users of same level) or vertical (higher level). Intruders can even erase their logs making it difficult to get tracked.
Tampering	Web-based attack where the attacker changes the URL to gain the sensitive information of the user and manipulate them.
Spyware	Malevolent software being downloaded to the individuals device without their consent and is capable of spying on all the internet activities.
Social engineering	A high bandwidth attack where the perpetrator attacks the system stepwise and by exploiting the psychological mind frame of the victim to siphon the data.
Direct access attacks	Intruder gains access to the system and can download the data directly; he is also capable of adding loggers and manipulation of the software.
Spear Phishing	It is a targeted attack which is aimed to a known individual or organization instead of some random user.
Clone Phishing	A legitimate email is being cloned and malicious links are put into which directs the user to a fake website.

(*Continued*)

Table 13.2 Active attacks. (*Continued*)

Active threats	Description
Signature wrapping	Attacker appears as an authentic user and is able to accomplish certain tasks. Malicious objects are wrapped inside the legitimate message structure.

the issues related to security in IoT ecosystem were being made using traditional approach. However, these solutions are not efficient enough to circumscribe the entire network. Hence, ML/DL technologies are being explored in this chapter to accommodate the security spectrum of IoT space.

Development in the ML and DL field have emerged a new scope in solving problems [44]. As IoT devices generate huge data and need sophisticated algorithms, ML/DL can significantly improve the detection task. ML/DL algorithms require large amounts of data for training and testing. They prove more efficient in threat detection in IoT systems, which are continuously generating un-processed data. Table 13.1 shows a summary of studies on ML/DL for securing IoT.

The following subsections discuss the ML/DL algorithms with respect to IoT security.

13.7.1 Machine Learning Methods

ML facilitates computers to learn and act like humans. Every time a machine comprehends something takes it as a new learning and act accordingly [45]. In this sub section potential ML algorithms are discussed for securing IoT devices. Table 13.3 shows ML models implemented for IoT security.

13.7.1.1 Decision Trees (DTs)

It is a supervised learning method that has been broadly used to classify samples with respect to their certain parameters in data mining. It repetitively splits the samples as per their attributes and it will perform the operation till the stopping condition is met. Every Feature is represented by a respective node and value associated to the node is a branch. Samples are grouped and ordered depending upon the feature value. The initial

Table 13.3 Summary of studies on ML.

Models	Working proposition	Implementation in IoT security	Advantages
DT	A supervised prediction model, where branches and leaves are used to represent the training data for classification of new samples.	• Misuse detection using C4.5 DT [46] • IDS to reduce false positive [47]	Simple and easy to implement.
KNN	Classification of unknown samples with the help of neighboring nodes to predict the instance. A supervised model can be used for classification and regression.	• Intrusion detection mechanism [48] • "Privacy-Preserving KNN classification scheme" for securing the cloud data [49] • IDS system for "forged commands" in industrial space [50]	Effective and can be combined with other methods for intrusion detection.
RF	DTs are combined to construct an RF, using a "bagging" method for classification.	• Anomaly Detection [51] • "Rules discovery and real-time anomaly detection" [52]	No problem of over-fitting. Less input parameters are required.
PCA	An unsupervised algorithm, transforming correlated attributes to the Uncorrelated sets.	• Anomaly Detection in IoT network [53] • Intrusion detection [54]	Capable of reducing overall dimensionality of the sample set. Hence, reducing the complexity.

(*Continued*)

Table 13.3 Summary of studies on ML. (*Continued*)

Models	Working proposition	Implementation in IoT security	Advantages
NB	NB is based on Bayes' theorem to predict the probability whether a particular feature set belongs to the specified label or not. It gives a posterior probability.	• Intrusion detection [55]	Less number of samples are required to train the model.
SVM	It is a supervised classification algorithm that will segregate the features by using the hyper-plane.	• "Privacy-preserving" in smart city [56]	Generalization Capability.

superlative classification of samples is considered the origin node of the DT, this gives an optimal split to the samples [44]. The drawback associated with DTs is that they require more storage because of their architecture and become complicated when the number of DTs increases [57]. It is difficult to use DTs classifier standalone for security applications as the data is massive and they are prone to over fitting. However, they can be used as classifiers to analyze the suspicious traffic. A hybrid detection model was proposed by Kim *et al.* [46], where a normal dataset is organized into subsets to form a misuse detection model. The model proposed uses DT to build a misuse detection framework, which decomposed the dataset. Since DTs are not capable to descry the unknown threats, they then trained SVM with decomposed subsets of data to make IDS. The above model was trained on NSL-KDD dataset. DTs are easy to understand and they provide all the possible solutions for a decision.

13.7.1.2   *K-Nearest Neighbor (KNN)*

This learning method works on the principle that features having similar properties will subsist adjacent in a dataset. It classifies new attributes according to the similarity assessment of the neighbor. Figure 13.4 depicts the classification of normal and abnormal behavior. To know the class

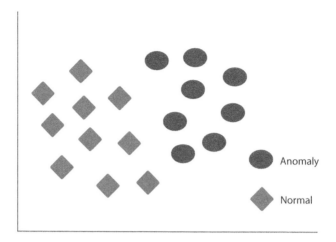

Figure 13.4 KNN for IoT security.

of a particular feature can be decided by noticing the nearest neighbors, KNN finds the k nearest occurrences to determine the label of the inquired instance by recognizing and determines its class by identifying the most recurrent class [58]. The nearest neighbor is often determined by calculating the Euclidean distance [59]. KNN can be used to train large dataset [60], although cross validation becomes important as it simply works on seeing the label of nearest neighbor, if it is normal then it would classify it as a normal node and if the neighbor nodes are malicious it would be labeled as abnormal.

13.7.1.3   Random Forest

It consists of DTs interconnected together to form a large network which is capable of giving a more sophisticated output. Collection of trees is used to form RF and these trees will vote for the most favored class [61]. RF is not vulnerable to over fitting as the output of classification is an average of all the results that are generated by various subsets of the voted class [62]. In certain cases, where the center frequency is unknown RF has given better results than DNN [63]. An RF based IDS is proposed by Nawir *et al.* [41]. Authors checked the performance of the system by using 3 public datasets (UNSW-NB15, GPRS and NSLKDD), experiments results showed that RF-800 was significantly better than other.

13.7.1.4   *Principal Component Analysis (PCA)*

It is a semi-supervised technique which is useful for feature reduction and is capable of preserving key features to retain the information of large sets. Detecting anomalies in the IoT system entails large scale data that includes diverse elements accumulated from networks. This high dimension data requires some technique to reduce the dimensionality. In PCA, Principal Components are deduced, by calculating statistical distance, Euclidean distance which are the uncorrelated features [64]. A malware detection scheme was proposed by Hussain *et al.* [65], where the authors used PCA to discern the anomalies in home routers and was successful to detect popular attacks like Mirai with 100% accuracy.

13.7.1.5   *Naïve Bayes*

NB algorithm is used for predictive modeling; it predicts the feature of a class independent of any other feature. This algorithm uses Bayes' method, which suggests that to calculate the probability of any event X occurring based upon that other event Z has happened is $P(X|Z) = P(Z|X)P(X) / P(Z)$, that can be used to predict the normal and abnormal traffic by calculating the conditional probability of the attack happened over the preceding data [66]. It is a supervised method of classification and all the labels will individually confer to foretell the possibility of anomalous traffic in the network. It has found its application in anomaly detection [67] and intrusion detection [68]. NB is easy to implement, requiring low training samples and is applicable to classify multi and binary classes. However, they aren't capable of finding the interconnection between labels.

13.7.1.6   *Support Vector Machines (SVM)*

SVM is a discriminative classifier that separates different points by utilizing superlative hyper-plane. It can be used at places where the number of samples is lower than the number of dimensions. It is memory efficient and has versatile uses. The usefulness of SVMs is their flexibility and their competency to amend the training samples during run time which make them efficient to be used in real-time IDS. SVMs can be applied to unknown distributions and they perform well on both multi and binary classes [63]. New active learning for SVMs where pool-based methodologies have been adopted to decrease the requirement for labeled training samples [69]. A hybrid scheme for malware detection based on SVM and directed acyclic networks was proposed by Sahu *et al.* [70]. First step was to reduce the dataset into subsets of independent features to model directed acyclic graphs. SVM utilized the Euclidean distance to classify the attacks, KDD cup-1999 dataset was used to perform the experiments. It becomes really important to evaluate SVM using the latest dataset samples and to check their efficiencies by integrating them with other techniques too.

13.7.2 Deep Learning Methods

The additional benefit of using DL for IoT systems over conventional ML that it can be conveniently used on large datasets. Since these systems produce ample data and extracting complex features by hand-engineering becomes difficult which in case of DL can be done automatically [71].

Table 13.4 shows DL model implemented for IoT security.

The following subsections discuss the DL algorithms with respect to IoT security.

Table 13.4 Summary of studies on DL.

Models	Working proposition	Implementation in IoT security	Advantages
CNN	Supervised method to extract the features and uses the sparse connection between the layers.	Classification accuracy for Side channel attacks [72] "Privacy-Preserving" using CNN inference for IoT edge devices [73]	CNNs have the capability to acquire the features from raw dataset.
RNN	Works on Sequential data to extract the variations in datasets by implementing a temporal layer. Supervised and unsupervised	Malicious behavior of nodes [74]	RNNs can be used to detect time series threats.

(Continued)

Table 13.4 Summary of studies on DL. (*Continued*)

Models	Working Proposition	Implementation in IoT security	Advantages
SAE	An unsupervised method that extracts features without the use of manual engineering. It takes the data, compresses it and encodes it in the first part and then learns to reconstruct the data from the coded representation.	"Un-Authorized Traffic" [75] False positive and scalability [76] Profiling abnormal behavior [77]	Used for feature selection and can be combined with other DL method e.g. DBN to detect the anomaly
RBM	An unsupervised deep generative model which is stochastic in nature with exactly two layers. No two nodes in the same layer are connected.	"Privacy-Preserving" using "optimal homomorphic encryption" [78]	RBM can be used to construct DBN for anomaly detection.
DBN	DBNs constitute stacked RBMs. Top down and generative weights are learned by employing greedy learning algorithms. Unlabeled dataset is trained for feature extraction.	Temporal attacks [79]	Malicious attack detection.

13.7.2.1   Convolutional Neural Networks (CNNs)

Convolutional neural networks [80] have been successfully implemented in the areas of image categorization and speech evaluation [81]. CNN incorporates an alternate convolutional layer and pooling layer, data features are convoluted by using numerous filers [82], as shown in Figure 13.5. Pooling layer will down-sample the size of successive layers

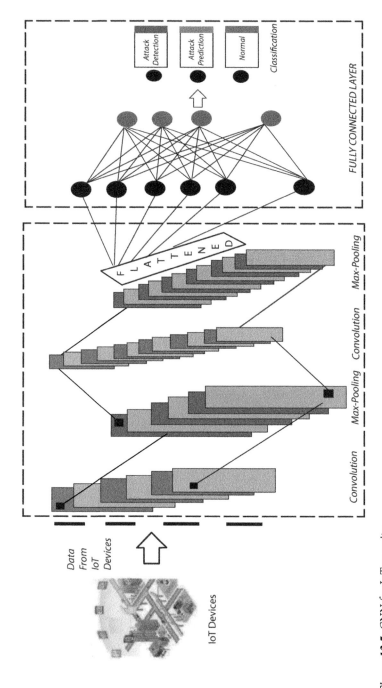

Figure 13.5 CNN for IoT security.

by max, global or average pooling [83]. A non-linear activation function is applied on every component of NN to determine if that element will fire or not. CNNs are capable of discerning attributes from large unlabeled samples. Multi CNN fusion model [84] is proposed to make IDS for IoT systems, the proposed methodology used data clustering to avoid the added relevance in dataset that usually occurs because of mapping one-dimensional features to two-dimensional and padding the redundant segment with zeros. Although the dataset used is NSL-KDD which is not a proper IoT dataset.

13.7.2.2   Auto Encoder (AE)

Auto Encoders comprise three layers: an input, at least one hidden, which is also known as code layer and an output layer [80], as shown in Figure 13.6. These are unsupervised Neural Network models and pick the important and unique details from the input to comprehend the mapping. The auto encoder model is bifurcated into two parts, encoder function and decoder function [85]. Encoder function f, will map the input data into a coded form, which can be illustrated by $h = f(x)$ and the decoder function, g, will recreate the input from the coded representation. The output is an approximate copy of input, where the model has to decide what features are to be imitated. Aminanto *et al.* [75] used AEs as classifier to build an IDS system Deep auto encoders were used to detect intrusion in the system. AEs were successful to assimilate latent characteristics and are capable of narrowing down the dimensionality.

13.7.2.3   Recurrent Neural Networks (RNNs)

Recurrent Neural Networks [86] are essentially developed to handle sequential data. RNNs are applied to a sequence of vectors, $x(t)$, t is time step indices, which ranges from 1 to τ [85]. RNNs are capable of memorizing the previous attributes and use the same to detect the features from current samples. As IoT devices generate huge amounts of sequential data, RNNs have been explored to detect the malicious nodes in network traffic. An IDS system has been proposed using RNN which outperformed traditional ML methodologies [87]. RNN-LSTM can be applied to detect four distinctive real time attacks [88], LSTM was trained to forecast new data features, and erratum were utilized to find anomalies. An architecture for IDS is proposed in [89] which is based on LSTM, authors have used KDD-cup 99 dataset to train the deep network. 41 attributes were being

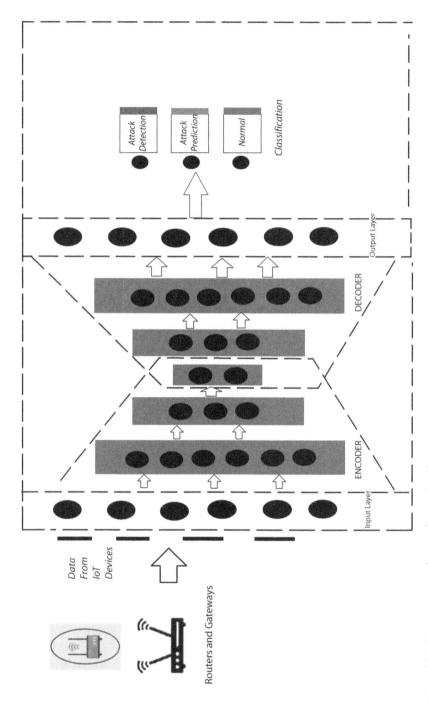

Figure 13.6 Deep auto encoders working principle.

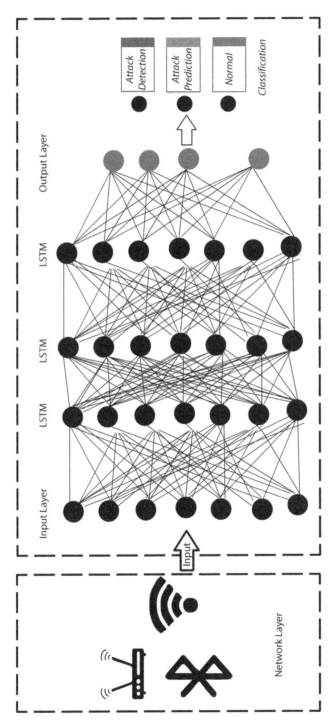

Figure 13.7 Illustration of RNN for IoT security.

used as an input to the neural network and the system performance was found to be 98.8%. Loukas *et al.* [90] proposed an IDS that evaluated RNN and deep MLP to for the cyber-physical intrusions for robotic vehicles. The proposed system gave more accuracy as compared to ML techniques. Figure 13.7 illustrates the use of RNN for IoT security.

13.7.2.4 *Restricted Boltzmann Machines (RBMs)*

Restricted Boltzmann machines [91] is a network of both visible and hidden layers, with no interconnection amongst the nodes of same layers, as shown in Figure 13.8. They can be deployed for classification and regression, and reduction of dimension for effective feature learning. Contrastive divergence technique is employed to train RBM networks. The said property of RBM is being used to discern the abnormality in the dynamic and unlabeled data. As RBMs have exactly a single hidden layer it is quite limited to develop an eloquent IDS system. However, by implementing more RBMs to form DBN which has been successful to realize powerful IDS.

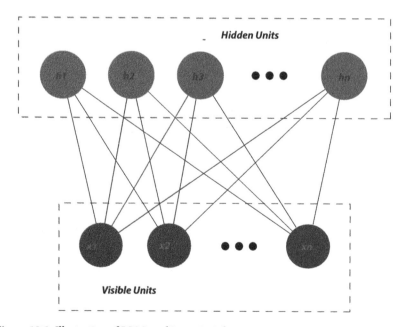

Figure 13.8 Illustration of RBM working principle.

13.7.2.5   Deep Belief Networks (DBNs)

DBN [86] is an unsupervised learning methodology, where more than two RBMs are stacked to form the network. Zhang and Wang [12] described an IDS based on GA and DBN, where the DBN were split in two steps for training, in first phase each RBM was trained distinctly and every trained layer formed as input to next layer this formed the stack of RBM once the appropriate criteria is met training is stopped, in next phase topmost layer of DBN is made as Back-Propagation NN. Proposed IDS system was able to reach 99% of detection. Each layer is trained in a greedy manner with unlabeled datasets. DBM is exploited for malware detection for edge computing [92], system was trained using 10 datasets and 500 malicious features, total 512 hidden layers were there in the NN. Another IDS using stacked RBM to form a DBN is proposed by Alom *et al.* [93]. NSL-KDD dataset was being used and five categories of attacks were classified. System was able to provide 97.5% accuracy in detecting anomalous activity.

13.7.2.6   Generative Adversarial Networks (GANs)

GANs [85] are generative framework that concurrently trains generative and discriminative models. Generative models are efficient to procreate data using random samples which are then fed into the discriminative model to adjudge the closeness with the authentic samples, as illustrated in Figure 13.9. This property of GANs make them useful to synthesize new attack samples for IDS systems. A "supply chain risk management architecture" [94] is proposed using GANs. An "operator-in-the-loop" architecture has been proposed which has consolidated various learning techniques to mitigate the vulnerabilities. Authors were able to get 91.83% accuracy in classifying the dataset.

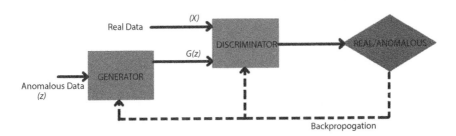

Figure 13.9 GAN working principles.

13.8   Challenges

This section enumerates concerns associated with ML/DL methodologies to extenuate security challenges of IoT systems, adequacy of datasets and computational complexities are discussed. Diverse ML/DL algorithms are there to choose from for the application. On that account, it is crucial to adopt an algorithm appropriate for securing the data. If the algorithm selected is not capable of doing the deliberate task it would not only be squander of efforts but the loss of effectiveness and reliability. Similarly, not just the algorithm but the dataset used for training should also be pre-processed properly (in case of ML) and must be free of ambiguous outliers. In this section we have discussed issues associated with using ML/DL algorithms.

13.8.1   IoT Dataset Unavailability

The biggest concern to develop an IDS system using ML/Dl algorithms is the availability of proper IoT datasets. As these algorithms learn the patterns and features from existing datasets, which is called as training of a model, for this purpose a security related dataset which is for IoT devices is the prior requirement. Many datasets have been artificially generated but they are not capable of providing the intricacies convoluted in real-time scenarios [95]. Particularly, to build a model for the supervised ML/DL methods the dataset should have a diverse pool of attacks. Although having an extensive dataset which is updating continuously is the major requirement, it is not feasible technically due to heterogeneity of IoT devices. Also, industries are skeptical in sharing these datasets to third parties for development as the intel present in these datasets are critical and can have sensitive information. Therefore, it becomes imperative to select a proper dataset for the training and evaluation purpose.

Table 13.5 shows the datasets available with their description and issues related to them.

13.8.2   Computational Complications

ML/DL deployment on IoT platforms not only requires memory, but it will consume more energy to implement for real time application [96]. Most of the studies that we have seen have used advanced GPUs for fast processing of these algorithms and employing them over light weight nodes is difficult. IoT devices deployed outside have limited resources and are power

Table 13.5 Datasets available for intrusion detection system.

Datasets	Description	Issues
KDD99	• Labeled dataset • 41 features • Dos, remote to user, Probing attacks are implemented	Obsolete and no proper classification
NSL-KDD	• Advanced version of KDD 99 dataset. • No duplicate records	No advanced attacks and not for IoT systems
UNS-WNB15	• Nine different attacks • Modern and contemporary synthetic attacks	Complex in nature as compared to KDD99
Sivanathan et al. [110] Dataset	• Real world dataset • Network layer data	Unlabeled data but for traffic characterization
CICIDS	• Labeled Dataset • Machine and deep learning purpose. • Implements attacks such as Brute Force FTP, Brute Force SSH, DoS, Heartbleed, Web Attack, Infiltration, Botnet and DDoS.	Private data not available to public

hungry devices, which will restrict the acceptance of these techniques. The current security measures for IoT devices is to move it to cloud computing but it is an overhead for cloud and is completely relying upon the network operability. Latency is also high when data is moved to cloud and some critical applications that need immediate response cannot wait for cloud to take the decision and send it back. Hence, if the network is not available or weak it would lead to unreachable end nodes. Another solution could be implementation of mobile GPUs [97], which is again energy consuming. Thus, needs for developing an IDS system which is computationally inexpensive and can also anticipate real time attack detection.

13.8.3   Forensics Challenges

IoT will soon be managing every aspect of our livelihood not just the smart cities or homes but the individuals too. IoT has its presence across various zones like, cloud, network and physical nodes [98]. These devices will be useful in discovering unknown facts for better investigation in case of any offense. However, as the heterogeneity and vast number of IoT devices which are laid down at various locations it would become strenuous for the forensic team to get the hold of evidence. Moreover, the new IoT devices do not succor to current digital forensics tools which will make it difficult to unsheathe the data from these devices. Also, this will open a complete new paradigm for intruders to attack and hamper the device [99] discussed prime forensics issues and proposed a reassuring solution to deploy a secure IoT system. Scouring the evidence and preserving them for further examination is a major step for identifying the crime that occurred. As IoT devices are spread across the system and are designed to work autonomously [99], there is no proper tool to gather the vestigial evidence. Moreover, restricted sources are available to collect data from IoT devices without invading the privacy of others in a multi-user environment. Also, preserving the scene of interest becomes non-viable owing to the no well-defined boundaries. For analyzing any crime scene knowing the temporal information is must. And most of the IoT end nodes do not store any time related information like when it got initiated retrieved or modified its challenging to gather the information and co relate it. Apart from correlation challenges, limiting the boundaries and getting the information without hampering personal data is a major problem [99].

13.9   Future Prospects

In the following section we will discuss future prospects that can be implemented to mitigate the challenges encountered to deploy ML/DL in the IoT systems. ML/DL have so far proved to be promising technologies however due to the lack of resources in IoT it becomes difficult to have a full-fledged IDS for the resource constrained IoT nodes. Kumari *et al.* [100] suggested link prediction method for fraud detection in social media. Moreover, ML technologies are found to be good at breaking encrypted systems which can also attract new kind of vulnerabilities to the IoT systems. To avoid such problems, we can implement other techniques in collaboration with the ML/DL methods to have a secured and robust system such as blockchain, edge or fog computation to get the desired result.

The following section discusses future opportunities in the security framework. Figure 13.10 shows the implementation of ML/DL with other advanced technologies.

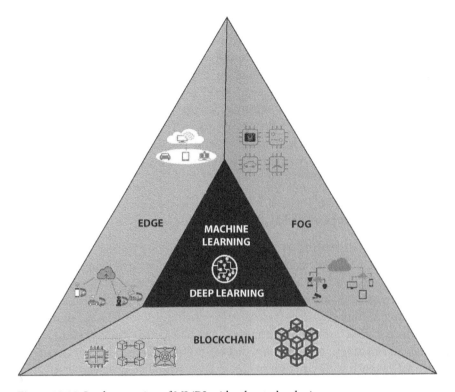

Figure 13.10 Implementation of ML/DL with other technologies.

13.9.1   Implementation of ML/DL With Edge Computing

Data transmission from IoT nodes to centralized cloud with restricted network availability and doing computations at centralized structure makes it difficult to realize the security framework at distinct layers of IoT environment. Use of edge computing transfers computing assignment to nearby nodes and will reduce the overhead of the cloud by processing the data locally. Edge server is positioned between the end-user and cloud, processing of data will take place at the edge server. IoT applications create a large amount of information at an immense rate. Majority of this information is unprocessed and are comparatively insignificant. Transmitting all the information over the cloud would consume more bandwidth, and would poses more security threats. If edge computing is used, then a lot of data cleaning and aggregation can be done at the edge nodes and only the summarized data, if required, needs to be sent to the cloud. The edge computing can perform well when the intermediate data size is smaller than the input data size and as we talk about DL owing to the architecture of deep neural network, they are capable of reducing data size by individual layer and also finding the important features required. Moreover, implementing ML/DL at the edge has become crucial to minimize network delays and provide as good as real time realization of attack detection. Edge computing relocates security allocation to the edge from the cloud, which could be a prospective answer to security solution [71]. Though, this technology is at inception and an exhaustive research in edge computing is required to find a promising solution for the lightweight nodes of IoT.

13.9.2   Integration of ML/DL With Blockchain

Blockchain is emanating as a promising technology to provide a secured operation in a network using cryptography. A blockchain provides a "digital ledger" [101], which is known to every device present in the network. It is a decentralized way of authorizing and authenticating the transactions, providing a more robust infrastructure which does not depend upon single consent. It is formed by a series of data blocks that are timestamped to store data of assets and transactions on the network where continuity is formed by hash to the previous block. Each stored transaction is verified and validated by consensus of miner nodes on the network [14]. This also enables blockchain technology to eliminate involvement of trusted third parties which could also be vulnerable at times. Smart city security framework proposed by Biswas and Muthukkumarasamy [102] suggested the use of multiple blockchains in the access layer for integration of existing communication protocols and private ledgers for database. The classic features provided by blockchain included resiliency against attacks, reliability, speed of operations, efficiency and scalability.

As IoT systems are heterogeneous updating the software and developing a trusted management it is preferable to implement a system that is not centralized in nature. Hence, blockchain is more advisable to have a 'tamper-proof transaction" [103]. The objective of ML/DL technology is to make the devices independent and intelligent so that they can act spontaneously for making it smart and secure [104]. Blockchain based scheme is proposed by Bahga and Madisetti [105] for industrial IoT, experiments were performed on Arduino Uno board and Ethereum smart contracts to demonstrate the working of smart transactions and maintenance. Another study [106] proposed a bitcoin ledger as per smart home perspective for smart transactions and an analysis was done for secured and private framework. Blockchain based smart home case study was carried out with analysis of security and privacy. They successfully achieved user control and authorization with blockchain in addition to CIA.

13.9.3 Integration of ML/DL With Fog Computing

Fog computing is arising as a promising technology to compliment the cloud technology, as the number of IoT devices is growing day-by-day data generated from these devices is increasing multifold. This is becoming an overhead for cloud to store and process the data. Storing this data at cloud and processing this high volume of data at real time is not reasonable. The benefit of having Fog architecture is to manage all time critical information locally in an efficient way [107]. In many scenarios it is required to have an instantaneous feedback, e.g., in case of an accident air bags must deploy immediately as soon as the sensors senses it, and waiting for the decision to come from cloud could be lethal. Fog Computing enables instant decision-making [108]. It prevents data theft likely to occur during transaction from IoT nodes to cloud by processing it at fog nodes. Fog computing was first introduced by CISCO in 2012, which can handle the huge data locally for prudent management. Fog computing can be realized as Fog-Device or Fog-Cloud-Device architecture [109]. The first framework has fog and devices, services are provided by fog nodes and there is no involvement of cloud while as latter one has cloud, fog and devices, only simple decisions are made at fog and decisions requiring complex computation and more storage can be send to cloud. As we are aware that IoT devices have limited resources which makes it difficult to deploy advanced and heavy computational algorithms in them, and hence they rely on cloud but when information needs to get processed early and is time critical then employing fog nodes can provide immediate response. Many attacks such as Man-in-the-middle, eavesdropping, transit attacks, etc. can also be avoided by saving the information at fog nodes.

13.10 Conclusion

The emanation of the IoT standard has opened various windows for intruders to breach the security. As per the various studies, a systematic organization of security threats is lacking. The security of IoT devices depends upon various factors, physical nodes, cloud transmission and end users' application. It is challenging to deploy updated algorithms that can provide security without consuming more energy and resources on the IoT environment. Security requirement at every layer of IoT has added to the complexity to develop a powerful IDS system. Smart Cities are prone to various attacks and the requirement to make a robust and secured architecture is the need of the hour. Developments in the field of ML/DL have shown a reassuring solution to depict the anomalies in the IoT environment. This chapter has done a comprehensive study of IoT attacks with the potential ML/DL methods that are already proposed by various researchers or can be further developed to have a secured IoT system. Lastly, an exhaustive list of various ML/DL techniques is presented which can be independently or connected with other methodology to secure the IoT environment to make a secured "Smart City". In this chapter we discussed the principal security threats seen by IoT while focusing on its application in smart cities. In order to consider all possible security incidents, we took into account a layered architecture of IoT and classify attacks and vulnerabilities discussed in the literature. However, the key contribution of this chapter includes providing a comprehensive review of methods proposed to provide ML/DL based models for secure IoT environment. The analysis is presented by comparison of advantages of the various algorithms and their application scenarios. The sole objective of this chapter is to evaluate the issues that are found at various levels of IoT and how ML/DL technologies can help in mitigating the issues. Owing to memory and energy consumption an exhaustive detection techniques cannot be deployed to the physical devices of IoT, hence a lightweight and flexible IDS needs to be developed.

References

1. Solanki, A. and Nayyar, A., Green Internet of Things (G-IoT): ICT Technologies, Principles, Applications, Projects, and Challenges, in: *Handbook of Research on Big Data and the IoT*, G. Kaur, and P. Tomar, (Eds.), pp. 379–405, IGI Global, Hershey, PA, USA, 2019.
2. Ullah, F., Al-Turjman, F., Nayyar, A., IoT-based green city architecture using secured and sustainable android services. *Environ. Technol. Innov.*, 20, 101091, 2020.
3. Yavuz, F.Y., *Nesnelerin İnternetinin Siber Güvenliği için Derin Öğrenme*, Tübitak, Istanbul, 2018.
4. Al-garadi, M.A., Mohamed, A., Al-ali, A., Du, X., Guizani, M., Surveys, in: *Underst. Commun. Res. Methods A Theor. Pract. Approach*, pp. 222–237, 2014.
5. Bandyopadhyay, S., Sengupta, M., Maiti, S., Dutta, S., Role Of Middleware For Internet Of Things: A Study. *Int. J. Comput. Sci. Eng. Surv.*, 2, 3, 94–105, 2011.

6. *I. Security and T. Report*, no. April, p. 10, ISTR Symantec, Mountain View, CA, United Stated of America, 2017, [Online]. Available: https://www.symantec.com/content/dam/symantec/docs/reports/istr-22-2017-en.pdf.

7. Abomhara, M. and Køien, G.M., Cyber security and the internet of things: Vulnerabilities, threats, intruders and attacks. *J. Cyber Secur. Mobil.*, 4, 1, 65–88, 2015.

8. Ray, S., Jin, Y., Raychowdhury, A., The Changing Computing Paradigm with Internet of Things: A Tutorial Introduction. *IEEE Des. Test*, 33, 2, 76–96, 2016.

9. Hou, J., Qu, L., Shi, W., A survey on internet of things security from data perspectives. *Comput. Networks*, 148, 295–306, 2019.

10. Yavuz, F.Y., Ünal, D., Gül, E., Deep learning for detection of routing attacks in the internet of things. *Int. J. Comput. Intell. Syst.*, 12, 1, 39–58, 2018.

11. Rathore, S. and Park, J.H., Semi-supervised learning based distributed attack detection framework for IoT. *Appl. Soft Comput. J.*, 72, 79–89, 2018.

12. Zhang, Y., Li, P., Wang, X., Intrusion Detection for IoT Based on Improved Genetic Algorithm and Deep Belief Network. *IEEE Access*, 7, 31711–31722, 2019.

13. Greenstein, B., Kohno, T., McCoy, D., Seshan, S., Pang, J., Wetherall, D., Improving wireless privacy with an identifier-free link layer protocol. *MobiSys'08 - Proc. 6th Int. Conf. Mob. Syst. Appl. Serv*, pp. 40–53, 2008.

14. Khan, M.A. and Salah, K., IoT security: Review, blockchain solutions, and open challenges. *Future Gener. Comput. Syst.*, 82, November, 395–411, 2018.

15. Ferrag, M.A. and Maglaras, L., DeepCoin: A Novel Deep Learning and Blockchain-Based Energy Exchange Framework for Smart Grids. *IEEE Trans. Eng. Manag.*, 67, 1–13, 2019.

16. Yang, L., Elisa, N., Eliot, N., Privacy and security aspects of E-government in smart cities, in: *Smart Cities Cybersecurity Priv*, no. June, pp. 89–102, 2018.

17. Wickramasinghe, C.S., Marino, D.L., Amarasinghe, K., Manic, M., Generalization of deep learning for cyber-physical system security: A survey. *Proc. IECON 2018—44th Annu. Conf. IEEE Ind. Electron. Soc*, no. May 2019, pp. 745–751, 2018.

18. Shafique, M., Khalid, F., Rehman, S., Intelligent security measures for smart cyber physical systems. *Proc.—21st Euromicro Conf. Digit. Syst. Des. DSD 2018*, pp. 280–287, 2018.

19. Kumar, V., Jha, R.K., Jain, S., NB-IoT Security: A Survey. *Wireless Pers. Commun.*, 113, 2, 1–48, 2020.

20. Alaba, F.A., Othman, M., Hashem, I.A.T., Alotaibi, F., Internet of Things security: A survey. *J. Netw. Comput. Appl.*, 88, 10–28, 2017.

21. Ezema, E., Abdullah, A., Mohd, N.F.B., Open Issues and Security Challenges of Data Communication Channels in Distributed Internet of Things (IoT): A Survey. *Circ. Comput. Sci.*, 3, 1, 22–32, 2018.

22. Hassija, V., Chamola, V., Saxena, V., Jain, D., A Survey on IoT Security: Application Areas, Security Threats, and Solution Architectures. *IEEE Access*, 7, 82721–82743, 2019.

23. Hamad, S.A., Sheng, Q.Z., Zhang, W.E., Nepal, S., Realizing an Internet of Secure Things: A Survey on Issues and Enabling Technologies. *IEEE Commun. Surv. Tutorials*, 22, 2, 1372–1391, 2020.

24. Krishnamurthi, R., Nayyar, A., Solanki, A., *Innovation Opportunities through Internet of Things (IoT) for Smart Cities. Green and Smart Technologies for Smart Cities*, pp. 261–292, CRC Press, Boca Raton, FL, USA, 2019.

25. Rathee, D., Ahuja, K., Nayyar, A., Sustainable future IoT services with touch-enabled handheld devices, *Security and Privacy of Electronic Healthcare Records: Concepts, Paradigms and Solutions*, 131, 131–152, 2019.

26. Al-Fuqaha, A., Guizani, M., Mohammadi, M., Aledhari, M., Ayyash, M., Internet of Things: A Survey on Enabling Technologies, Protocols, and Applications. *IEEE Commun. Surv. Tutorials*, 17, 4, 2347–2376, 2015.

27. Jabraeil Jamali, M.A., IoT Security—Huawey, in: *Towar. Internet Things*, pp. 33–83, 2020.

28. Kumar, A., Sangwan, S.R., Nayyar, A., *Multimedia Big Data Computing for IoT Applications*, vol. 163, no. July 2019, Springer, Singapore, 2020.

29. Nayyar, A., Jain, R., Mahapatra, B., Singh, A., Cyber Security Challenges for Smart Cities, *Driving the Development, Management, and Sustainability of Cognitive Cities*, pp. 27–54, IGI Global, Hershey, PA, USA, 2019.

30. Sethi, P. and Sarangi, S.R., Internet of Things: Architectures, Protocols, and Applications, *J. Electr. Comput. Eng.*, 2017, 9324035:1-9324035:25, 2017.

31. Zeng, D., Guo, S., Cheng, Z., The web of things: A survey. *J. Commun.*, 6, 6, 424–438, 2011.

32. Neely, S., Dobson, S., Nixon, P., Adaptive middleware for autonomic systems. *Ann. Telecommun. Telecommun.*, 61, 9–10, 1099–1118, 2006.

33. Almiani, M., AbuGhazleh, A., Al-Rahayfeh, A., Atiewi, S., Razaque, A., Deep recurrent neural network for IoT intrusion detection system. *Simul. Model. Pract. Theory*, 101, Article 102031, November, 2020.

34. Aly, M., Khomh, F., Haoues, M., Quintero, A., Yacout, S., Enforcing security in Internet of Things frameworks: A Systematic Literature Review. *Internet Things*, 101, 6, 100050, 2019.

35. Carlin, A., Hammoudeh, M., Aldabbas, O., Defence for Distributed Denial of Service Attacks in Cloud Computing. *Procedia Comput. Sci.*, 73, 490–497, 2015.

36. Porter, T. and Gough, M., Chapter 7—Active Security Monitoring, in: *How to Cheat*, T. Porter, M.B.T.-H. @ to C, V.S. Gough, (Eds.), pp. 185–206, Syngress, Burlington, 2007.

37. Zhao, D. Traore, I., Sayed, B., Lu, W., Saad, S., Ghorbani, A., & Garant, D., Botnet detection based on traffic behavior analysis and flow intervals. *Comput. Secur.*, 39, 2–16, 2013.

38. Babar, S., Stango, A., Prasad, N., Sen, J., Prasad, R., Proposed embedded security framework for Internet of Things (IoT). *2011 2nd Int. Conf. Wirel. Commun. Veh. Technol. Inf. Theory Aerosp. Electron. Syst. Technol. Wirel. VITAE 2011*, no. February, 2011.

39. Altawy, R. and Youssef, A.M., Security Tradeoffs in Cyber Physical Systems: A Case Study Survey on Implantable Medical Devices. *IEEE Access*, 4, 959–979, 2016.

40. Li, S., *Security Requirements in IoT Architecture*, Elsevier Inc., Virginia, USA, 2017.

41. Nawir, M., Amir, A., Yaakob, N., Lynn, O.B., Engineering, C., *2016 3rd International Conference on Electronic Design, ICED 2016, 2016 3rd Int. Conf. Electron. Des. ICED 2016*, pp. 321–326, 2017.

42. Fosso Wamba, S., Anand, A., Carter, L., A literature review of RFID-enabled healthcare applications and issues. *Int. J. Inf. Manage.*, 33, 5, 875–891, 2013.

43. Malasri, K. and Wang, L., Securing wireless implantable devices for healthcare: Ideas and challenges [Accepted from Open Call]. *IEEE Commun. Mag.*, 47, 7, 74–80, 2009.

44. Jordan, M.I. and Mitchell, T.M., Machine learning: Trends, perspectives, and prospects. *Science*, 17, 349, 6245, 255–260, 2015.

45. Alzubi, J., Nayyar, A., Kumar, A., Machine Learning from Theory to Algorithms: An Overview. *J. Phys. Conf. Ser.*, 1142, 1, 012012, 2018.

46. Kim, G., Lee, S., Kim, S., A novel hybrid intrusion detection method integrating anomaly detection with misuse detection. *Expert Syst. Appl.*, 41, 4 PART 2, 1690–1700, 2014.

47. Goeschel, K., Reducing false positives in intrusion detection systems using data-mining techniques utilizing support vector machines, decision trees, and naive Bayes for off-line analysis. *Conf. Proc.—IEEE SOUTHEASTCON*, vol. 2016-July, 2016.

48. Syarif, A.R. and Gata, W., Intrusion detection system using hybrid binary PSO and K-nearest neighborhood algorithm, in: *2017 11th International Conference on Information & Communication Technology and System (ICTS)*, pp. 181–186, 2017

49. Liu, L. *et al.*, Toward Highly Secure Yet Efficient KNN Classification Scheme on Outsourced Cloud Data. *IEEE Internet Things J.*, 6, 6, 9841–9852, 2019.

50. Derhab, A. *et al.*, Blockchain and Random Subspace Learning-Based IDS for SDN-Enabled Industrial IoT Security. *Sensors (Switzerland)*, 19, 14, 1–24, 2019.

51. Primartha, R. and Tama, B.A., Anomaly detection using random forest: A performance revisited, in: *2017 International Conference on Data and Software Engineering (ICoDSE)*, pp. 1–6, 2017.

52. Domb, M., Bonchek-Dokow, E., Leshem, G., Lightweight adaptive Random-Forest for IoT rule generation and execution. *J. Inf. Secur. Appl.*, 34, 218–224, 2017.

53. Hoang, D.H. and Nguyen, H.D., A PCA-based method for IoT network traffic anomaly detection. *Int. Conf. Adv. Commun. Technol. ICACT*, vol. 2018-Febru, no. February, pp. 381–386, 2018.

54. Swarna Priya, R.M. *et al.*, An effective feature engineering for DNN using hybrid PCA-GWO for intrusion detection in IoMT architecture. *Comput. Commun.*, 160, May, 139–149, 2020.

55. Mukherjee, S. and Sharma, N., Intrusion Detection using Naive Bayes Classifier with Feature Reduction. *Procedia Technol.*, 4, 119–128, 2012.

56. Shen, M., Tang, X., Zhu, L., Du, X., Guizani, M., Privacy-Preserving Support Vector Machine Training Over Blockchain-Based Encrypted IoT Data in Smart Cities. *IEEE Internet Things J.*, 6, 5, 7702–7712, 2019.

57. Bielza, C. and Shenoy, P.P., Comparison of graphical techniques for asymmetric decision problems. *Manage. Sci.*, 45, 11, 1552–1569, 1999.

58. Kotsiantis, S.B., Zaharakis, I.D., Pintelas, P.E., Machine learning: A review of classification and combining techniques. *Artif. Intell. Rev.*, 26, 3, 159–190, 2006.

59. Soucy, P. and Mineau, G.W., A simple KNN algorithm for text categorization. *Proc.—IEEE Int. Conf. Data Mining, ICDM*, pp. 647–648, 2001.

60. Deng, Z., Zhu, X., Cheng, D., Zong, M., Zhang, S., Efficient kNN classification algorithm for big data. *Neurocomputing*, 195, 143–148, 2016.

61. Breiman, L., ST4_Method_Random_Forest. *Mach. Learn.*, 45, 1, 5–32, 2001.

62. Buczak, A.L. and Guven, E., A Survey of Data Mining and Machine Learning Methods for Cyber Security Intrusion Detection. *IEEE Commun. Surv. Tutorials*, 18, 2, 1153–1176, 2016.

63. Jagannath, J., Polosky, N., Jagannath, A., Restuccia, F., Melodia, T., Machine learning for wireless communications in the Internet of Things: A comprehensive survey. *Ad Hoc Networks*, 93, arXiv:1901.07947, 2019.

64. Wold, S., Esbensen, K., Geladi, P., Decret_Du_7_Mai_1993_Fixant_Les_Modalites_D_Application_De_La_Loi_Relative_Aux_Recensements_Et_Enquetes_Statistiques.Pdf. *Chemom. Intell. Lab. Syst.*, 2, 1–3, 37–52, 1987.

65. Hussain, F., Hussain, R., Hassan, S.A., Hossain, E., Machine Learning in IoT Security: Current Solutions and Future Challenges. *IEEE Commun. Surv. Tutorials*, 22, 3, 1–23, 2020.

66. Mehmood, A., Mukherjee, M., Ahmed, S.H., Song, H., Malik, K.M., NBC-MAIDS: Naïve Bayesian classification technique in multi-agent system-enriched IDS for securing IoT against DDoS attacks. *J. Supercomput.*, 74, 10, 5156–5170, 2018.

67. Agrawal, S. and Agrawal, J., Survey on anomaly detection using data mining techniques. *Procedia Comput. Sci.*, 60, 1, 708–713, 2015.

68. Panda, M., Abraham, A., Das, S., Patra, M.R., Network intrusion detection system: A machine learning approach. *Intell. Decis. Technol.*, 5, 4, 347–356, 2011.

69. Tong, S. and Koller, D., Support vector machine active learning with applications to text classification. *J. Mach. Learn. Res.*, 2, 1, 45–66, 2002.

70. Sahu, M.K., Ahirwar, M., Shukla, P.K., Improved malware detection technique using ensemble based classifier and graph theory. *Proc.—2015 IEEE Int. Conf. Comput. Intell. Commun. Technol. CICT 2015*, pp. 150–154, 2015.

71. Li, H., Ota, K., Dong, M., Learning IoT in Edge: Deep Learning for the Internet of Things with Edge Computing. *IEEE Network*, 32, 1, 96–101, 2018.

72. Picek, S., Samiotis, I.P., Kim, J., Heuser, A., Bhasin, S., Legay, A., On the performance of convolutional neural networks for side-channel analysis. *Lect. Notes Comput. Sci. (including Subser. Lect. Notes Artif. Intell. Lect. Notes Bioinformatics)*, 11348 LNCS, 157–176, 2018.

73. Tian, Y., Yuan, J., Yu, S., Hou, Y., LEP-CNN: A Lightweight Edge Device Assisted Privacy-preserving CNN Inference Solution for IoT, arXiv:1901.04100, 2019. [Online]. Available: http://arxiv.org/abs/1901.04100.

74. Torres, P., Catania, C., Garcia, S., Garino, C.G., An analysis of Recurrent Neural Networks for Botnet detection behavior. *2016 IEEE Bienn. Congr. Argentina, ARGENCON 2016*, 2016.

75. Aminanto, M.E. and Kim, K., Deep Learning-based Feature Selection for Intrusion Detection System in Transport Layer 1, *Proceedings of the Summer Conference of Korea Information Security Society (CISC-S'16)*, 535–538, 2016.

76. Abeshu, A. and Chilamkurti, N., Deep Learning: The Frontier for Distributed Attack Detection in Fog-To-Things Computing. *IEEE Commun. Mag.*, 56, 2, 169–175, 2018.

77. Li, L., Hu, X., Chen, K., He, K., The applications of WiFi-based Wireless Sensor Network in Internet of Things and Smart Grid. *Proc. 2011 6th IEEE Conf. Ind. Electron. Appl. ICIEA 2011*, pp. 789–793, 2011.

78. Kalyani, G. and Chaudhari, S., An efficient approach for enhancing security in Internet of Things using the optimum authentication key. *Int. J. Comput. Appl.*, 42, 3, 306–314, Apr. 2020.

79. He, Y., Mendis, G.J., Wei, J., Real-Time Detection of False Data Injection Attacks in Smart Grid: A Deep Learning-Based Intelligent Mechanism. *IEEE Trans. Smart Grid*, 8, 5, 2505–2516, 2017.

80. Lecun, Y., Bottou, L., Bengio, Y., Haffner, P., Gradient-based learning applied to document recognition, in *Proceedings of the IEEE*, vol. 86, no. 11, pp. 2278–2324, 1998.

81. Zhang, Q., Zhang, M., Chen, T., Sun, Z., Ma, Y., Yu, B., Recent advances in convolutional neural network acceleration. *Neurocomputing*, 323, 37–51, 2019.

82. Chen, X.W. and Lin, X., Big data deep learning: Challenges and perspectives. *IEEE Access*, 2, 514–525, 2014.

83. Cires, D.C., Meier, U., Masci, J., Gambardella, L.M., IJCAI11-210.pdf. *Proc. Twenty-Second Int. Jt. Conf. Artif. Intell. Flex*, pp. 1237–1242, 2003.

84. Li, Y. *et al.*, Robust detection for network intrusion of industrial IoT based on multi-CNN fusion. *Meas. J. Int. Measurement Confederation*, 154, 107450, 2020.

85. LeCun, Y., Bengio, Y., Hinton, G., Deep learning. *Nature*, 521, 7553, 436–444, 2015.

86. Rumelhart, D.E., Hinton, G.E., Williams, R.J., Learning representations by back-propagating errors. *Nature*, 323, 6088, 533–536, 1986.

87. Yin, C., Zhu, Y., Fei, J., He, X., A Deep Learning Approach for Intrusion Detection Using Recurrent Neural Networks. *IEEE Access*, 5, 21954–21961, 2017.

88. Guizani, N. and Ghafoor, A., A network function virtualization system for detecting malware in large IoT based networks. *IEEE J. Sel. Areas Commun.*, 38, 6, 1218–1228, 2020.

89. Kim, J., Kim, J., Thu, H.L.T., Kim, H., Long Short Term Memory Recurrent Neural Network Classifier for Intrusion Detection. *2016 Int. Conf. Platf. Technol. Serv. PlatCon 2016 - Proc*, September 2017, 2016.

90. Loukas, G., Vuong, T., Heartfield, R., Sakellari, G., Yoon, Y., Gan, D., Cloud-Based Cyber-Physical Intrusion Detection for Vehicles Using Deep Learning. *IEEE Access*, 6, 3491–3508, 2017.

91. Smolensky, P., *Information Processing in Dynamical Systems: Foundations of Harmony Theory*, University of Colorado at older Information Processing in Dynamical Systems: Foundations of Harmony, no. 667, University of Colorado at Boulder, 1986.

92. Chen, Y., Zhang, Y., Maharjan, S., Deep Learning for Secure Mobile Edge Computing. 1–7, arXiv:1709.08025 v1, 2017. [Online]. Available: http://arxiv.org/abs/1709.08025.

93. Alom, M.Z., Bontupalli, V., Taha, T.M., Intrusion detection using deep belief networks, in: *2015 National Aerospace and Electronics Conference (NAECON)*, pp. 339–344, 2015.

94. Hiromoto, R.E., Haney, M., Vakanski, A., A secure architecture for IoT with supply chain risk management. *Proc. 2017 IEEE 9th Int. Conf. Intell. Data Acquis. Adv. Comput. Syst. Technol. Appl. IDAACS 2017*, vol. 1, pp. 431–435, 2017.

95. Jain, A. and Nayyar, A., Machine Learning and Its Applicability in Networking, in: *New Age Anal*, no. May, pp. 57–79, 2020.

96. Lane, N.D. *et al.*, DeepX: A Software Accelerator for Low-Power Deep Learning Inference on Mobile Devices, in: *2016 15th ACM/IEEE International Conference on Information Processing in Sensor Networks (IPSN)*, pp. 1–12, 2016.

97. Sha, K., Yang, T.A., Wei, W., Davari, S., A survey of edge computing-based designs for IoT security. *Digit. Commun. Netw.*, 6, 2, 195–202, 2020.

98. Alabdulsalam, S., Schaefer, K., Kechadi, T., Le, N.A., Internet of Things Forensics: Challenges. no. June, 1–13, arXiv:1801.10391, 2017.

99. Conti, M., Dehghantanha, A., Franke, K., Watson, S., Internet of Things security and forensics: Challenges and opportunities. *Future Gener. Comput. Syst.*, 78, 544–546, 2018.

100. Kumari, A., Behera, R., Sahoo, K., Nayyar, A., Luhach, A., Sahoo, S., Supervised link prediction using structured-based feature extraction in social network. *Concurr. Comp. Pract. E.*, Special Issue Paper, Jun. 2020.

101. Zyskind, G. and Pentland, A.S., Decentralizing Privacy: Using Blockchain to Protect Personal Data, *IEEE Symposium on Security and Privacy Workshops*, pp. 180–184, 2015.

102. Biswas, K. and Muthukkumarasamy, V., Securing Smart Cities Using Blockchain Technology, in: *2016 IEEE 18th International Conference on High Performance Computing and Communications; IEEE 14th International Conference on Smart City; IEEE 2nd International Conference on Data Science and Systems (HPCC/SmartCity/DSS)*, pp. 1392–1393, 2016

103. Kshetri, N., Can Blockchain Strengthen the Internet of Things? *IT Prof.*, 19, 4, 68–72, 2017.

104. Nayyar, A., Rameshwar, R., Solanki, A., Internet of Things (IoT) and the Digital Business Environment: A Standpoint Inclusive Cyber Space, Cyber Crimes, and Cybersecurity, *The Evolution of Business in the Cyber Age*, 10.1201/9780429276484-6, January. 2020.

105. Bahga, A. and Madisetti, V.K., Blockchain Platform for Industrial Internet of Things. *J. Softw. Eng. Appl.*, 09, 10, 533–546, 2016.

106. Dorri, A., Sydney, U., Dorri, A., Kanhere, S.S., Jurdak, R., Gauravaram, P., Blockchain for IoT Security and Privacy: The Case Study of a Smart Home, *IEEE Percom Workshop on Security Privacy and Trust in the Internet of Thing*, January, 2017.

107. Singh, S.P., Nayyar, A., Kumar, R., Sharma, A., Fog computing: From architecture to edge computing and big data processing. *J. Supercomput.*, 75, 4, 2070–2105, 2019.

108. Kaur, A., Singh, P., Nayyar, A., Fog Computing: Building a Road to IoT with Fog Analytics Fog Computing: Building a Road to IoT, *Fog Data Analytics for IoT Applications*. pp. 59–78, August, 2020.

109. Ren, J., Guo, H., Xu, C., Zhang, Y., Serving at the Edge: A Scalable IoT Architecture Based on Transparent Computing. *IEEE Network*, 31, 5, 96–105, 2017.

110. Sivanathan, A., Sherratt, D., Gharakheili, H. H., Radford, A., Wijenayake, C., Vishwanath, A., & Sivaraman, V. (2017, May). Characterizing and classifying IoT traffic in smart cities and campuses. In *2017 IEEE Conference on Computer Communications Workshops (INFOCOM WKSHPS)* (pp. 559-564). IEEE.

14

Role of Smart Buildings in Smart City— Components, Technology, Indicators, Challenges, Future Research Opportunities

Tarana Singh*, Arun Solanki and Sanjay Kumar Sharma

Department of CSE, Gautam Buddha University, Greater Noida, India

Abstract

The connected future of smart cities starts with smart buildings. Nowadays, "Smart City" initiatives are growing around the globe. In order to have smart cities, it's important to understand the most fundamental part of them that is smart buildings. Smart Building is the foundational "building block" that will enable a true transformation of our cities through which one can have safe, sustainable, connected, and smart environments for the majority of the world's population as the buildings get smarter across the world. Behind the smartness of the buildings in the smart cities, there are various indicators involved. There are various supporting technologies and requirements of Smart Buildings for Smart cities. There are various factors also which buildup a smart building for a smart city. This chapter represents various indicators, technologies, components, features of smart buildings in smart cities. Then general architectures are being discussed. At the end of the chapter, different challenges followed by future research opportunities in the domain are being discussed.

Keywords: Smart city, smart building, Internet of Things, machine learning, deep learning, security and privacy

14.1 Introduction

Smart Buildings are the brain of Smart city (SC). Without smart structures, a genuinely smart city can't exist. These structures utilize computerized

*Corresponding author: taranasingh14@gmail.com

Arun Solanki, Adarsh Kumar and Anand Nayyar (eds.) Digital Cities Roadmap: IoT-Based Architecture and Sustainable Buildings, (449–476) © 2021 Scrivener Publishing LLC

cycles to naturally control the structure's activities like warming, ventilation, cooling, lighting, security and different frameworks. These structures are otherwise called the self-ruling structures and are the vital chess pieces that form the establishment of a genuinely (SC) [1]. Smart structures collaborate with the individuals, frameworks and outside components around them. These structures gain knowledge from the past encounters and ongoing data sources and receive to the need of individuals and organizations inside them by expanding comfort, productivity, flexibility and security. Today, there is another need to shield individuals from COVID-19. At the point when the innovation is being utilized to help the individuals in structures, this makes a domain which thinks about the predetermined destinations. The smart structures empower contact following, space use, without settling on prosperity. Healthcare associations and organizations around the globe have gone to contact following and physical separating measures to stop the chain of transmission of the infection. At the point when the IoT sensors are coordinated, physical separating measures set up can likewise be overseen by building administrators through experiences gave by information on the usage of rooms or regular office spaces. The comfortable workspace application permits structures administrators and owners to draw in with inhabitants and keep them educated, protected and gainful [2].

The smart buildings help to make the structures a solid and safe spot for the individuals. The estimates are taken against the spread of the COVID power building administrators and office directors to re-examine building a work environment technique. The health and security of representatives, collaborators and buyers is the primary goal. The activities of the people practicing physical separating and expanded cleanliness measures can be hugely supported by smart building innovation. The contributions on warming, ventilation and cooling, room robotization and building the board frameworks help make sound, profitable, maintainable situations and safe working environments for individuals to re-visitation of after the emergency and beyond [3]. Smart Buildings framework empowers reliable quality and flexibility of the structure's foundation. To see how advancements can uphold the virtual workplaces, the information abilities of smart structures along with building mechanization empower online tasks which demonstrate its significance in the current pandemic.

Advancements in smart buildings reinforce identification and restricting the spread of infection. The requirement for internal heat level discovery will end up being critical as work environments, air terminals and restaurants re-opening. To moderate any dangers brought about by the spread of the infection, innovations which take into consideration productive scanning of temperatures as inhabitants and guests enter the building will be deployed. The association of the human body internal heat level recognition with access control empowers an exceptionally secure and uncountable arrangement [4]. The information produced from smart structures might be changed into financial advantages. Smart foundation can change urban communities and enterprises. In any case, quickening mechanical progress will require a private scheme, including a differing scope of financing models behind the imaginative advances. From smart building frameworks to energy effectiveness innovation, finance is assumed to be a key part in helping structures from clinics, schools, to business and government structures, tackle feasible capital for development and advancement while obtaining future-verification mechanical advantages. Technology empowers the information gathering and examination, network, checking, and control is turning into the new benchmark for smart structures of tomorrow [5]. To plan a smart framework requires the worldwide aptitude and neighborhood understanding that is at the core of structures, and that can adjust after some time. Over 170 years of experience gives a strong establishment to understand how to make a move and transform incorporating information with substantial worth. Assuming control over the control of information to change the activities, this empowers the automation of structures to make them more proficient, responsive and versatile. Through control, security and energy, the board framework, the control of information and change might be picked up to support production lines and workplaces better help them. Accordingly, with regards to expanding resource and framework execution over the whole structure lifecycle, associated and information-driven structures, innovation is the key. Digitalization of administrations permits to meet all business objectives more viably [6].

IoT is continually making the gadgets smarter and more associative. This doesn't end at the gadgets yet stretches out to the Smart Buildings as the structures are turning into a focus of developments where its effect might be seen around the world. Barely any instances of unimaginably smart structures over the world are the Edge Building in Amsterdam, Capital Tower in Singapore, Glumac in Shanghai, DPR Construction in San Francisco, Hindmarsh Shire Council Corporate Center in Melbourne, Duke Energy Center in Charlotte, the Crystal Building in London and so forth. As IoT sensors and associated gadgets become more common, smart structures will turn out to be more generous. There are conclusively numerous significant financial and social motivations to make smart innovation in the workspace is a definitive objective [7].

SC rolls around information specifically and incorporating the information together so as to produce experiences and to predict outcomes. The development of a number of IoT applications and gadgets, for example, sensors, surveillance camera, advanced counter, have begun in another time of huge information based on everything. Gathering the information is just not sufficient. What should be possible utilizing that information through the smart utilization of examination and applications is significant. This offers some benefit and permits urban areas and unified order and control stages to help screen, supervise and control framework over its unique networks. Few out of every odd city should be designed starting from the earliest stage to be smart. Rather, old structures and urban areas can be retrofit in smaller, however significant manners. Smart structures frequently permit their owners and administrators to separate better information out of the structures and make nonstop changes to their energy utilization [8]. Dealing with the massive inflow of information from around a city frequently implies using an incorporated order, control and utilizing the bits of knowledge from the information to settle on choices at a structure administrator or even at a citywide level. The new Egyptian capital, for example, hopes to convey citywide security and investigation frameworks into a solitary purpose of control, known as a coordinated order and control focus. The control community will intend to associate recordings takes care of from a few thousand IP cameras, and run advanced video examination to help screen groups and gridlock, recognize episodes of robbery, watch dubious individuals or articles, and trigger mechanized alerts in crisis circumstances.

To accomplish the smart urban areas will take an insightful association of task engineers, government offices, metropolitan organizers, innovation suppliers, industry specialists, and residents. First, it is important to change the previously established inclinations of what engineering is and the desires for what it can or should do. For quite a long time, numerous structures were planned and built likewise. There was the result of modern cycles, practically hidden and slow to the changing condition [9]. At last, to expand the worth related with and produced by huge structures, engineers and designers must grasp a structure and arranging suggestion that goes past steel or cement. Our structures must become living articles more sensitive to the earth and the necessities of that inside. This will help lead to more smart urban areas that are more receptive to individual and aggregate needs.

14.1.1 Chapter Organization

The chapter is organized into eight different sections to explain various different areas related to the smart city. The chapter will discuss the importance of the role of smart buildings in smart cities. Section 14.2 discusses the literature review representing the works of researchers in the domain. Section 14.3 explains different components of the smart cities like smart infrastructure, smart water management system, smart energy management system, etc. which is being observed as the brain of the smart cities. Section 14.4 explains different characteristics of the smart city, for example, minimal human control, optimization, and quality of life, etc. These characteristics make it possible to achieve the objectives of the smart city. Section 14.5 highlights different supporting technologies of the smart cities, i.e. big data, Internet of things, machine learning, robotics etc. Section 14.6 describes different key performance indicators to evaluate whether the smart city is working up to the required set targets, there exist various performance indicators. These performance indicators help to evaluate the impact of a smart city. These indicators are the smart economy, smart governance, smart people, and smart living etc. Section 14.7 explains various challenges in the way of the development of smart cities. These challenges are retrofitting the existing legacy of city infrastructure to make it smart, financing, city development plan, technical constraints, governance, dealing with the multivendor environment, and reliability of services, etc. All the different challenges raise various futuristic opportunities for the researchers. Section 14.8 discusses future research opportunities in the domain of the smart city. These research opportunities are IoT management, data management, smart city assessment framework, security, smart city enabler, information system risks, etc.

14.2 Literature Review

Nowadays, lots of research work is going on in the domain of the smart city. There are various components of any smart city which require further development for better performance. This section of the chapter discusses some latest research work which is being done by the researchers and presented in their research papers of the smart city domain.

In 2018, Pan and Cheng [10] presented a research paper, assessment of the quality of encoded YouTube adoptable streaming for saving energy. In his work, the author proposed a machine learning-based bitrate Estimation approach. The author evaluated this approach with 95% accuracy. In 2018,

Quero *et al.* [11] presented a research paper, Forecasting the urgent demand of COPD patients. The author proposed a methodology to predict COPD from Sensors. The author analyzed the improved performance based on quantitative regression analysis. In 2018, Vo *et al.* [12] proposed a framework for 5G optimized caching and downlink resources sharing. In this work, authors proposed a joint caching and downlink resource sharing optimization framework. Authors evaluated the proposed work and obtained the best performance in terms of hit rate and system delivery capacity.

In 2019, Rodriguez-Hernandez *et al.* [13] proposed a model for telecommunication traffic management and to advance the value of services in a smart city. Authors used the well-known simulator OMNET++ for the simulations and obtained the correct estimations of the communication needs and cost before service deployment. In 2019, Kulandaivel *et al.* [14] proposed a smart information transfer method for the smart city. Authors proposed a new technology-based routing structure; this intended routing plot provides much spectacle than existing protocols for real-time applications. In 2019, Gheisari *et al.* [15] proposed architecture for preserving the privacy in IoT based Smart Cities. Authors proposed a real-time privacy-preserving method. The proposed system provides privacy in real-time. In 2019, Oughton *et al.* [19] proposed an open-source framework for technical and economic assessment for 5G deployment. The author performed all the simulation on PySim 5G simulator and observed the cost reduction by 30% in deployment. In 2019, Li *et al.* [16] developed a vehicular network framework to perform non-real-time data collection tasks in a smart city. Authors developed a location-based urban vehicle network. When evaluated his work, the author observed reliability and predictability simplifies the topology in wireless connectivity. In 2019, Garcia-Roger *et al.* [17] proposed a 5G architecture and signal improvement to support path management for eV2X. Authors proposed a new network function and a method to present the current abilities of the 3GPP 5G framework. The author observed the improved results of the proposed system. In 2019, Jamshidi *et al.* [18] proposed a framework by utilizing time-location tags and watchdog nodes to protect the nodes against the node duplication attack in the mobile Wireless Sensor Network. Authors proposed a novel algorithm using watchdog node and used J-SIM Simulator to perform the simulations. Authors evaluated the system and observed that the system detects 100% replicated nodes, and the false detection rate is 0.5%.

In 2020, Mroue *et al.* [20] proposed the extension of LoRaWAN protocols to decrease the infrastructure expenses by enlightening the superiority of the service. Authors modified the LoRaWAN in the MAC

Layer and used MATLAB to perform simulations. Authors evaluated and analyzed that the model is effective in different complex situations. In 2020, Martins *et al.* [21] developed a smart city platform architecture. The author proposed an approach named CityAction, which works for the reduced rejected packet rate and PER by up to 30%. In 2020, Fallis *et al.* [22] proposed an energy effective audio achievement system for SC applications. Authors designed a testbed for smart microphone systems and observed the technologies, i.e. Wi-Fi, Bluetooth and ZigBee, etc. For better discussions in the smart city management, the author observed the improved response time, safety, and well living. In 2020, Fernandez-Ares *et al.* [23] detected and analyzed the irregularities in-person gathering and movement via radio smartphones tracing. Authors proposed a method to spot the movement of persons from the data communicated by smart mobile gadgets. Authors evaluated the model and observed that the power consumption is lowered by 97%. In 2020, Ali *et al.* [24] proposed a model for secure smart City Surveillance. Authors used the lightweight symmetric vital primitives and temporal identifications (iTCALAS System). Authors stated that the system provides correct and cost-effective air quality assessment, and provides a recognized safety feature and complete verification in just 2.295 ms.

14.3   Components of Smart Cities

In the present time, the utilization of IoT in SC and associated innovation advances financial turn of events, improve framework and condition, upgrade transportation frameworks and advance expenses of overseeing public resources. There are different segments of SC and their effect in the IoT period. Some of the components are presented in Figure 14.1 and will be discussed in the following section.

14.3.1   Smart Infrastructure

The worldwide market for the smart metropolitan foundation in smart urban areas, incorporate associated smart roads, stopping, lighting, and other transportation developments. With smart lights, city specialists can keep ongoing following of lighting to guarantee enhanced illumination and convey request-based illumination in various zones. This additionally helps in sunlight gathering and spare energy by fading out parts without any inhabitancies for example parking areas can be moderated during work hours, and when a vehicle is entering, it will be identified, and fitting parts

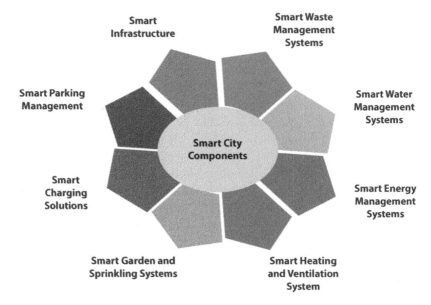

Figure 14.1 Components of Smart City.

can be enlightened, while others can be kept at diffused setting. Associated and smart roads are fit for securing information and conveying data and administrations to and from many gadgets, which incorporates data about traffic, street blockages, roadworks, and so forth. This aides in the proficient administration of assets and individuals to upgrade public transportation and the metropolitan scene [25].

14.3.2   Smart Parking Management

This framework can be utilized to locate the empty area for a vehicle at various public spots. This system's in-Ground Vehicle Detection Sensors are core techniques; having a key impact in the Smart Parking arrangement that is changing how drivers in the shopping centers and downtown areas can locate an accessible parking spot. Remote sensors are implanted into parking spots, communicating information on the circumstance and length of the space utilized by means of neighbourhood signal processors into a focal stopping the executive's application. Smart Parking diminishes blockage and vehicle outflows, brings down authorization expenses and reduces driver stress. For a successful arrangement of smart parking technologies, every gadget needs to have a solid availability with the cloud servers [26].

14.3.3   Connected Charging Stations

Smart frameworks incorporate executing charging stations in parking areas, city fleets, malls, buildings, airports, and bus stations over the city. Electronic vehicle (EV) charging points can be coordinated with IoT to smooth streamline the tasks of EV charging and addresses the effect of the power network [27].

14.3.4   Smart Buildings and Properties

Smart structures use various frameworks to guarantee the security of structures, support of advantages and in the general strength of the encompassing. Health and security frameworks incorporate executing distant observing, biometrics, IP observation cameras, and remote cautions to decrease unapproved admittance to structures and odds of robberies. It likewise incorporates using Perimeter Access Control to stop admittance to limited zones of the property and identify individuals in non-approved areas [28].

14.3.5   Smart Garden and Sprinkler Systems

Smart sprinkler framework adjusted with associated innovations and cloud can be utilized to watering plants with the confirmation that plants get the perfect measure of water. Smart nursery gadgets can likewise perform assignments, for example, estimating soil dampness and levels of compost, assisting the city specialists with saving money on water charge (smart sprinkler gadgets utilize climate forecasts and consequently modify their timetable to remain off when it rains), and shield the grass from congesting in an advantageous manner (robot lawnmowers) [29].

14.3.6   Smart Heating and Ventilation

Smart warming and ventilation frameworks monitor different boundaries, for example, temperature, pressure, vibration, dampness of the structures and properties, for example, cinemas, and historical landmarks. Remote sensor network sending is the way to guaranteeing suitable warming and ventilation. These sensors additionally gather information to upgrade the HVAC frameworks, improving their productivity and execution in the structures [30].

14.3.7   Smart Industrial Environment

This present one-of-a-kind open door for creating applications related to the Internet of things and associated advances which can be used in the territories like Forest Fire Detection. This helps in checking of burning gases and pre-emptive fire conditions to characterize ready zones and Air/Noise Pollution; which helps in controlling of CO_2 outflows of plants, contamination radiated via vehicles and poisonous gases produced on ranches. Some different regions are Snow Level Monitoring, Landslide and Avalanche Avoidance, Earthquake Early Detection, Liquid Presence, Radiation Levels, Explosive and Hazardous Gases, etc. [31].

14.3.8   Smart City Services

IoT answers for Smart city incorporate administrations for public wellbeing and crises. There are different key regions where IoT and associated advancements can help, for instance, Smart Kiosk assumes a significant part in giving diverse city administrations to the public, for example, Wi-Fi administrations, 24×7 IP investigation cameras and examination, Digital signage for notice and public declarations. Different administrations of Smart City are observing unsafe territories, public security, fire/blast the executives, and programmed medical services dispatch and so on [32].

14.3.9   Smart Energy Management

IoT arrangements can likewise be actualized for smart energy executive in various manners like; Smart Grids and Smart Meters. These grids are carefully checked, self-mending energy frameworks that convey power or gas from age sources. These arrangements can be across industrial, private, as well as in transmission and broadcasting schemes. Different IoT arrangements like passages can be utilized to accomplish energy protection at both the transmission level and customer level. For e.g., doors can give a more extensive perspective on energy dissemination examples to service organizations with high network and ongoing investigation. Additionally, it builds up a Demand–Response instrument for the utility suppliers to upgrade energy appropriation dependent on the utilization designs. Smart Meters can be utilized in private and public metering segments for power and gas meters where there is a need to distinguish the continuous data on energy use. Customers and utilities with smart meters can screen their energy utilization. Besides, energy examination, reports, and public dashboards can be likewise accessed over the web utilizing portable applications incorporated with these meters [33].

14.3.10 Smart Water Management

IoT and Connected gadgets empower smart water arrangement in various manners like compact water observing for checking the nature of outlet water in the urban communities, compound spillage to distinguish the spillages and misuses of manufacturing plants in waterways, pools far off estimations to control the pool conditions distantly, contamination levels in the ocean to control the event of spillages and misuses in the ocean, water outpourings to identify the presence of fluid external the tanks and weight varieties along pipes, stream floods to screen the water level varieties in waterways, dams, and supplies and so forth [34].

14.3.11 Smart Waste Management

IoT Solutions for following misuses help regions and waste administrations directors the capacity to enhance squanders, decrease operational expenses, and better location the natural issues related with a wasteful waste assortment [35].

Usage of an SC accompanies massive chances to change the lives of individuals and improve the general city foundation and activities. Smart sensor organizations, IoT and associated innovations are the key answers for SC usage.

14.4 Characteristics of Smart Buildings

To make a building smart means to automate the building. This requires a number of smart devices installed in the building. Fundamentally, a smart structure is a structure that, with the insignificant human control, streamlines characterized characteristics. There are three key qualities of an ideal smart building, which are:

14.4.1 Minimal Human Control

The substance here is self-governance, and there are two explanations behind this; first, for a structure to be smart, the client anticipates that it should oversee itself, at any rate to a serious extent. Second, with an elevated level of complexity because of broad utilization of advanced arrangements, it will be for all intents and purposes incomprehensible for a human administrator to deal with the structure's different frameworks physically [36, 56].

14.4.2   Optimization

This is the main explanation because of which the smart structures are fascinating in any case. Their structures are relied upon to show improvement over the customary structure. In down to earth, streamlining includes the utilization of cutting-edge computerized frameworks [36].

14.4.3   Qualities

The two instances of building-related characteristics that get a great deal of consideration are the adequacy of energy the executives and space usage. There are numerous different characteristics that can be improved, for example, working proficiency, representative prosperity, natural effect, waste management, etc. [36].

The above attributes of smart structures can't characterize the smart structure actually. Smart building is one that is utilizing innovation to share data about what goes on in the structure between frameworks to advance the structure's presentation. This data is then used to computerize different cycles, for warming and ventilation to cooling and security. Along these lines, the following are some primary highlights of Smart Buildings which can characterize the smart structure in fact.

14.4.4   Connected Systems

The most crucial element of smart structure is that the center frameworks inside it are connected. Thus, water meters, pumps, fire alarms, power, lighting and so on are totally associated. This is the thing that makes a structure "smart"—the capacity of the frameworks inside it to converse with each other [37].

14.4.5   Use of Sensors

Sensors are a vital piece of smart structures and assume a significant function in gathering information to advise choices about where to distribute assets. In this way, for instance, footfall counters might be incorporated into the structure to give data on where individuals are at certain times and which regions are high traffic [38, 57].

14.4.6   Automation

Data is assembled and dissected by the frameworks that have been set up in a smart building—critically, this is done continually and progressively. This progressing observation takes into account robotized alterations that can control conditions over a whole structure [37].

14.4.7   Data

Smart structures create a huge volume of significant information about their own utilization, which is something that usual structures essentially don't do [37].

14.5   Supporting Technology

SC around the globe is executing activities to advance greener and more secure metropolitan conditions, with cleaner air and water, better portability, and effective public administrations. These activities are maintained by innovations like the IoT and large information examination, that structure the base of the SC model. Smart urban communities influence innovation answers to improve city administrations and the living experience of occupants. Districts use IoT sensors, organizations, and applications to accumulate important information, for example, gridlock, energy use, and air quality. This information would then be able to be utilized by innovative answers to improve city administrations, including utilities, transportation, and public administrations. Urban areas around the globe are turning out to be more perceptive [38, 58]. They are actualizing activities to advance greener and more secure metropolitan conditions, with cleaner air and water, better portability, and proficient public administrations. These activities are upheld by smart innovations, for example, the IoT and ICT that give the specialized structure to actualize SC ventures.

14.5.1   Big Data and IoT in Smart Cities

IoT is a fundamental innovation without which SC can't exist. The "things" of the IoT gadgets, sensors, applications gather the information that empowers the innovation answers for being powerful. For instance, smart water meters revealing water quality and use, alarming the water organization of breaks, or likely defilement. This speaks to that brilliant city activities need huge information examination to work. The IoT produces incredible datasets that must be examined and prepared to execute brilliant city administrations. Huge information stages, part of the city ICT foundation, need to sort, break down, and measure the information assembled from the IoT. City administration coordinates ICT answers for interconnecting public administrations, simultaneously captivating networks in nearby administration, in this way advancing participation [39, 59]. One case of this is the Greater London Authority activity, where city lobby is utilizing an open, basic stage to impart information to neighbourhood networks. Instances of the utilization of IoT in smart urban communities incorporate city lighting, squander the executives, associated public vehicle, etc.

As indicated by definition, the SC is information-driven. Enormous Data and investigation assume a significant function in city management, with numerous information collection, a city having a Chief Data Officer in the organization. The mix of huge information examination and SC arrangements assist urban areas with improving the administration in basic portions, for example, brilliant city energy the executives, SC transport the board, SC framework, etc.

14.5.2 Sensors

Sensors are at the center of each gadget in the IoT framework. From associated vehicles to traffic signals and smart homes, pretty much every gadget today has sensors that accumulate and send information to the cloud. This interconnectivity is the thing that makes conceivable IoT framework. For instance, closeness sensors make conceivable improvement of robotized vehicle frameworks. Smart urban communities use sensors to measure a crowd of qualities from gridlock to contamination levels, water quality, and energy use [40, 60].

14.5.3 5G Connectivity

SC advancements expect the network to work. 5G cells give metropolitan territories a solid association between a large number of gadgets and sensors, empowering the IoT to work effectively. In this manner, urban areas like London are introducing 5G cells over the city, utilizing automatons to recognize accessible spaces [39].

14.5.4 Geospatial Technology

Metropolitan planning requires geolocation precision and point by point, geographic information. Smart urban communities depend on innovations, for example, Global Positioning System (GPS) for transportation the board and associated vehicles. Geographical Information System (GIS) causes city organizers to construct a metropolitan computerized model with georeferenced information. This empowers building engineers, for instance, to decide the best course for bike paths or where to find multimodal transport stations. On account of new urban areas, for example, Belmont, USA, city organizers use geospatial innovations to plan private and metropolitan regions in a manner that advances walking driving [38].

14.5.5   Robotics

Robots left science fiction films to turn out to be important for regular existence. The coordination of mechanical technology plans to improve city activities, for example, utilizing drones for postal administrations. Urban areas, for example, Dubai, Singapore, and Tokyo, are at the front line of this pattern, presenting humanoids for administrations, for example, room administration in inns, investigation and to go to the data work area at public workplaces. For instance, guests to the 2020 Tokyo Olympics will find support to convey in Japanese from humanoid mechanical interpreters. Then, in Dubai, Robocop isn't a dream any longer, since the city is trying humanoid cops with the expectation to supplant 25% of their police power by 2030 [40, 61].

14.6   Key Performance Indicators of Smart City

To assess the effect of SC, both every day toward the finish of every period through the foundation of a progression of nearby performance indicators evaluates the advancement in each division. In choosing the proper indicators, one needs to talk with the most helpful assets which are as of now accessible [41]. The local indicators for smart urban areas can be assembled into six divisions that are economy, administration, versatility, condition, individuals, and personal satisfaction. Fundamentally, three kinds of performance indicators are built up in every division that is data sources, yields and effects. Following are a portion of the presentation markers of the SC.

14.6.1   Smart Economy

Among the numerous government PIs that have to do with the economy are those identified with the expense of an SC venture and the structures it produces, just as broad miniature and large-scale financial boundaries. A few models would be the development of innovation and science parks, number of new businesses every year, joblessness rate, number of occupations made every year, joblessness rate in innovation and inventive segments, and so forth.

14.6.2   Smart Governance

The territory of administration unites the nearby government PIs pertinent to the organization of the SC. Here one can control perspectives, for example, the execution of electronic frameworks to direct the organization resident relationship, a number of foundations with associated sensors, a measure of online data accessible to city occupants, and so forth.

14.6.3   Smart Mobility

The nearby government PIs identified with metropolitan versatility consider both vehicle and ICT. Metropolitan versatility pointers incorporate the number of electric vehicles charging stations, number of public Wi-Fi zones, number of public transportations travels every year, kilometres of bicycle paths per 100,000 occupants, level of the domain with broadband web inclusion, and so forth.

14.6.4   Smart Environment

With respect to nature, it's tied in with checking energy utilization and the impacts of human movement on the earth. To screen these, there are the PIs for smart urban areas, for example, the number of smart streetlights, water contamination levels, disorder contamination levels, level of energy expended originating from sustainable power sources, the pace of constant respiratory illnesses per 100,000 occupants, the extent of strong waste that is reused, and so forth.

14.6.5   Smart People

Given that the improvement of everyday environments for its occupants is a definitive objective of any SC, nearby government KPIs for brilliant urban areas additionally centre around estimating the preparation and aptitudes obtained by residents, ascertaining information, for example, the number of PCs per understudy, school dropout rate, level of the population with a college degree, utilization of ICT in instruction, the sufficiency of neighbourhood preparing to fulfil the needs of the work market, openness to instructive assets, and so forth.

14.6.6   Smart Living

To decide the personal satisfaction in the SC, performance indicators may be utilized related to wellbeing, security and prosperity. Here are a few thoughts like the normal holding up time at clinical focuses, normal crisis administration reaction time, Gini coefficient of monetary imbalance, a record of energy destitution, self-destruction rate per 100,000 occupants, the pace of malicious wrongdoing per 100,000 occupants, execution of online wellbeing administrations, level of network protection, and so on.

14.7   Challenges While Working for Smart City

At the point when anybody hears the expression "Smart City" one may picture the well-known science fiction films. While fast mechanical headways still can't seem to give us business flying vehicles. The clients will have the option to get to many transportation techniques with their cell phones, all while accessing those telephones utilizing facial examining and confirmation innovation. Presently, individuals are living in a reality that was previously the creative mind of skilled screen journalists. As all are drawing nearer to the advanced urban communities with apparently incomprehensible effortlessness, the interest for smart innovation improvement and IT critical thinking just keeps on developing [42, 62]. Despite the fact that the quantity of engineers and trailblazers handling Smart City advancements is expanding, there still stays a progression of issues all designers face sooner or later in their answers. Here are some basic difficulties confronting Smart City arrangements today and how designers can start to deliver these obstructions to progress.

14.7.1   Retrofitting Existing Legacy City Infrastructure to Make it Smart

There are various inactive issues to consider while exploring an SC procedure. The most significant is to decide the current city's powerless territories that need the most extreme thought, for example, 100% appropriation of water gracefully and disinfection. The incorporation of earlier disengaged inheritance frameworks to accomplish citywide efficiencies can be a noteworthy test [42, 63].

14.7.2   Financing Smart Cities

The High-Power Expert Committee (HPEC) on Investment Estimates in Urban Infrastructure has evaluated a for each capita venture cost (PCIC) of Rs 43,386 for a 20-year time span. Utilizing a normal figure of 1 million individuals in every one of the 100 brilliant urban communities, the absolute gauge of venture prerequisites for the SC comes to Rs 7 lakh crore more than 20 years (with a yearly acceleration of 10% from 2009–20 to 2014–15). This converts into a yearly necessity of Rs 35,000 crore. One needs to perceive how these ventures will be financed as most of the task need would travel through complete private speculation or through PPPs (public-private association) [36, 64].

14.7.3   Availability of Master Plan or City Development Plan

A large portion of our urban areas don't have all-inclusive strategies or a city advancement plan, which is the way to SC arranging and usage and embodies everything a city requires to improve and give better chances to its residents. Shockingly, 70–80% of Indian urban areas don't have one [37, 65].

14.7.4   Financial Sustainability of ULBs

Most ULBs are not monetarily self-economical and tax levels fixed by the ULBs for offering types of assistance regularly don't reflect the expense of providing the equivalent. Regardless of whether extra speculations are recouped in a staged way, lacking cost recuperation will prompt proceeded with budgetary misfortunes [36, 37].

14.7.5   Technical Constraints ULBs

Most ULBs have restricted specialized ability to guarantee convenient and smart usage and ensuing activities and support attributable to restricted enrolment over various years alongside powerlessness of the ULBs to draw in best of ability at market serious remuneration rates [37, 38].

14.7.6   Three-Tier Governance

Fruitful execution of brilliant city arrangements needs viable even and vertical coordination between different organizations giving different metropolitan luxuries just as viable coordination between focal government (MoUD), state government and nearby government offices on different issues identified with financing and sharing of best practices and administration conveyance measures [36, 38].

14.7.7   Providing Clearances in a Timely Manner

For opportune finishing of the undertaking, all clearances should utilize online cycles and be cleared in a period bound way. An administrative body ought to be set up for every utility assistance, so a level battleground is made accessible to the private area and duties are set in a way that offsets budgetary manageability with quality [36, 37].

14.7.8   Dealing With a Multivendor Environment

Another significant test in the Indian brilliant city space is that (generally) programming framework in urban communities contains segments provided by various merchants. Henceforth, the capacity to deal with complex blends of brilliant city arrangements created by numerous innovation merchants turns out to be critical [37, 38].

14.7.9   Capacity Building Program

Building limit with regards to 100 keen urban communities isn't a simple undertaking and most goal-oriented ventures are postponed attributable to the absence of value labour, both at the middle and state levels. Regarding reserves, just around 5% of the focal distribution might be apportioned for limit building programs that attention on preparing, relevant exploration, information trade and a rich data set. Interests in limit building programs have a multiplier impact as they help in the time-bound culmination of activities and in planning programs, creating workforce, building information bases just as planning toolbox and choice emotionally supportive networks. As all these make some slack memories, limit assembling should be reinforced right toward the start [36, 37, 66].

14.7.10   Reliability of Utility Services

For any SC on the planet, the emphasis is on the dependability of utility administrations, regardless of whether it is power, water, phone or broadband administrations. Smart urban communities ought to have all-inclusive admittance to power 24×7; this is preposterous with the current flexibly and circulation framework. Urban areas need to move towards inexhaustible sources and spotlight on green structures and green vehicle to diminish the requirement for power [38].

While most everybody can concur, that smart innovation has the ability to make individuals lives a lot less complex, particularly in exceptionally populated metropolitan zones, executing that innovation must be done in a deliberately arranged and profoundly secure way. As opposed to simply zeroing in on what the arrangement can do, designers and specialized organizations mush additionally consider how it will influence the individuals that come into contact with it [67, 68]. At the point when innovation, city administration, and networks of individuals meet up to improve the personal satisfaction for everybody included, that is the point at which a city really becomes "Smart".

14.8   Future Research Opportunities in Smart City

There are lots of research opportunities in the SC area. Here are a few points which are open in future opportunities in the area of a smart city.

14.8.1   IoT Management

IoT needs effective, secure engineering that upgrades metropolitan information collecting. As it has been informed that universal and community-oriented metropolitan detecting coordinated with brilliant articles can give a keen situation. Something else, parcel latencies and bundle misfortune are definitely not controllable [42]. One such proposition is the Mobile Ad hoc Networks coordination convention to sharply abuse MANET hubs as versatile transfers for the quick assortment of pressing information from remote sensor networks without giving up battery life. Recreation results show that their bunch development convention is dependable and consistently conveys over 98% of the bundles in road and square situations [43]. Different issues, including the assembly of IoT and wise transportation frameworks, require further examination.

14.8.2   Data Management

Information assumes a key function in Smart Cities. An enormous amount of information will be created by smart urban areas; getting, dealing with, and treating it will be a test. Be that as it may, cell phone information can help accomplish a few brilliant urban areas destinations. This cell phone information can be utilized to build up an assortment of metropolitan applications [44]. For instance, transportation investigation for assessing the traffic volume on the streets and the vehicle requests, and so on. Ongoing data from cell phone information about the sources of guests joined with taxi's Global Positioning System could help oversee transportation assets, that is it very well may be said that the public's future interest for taxis [44, 45].

14.8.3   Smart City Assessment Framework

Reasonable urban communities must be checked through nature of-living record, estimating the wellbeing, security, and success in the city. An appraisal structure must contemplate different trademark, including smart procedure and the interests of all partners, for example, execution evaluators, ICT frameworks, legitimate and administrative strategies, administrations, plans of action, and supportability, and so on. The goals of such a system are to look at the attributes of various smart urban communities to recognize new difficulties, measure benefits, and assess execution [44, 46].

14.8.4   VANET Security

In brilliant urban areas, proficient security uphold is a significant necessity of VANETs. One thought is the manner by which to make sure about them by planning arrangements that decrease the probability of organization assaults or even how to lessen the impact an effective assault could have on them. Loads of security challenges are there as for the confirmation and decreasing the various sorts of assaults, and if there is any sort of challenge in accomplishing any of the undertakings, there are bunches of modern open doors which tags along for the scientists of the space [44, 47].

14.8.5   Improving Photovoltaic Cells

Accomplishing a manageable fuel source in an SC must incorporate sustainable power source. Sun oriented innovation has made critical walks, for example, photovoltaic cells that convert light energy into power. Still more proficient sun-oriented energy-gathering methods are needed to improve the sunlight-based cells [44, 48].

14.8.6   Smart City Enablers

Innovation progress are making a business opportunity for SC items and arrangements, yet smart urban communities need proficiency and maintainability. Numerous creators proposed the conjuncture of four powers that are metropolitan future, advances, applications and developing economy. To create, smart urban areas must use mechanical headways and the advancement of information and development organizations. Huge numbers of the analysts proposed diverse creative strategies to help the brilliant urban communities in various regard, yet this zone is as yet open for the specialists with the immense future work [44, 49].

14.8.7   Information System Risks

In Smart City, everything is interconnected, including the public water framework, traffic signal, public transportation, and basic foundation. Every one includes its own weaknesses. Although an SC is a confusing framework, its interconnected nature implies a solitary weakness could significantly influence residents security, for instance, an aggressor may have the option to interface with the electric force framework to access the organize and adjust public transportation to possibly incapacitate insightful transportation frameworks, with a great many travellers on board at times of heavy traffic. The aggressor could likewise dispatch bogus cautions and adjust traffic signals and regulators. Finding functional arrangements is basic; in any case, the public won't trust keen city extends or regard them suitable [44, 50].

Scientific people group must address these network safety ventures. Uncertain difficulties and open doors for investments include DoS-Attack recognition for dissemination frameworks, cryptographic countermeasures, and validations in IoT and basic foundation, just as in key administration. There are heaps of more open examination openings in the field of Smart City in various—various spaces [51, 52].

14.9   Conclusion

The concept of Smart Building and Smart Cities and the smart buildings are the core of Smart Cities. Smart buildings and cities have a different component which is completely interconnected with each other. Various services are being performed autonomously in smart cities with the help of technologies. There are various supporting technologies of smart cities which are briefly discussed in this chapter, and different key performance indicators are also being discussed for evaluation of the smart cities [53]. The smart buildings are beneficial in smart cities for different reasons like:

- The smart structures make the tenants more profitable as the air quality, physical solace, security, sterilization, lightning and even room and space accessibility would all be able to be conveyed at an ideal level to empower inhabitants to perform well.
- The brilliant structures diminish energy utilization, and these structures are greener, more energy proficient and smart.
- The utilization of sensors and cameras gives exact information on how the structure is being utilized, which can be changed over into a sagacious dynamic. Space used can be improved dependent on genuine information, as the structure produces noteworthy, living knowledge consequently.
- The brilliant structures empower the huge operational sparing as it incorporates the sparing that can be made as far as ordinary spend and upkeep on hardware.
- Equipment's, for example, warm sensors, measures information without utilizing recognizable pictures of staff or the public which empower the information assurance.

There is a huge number of benefits of Smart City Solutions of the smart city. Name of few of them is public safety, faster communication, economic prosperity, greener environment, etc. Most importantly, the keen city innovations and applications help urban areas to change into greener, more secure and adequately arranged metropolitan condition [54]. It is nothing unexpected then that the keen city model is furnishing effective with more than 50 smart urban communities around the globe utilizing smart advancements to improve the personal satisfaction of its inhabitants [55].

References

1. Alotaibi, S.S., Registration Center Based User Authentication Scheme for Smart E-Governance Applications in Smart Cities. *IEEE Access*, 7, 819–833, 2019.

2. Shah, S.A. *et al.*, Towards Disaster Resilient Smart Cities: Can Internet of Things and Big Data Analytics Be the Game Changers? *IEEE Access*, 7, 529–548, 2019.

3. Tian, L., Wang, H., Zhou, Y., Peng, C., Video big data in smart city: Background construction and optimization for surveillance video processing. *Future Gener. Comput. Syst.*, 86, 1371–1382, 2018.

4. Cui, L., Xie, G., Qu, Y., Gao, L., Yang, Y., Security and privacy in smart cities: Challenges and opportunities. *IEEE Access*, 6, 345–364, 2018.

5. Mohamed, N., Al-Jaroodi, J., Jawhar, I., Lazarova-Molnar, S., Mahmoud, S., SmartCityWare: A service-oriented middleware for cloud and fog enabled smart city services. *IEEE Access*, 5, 438–457, 2017.

6. Rahman, M.A. *et al.*, Blockchain and IoT-Based Cognitive Edge Framework for Sharing Economy Services in a Smart City. *IEEE Access*, 7, 18611–18621, 2019.

7. Kotevska, O., Kusne, A.G., Samarov, D.V., Lbath, A., Battou, A., Dynamic Network Model for Smart City Data-Loss Resilience Case Study: City-to-City Network for Crime Analytics. *IEEE Access*, 5, 20524–20535, 2017.

8. Morello, R., Mukhopadhyay, S.C., Liu, Z., Slomovitz, D., Samantaray, S.R., Advances on sensing technologies for smart cities and power grids: A review. *IEEE Sens. J.*, 17, 7596–7610, 2017.

9. Xu, L. *et al.*, DIoTA: Decentralized-Ledger-Based Framework for Data Authenticity Protection in IoT Systems. *IEEE Netw.*, 34, 38–46, 2020.

10. Pan, W. and Cheng, G., QoE Assessment of Encrypted YouTube Adaptive Streaming for Energy Saving in Smart Cities. *IEEE Access*, 6, 687–705, 2018.

11. Quero, J.M., Lopez Medina, M.A., Salguero Hidalgo, A., Espinilla, M., Predicting the Urgency Demand of COPD Patients from Environmental Sensors Within Smart Cities with High-Environmental Sensitivity. *IEEE Access*, 6, 767–779, 2018.

12. Vo, N.S., Duong, T.Q., Guizani, M., Kortun, A., 5G optimized caching and downlink resource sharing for smart cities. *IEEE Access*, 6, 31457–31468, 2018.

13. Rodriguez-Hernandez, M.A., Jiang, Z., Gomez-Sacristan, A., Pla, V., Intelligent municipal heritage management service in a smart city: Telecommunication traffic characterization and quality of service. *Wirel. Commun. Mob. Comput.*, 2019, 1038–1065, 2019.

14. Kulandaivel, R., Balasubramaniam, M., Al-Turjman, F., Mostarda, L., Ramachandran, M., Patan, R., Intelligent data delivery approach for smart cities using road side units. *IEEE Access*, 7, 2019.

15. Gheisari, M., Pham, Q.V., Alazab, M., Zhang, X., Fernández-Campusano, C., Srivastava, G., ECA: An Edge Computing Architecture for Privacy-Preserving in IoT-Based Smart City. *IEEE Access*, 7, 155779–155786, 2019.

16. Li, H., Liu, Y., Qin, Z., Rong, H., Liu, Q., A Large-Scale Urban Vehicular Network Framework for IoT in Smart Cities. *IEEE Access*, 7, 1345–1369, 2019.

17. Garcia-Roger, D., Roger, S., Martín-Sacristán, D., Monserrat, J.F., Kousaridas, A., Spapis, P., Zhou, C., 5G functional architecture and signaling enhancements to support path management for eV2X. *IEEE Access*, 7, 20484–20498, 2019.

18. Jamshidi, M., Esnaashari, M., Darwesh, A.M., Meybodi, M.R., Using Time-Location Tags and Watchdog Nodes to Defend Against Node Replication Attack in Mobile Wireless Sensor Networks. *Int. J. Wirel. Inf. Netw.*, 27, 102–115, 2020.

19. Oughton, E.J., Frias, Z., van der Gaast, S., van der Berg, R., Assessing the capacity, coverage and cost of 5G infrastructure strategies: Analysis of the Netherlands. *Telemat. Inform.*, 37, 50–69, 2019.

20. Mroue, H. *et al.*, LoRa+: An extension of LoRaWAN protocol to reduce infrastructure costs by improving the Quality of Service. *Internet Things*, 9, 100176, 2020.

21. Martins, P., Albuquerque, D., Wanzeller, C., Caldeira, F., Tome, P., Sa, F., *CityAction a Smart City Platform Architecture*, pp. 874–892, Springer, Cham, 2020.

22. Fallis, E., Spachos, P., Gregori, S., A power-efficient audio acquisition system for smart city applications. *Internet Things*, 9, 100155, 2020.

23. Fernandez-Ares, A., Garcia-Sanchez, P., Arenas, M.G., Mora, A.M., Castillo-Valdivieso, P.A., Detection and Analysis of Anomalies in People Density and Mobility through Wireless Smartphone Tracking. *IEEE Access*, 8, 54237–54253, 2020.

24. Ali, Z., Chaudhry, S.A., Ramzan, M.S., Al-Turjman, F., Securing Smart City Surveillance: A Lightweight Authentication Mechanism for Unmanned Vehicles. *IEEE Access*, 8, 43711–43724, 2020.

25. Mohanta, B.K., Jena, D., Satapathy, U., Patnaik, S., Survey on IoT Security: Challenges and Solution using Machine Learning, Artificial Intelligence and Blockchain Technology. *Internet Things*, 9, 100227, 2020.

26. Zhang, Y., Xiong, Z., Niyato, D., Wang, P., Han, Z., Information Trading in Internet of Things for Smart Cities: A Market-Oriented Analysis. *IEEE Netw.*, 34, 122–129, 2020.

27. Hakak, S., Khan, W.Z., Gilkar, G.A., Imran, M., Guizani, N., Securing Smart Cities through Blockchain Technology: Architecture, Requirements, and Challenges. *IEEE Netw.*, 34, 8–14, 2020.

28. Mocrii, D., Chen, Y., Musilek, P., IoT-based smart homes: A review of system architecture, software, communications, privacy and security. *Internet Things*, 1–2, 81–98, 2018.

29. Mohanta, B.K., Jena, D., Panda, S.S., Sobhanayak, S., Blockchain technology: A survey on applications and security privacy challenges. *Internet Things*, 8, 100107, 2019.

30. Basford, P.J., Bulot, F.M.J., Apetroaie-Cristea, M., Cox, S.J., Ossont, S.J.J., LoRaWan for smart city IoT deployments: A long term evaluation. *Sensors Switzerland*, 20, 2049–2072 2020.

31. Venkatesh, J., Aksanli, B., Chan, C.S., Akyurek, A.S., Rosing, T.S., Modular and Personalized Smart Health Application Design in a Smart City Environment. *IEEE Internet Things J.*, 5, 614–623, 2018.

32. Sivrikaya, F., Ben-Sassi, N., Dang, X.T., Görür, O.C., Kuster, C., Internet of Smart City Objects: A Distributed Framework for Service Discovery and Composition. *IEEE Access*, 7, 14434–14454, 2019.

33. Nelson, A., Toth, G., Linders, D., Nguyen, C., Rhee, S., Replication of Smart-City Internet of Things Assets in a Municipal Deployment. *IEEE Internet Things J.*, 6, 6715–6724, 2019.

34. Mohammad, N., Muhammad, S., Bashar, A., Khan, M.A., Formal Analysis of Human-Assisted Smart City Emergency Services. *IEEE Access*, 7, 60376–60388, 2019.

35. Kulkarni, P. and Farnham, T., Smart City Wireless Connectivity Considerations and Cost Analysis: Lessons Learnt from Smart Water Case Studies. *IEEE Access*, 4, 660–672, 2016.

36. Javidroozi, V., Shah, H., Feldman, G., Urban Computing and Smart Cities: Towards Changing City Processes by Applying Enterprise Systems Integration Practices. *IEEE Access*, 7, 108023–108034, 2019.

37. Jablonski, I., Graph Signal Processing in Applications to Sensor Networks, Smart Grids, and Smart Cities. *IEEE Sens. J.*, 17, 7659–7666, 2017.

38. Hu, L. and Ni, Q., IoT-Driven Automated Object Detection Algorithm for Urban Surveillance Systems in Smart Cities. *IEEE Internet Things J.*, 5, 747–754, 2018.

39. Gyrard, A., Zimmermann, A., Sheth, A., Building IoT-Based Applications for Smart Cities: How Can Ontology Catalogs Help? *IEEE Internet Things J.*, 5, 3978–3990, 2018.

40. Du, R., Santi, P., Xiao, M., Vasilakos, A.V., Fischione, C., The sensable city : A survey on the deployment and management for smart city monitoring. *IEEE Commun. Surv. Tutorials*, 5, 1, 2018.

41. De Filippi, F. *et al.*, MiraMap: A We-Government Tool for Smart Peripheries in Smart Cities. *IEEE Access*, 4, 3824–3843, 2016.

42. Brisimi, T.S., Cassandras, C.G., Osgood, C., Paschalidis, I.C., Zhang, Y., Sensing and Classifying Roadway Obstacles in Smart Cities: The Street Bump System. *IEEE Access*, 4, 1301–1312, 2016.

43. Ansari, M. and Almalki, F., Survey on Collaborative Smart Drones and Internet of Things for Improving Smartness of Smart Cities. *IEEE Access*, 4, 1–29, 2019.

44. Al-Ali, A.R., Zualkernan, I.A., Rashid, M., Gupta, R., Alikarar, M., A smart home energy management system using IoT and big data analytics approach. *IEEE Trans. Consum. Electron.*, 63, 426–434, 2017.

45. Aznavi, S., Fajri, P., Asrari, A., Harirchi, F., Realistic and Intelligent Management of Connected Storage Devices in Future Smart Homes Considering Energy Price Tag. *IEEE Trans. Ind. Appl.*, 56, 1679–1689, 2020.

46. Dinh, H.T., Yun, J., Kim, D.M., Lee, K.H., Kim, D., A Home Energy Management System with Renewable Energy and Energy Storage Utilizing Main Grid and Electricity Selling. *IEEE Access*, 8, 49436–49450, 2020.

47. Dryjanski, M., Buczkowski, M., Ould-Cheikh-Mouhamedou, Y., Kliks, A., Adoption of Smart Cities with a Practical Smart Building Implementation. *IEEE Internet Things Mag.*, 3, 58–63, 2020.

48. Hou, X., Wang, J., Huang, T., Wang, T., Wang, P., Smart Home Energy Management Optimization Method Considering Energy Storage and Electric Vehicle. *IEEE Access*, 7, 144010–144020, 2019.

49. Li, W., Logenthiran, T., Phan, V.T., Woo, W.L., Implemented IoT-based self-learning home management system (SHMS) for Singapore. *IEEE Internet Things J.*, 5, 2212–2219, 2018.

50. Shareef, H., Ahmed, M.S., Mohamed, A., Al Hassan, E., Review on Home Energy Management System Considering Demand Responses, Smart Technologies, and Intelligent Controllers. *IEEE Access*, 6, 24498–24509, 2018.

51. Sivapragash, C., Padmanaban, S., Eklas, H., Holm-Nielsen, J.B., Hemalatha, R., Location-based optimized service selection for data management with cloud computing in smart grids. *Energies*, 12, 1178–1197, 2019.

52. Stamatescu, G., Făgărăşan, I., Sachenko, A., Sensing and Data-Driven Control for Smart Building and Smart City Systems. *J. Sensors*, 2019, 1095–1125, 2019.

53. Stepaniuk, V., Pillai, J., Bak-Jensen, B., Padmanaban, S., Estimation of Energy Activity and Flexibility Range in Smart Active Residential Building. *Smart Cities*, 2, 471–495, 2019.

54. Zafar, U., Bayhan, S., Sanfilippo, A., Home Energy Management System Concepts, Configurations, and Technologies for the Smart Grid. *IEEE Access*, 7, 1–1, 2020.

55. Zekić-Sušac, M., Mitrović, S., Has, A., Machine learning based system for managing energy efficiency of public sector as an approach towards smart cities. *Int. J. Inf. Manage.*, 8, 102074, 2020.

56. Singh, T., Nayyar, A., Solanki, A., Multilingual Opinion Mining Movie Recommendation System Using RNN, in: *Proceedings of First International Conference on Computing, Communications, and Cyber-Security (IC4S 2019)*, Springer, Singapore, pp. 589–605, 2020.

57. Solanki, A. and Singh, T., An Efficient Flower Species Recognition System Using Deep Convolutional Neural Networks, Accepted for publication in. *International Conference on Evolving Technologies for Computing, Communication and Smart World (ETCCS-2020)*, 31 Jan to 01 Feb. 2020, CDAC Noida.

58. Tayal, A., Solanki, A., Singh, S., Integrated Frame work for Identifying Sustainable Manufacturing Layouts based on Big Data, Machine Learning, Meta-Heuristic and Data Envelopment Analysis, Accepted for Publication in. *J. Sustain. Cities Soc.*, vol. 7, pp. 1136–1156, Elsevier Publication, IF=5.2 SCIE, 2019.

59. Pramanik, P., Solanki, A., Debnath, A., Nayyar, A., El-Sappagh, S., Kwak, K., Advancing Modern Healthcare with Nanotechnology, Nanobiosensors, and Internet of Nano Things: Taxonomies, Applications, Architecture, and Challenges. *IEEE Access*, IF=4.09, 9, 987–1012, 2019.

60. Tayal, A., Kose, U., Solanki, A., Nayyar, A., Marmolejo Saucedo, J.A., Efficiency analysis for stochastic dynamic facility layout problem using meta-heuristic, data envelopment analysis and machine learning. *Computat. Intell.*, vol. 8, pp. 1467–1489, Wiley Online Library, SCI Publication, 2020, https://doi.org/10.1111/coin.12251 IF=1.196.
61. Nayyar, A., Jain, R., Mahapatra, B., Singh, A., Cyber security challenges for smart cities, in: *Driving the Development, Management, and Sustainability of Cognitive Cities*, pp. 27–54, IGI Global Hershey, PA, USA, 2019.
62. Singh, P., Nayyar, A., Kaur, A., Ghosh, U., Blockchain and Fog Based Architecture for Internet of Everything in Smart Cities. *Future Internet*, 12, 4, 61, IGI Global, Hershey, PA, USA, 2020.
63. Krishnamurthi, R., Nayyar, A., Solanki, A., *Innovation Opportunities through Internet of Things (IoT) for Smart Cities. Green and Smart Technologies for Smart Cities*, pp. 261–292, CRC Press, Boca Raton, FL, USA, 2019.
64. Solanki, A. and Nayyar, A., Green internet of things (G-IoT): ICT technologies, principles, applications, projects, and challenges, in: *Handbook of Research on Big Data and the IoT*, pp. 379–405, IGI Global Hershey, PA, USA, 2019.
65. Ullah, F., Al-Turjman, F., Nayyar, A., IoT-based green city architecture using secured and sustainable android services. *Environ. Technol. Innovation*, 6, 101091, 2020.
66. Anavangot, V., Menon, V.G., Nayyar, A., Distributed big data analytics in the Internet of signals, in: *2018 International Conference on System Modeling & Advancement in Research Trends (SMART)*, 2018, November, IEEE, pp. 73–77, 2018.
67. Kumar, A., Sangwan, S.R., Nayyar, A., Multimedia social big data: Mining, in: *Multimedia Big Data Computing for IoT Applications*, pp. 289–321, Springer, Singapore, 2020.
68. Bhatia, J., Dave, R., Bhayani, H., Tanwar, S., Nayyar, A., Sdn-based real-time urban traffic analysis in VANET environment. *Comput. Commun.*, 149, 162–175, 2020.

15

Effects of Green Buildings on the Environment

Ayushi Nain*, Ankita Banerjee and N.P. Melkania

*School of Vocational Studies and Applied Sciences, Gautam Buddha University,
Greater Noida, India*

Abstract

Concerns on environmental and sustainability issues like urbanization, climate change, loss of biodiversity and resources degradation are increasing rapidly, so there is the need of advancement in housing. When various other urban stresses combine with building oppressiveness, the compact cities become unsustainable. Green buildings represent the science and styling of buildings with a planned construction following minimum impact on the surroundings by the reduction in utilization of water, energy, and disturbances in the surrounding environment by the building location. Green buildings aim on providing several efficient means to attain a range of global aims, such as, arresting climate change, building sustainable and advanced communities, and pushing inclusive economic growth. Green buildings improve human health by creating healthy indoor environment, enhance occupant's health comfort, and improve overall quality of build environment and life. According to the recent Report of IPCC, building industry is responsible for 40 per cent of global carbon footprint is caused by usage of fossil fuels, and perform a major function in a sustainable transformation. Developing countries people lack awareness about the green buildings. Research work in developing countries is far away as compared to developed countries in green buildings. This contribution is an attempt to appraise the value of green buildings, compared to standard buildings. Attempts are also made to illustrate good practices as available regarding green structures in India.

Keywords: Green buildings, sustainability, environmental issues, carbon footprint, bio-diversity, ecosystem, urbanization

*Corresponding author: ayushinain3@gmail.com

Arun Solanki, Adarsh Kumar and Anand Nayyar (eds.) Digital Cities Roadmap: IoT-Based Architecture and Sustainable Buildings, (477–508) © 2021 Scrivener Publishing LLC

15.1   Introduction

Smart city consists of intelligent infrastructure that provides a good quality life with affordable building designs. It takes into account the cleanliness of air, efficiency in energy usage and water quality, continuous supply of electricity, proper sanitation, health protection, quality education, digital working, and good speed of internet and fast mobility sources. Smart city aims to provide good living standards for every resident but the rate with which humans are moving forward, it is not sustainable. That means, in a short time span, society will begin to run out of natural resources especially for survival.

What is green building? A green building is a designing method of structures and processes which are feasible for environment, having facilities that are built in a resource-efficient way by reducing the consequences on the health of human beings, environment and building life cycle. The green building concept goes beyond the walls of buildings and includes the site and land use planning as well. It is created in a manner to meet certain goals like using energy and water efficiently, increasing human productivity, and reducing the impact on human health and environment.

Why do we build green? The adverse effect of pollutants and greenhouse gases on the environment is a major issue nowadays which is deliberating us to think and work sustainably with more efficient practices of energy use, with less dependency on fossil fuels and striving for pollution-free land, water, and air. The building industry dominates in creating an enormous amount of pollution and absorbs great amount of resources. According to Environment Protection Agency (EPA) of the United States, indoor air of buildings could be as much as 100 times polluted than the outside air [20, 21].

How do we build green? The process of building green needs proper architecture, planning, and developers to examine the connections between the buildings, environment, and their communities with a mindset of conserving nature. Several limitations and challenges like short of consciousness in people, more high-priced costs, rules, and regulations, etc. [1] which restricts the implementation of green buildings. Most significant objection to accept green in society is the requirement to be well knowledgeable, motivated, and informed towards the sustainability. Hence, developers perform an essential part in establishing a much required ingenious policy [2]. The environmental demands of nations are distinct relying on their cultures, environment, and building types.

Furthermore, various developers of distinct countries play a noteworthy role in the implementation of green building protocols relying upon the type of structure. For instance, in case of novel buildings, a major role can be played by the developers in decreasing the consumption of energy by 20 to 60%. But in the case of conventional buildings, owners, occupants, and other partners of the buildings can diminish the consumption of energy by only 25 to 50%. Being highly effective in cost in order to achieve energy-efficacy in new buildings, 60% of the building structure is still to occur that models a massive possibility to implement green building structures and limit the carbon footprint on the surrounding environment for the future in developing countries like India. As per the explanation by Hong et al. [2] the essential policy-mix is supposed to have the supervisory "push" by administration and should be followed by a gushing "pull" from the market of business with non-regulatory devices to raise the knowledge and encourage the investment. In their work an interspersed method is recommended to uncover a policy-mix including several protocols that consolidate to deliver "push" and claim a "pull" impact [3]. In their research, study on the impact of institutional factors on green actions is also included. Acknowledgment of Government is an essential institutional element to encourage green actions. Further support from the green developers' theory [4] and assert that developer's pressure urges organizations to adopt green actions. In 2017, Darko et al. [27] studied the classification structure of green building operators with the submission of those distinct operators that will stimulate various green partners. Many shreds of evidence are specified in the considerations that stand the government reflects the most efficient operator that drives other producers to strive in the direction of sustainability. An essential requirement in order to generate a structure or recognize practices or the evolution tools of buildings is unanimously realized to have a higher emphasis that is required to distinguish green buildings implementation obstacles in the developing countries or countries like India [5]. In 2017, Darko et al. [27] studied that the choice to go green and its preference decision is affected by the time, budget, threat, external factors, corporate operators, property operators, project operators, and individual operators. Knowledge of these challenges is required to find an explication. Major barriers found are political & structural restraints, economic or financial restraints, behavioral and cultural restraints, and knowledge and skill restraints. In Malaysia, the main barricades in promoting green building were recognized as a result of shortage of credit assets to coat the upfront price, threat of investments, and demand shortage plus the greater ultimate rate. In Saudi Arabia, the main challenges identified for the implementation of green constructions recognized were monetary, cultural, political, technical, and market [16]. These challenges categorized into three main groups: product information, builder incentive, and source. According to Shafi and Othman major limitations in Asia are the need for awareness, confined training and knowledge of sustainability, more high-priced cost, appropriate materials, laws, representation and technology shortage, and inadequate demand. As per the studies following are the challenges that have been chosen: technological problems throughout the development procedure and higher green design of the product and expenses of the energy-efficient source [6]; confined consciousness and knowledge regarding the green construction. According to the Energy and Resource Institute, 2006 confined integrated construction rules and by laws within the green structure; lack of motivation from consumers and inadequate policy implementation practices [7]. The various processes in regard to green buildings are discussed in detail in this chapter.

15.2   Sustainability and the Building Industry

Sustainability is defined as as the meeting demands of current generation without compromising the ability of the upcoming generations and fulfilling their own desires. The idea of sustainable development took birth in 1985 due to concerns of environmental pollution and crisis in energy. The green building movement has basically US-origin which aroused during the necessity for a more energy-efficient and environment-friendly building system. Investment in buildings has a long-term impact on the competitiveness of the cities. These green buildings are planned to use less materials, use recycled materials whenever possible, and use only environment-friendly and clean building practices. If one invests 5% in designing the green construction, it could result in a 25% life cycle saving of the total primary construction cost. This is more than 10 times the original investment when compared with the cost–benefit analysis amid conventional and green construction which is highly noticeable and includes approximately 10% decline in operating cost, 15% increment in the construction rate, 10% boost in building value, and many other economic benefits [11]. Residents of green buildings are more productive and healthy. A barrier to the green building industry is that builders and architect lack knowledge about green products, and have inadequate accessible knowledge of high-performance building systems. This leads builders to buy risky and costly setups to replace green products that don't operate well. In a green building the sustainable design combines the life cycle of the building with each applied green method with a purpose of designing in order to form a synergy between the methods applied. The interest caused by distinct developers and the government's intention to thrust for the green construction will result in the evolution of sustainable structures. UNESCO's (2005) explanation of sustainable development describes economic, environmental, and social dimensions [8]. The environment is attributed to sustainable urbanization, resources, change in climate, disaster prevention, rural development, mitigation and is also assigned to the susceptibility of the physical environment. The economy involves a decline in poverty, corporate liability, and market economics. It correlates to how they result in the society and environment. Society is a system that is based on emancipation that allows gives opportunity to the citizens to enthusiastically competing in the policy of life, revealing diverse viewpoints, and choosing governments. Environment, society, and economy have been seen as three mainstays of sustainable development that are implemented by many studies on the sustainable development. According to Biasutti and Frate in 2016 education is thought to be the most imperative for budding the ethical consciousness in society in the dimensions of sustainability [9]. GRIHA Manual, 2010 suggests that sustainability also formulates a competitive benefit and improves process innovation [10]. Green buildings are evolving rapidly and differ from region to region. Benefits and motives of green buildings, environmental, social and economic are briefly discussed below.

15.2.1   Environmental Benefits

Reducing Environmental Impact—Global carbon emissions have rapidly increased over the past years. Buildings play a significant role in contributing to carbon footprint. Around 70% of the worldwide carbon footprint is caused by the use of fossil fuels. A large part of fossil fuel consumption is caused by heating systems in buildings.

Benefits—If the buildings are built green, the worldwide carbon footprint could drop by 15–20% every year. This would play an important role in reducing the adverse effects as a result of changes in climate. The U.S. Green Building Council has produced the Leadership in Energy and Environmental Design (LEED), a rating system for green building. The LEED buildings are capable of reducing climate change. LEED portrays a key contribution in decreasing the negative impacts of the changes in climate on environment.

Conserving Biodiversity and Ecosystems—Green buildings reduce the disruption of existing biotic species. With a thoughtful planning and construction methods, valuable plant biodiversity can be conserved.

Benefits—Conserving nature as a whole and existing trees and other plant species in particular helps in natural cooling, reducing noise pollution, prevents soil erosion, conserves nature, distracts waste from landfills, and retains the sole character of their biological communities.

Protecting Regional Soil—When the non-ligneous and ligneous species are removed, the surface of the ground is set on sub-soil; it leads to a cycle of high demand for water and chemical dependence.

Benefits—Green buildings help in maintaining the soil health, reduction in demand of fertilizers and pesticides, reduce storm water runoff, and conserve water quality.

Minimization of Wastes—Reducing of wastes is the biggest challenge the society facing today especially in urban areas. Minimization of materials for constructing a building possibly reduces the potential waste and aids in an energy-efficient construction. Instruments are used to lessen the risk of wastes and make it more environmental friendly.

Benefits—It reduces the toxic effects of hazardous and solid wastes generation. It keeps cost of waste low, and supports other businesses because the waste of one business could be resource for the other business.

Reduction in Wastage of Water—Modern irrigation technologies apply water to the soil at the plant root zone so that soil can optimally absorb water. This significantly helps in reducing water wastage from spraying over. Some applications are: installation of sub-surface drip, low-flow drip, or low-flow sprinklers instead of sprinkler systems for all landscape patterns and rainwater harvesting.

Benefits—High-efficiency irrigation systems reduce wastage of water, minimize weed growth, and prevent critical diseases that happen due to open water storage.

Improve Indoor Air Quality—It is the air that the inhabitants breathe throughout life inside a building. The quality of indoor air relates to the standard of the air that is in circulation inside a building. Negative impacts of a building sickness are fatigue, anxiety, distractions and stress, coming from poor indoor air quality. About 15–16 cfm outdoor air is necessary per person for ventilation and maintaining a healthy and comfortable environment inside a building. Ventilation can lower down the carbon dioxide production rate which is as a result of respiration by building occupants.

Benefits—Green buildings provide good ventilation by the flow of fresh air into the building and lowering carbon dioxide concentration. The installed exhaust systems help in removal of noxious gases, dodging wood products that have formaldehyde, controls the temperatures of buildings and have strong positive effects.

15.2.2   Social Benefits

Green buildings are socially-beneficial, as they improve the health occupants and enhance the overall quality of life. This includes building security, knowledge transfer, community restoration, etc. Comfort and satisfaction, are psychical results which are caused by perceptual and sensory processes that represent environmental information in terms of its impact on contemporary needs, activities, and preferences. Occupant's productivity and stress give a psychological interpretation of the environment [22]. Same environmental conditions may affect each person differently due to the inherent variability of psychological responses. Occupants who encounter increased satisfaction in their jobs, higher work productivity, and good health will take these experiences back to their home, and affect the overall well-being. The advantages of green buildings can potentially go beyond the workplace. It includes increased adoption of sustainable design practices and change in the occupant's well-being in the community at large. Sustainable buildings set examples for others to follow. For example, some sustainable buildings allow people to see the difference between conventional or green buildings. They provide tours and arrange programs for professionals and local people who are planning to construct their own buildings.

15.2.3   Economic Benefits

Green buildings have several economic and financial benefits. These include savings of household utility bills by energy and water efficiency, cutting down construction costs and more eminent property price for building developers, and high occupancy rates or operating costs for building proprietors.

At global level: Global energy efficiency standards for cost-effective estimated to be \$25,000 to 36,000 billion in profits on spending energy (that is equal to nearly double the annual electricity expenditure of the United States) [13].

At nation level: The green building industry of Canada contributed \$ 23.45 billion in GDP and served nearly 3,00,000 full-time employment in

2014 [14], Green building industry estimated for more than 3.4 million in United States jobs by 2018.

At building level: Local building proprietors state that green buildings, either brand-new or refurbished, set a 7% gain in asset cost over conventional buildings [15].

15.3   Goals of Green Buildings

In recent years, the global surge has begun concern about climate change; consequently, the organizations are linking themselves in social corporate responsibilities. Several procedures have been discussed earlier in order to decrease the environmental impacts, from installing green products to lowering down the release of the amount of carbon dioxide from buildings. Green buildings are a rapid way to minimize long-term costs and resource consumptions. Seven goals or components of green building are discussed below with the objective to optimize of one or more of these goals (Figure 15.1).

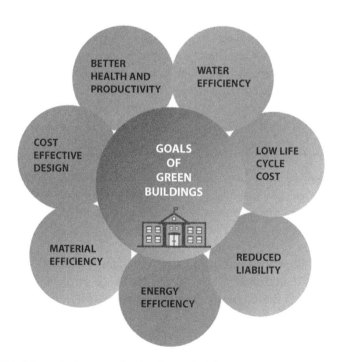

Figure 15.1 Schematic diagram of goals of green buildings.

15.3.1 Green Design

The green design intends to reduce the environmental effects related to the life-cycle processes of the buildings. The concept of green designing for sustainable buildings has the most extensive impression on cost and production. The base of any building plan is rooted in the idea and designing processes. According to the Environment Protection Agency of the United States (2014), the idea or concept stage is the key step in a life-cycle plan, since it has the most valuable influence at production and cost. Nevertheless, building processes vary from one building to another and are not as aerodynamic as an industrial process. Designing a green building is not about compiling the most advanced green components and technologies, willingly, it's a method in which each part of designing is firstly optimized and after that impact of several elements within the system is combined, optimized, and evaluated as a building explication [19]. For instance, inter-relationships among the sites of the construction regarding the green building, tacking of the sun path, details of the building, like windowpanes, and outer shading patterns hold a meaningful result on the nature of daylight. Certain factors also induce linear solar content and the total usage of energy for the growth of the green building. More elements originate under Green architecture applying vegetation as their principal element of the building covering and roof arrangements; it tries to remove the boundaries between internal and external areas by designing [12]. A change in design variability may influence the conditions through each of the buildings' relative life process levels. The main key points are:

- functionality and matching the demands of occupants,
- safety and security,
- constant with a high adequate indoor environment,
- institutional property and providing advanced building systems service time,
- cost-effective and efficient operation and maintenance,
- low operating and maintenance costs for overall life of the facilities, and
- comprised of environmental-friendly and recyclable materials (Figure 15.2).

15.3.2 Energy Efficiency

According to International Energy Agency (2015), energy efficiency is the lowering of energy usage to provide quality of services. Energy efficiency is

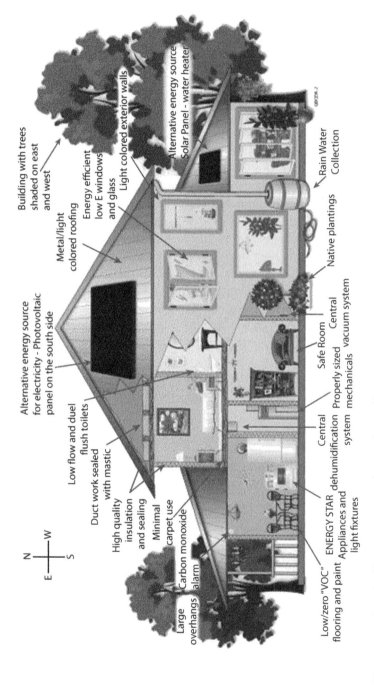

Figure 15.2 Green building optimization (Source: https://blogs.umass.edu/natsci397a-eross/optimizing-conventional-buildings/).

an essential component to attain sustainability in green buildings. Reducing energy consumption in the buildings is commencing a significant growth for many companies and businesses. Furthermore, energy efficiency helps to achieve values and enhance the competitiveness of the green buildings.

Solar photovoltaic (PV) panels—Installation of renewable source of energy like solar photovoltaic (PV) panels converts solar energy into usable electricity.

Cross ventilation—Use of cross-ventilation aims to achieve energy efficiency or developing passive designs, such as, windows to reduce the indoor temperature. Consequently, the usage of air conditioners will be limited and overcome the problem of GHGs emissions. The air pollution problems and anthropogenically-induced climate change can be overcome at the same time. Decreasing the total amount of GHGs in the atmosphere is a necessary step in mitigating the consequences of climate change.

Automated lighting system—Inside a building, not every spot and appliance need 24-hour energy usage, e.g., lighting of a bulb. In high-efficiency buildings, sensor systems (automated lighting systems) are used to save electricity. The sensor systems use movement detection to operate, and are generally installed on the ceilings to overcome unnecessary wastage.

Passive design—Designing of external shading devices and passive solar orientation can minimize unwanted solar lighting through the summer time and can maximize during the winter season. Furthermore, with proper designing of planting green, balconies, awnings and roofs, tend to give shade to walls, and windows in the summers and increase the solar radiation during winters. Choosing a specific orientation and building optimization, interiors and colors can control the natural daylighting. Natural daylighting decreases unnatural lighting energy usage in the building. It also reduces the load in energy usage and cooling. A different approach for passive solar designs comprises the use of energy-efficient appliances (Energy Star Certified), sensor systems, a light-emitting diode (LED) bulb that are implemented in low-energy homes [18].

15.3.3 Water Efficiency

The primary objectives of a water-efficient green building are a reduction in water consumption and enhanced water quality.

It can be practiced by moderating the true characteristic of the water cycle and planning building improvement with the end goal that they intently imitate every site's original "pre-development" hydrological practices. The focus should establish on the on-premises filtration and groundwater recharge to conserve essential natural hydrological characteristics.

The US Green Building Council LEED is associated in this action. It incorporates certain guidelines to have the key elements for sustainable buildings including, the use of indigenous plants, bioswale, essential porous pavement, rainwater harvesting, rooftop water collection, reservoirs, biofiltration planters, a rain garden, etc.

Rainwater harvesting—In areas that are thick with concrete structures, the water that falls, streams away, and is lost forever. That is the reason for even the smallest of buildings to have introduced a water collecting system. That can give a consistent source of water which can be separated and re-filtered to make it portable enough for human utilization. Apart from being utilized in the bathrooms and for watering the nursery, the harvested water can be filtered using simple methods to make it sufficiently safe to drink. There are many kinds of rainwater harvesting systems used everywhere throughout the world, with the expense contingent upon the size and the innovation being conveyed. Though, all systems have one extreme objective—to conserve water and make the best out of it, the benefit of rainwater harvesting is that it can be done at a remarkably small scale as well as a high scale with several liters of water harvested.

Indigenous plants—Indigenous (native) plants generally occur in a particular habitat adapted to the regional environment. Species directly or indirectly introduced by humans, spread aggressively and are called exotic or non-native plants. Indigenous plants require the least attention, maintenance and improve ecosystem stability. Many indigenous plant species entice birds and beneficial insects. They help in xeriscaping, a method of landscape-gardening, planned to reduce the requirement for irrigation as well as rainwater utilization.

Pervious paving—Standard impervious paving makes water to instantly outflow across the surface and into rainwater drains, sewers, and frequently causes flooding during heavy rains. The pervious paving permits vertical water flow through the paving body to gradually infiltrate, recharge and restore groundwater. Water moves into the connections within gravel sub base, filters, pavers, penetrates the regional sub-grade, and eventually recharges ground water. In urban areas, pervious paving formulates a clearer environment and it saves expensive rainwater filtration and infrastructure and system.

Roof rainwater collection—Using present sewer and drainpipe practices, re-routing of rain water can be possible by rain vessels and cisterns. They enable reusing of water otherwise that would be flowing inside the storm watercourse. Harvested rainwater in irrigating green roofs gives recreational convenience via rooftop gardens, decreases periodic thermal gain, and reduces urban heat island effect with lower energy intake than regular the cooling methods.

Cisterns—Adopting cisterns for the rainwater collection gives it more likely to reduce dependence on drinkable water. The building's rainwater stating from rooftop downpipe, pervious paving, drain tubes, and the passages of rain garden, bioswale and biofiltration tree planters, all are managed and cisterns are collected under the ground. Before entering the water into cisterns, waterspout filters separators clean it out, excluding minute debris and it is utilized for the irrigation practices.

Biofiltration planter—Biofiltration planter or storm water planter contains vegetation that collects stormwater runoff. Using biofiltration methods, these planters accumulate and filter water into various courses of vegetation and soils. One can commonly see biofiltration plants in cities along streets and sidewalks varying in sizes and shapes depending on the location and available space. It consists of a gravel layer, and soil layer for planting for species, like ferns, shrubs, herbs, even small trees and bonsai. Water flows through inlet pipe or naturally from a slope gradient into the planter's soil and plant roots ultimately flowing into the groundwater system below. In case an extra amount of runoff enters the planter, an overflow pipe is located to redirect the excess.

15.3.4   Material Efficiency

Building material efficiency is useful in lowering the usage of non-renewable building substances and other sources, for instance, water and energy through effective planning, designing, engineering, and construction, and efficient recycling of construction debris, extending the utilization of recycled materials and the latest resource-efficient engineered products, maximum utilization of renewable, reusable, high performance sustainably engineered and bio-based products. Green materials commonly include renewable and green elements like bamboo (bamboo tend to grow fast) and straws, logs from forests that are permitted for managing sustainably, natural rocks materials, metals, reclaimed stones, and non-toxic products. The maximum utilization of renewable, reusable, high performance sustainably engineered, and bio-based products (e.g. are the clay, trass, sheep wool, paper flakes panels, compressed earth blocks, linoleum, calcium sandstone, wood fiber plates, sisal, baked earth, coconut shells, rammed earth, clay, flax linen, sea grass, cork, expanded clay grains, vermiculite, roman self-healing concrete and high-performance pavement). For in case, void fly ash blocks would work in wall construction as it has good insulating properties. The Environmental Protection Agency United

States also recommends adopting industrial products which are recycled, like as foundry sand, coal combustion products, and construction debris of projects. The adoption of green goods, for example, different varieties of agriboard (covering slat made from horticultural scrap and by-products like peanut shells, sunflower shells, straw, barley, soy, wheat, and other elements) can also be used. Any primary insulated panels salvaged from bio products use wood materials from certified forests wherever the forests are maintained and timber store is done applying sustainable methods. Building materials extraction and manufacture should be limited to the building site to reduce the energy loss in their shipment. Increasing the values of the off-site rendering including reduction in waste, recycling maximization (due to on location manufacturing), using high-quality components, better OHS command, sawdust, less noise should also be considered.

15.3.5   Improved Internal Environment and Air Quality

World Health Organization (WHO) states that the fundamental requirement for individual's safety and health is the clean air. Generally, a normal human breathe around 12,000 L of air per day. It is, thus, necessary for the health of human's health to breathe pure air in the surrounding environment. Indoor air quality (IAQ) is the eminence of air that is interior of the buildings and is determined by the pollutant concentration and the thermal environment (like relative humidity and temperature) which influences the healthiness and performance of the inhabitants. A major factor, to measure the quality of air in green constructions is the IAQ. Green buildings avoid contaminants causing air pollution control, thermal comfort and upgrade the maintenance. A green building certification can be achieved by maintaining a 7.5% healthy environment inside the building. The main components contributing to unhealthy air quality are carbon-dioxide (CO_2) carbon mono-oxide (CO) volatile organic compounds (VOCs), particulate matters (PMs), sulfur oxides (SOx), nitrogen oxides (NO_x), environmental tobacco smoke (ETS), ozone (O_3) and biological agents (Table 15.1). These are all related to poor health consequences, including ischemic heart diseases, chronic obstructive pulmonary disease (COPD), strokes, asthma, and lung cancer. Around half of the deaths of children below then five years occur due to pneumonia fever caused by particulate matter inhaled from the indoor air. Researchers found that there is a good relationship between ventilation and IAQ, and with high-grade ventilation techniques we can attain a good IAQ [23]. High-level automated ventilating systems have been utilized to surge the

Table 15.1 An enumeration of major indoor air pollutants.

Pollutant	Source	Health effects
Volatile organic compounds (VOCs)	Building materials, furnishings, office, cleaning products and HVAC equipment's people and their personal care products, ETS, and exterior air	Acuity of objectionable odors, asthma, irritation in mucous membrane, fatigue, cancers
Nitrogen oxides	Cooking, cooking appliances, unvented heaters and pilot lights	Lung damage, increase of host susceptibility to respiratory infections
Ozone	Coronal or electrical discharges from office equipment's, for instance photocopiers and laser printers	Acute and chronic respiratory tract health effects
Sulfur dioxide	Heating oil, gasoline and coal or burning any Sulphur containing material	Respiratory tract infections, irritant of the upper respiratory mucosa
Carbon dioxide	Human respiration, emission from gasoline and diesel engines	Central nervous system dysfunction, shortness of breath
Carbon monoxide	Gas furnace, hot water heater, attached garage, weather inversion, kerosene, gas stoves, lantern and heater, sidestream and mainstream tobacco smoke, woodstove, and unvented or improperly ventilated burning sources	Headache, dizziness, negative change in the oxygen dissociation curve, inhibiting the oxygen transportation in the blood by the formation of carboxyhemoglobin

(Continued)

Table 15.1 An enumeration of major indoor air pollutants. (*Continued*)

Pollutant	Source	Health effects
Refrigerants	Leaks from refrigeration, HVAC equipment's and refrigerant storage containers, poor practice of servicing refrigeration equipment's	Cardiotoxicity, arrhythmia, Central nervous system (CNS) depression and asphyxia
Particulate matters	Demolition, blasting, drilling, shoveling, screening, sweeping, tobacco smoke, combustion of wood coal, oil, and other carbonaceous materials	Early death with lung or heart diseases, irregular heartbeat, non-fatal heart attacks

air flow and minimize inhabitant intercommunication with the air-borne contagious agents.

15.3.6   Minimization of Wastes

Material efficiency can be achieved in green architectural designs by reducing waste and materials usage during construction. During the construction period, one should aim to minimize the kind and amount of waste matter moving to the landfills. Highly efficient buildings serve to decrease the quantity of waste produced by the inhabitants along with giving on-site explications, like as, compost bags to lessen the amount of waste moving to landfills managing at source inhabitant waste, and transferring it to a semi-centralized biogas plant with other biological wastes, it could also produce liquid fertilizers. Systems like these makes them soil nutrients rich and it creates carbon sinks further making inorganic fertilizers more cost ineffective, compared to the processes cited here.

15.3.7   Operations and Maintenance Optimization

Using methods that are necessary in designing or constructing, the green building would only be accountable if these are managed responsibly and sustained well. Operations and maintenance (O&M) is the most important part of the project's development and planning that will support and maintain the green standards planned in the beginning of the project. All features of green building are combined within the O&M stage of a building's life. As a part of O&M, life cycle assessment (LCA) is adopted to examine and value the social, economic and environmental impacts of services or the product of the green buildings [28]. The LCA assesses buildings supplies of high efficient buildings entirely throughout the buildings' lives and examines the entire range of environmental impacts, including efficiencies, waste reduction and disposal, indoor air quality and global-warming potential, etc. The LCA is an imperative mechanism as it can validate weather a material employed in a building is positively green or not [24].

15.4   Impacts of Classical Buildings that Green Buildings Seek to Rectify

Conventional building construction is the traditional method of making buildings where the construction experience is passed from one generation to another associated with in-site constructions using augmented concrete. In this chapter, so far we have discussed green buildings to a great extent, which use less water, optimize energy efficiently, restore natural flora and fauna, generate less amount of waste, use scientific waste disposal, and provide healthy space and quality of life if we compare it to classical or conventional buildings. According to Environment Protection Agency (2018) in developed countries buildings estimated more than 40% for consumption of energy [20, 21]. Researchers have concluded that unsatisfactory indoor environment quality in conventional buildings degrade work quality. Conventional buildings work on a large amount of area, water, energy usage, and poor quality materials for their planning and construction. Conventional building produces high amount of greenhouse gases (GHG) and other harmful pollutants. Generation of construction and demolition (C&D) waste is high and have a severe effect on wild animals and plants. Truth is that a large amount of buildings are not green, and these buildings will stay the same and will be used for several coming years. The U.S. Green Building Council has an existing building rating system, i.e., LEED-EBOM (Existing Buildings Operation and Maintenance). A deep investigation of the matters illustrates the scope of the problem.

15.4.1   Energy Use in Buildings

Globally, constructions utilize extensive energy amounts. As per the reports of United Nations Environment Program (UNEP) buildings consume 30–40% major energy produced globally. In the year 2008, the International Energy Agency published that from the total energy consumption greater than 40% is attributed to the existing constructions and 24% to global CO_2 emissions. Several ways for the reduction of energy consumption include construction of high-efficacy windows, ceilings, insulating walls, and floors. The building layouts, for instance, placement of window, can be strategized in order to permeate the natural light for auxiliary warmth [25, 26]. The use of energy in commercial and green building is demonstrated in Figure 15.3.

15.4.2   Green House Gas (GHG) Emissions

Greenhouse gases (CO_2, CH_4, and CFCs prominently) aggregate all the heat and make the planet the hottest. The incineration of fossil fuels is responsible for the production of major energy in the conventional buildings that are accountable for emission of millions of tons of GHG annually. The two most obvious sources of energy for buildings are electricity and the immediate consumption of natural gas and petroleum for heating and cooking. Others are heat and transportation. Electricity accounts more in total building energy dissipation and largely contributes to GHG emissions. The greenhouse gases are short-wave infra-red radiations (heat from the sun). They allow sun rays to enter the atmosphere and heat the Earth's surface. Sources of GHG emissions are:

- production and transport of building supplies,
- consumption of energy for resource processing,
- consumption of energy by construction materials, and
- disposal of construction waste.

The emission of GHG in building structures can be illustrated as follows (Figure 15.4).

15.4.3   Indoor Air Quality

Reduction of volatile organic compounds (VOCs) and providing satisfactory exposure to air by culling the right materials for construction and

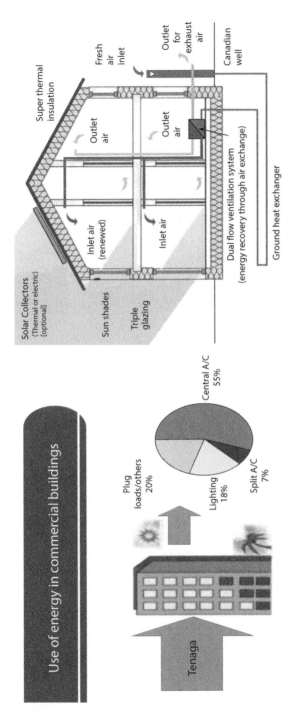

Figure 15.3 Use of energy in commercial buildings and green buildings (Source: Energy audit in Government buildings by Pusat Tenage Malaysia/Greentechmalaysia).

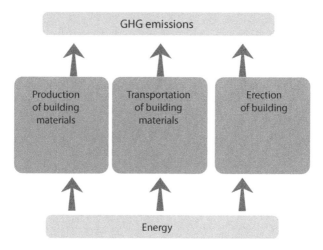

Figure 15.4 Emission of GHG in building structure.

internal products of a building with low zero emissions are key components for quality air. This will greatly improve the indoor air quality.

15.4.4   Building Water Use

Reduction in water consumption and protecting water property needs to be fundamental in green building structures. Builders should choose the practices to reuse of collected and purified water. They should create an aim to decrease wastewater by utilizing green products like, ultralow flush restrooms and low flow bathrooms.

15.4.5   Use of Land and Consumption

Construction of buildings globally covers billions of acres of land. Having a large amount of land is not the primary issue in building construction, compared to poorly assembled buildings using a large amount of land, and consuming large quantity of diverse resources. For example, buildings that are in construction mode and away from existing residential or commercial areas need to construct new roads, sewer channels, and utility services which can lead to habitat disruption or extinction. In addition, if they are not reachable by public transportation, it could require modes to transportation and construction of garages or parking lots. Most importantly, buildings constructed on the borders of urban or sub-urban areas usually add to the dilemma of sprawl (spreading of a city, undeveloped or lightly developed areas). Forestlands, croplands and wetlands developing into sub-urban areas are not a good sign to environmental quality.

15.4.6   Construction Materials

The building industry demands a lot of raw material production. A variety of materials needs constant production. Globally, around 3 billion tons of raw materials are used in constructive activities every year, and it has been consuming around half of all the products formed by the volume. A significant fraction of green buildings is the products and materials utilized in their construction. Materials of green buildings are usually made of exhaustible with respect to non-exhaustible resources, and are environmental-efficient due to their impressions that are analyzed over the product life [28]. Besides, materials for green construction usually results in lower alternative costs and controlled maintenance throughout the building life, save energy, and enhance occupant productivity and health. Materials of green buildings can be chosen by estimating properties like reused and recycled contents, sustainable and rapid renewable harvested materials, negligible toxicity, and negligible off-gassing of detrimental air emissions, high longevity, robustness, and local production. Figure 15.5 illustrates comparison between construction material used in green and conventional buildings.

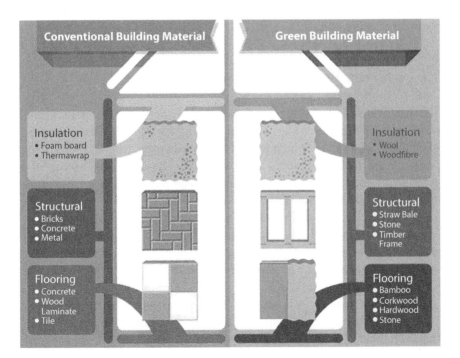

Figure 15.5 Comparison between construction materials used in green and conventional buildings (Source: https://inhabitat.com/conventional-building-materials/).

15.4.7   Construction and Demolition (C&D) Wastes

Wastes from construction originally comprised of wood products and lumber (35%), drywall (15%), masonry material (12%), and cardboard (10%); rest is a mixture of plastics, roofing materials, plaster, metals, foam, textiles, glass, insulation, and packaging. Many of these materials are eco-friendly and maximum part of the material gets transferred into sanitary landfills. Generally green construction attempts to reduce the C&D wastes amounts they produce. It is achieved by reusing or recycling C&D wastes, for instance, using inert devastation materials as a fundamental material for roadways and parking lots. Plans can be developed early in designing for managing and reuse purposes for the deconstruction, demolition, and construction processes for sites that embrace the destruction of existing structures. Demolition produces generous amount of reused or recycled materials; primarily concrete, wood, and other kinds of masonry, and drywall. Prior to destruction of a whole building, all the parts of a building can be deconstructed. Deconstruction of a building is the systematic dismantling of parts of building for the purpose of recycling or reuse. In contradiction to the demolition of a building, deconstruction requires separation of portions of buildings or eliminating their parts with the main purpose of being reused.

15.5   Green Buildings in India

The Earth is facing severe degeneration as rising in global mean temperature bleaching of coral reefs and melting ice caps. Because of green structures, the world can make a stride towards preparing and saving the deteriorating Mother Nature. India is among the countries starting the green structure development. The Indian Green Building Council's (IGBC) vision is to build a feasible environment for India by 2025. A glance of the top 10 green buildings of India is given in Table 15.2.

India According to GRIHA Manual, 2010 [10] India is observing a growth in the landed properties, construction, and development area which is increasing at the pace of 9% versus the global standard of 6.5 and 5.5% contributing to the GDP.

A fast increment in urbanization and it is expected to be normal by 2050, 66% of the total population will be living in the urban areas. Other than as indicated by the United Nations Report 2013, India is presumed to be the most populated nation by 2028 and that would put great pressure on

Table 15.2 Green buildings in India.

Name of green building	Location	Key features
Suzlon One Earth	Pune	Office in the garden, it has cent per cent onsite and offsite renewable sources, seven per cent of energy consumption is fulfilled by 18 hybrid wind turbines; another energy demand brought by offsite wind turbines, designed in a form to ensure the greatest sunshine exposure thereby diminishing unnatural lighting utilization; inside the campus, infrastructures are intended to let water permeation and for control of stormwater overflow, along these lines, including towards an elevated water table level.
Rajiv Gandhi International Airport	Hyderabad	Utilizes less water, power, and conserves natural resources; it has a green belt of 273 hectares with numerous plant species; it has a green belt of 273 hectares with various plant species; saves energy for almost 3.97 million kWh, 3,331 tons reduction in carbon footprint.
Infosys Limited	Mysore	Platinum rating, area of 780,000 sq ft. The five-level structure has been built remembering a comprehensive way to deal with sustainability in five fundamental regions, including—conservation of water, energy-efficient building, sustainable site improvement, materials effectiveness, and indoor environment quality. Prompting 40% of less energy utilization.

(Continued)

Table 15.2 Green buildings in India. (*Continued*)

Name of green building	Location	Key features
CII-Sohrabji Godrej Green Business Centre	Hyderabad	An architectural showpiece. Outside of the US it is the first structure to be granted LEED platinum rating at the time of its inauguration. This building recycles its own waste.
Infinity Benchmark	Kolkata	Twenty levels building covering 5, 60,000 sq. ft. area; 7th building to receive LEED platinum rating. a building equipped with carbon dioxide monitor sensors, a system of wastewater recycling, a rainwater harvesting system, and controls of humidification. Building covering is comprised of brick wall block while the rooftop contains deck thick polyurethane froth for more prominent protection.
I-Gate Knowledge Centre	Noida	LEED platinum rated. Built over 4, 60,000 sq. ft. In sub-urban Noida and planned such that it gets 73% of sunshine inside the workplace. Almost 50% of the land is covered with grass which doesn't let waste and sewage water go out.
Bank of India	Goa	Equipped with eco-friendly air-conditioning and lightning, modern capsule lifts, intelligent glazing, and indoor fountains. The building contains Nano Misty Blue and softening color glass manufactured by Saint Gobin Glass, India for formulating the conserving energy and cool effect. It has thermal insulated and solar control glasses.

(*Continued*)

Table 15.2 Green buildings in India. (*Continued*)

Name of green building	Location	Key features
Ansal Esencia	Gurugram	A Green Eco Revolution, energy efficient building; electronics are made for the greatest energy savings, environ seats, stunning bike ways, canisters, drought-resistant campus and transport stops.
Biodiversity Conservation India Ltd.	Bangaluru	Founded in 1994, it is an astonishing model where mobile phones are used for switching off the lights. Greywater is steered to the toilets, gardens and used for washing cars. Central reverse osmosis system for purifying the water with no use of chemicals. The building has 44 interconnected rainwater percolation wells that lead to 400,000 L water in the water tank.
Olympia Tech Park	Chennai	Rated largest. This building is most popular and has the best estate hundred companies operating in it. LEED Gold Rated, most solicited and one of the biggest IT parks in Chennai. It has a grand structure of its size i.e. 1.8 million sq. ft. It has the high natural lighting systems, lowest energy consumption, cent percent water recycling, and different environment-friendly practices.

Photo of CII Sohrabji Godrej Green Business Centre,
(Source:https://www.facebook.com/greenbusinesscentre/photos/)

energy demands [17]. The Green Building effort in India got an immense force when the CII-Sohrabji Godrej Green Business Center structure in Hyderabad was granted the first and the esteemed Platinum evaluated green structure rating outside of United States by the US Green Building Council after that there is no turning back market-driven deliberate adoption mode approach is utilized by the legislature of India and the key makers to support interest for green structures which has diminished the expense and today a Certified Green Building can built at the comparable cost as a regular. A ton has been done by India regarding green structures yet a great deal should be done.

The government is understanding the environmental perspectives of the building sectors and is exerting attention on several policies actions with the initiation of the green building rating systems and Bureau of Energy Efficiency (BEE) and National Building Code (NBC), which constitute the Green Rating Integrated Habitat Assessment (GRIHA), developed by the Ministry of New and Renewable Energy, The Energy and Resource Institute (TERI) and Leadership in Energy and Environment Design (LEED), operated by the Association for Development and Research of Sustainable Habitats (ADaRSH) and Indian Green Building Council (IGBC), for smaller structures; the Star Rating Programme for Buildings of the Bureau of Energy Efficiency and the Eco-Housing rating system developed for Pune. IGBC also has rating systems for houses, landscapes, townships, and special economic zones factories [29]. Many of the certified green buildings in India belong to the government or private firms, and residential interest is extremely inadequate. In 2011 European Commission published a document "Smart Cities & Communities", which explained that demand to arrange economy and ecology indicated the necessity to generate synergy among environment development and protection of modern technology. Nearly 60% of development yet to take place India can goes a long way in sustainability.

15.6 Conclusion

Buildings are possibly the sole most prominent stress on the environment, considering these around 1/6th of the global freshwater recession, 1/4th of its wood consumption, and 2/5th of its element and energy flows, putting the biodiversity into peril. Barriers in choosing a green building in which human survival depends on threatening deficiencies of freshwater and other elements and the risk of disastrous climate change. In a world full of stress, the green buildings are shifting from an unfamiliar interest to a constraint. Besides the expanding knowledge of green buildings, the green building campaign is completely inclined towards attaining a bigger rise. The increasing green footprints offer many challenges and at the same time offer a lot of possibilities. The collaborator of the green buildings industries needs to be fully outfitted to cover up to certain possibilities. The green buildings must have environmental favorable components; their design needs to be required to verify the environmental benefits as it claims. The beliefs of Green architects prefer buildings as combined entities that are visually delightful on the encircled environment, extremely operative for everyday practices, and environment-friendly. The true and future greens would be where the designers can easily combine details around 'true nature' with the idea of a human-made environment. Later, the limit between natural and unnatural is most likely to become hazy as structures shift to consistency with natural processes. Furthermore, rather than being a disruptor to ecosystems and large consumption of energy, constructions are growing towards a regulated and healthy environment. Strong recognition of the benefits of green buildings, a deliberate attempt to shift will promote this approach forward.

Acknowledgement

The authors first and foremost express gratitude to the almighty for his grace and blessings. We owe thanks to faculty of Department of Environment Science, SoVSAS for support in developing the manuscript.

I, Ayushi Nain could not imagine my success in my life without the cooperation and encouragement of my father Shri Vikas Nain and mother Smt. Monika. Their support assists me to do better and I owe all my achievements to them.

Acronyms

EPA	Environment Protection Agency
LEED	Leadership in Energy and Environmental Design
Cfm	Cubic Feet per Minute
IEA	International Energy Agency
SP	Solar Photovoltaic
IGBC	Green Rating Integrated Habitat Assessment
GHG	Green House Gas
LED	Light-emitting diode
OHS	Occupational Health and Safety
GRIHA	Green Rating Integrated Habitat Assessment
WHO	World Health Organization
IAQ	Indoor Air Quality
VOC	Volatile Organic Compounds
PM	Particulate Matter
ETS	Environmental Tobacco Smoke
NBC	National Building Code
COPD	Chronic Obstructive Pulmonary Disease
O&M	Operations and Maintenance
BEE	Bureau of Energy Efficiency
LCA	Life Cycle Assessment
C&D	Construction and Demolition Waste
LEED-EBOM	Existing Buildings: Operations & Maintenance
UNEP	United Nation Environment Programme
CFCs	Chlorofluorocarbons
IR	Infra Radiation
IGBC	Indian Green Building Council

ADaRSH   Association for Development and Research of Sustainable Habitats

References

1. Shafii, F. and Othman, M.Z., Sustainable building in the Malaysian context, in: *The International Conference on Sustainable Building Asia*, Seoul, Korea, November, 2007.

2. Hong, W., Chiang, M.D., Shapiro, R.A., Clifford, M.L., *Building Energy Efficiency: Why Green Buildings Are Key to Asia's Future. An Asia Business Council Book*, Inkstone Books, Hong Kong, 2007, http://www.iisbeportugal. org/documents/BEEBook.pdf/ (Accessed 12-08-2020).

3. Ling, T.C., Nee, G., Seng, C.H., A model linking institutional factors and green initiatives: A study among the private higher education institutions. *J. Sustain. Sci. Manag.*, 10, 2, 52–64, 2015.

4. Buysse, K. and Verbeke, A., Proactive Environmental Strategies: A Stakeholder Management Perspective. *Strategic Manage. J.*, 24, 5, 453–470, 2003.

5. Amos, D. and Chan, A.P., Critical analysis of green building research trend in construction. *J. Habitat Int.*, 57, 53–63, 2016.

6. Tagaza, E. and Wilson, J.L., *Green buildings: drivers and barriers and lessons learned from five Melbourne developments*, Report Prepared for Building Commission by University of Melbourne and Business Outlook and Evaluation, *Aust. J. Struct. Eng.*, 2004.

7. Zhang, X., Shen, L., Wu, Y., Green strategy for gaining competitive advantage in housing development: A China study. *J. Cleaner Prod.*, 19, 2–3, 157–167, 2011.

8. Khan, M.A., Concepts, definitions and key issues in sustainable development: The outlook for the future, *Proceedings of the 1995 International Sustainable Development Research Conference,* Manchester, England, pp. 2–13, 1995.

9. Biasutti, M. and Frate, S., A validity and reliability study of the attitudes toward sustainable development scale. *Environ. Educ. Res.*, 23, 2, 214–230, 2017.

10. GRIHA Manual, in: *Introduction to National Rating System—GRIHA. An evaluation tool to help design, build, operate, and maintain a resource-efficient built environment*, Ministry of New and Renewable Energy, Government of India, and The Energy and Resources Institute, 2010, http://www .grihaindia. org/files/Manual_ VolI.pdf /(accessed 29-08-2020).

11. Howe, J.C., Overview of green buildings. *Natl. Wetl. Newsl.*, 33, 1, 3–14, 2010.

12. Pushkar, S., Becker, R., & Katz, A. A methodology for design of environmentally optimal buildings by variable grouping. *Build. Environ.*, 40, 8, 1126–1139, 2005.

13. Annual activity report, https://ec.europa.eu/info/publications/annual-activity-reports-2015_en. (Acceded on date 14-08-2020).

14. Canada Green Building Council, https://www.cagbc.org/ (Acceded on date 15-08-2020).

15. U.S. Green Building Council, Green Building Facts. Online at, http://www. usgbc. org/DisplayPage.aspx?CMSPageID=1718, 2009.

16. Jones, S.A. and Laquidara-Carr, D., *World Green Building Trends 2016— Developing Markets Accelerate Global Green Growth*, Dodge Data & Analytics, Bedford (US), 2016.

17. Sharma, M., Development of a 'Green building sustainability model' for Green buildings in India. *J. Cleaner Prod.*, 190, 538–551, 2018.

18. Rathee, D., Ahuja, K., Nayyar, A., Sustainable future IoT services with touch-enabled handheld devices, in: *Security and Privacy of Electronic Healthcare Records: Concepts, Paradigms and Solutions*, 131, 2019.

19. Solanki, A. and Nayyar, A., Green internet of things (G-IoT): ICT technologies,principles, applications, projects, and challenges, in: *Handbook of Research on Big Data and the IoT*, Green Building Management and Smart Automation, United States, IGI Global, 379–405, 2019.

20. U.S. Environmental Protection Agency, Green building basic information, 2009, http://www.epa. gov/greenbuilding/pubs/about.html (Acceded on date 19-08-2020).

21. Environmental Protection Agency, Green building materials, 2014, http:// www.epa.gov/greenbuilding/pubs/components.html (Acceded on date 19-08-2020).

22. Nayyar, A., Rameshwar, R., Solanki, A. Internet of Things (IoT) and the Digital Business Environment: A Standpoint Inclusive Cyber Space, Cyber Crimes, and Cyber security.

23. Persily, A.K. and Emmerich, S.J., Indoor air quality in sustainable, energy efficient buildings. *Hvac & R Res.*, 18, 1–2, 4–20, 2012.

24. Hajare, A., *Life cycle cost analysis of an energy efficient residential unit*, Doctoral dissertation, Purdue University Graduate School, Faculty of Purdue University. Department of Construction Management Technology. West Lafayette, Indiana, 2019.

25. Krishnamurthi, R., Nayyar, A., Solanki, A., Innovation Opportunities through Internet of Things (IoT) for Smart Cities, in: *Green and Smart Technologies for Smart Cities*, pp. 261–292, CRC Press, Boca Raton, FL, USA, 2019.

26. Rameshwar, R., Solanki, A., Nayyar, A., Mahapatra, B., Green and smart buildings: A key to sustainable global solutions, in: *Green Building Management and Smart Automation*, IGI Global, 146–163, 2020.

27. Darko, A., Zhang, C., & Chan, A. P. (2017). Drivers for green building: A review of empirical studies. *Habitat international*, 60, 34–49.

28. Kibert, C.J., *Sustainable construction: Green building design and delivery*, John Wiley & Sons, Germany, 2016.

29. Fazli, R.F. and Faridi, R.A., Green Buildings in India: A road ahead for sustainable environment. *J. Soc. Sci., India*, 1–8, 2010.

Index